Yale Broadway Masters

JEROME KERN

STEPHEN BANFIELD

With a Foreword by Geoffrey Block, General Editor

YALE UNIVERSITY PRESS   NEW HAVEN & LONDON

Published with assistance from the foundation established in memory
of Philip Hamilton McMillan of the Class of 1894, Yale College.

Frontispiece. Copyright Getty Images.

Set in Electra Roman by Tseng Information Systems.
Printed in the United States of America.

Library of Congress Cataloging-in-Publication Data
Banfield, Stephen, 1951–
Jerome Kern / Stephen Banfield ; with a foreword by Geoffrey Block, general editor.
p. cm. — (Yale Broadway masters)
Includes list of works by Jerome Kern (p.   ), bibliographical references (p.   ), and index.
ISBN-13: 978-0-300-11047-0 (alk. paper)
ISBN-10: 0-300-11047-2
1. Kern, Jerome, 1885–1945.   2. Composers—United States—Biography.   I. Title.
II. Series.
ML410.K385B36 2006
782.1′4092—dc22   2005035950

A catalogue record for this book is available from the British Library.
The paper in this book meets the guidelines for permanence and durability
of the Committee on Production Guidelines for Book Longevity of the
Council on Library Resources.

10 9 8 7 6 5 4 3 2 1

For Oscar

Contents

Foreword

In 1915, a thirteen-year-old Richard Rodgers heard in Jerome Kern tunes the "first truly American theatre music" and a standard in theatrical music that "pointed the way" Rodgers "wanted to be led." George Gershwin informed his first biographer, Isaac Goldberg, that from the moment he heard an orchestra play "You're Here and I'm Here" and "They Didn't Believe Me" from *The Girl from Utah* at the wedding of his Aunt Kate in 1914— George was fifteen at the time—Kern became "the first composer who made me conscious that popular music was of inferior quality, and that musical-comedy music was made of better material." After achieving his own considerable Broadway success, Gershwin expressed his view that Kern's *Show Boat* score was "the finest light opera achievement in the history of American music."

As a rehearsal pianist, Gershwin knew Kern's *Miss 1917* intimately. Rodgers spent most of his allowance in the winter of 1917 "listening to the score of *Love o' Mike.*" More recent students and practitioners of the Broadway musical and Hollywood devotees know Kern primarily as the composer of the stage classic *Show Boat* (1927), the Fred Astaire and Ginger Rogers film gem *Swing Time* (1936), and such unforgettable songs as "All the Things You Are," "Smoke Gets in Your Eyes," "The Way You Look Tonight," and "Ol' Man River." In *Jerome Kern*, Yale Broadway Masters, Stephen Banfield, the award-winning author of the seminal *Sondheim's Broadway Musicals* (1993), offers the first serious and much-needed exploration of Kern's musical and dramatic language and an accessible, comprehensive survey of an incalculably important Broadway and Hollywood career. The trajectory of this re-

markable career begins with "How'd You Like to Spoon with Me?," a hit
song interpolated in the Chicago production of Ivan Caryll's *The Earl and
the Girl* in 1905—recycled in 1971 in the long-running London revival of
Show Boat—and ends four decades later with "Nobody Else But Me," Kern's
final song for the New York *Show Boat* revival in 1946, completed shortly
before his death from a cerebral hemorrhage in November 1945.

Banfield presents both a persuasive and well-informed advocacy of such
little-known treasures as *Have a Heart* (1917), *Sitting Pretty* (1924), and the
under-appreciated and undeservedly obscure *The Cat and the Fiddle* (1931)
and new insights into familiar territory, including *Show Boat* and *Swing
Time*. While acknowledging the undeniable historical importance and canonic stature of *Show Boat*, for example, Banfield rigorously explores second act problems that have been recognized but rarely examined and finds
dramatic solutions to these infelicities in the Universal film version, with a
screenplay by Oscar Hammerstein, released in 1936 with several members
of the original Broadway and London casts.

In an interview that appeared in the *Dramatic Mirror* shortly after the
successful debut of *Oh, Boy!* in 1917, Kern expressed the then-novel but later
prevailing view that "musical numbers should carry on the action of the play
and should be representative of the personalities of the characters who sing
them" and that "songs must be suited to the action and the mood of the
play." Kern's quip to the biographer Alexander Woollcott that "Irving Berlin
has *no* place in American music, HE IS AMERICAN MUSIC" belongs to Broadway folklore. For composers as diverse as Gershwin, Rodgers, and Sondheim,
and for historians, critics, and audiences from his time to ours, Jerome Kern
occupies a similarly hallowed place in the American musical.

GEOFFREY BLOCK
General Editor

Acknowledgments

Because so much material is unpublished or out of print, this book simply could not have been written without the cooperation and generous assistance of the persons listed below in their private and institutional capacities. Most of them gave the impression, which I like to think may in some cases even have been genuine, that they enjoyed nothing more than to help a scholar research Jerome Kern. To them all go my heartfelt thanks. Nine or ten people in particular went far beyond the call of duty in helping me acquire or check out material; they know who they are. Two read drafts of the book and made helpful, encouraging comments. Three wrote time-consuming references for research grant applications. The complete list comprises Richard Abram (EMI), Sargent Aborn (Tams-Witmark Music Library), Amy Asch, Elizabeth Auman (Library of Congress), Frances Birch (Theatres Trust), Geoffrey Block (Yale Broadway Masters), Andrew Boose (Betty Kern Miller Literary Trust), Gerald Bordman, Lezlie Botkin, Tom Briggs (Rodgers and Hammerstein Organization), Samuel Brylawski (Library of Congress), Lauren Buisson (Young Library, UCLA), Rexton Bunnett, Tim Carter, Mary Ann Chach (Shubert Archive), Paul Charosh, Ned Comstock (Cinema-Television Library, USC), Keith Condon (Yale University Press), Jon Alan Conrad, Steve Cork (British Library), Jean Cunningham (Paramount Theatre Library, Oakland), Barry Day, Peter Dickinson, Jo Elsworth (University of Bristol Theatre Collection), Michael Feinstein, George Ferencz, James Fuld, Mark Trent Goldberg (Ira and Leonore Gershwin Trusts), Julie Graham (Young Library, UCLA), John and Roberta Graziano, William Harbach, Harry Haskell (Yale University Press), Murray

Hedgcock, Larisa Heimert (Yale University Press), Randi Hokett (Warner Bros. Collection, USC), Mark Eden Horowitz (Library of Congress), Sally Irwin (Josef Weinberger), Norman Josephs, Alexandra Kaprielian (42nd Street Moon Theatre), Robert Kimball, Raymond Knapp, Kim Kowalke, Miles Kreuger (Institute of the American Musical), Andrew Lamb, Valerie Langfield, Geri Laudati (Mills Music Library, University of Wisconsin), Kathy Lewis (NODA), Bob McCrea, Greg MacKellan (42nd Street Moon Theatre), Nick Markovich (Harburg Foundation), Richard Middleton, Larry Moore, Sally Plowright, Bruce Pomahac (Rodgers and Hammerstein Organization), J. R. Piggott (Dulwich College), Susan Pyzynski (Brandeis University Library), James Randall, Perry Robbins (University of Bristol Photographic Service), Jonathan Scott, Benjamin Sears, Wayne Shirley (Library of Congress), John Snelson, Donald J. Stubblebine, Claire Thomas (British Film Institute), Ernest Tomlinson (Light Music Society), Caroline Underwood (Warner Chappell, London), and Walter Zvonchenko (Library of Congress). My partner, Oscar Martinez, should be thanked separately for accompanying me on my research trips and doing much of the work, especially the boring bits, and for his patient support of the entire enterprise. On the material front, research for the book was facilitated by two British Academy Small Research Grants, a University of Birmingham research grant and study leave, a University of Bristol research grant and research fellowship, and an Arts and Humanities Research Board research leave award.

Editorial Method

1. The following shorthand for musical notation is used throughout the book where appropriate. Numbers indicate degrees of the major scale, and they move to the closest interval unless ↓ (down) or ↑ (up) is indicated. ♭ indicates a subsequent flattened scale degree, ♯ a sharpened one. The rhythmic unit is that of "oompah" beats, for example, eighth notes in 2/4; a hyphen indicates a silent or held beat, italics a half-beat, strikethrough a quarter-beat note. A dot indicates a dotted note; the first barline shows the start of the harmonic period.

2. Kern's show titles were rarely presented consistently. Thus we have *The Stepping Stones* on the sheet music and piano/vocal score covers, *Stepping Stones* on the latter's title page; *Good Morning Dearie* and *Good Morning, Dearie* on the respective artefacts for that show. *Zip, Goes a Million* has a comma on the sheet music covers, but since the show generated no published piano/vocal score there was no title page to confirm or conflict with this. *Oh, Lady! Lady!!* has the three exclamation marks on the sheet music covers, but the comma only on the piano/vocal score's title page. I have not been able to make a comprehensive check of theater programs for this purpose and have taken whichever form of the title seems grammatically most sensible. Where a music title page exists, I have followed it. The original ampersand has been outlawed for *Theodore and Co.*, though the original numeral for *90 in the Shade* has not.

Jerome Kern

CHAPTER 1

Introducing Kern

Prelude: The State of the Subject

THE NAME OF JEROME KERN IS WELL KNOWN; THE COMPOSER IS not. During his lifetime and for years after his death eulogists spoke of "no more gifted composer in the American scene . . . since the passing of the late Victor Herbert[;] . . . one of the truly great songwriters of all times"; of "the composer of *Show Boat* and many another great musical score" as one who enjoyed "a special place in the hearts of all music lovers everywhere" and wrote some of the "greatest classics of American songwriting." Kern and Oscar Hammerstein were "America's greatest team of composers," Kern's melodies "as much a part of us as our voices and our hearts, for which they were written"; Kern had earned "a lasting place in his nation's memory" and "many of his works will be written in[to] the folklore of American music." David Ewen, in the first book on Kern, called him "a great composer, a genius."[1] Commemorative postage stamps were issued for his centenary in 1985, and the Gramatan Masonic Lodge of Bronxville, New York, into which Kern had been initiated in May 1919, dubbed him "King of the American musical stage" in a first-day cover note that accompanied them.

Such reverential pronouncements were sometimes challenged, for example, when a review of Kern's 1946 "biopic," *Till the Clouds Roll By*, deplored lines like "Yours are the folksongs of a nation" as "alien corn."[2] But they have remained standard, with the effect of sacralizing a small number of Kern's songs as though, still more than folklore, they were favorite hymns.

Perhaps only "Ol' Man River" and "Smoke Gets in Your Eyes" could be hummed by the person in the street today, although "The Way You Look Tonight," "Look For the Silver Lining," "All the Things You Are," and one or two more might come to memory with prompting; others such as "She Didn't Say 'Yes,'" once heard or reheard, are never forgotten. At the same time the very familiarity of Kern's best-known songs militates against thinking about them. How often is it recognized that the end of "Smoke Gets in Your Eyes" lacks its proper verbal closure? Otto Harbach wanted to perfect his poetic conceit by twisting it to "It's when a lovely flame *dies*, / That smoke gets in your eyes" in his last two lines, but Kern was unwilling to supply two extra melody notes (for "it's" and "that").[3] Or did he realize that Harbach's proper emphasis would be musically insoluble?

Kern's music has not been critically investigated, or even conserved, whole. Only forty-six of his songs are easily available in print, plus a few more in the published piano/vocal score of *Show Boat*, whereas he wrote well over 1,000, probably nearer 1,350, though nobody knows for sure in the absence of an annotated thematic catalogue. Few of the mature ones are less than excellent, and Kern never repeated himself, though he reused many of his songs (most commonly the refrain portion). Almost all of these songs were first performed on the stage or on screen in dramatic presentations mixing sung music with spoken dialogue. Yet of the forty-odd stage shows for which Kern was principal or sole composer, none was ever published in a score that included the script; indeed, only four of the scripts were published at all, and only in England in Kern's lifetime, in editions so ephemeral that even the British Library lacks them. The music on its own has fared slightly better, for a complete piano/vocal score was published for fourteen of his shows, yet this still leaves nearly thirty of which major portions (ensembles, underscored scenes, and finales) exist only in manuscript or in hire-library photocopies or, worse, have perished, as with *Three Sisters*. As for the orchestrations, never produced by Kern himself but by right-hand men, notably Frank Saddler and Robert Russell Bennett, almost as many are lost as locatable, and none has been published. Nor is any Kern musical edition planned. An unannotated and incomplete reprint edition of his published songs has petered out, though one is thankful for its sixteen modest volumes. Perhaps eight hundred or more of Kern's songs were published as individual pieces of sheet music for voice and piano, but most if not all except the anthologized forty-six have long been out of print, now sought after as much for their delightful cover art as their musical content.

Kern is not alone in these respects: the outputs of George Gershwin, Cole Porter, Irving Berlin, and the earlier Richard Rodgers are scarcely more consolidated; Harry Warren is worse off. Even the Rodgers and Hammerstein scripts, once available in a handy bound volume, have now been taken out of retail circulation because of legal complications.[4]

The music for films has fared as badly as Kern's stage works. Nothing beyond individual songs, generally truncated, has been published as sheet music. There are no published screenplays. Worse, where underscoring and vocal or choral arrangements and general routing are concerned—and they constitute a much greater proportion of a film's music than within a stage score—one cannot even be sure what was written by Kern and what was supplied by the studio's musical director or the film's orchestrator, with or without Kern's involvement and approval. In many cases the film archives may eventually answer such questions, but the work has not yet been done, and in some cases may not yet (or may no longer) be possible. On the other hand, one can hear a film musical's songs as they sounded on the original soundtrack and as they graced the narrative, for many of the films remain available. This is untrue of the stage music, for with minor though important exceptions there are no surviving recordings by the original cast, orchestra, and musical director of Kern's Broadway musicals, and throughout Kern's lifetime such stars as Fred Astaire went into the recording studio not to recreate what they had sung on stage or screen but to make a song popular as vocalist for a dance-band arrangement. London treated its musical theater composers somewhat more generously during the years of Kern's prime, and *Show Boat, Oh, Boy!* (as *Oh Joy!*), and *Sally* were all extensively recorded with their original London casts. These are crucial historical documents, one of them, "Wedding Bells" from *Oh Joy!*, a Kern song apparently surviving on record but not in score; this number also includes a generous portion of spoken dialogue for George, Jim, and the Judge. London and Broadway performance practice—at least for Kern's type of show— was comparably anglophone in style in those days, but it is still galling to admit that we do not know what Kern's stage shows sounded like in New York at the time of their initial run. Singing, speaking, acting, and orchestral playing have all changed greatly since the 1920s and 1930s, and the intimate recorded sound of film rendered conditions and performance practice in the Hollywood studio different from the start from those of Broadway, which did eventually come into line, but slowly. Latter-day recordings of Kern's stage shows, even when restoring the original orchestration, have been performed by singers and players trained or experienced in different traditions, including those of the modern studio, the amplified Broadway stage, the postwar symphony orchestra, choir, and conservatoire, and even the early music movement. Few if any of them are the inveterate troupers of more artisanal times.

Latter-day recordings and concert performances there have at least been, and John McGlinn stands preeminent in the Kern historiography for his work of reclamation. The complete *Show Boat* is his major monument, *Sitting Pretty* and the *Jerome Kern Treasury* scarcely lesser ones. Other show recordings are in the offing. New York, London, and West Coast concert stagings of such musicals as *Very Warm for May*, *Music in the Air*, and *Sweet Adeline* have given those who attended them, over the past two decades or more, unexampled insights into the uncanonic Broadway Kern; but virtually all of Broadway Kern is uncanonic, *Show Boat* being the glaring exception. *Leave It to Jane* ran off Broadway some decades ago, left behind a recording, and like a few of the other shows very occasionally enjoys, or suffers, an amateur or student production. *Very Good Eddie* has been professionally revived, but with the usual paraphernalia of rewritten libretto, reorchestrated score, and interpolations that prevents critical assessment of the show in its full historical context and, worse, substitutes the new "book" for the old one in the rental library. Where does the old one go to? Too seldom does anyone know.[5]

Recordings, even McGlinn's of *Show Boat*, do not include all the spoken dialogue. A concert performance does, but one still needs to see the show fully staged to judge its emotional and dramatic potential. Not until a decent number of Kern's musicals have found their way back to the theater shall we really be able to say we know the composer.

Meanwhile, the Kern literature is naturally of considerable help to the critical musicologist, but in certain respects only. Gerald Bordman's *Jerome Kern* (1980) is a reliable, painstaking, and exhaustive monument, though with patent limitations, not least a publication date prior to the discovery of the Warner Bros. warehouse material in Secaucus, New Jersey, in 1982. Bordman researched fact and undermined the fiction of Kern mythology, untangled the songs in the shows (he indexes them all), and has something germane to say about most of them. We are lucky to have such a biography.[6] Yet Bordman is not a musician and cannot bring Kern the composer, Kern the Broadway master back to life. He also did relatively little research on the film music or the London shows. Most seriously for subsequent scholarship, his research is unfootnoted and there is no bibliography.

Bordman's is hardly a coffee-table book, indeed is distinctly dense in its attention to detail. Why scholarly apparatus is deemed anathema to such musical theater critiques is therefore a mystery, but it affects many of them, and this has queered the pitch for whole generations of scholars who are accordingly supposed to be in the know about the primary source repositories without the help of a documentary trail. Admittedly access to private collections and to Kern's contemporaries by way of interview accounts for much of Bordman's working material, but since the former can change hands (the residual holdings of Kern's daughter, Betty Kern Miller, who died in 1996, are now in the Library of Congress) and the latter are now dead, it is all the more important to be able to trace remarks and artefacts to their source.

Of the other four books solely devoted to Kern, one, Andrew Lamb's *Jerome Kern in Edwardian London* (1981, revised 1985), is more an essay in detective work on the young composer's movements than a rounded monograph, but exemplary in approach, content, and procedure, altogether fascinating, and invaluable. Ewen's two studies, *The Story of Jerome Kern* (1953), a modest introduction, and the somewhat larger *The World of Jerome Kern* (1960), while couched for the general reader of their period and sometimes responsible for spuriousness of fact that has died hard, should not be overlooked, for two reasons. First, he was close in time to his sources; second, while *The Story of Jerome Kern* is bland, Ewen is surprisingly candid, sometimes negative in *The World of Jerome Kern*, evidence of a long hard look at the subject fifteen years on from Kern's death by the composer's widow (who died in 1959) and daughter as well as the author. But again, Ewen does not cite his sources and occasionally makes a bad mistake. Michael Freedland's *Jerome Kern* (1978) lacks scholarly integrity and although readable is full of errors and largely superseded by the more accurate Bordman, though it includes some "hitherto untold family stories" from Betty Kern Miller and material from other interviewees that does not appear elsewhere.[7]

Beyond these, particular labors of love are Miles Kreuger's *Show Boat: The Story of a Classic American Musical* (1977), Steven Suskin's *Berlin, Kern, Rodgers, Hart and Hammerstein: A Complete Song Catalogue* (1990), which lists 938 copyrighted songs by Kern (in three ways: separately, by show, and by lyricist), and Lee Davis's *Bolton and Wodehouse and Kern* (1993). Davis, by quoting lyrics and portions of dialogue as well as reviews, gives more of the flavor of the shows than Bordman and is clearly in control of a wide range of unpublished sources, though he stops short of music examples and relies rather heavily on P. G. Wodehouse's and Guy Bolton's own account of their musical theater collaborations, *Bring on the Girls* (1954).[8] Who wouldn't? *Bring on the Girls* as hilarious reading will win out over more meticulous scholarship for a long while yet; one would relinquish many of its anecdotes, true or false, only with extreme reluctance. Given Wodehouse's and Hammerstein's importance in Kern's career, various documentary publications on the former—most recently Barry Day's *The Complete Lyrics of P. G. Wodehouse* (2004)—and the biography of the latter by Hugh Fordin, *Getting to Know Him* (1997), are indispensable, as is Stanley Green's *Rodgers and Hammerstein Fact Book* (1980). But by the same token the absence of any scholarship at all on Otto Harbach leaves a big gap, as does the paucity of journal articles on Kern. There have, however, been various American dissertations on him and his collaborators, mostly about the Princess shows; James Randall's *Becoming Jerome Kern* (2004) is superior, a significant contribution to the literature.[9] One primary source postdating Bordman in print was Robert Russell Bennett's autobiography, *The Broadway Sound* (1999, edited by George J. Ferencz). It contains so much on Kern and the creation of his shows and films as to be a major item of bibliography.

But what of published critical commentary on Kern's music? Alec Wilder, in his inimitable way, analyzed about forty of Kern's songs in *American Popular Song* (1972), Allen Forte six at greater length in *The American Popular Ballad* (1995) and one in *Listening to Classic American Popular Songs* (2001). For a contextual model of musicological investigation of Kern the composer, however, one has to turn to Geoffrey Block's chapter on *Show Boat* in *Enchanted Evenings* (1997). Block's work is the nearest thing to a model available to me.

Journeyman Kern

Jerome David Kern was born on 27 January 1885 in New York City to prosperous middle-class parents, both Jewish. He was the sixth and penultimate son—there were no daughters—of Henry and Fannie Kern, though four of Jerome's brothers were dead by the time he was a teenager (the careers of the other two, Joseph and Edwin, do not feature in anybody's narrative). Louis Hirsch, another musical theater composer, grew up next door on East 56th Street, in a neighborhood now extremely select. (Kern's birthplace does not survive.) Henry Kern was born in Germany in 1842, Fannie, whose maiden name was Kakeles, in New York ten years later, though both her parents came from Bohemia. She was a fine pianist, and it can hardly be by chance that Jerome Kern wrote magnificently tuneful and rhythmic polkas throughout his life as the 2/4 or 2/2 staples of his shows and films, which though mostly unlabeled and rarely recognized as such breathe the dance's phrasing and gesture at every turn. (See ex. 1.1, its tunes recast in 2/4 meter where necessary to make the point; fig. 1.5, "Two Dachshunds," is another excellent example.)

Henry Kern had run a stabling business in Manhattan but later turned to merchandizing. When Jerome was eleven or twelve the family moved across the Hudson to Newark, New Jersey, where Henry remained successful, even when his wayward son, working for the firm after leaving Newark High School, ordered two hundred pianos rather than two for onward sale. "You can't imagine what it looks like for two hundred pianos to come off vans," Jerome told his daughter.[10] Whether or not this persuaded his father that a musical career might be more appropriate than a business one, Kern had already showed talent and enterprise in that direction with a score for his school's minstrel show, *The Melodious Menu*, in 1901, and another, *Uncle Tom's Cabin*, for the Newark Yacht Club the following year on his seventeenth birthday.

The music for these shows does not survive, but we can guess at Kern's early influences and aptitude. After his death, Joseph Miron claimed to have been a school friend in Manhattan and testified that Kern was "a wistful, sensitive kid," subject to bullying because of his music but equally protected "because we respected his piano-playing."[11] The comment has been downplayed, fitting ill with Kern's extrovert image and with a period that wanted to normalize Jews and American musicians, but could well be true. Kern's father took him to his first Broadway musical as a tenth birthday present, and Bordman speculates that it may have been *Little Christopher Columbus* by Ivan Caryll and Gustave Kerker. As a boy he was enthusiastic about Victor Herbert's *The Wizard of the Nile*, which opened later the same year, though his later attitude to Herbert is not entirely clear.[12] He would almost certainly have known his Gilbert and Sullivan and possibly some Offenbach, immensely popular in New York in the decades before Kern's birth, from parlor usage, which also kept sentimental ballads such as Stephen Foster's and the usual residue of light classics in dog-eared circulation. Most of all, perhaps, Kern imbibed the homely (in the English sense) Germanic culture

The Gay Lothario (1908)

Polka from *Oh, I Say!* (1913)

from Why Don't They Dance the Polka? (1914)

Play Us a Polka, Dot (1929)

I've Told Ev'ry Little Star (1932)

Roll On, Rolling Road (1934)

Pick Yourself Up (1936)

from You and Your Kiss (1940)

Polka (*Portrait for Orchestra*) (1942)

Ex. 1.1. Some Kern polkas.

of his parents. They were both to die, in 1907 and 1908, before he was fully established, and this seems to have affected him deeply. He had continued living in Newark until this point, despite working on Broadway and traveling to Europe. *Sweet Adeline*, its setting and character Kern's idea and framed with a song in German, is almost certainly a tribute to the never fully Americanized musical preferences of his father, set as it is in Hoboken around the time the Kerns moved to New Jersey. Kern himself gravitated toward old world gentility on countless occasions and in various ways, eavesdropping on Episcopalian choir practice as a boy, borrowing from a German hymn tune for "Till the Clouds Roll By." In this he is much closer to Sullivan than to his American exemplar Herbert.

The German imperative supposedly climaxed with a period of private musical study near Heidelberg, and though this has never been verified there is again no reason to disbelieve it; it remains the most likely source of Kern's disciplined sense of harmony and part-writing and solidity of texture if he was tutored intensely. Bordman suggests the first half of 1902 as the date of Kern's European sojourn, before he started work at Lyceum Publishing and before entering the New York College of Music for part-time study in the autumn.

Kern got his first music-related job either through a chance meeting with William Hammerstein, Oscar II's father, or through a family friend, or possibly both.[13] He may have started out making bills and invoices, but Lyceum issued his first published composition, the piano piece "At the Casino," immediately, following it up with another, "In a Shady Bungalow," the following year. While neat and thoroughly competent, they are not great music, though "In a Shady Bungalow" contains an early enharmonic transformation. Overall there is no need to dwell on Kern's early works, since for a good ten years after this he turned out tuneful but not especially characteristic compositions, almost all of them theater songs interpolated into somebody else's score, and the stricture also applies to his own complete score for *The Red Petticoat*. Yet he clearly had an affection for his early pieces, reusing a number of them in later works, right back to "In a Shady Bungalow."

How do we square this with the smart, ambitious, sensitive, and teleological figure that we take Kern to have been? First, although bland in comparison with the later Kern, his early songs did and do stand out from the clumsy hand-me-downs of much of Broadway at the time. When, admittedly not until 1913, a Kern song, "Look in Her Eyes," is first reached after 163 generic tracks of *Music from the New York Stage* in contemporary record-

ings dating back to 1890, the effect is electrifying in its freshness. The critic
Alan Dale found something comparable as early as 1904 in Kern's contribution to *Mr. Wix of Wickham*, which, he said, "towers in such an Eiffel way,
above the average hurdy-gurdy, penny-in-the-slot, primitive accompaniment
to the musical show that criticism is disarmed."[14] Second, Kern's finer qualities were probably held back by bachelor sociability, dutiful behavior toward
family expectations, and perhaps insecurity. Like many heterosexual men
with good, normal prospects of career and family, he was not in a hurry.
His breakthrough took a long time, and one newspaper interview attributed
it more to his wife than himself: "Mr. Kern was young—he is only thirty-
two now—and modest, and since he was being well paid and was collecting
handsome royalties from the sale of his songs, the fact that he was unknown
to the theatergoing public worried him not at all. Enter Mrs. Kern. She held
no such modest notions about the value of fame and insisted that recognition
be a part of her husband's payment."[15]

Third, from 1902 onward Kern's musical theater activities were both creative and part of a business occupation in music publishing. In the latter
he was doubtless his father's son, and one might speculate further on the
parallels between his delight in the polishing and placing of a song and the
similar concerns of other predominantly Jewish trades centered on New York
at the time, especially the garment and jewelry industries, though as bourgeois German Jews he and his family would have distanced themselves from
the later waves of east European immigrants.[16] Thus he soon moved to a
better-paid job in music publishing, at T. B. Harms, became a junior business partner in Harms (probably in 1904), and found himself representing
Harms's song-publishing interests in London when Francis, Day and Hunter
could no longer be expected to do so because they had themselves set up a
New York office.

Kern went to London for the summer of 1905. Although by then he was
already enjoying American success with his first well-known song, "How'd
You Like to Spoon With Me?," added to Caryll's (British) musical *The Earl
and the Girl* as an interpolation in Chicago and New York, one can see
why so much has been made of his early experience in the Edwardian West
End. There, on this first occasion, he coauthored a song, "Won't You Kiss
Me Once Before You Go?," with Francis, Day and Hunter's literary editor,
Fred W. Leigh, joined that firm's annual staff outing to Box Hill in Sur-
rey, composed a number of songs which Hopwood and Crew published in
London in cooperation with Harms in New York, possibly attended Charles

Frohman's summer school for musical theater aspirants, and was contracted to write twelve songs a year for the actor-manager Seymour Hicks and the producer Frohman. He probably met Frohman, though probably not on the boat back to America and not as an ostensibly English composer, as legend has it. In Britain again for the first half of 1906, Kern reveled in a social existence presumably not available in New York while he was still living at home in New Jersey. Capturing this perfectly is the photograph, identified by Lamb, of Millie Legarde making a hit of "How'd You Like to Spoon With Me?" in Alfred Butt's Palace Theatre variety show on 12 February 1906. As Turn no. 14, she leans out across Herman Finck's orchestra pit and flirts with four friends in evening dress in a nearby box: Bertie Hollender, Raymond Howard, Powers Gouraud, and Kern (see fig. 5.7). All American except Hollender, they were denizens of a rented flat in Jermyn St. and perpetrators of bachelor pranks like the overnight motoring trip to High Wycombe with a bevy of Gaiety Girls which ended when the police came to break up a scene of mock-electioneering. Echoes of such escapades attach to Kern's much later haranguing of the public from a hotel balcony and impromptu laying off of London construction workers.

"How'd You Like to Spoon With Me?" was "possibly the very first public performance of his music in the British capital," though Max Dreyfus, "the legendary maharajah" of Harms and a highly discerning popular music publisher, had already given Kern healthy Broadway exposure.[17] A lifetime associate of the utmost importance, Dreyfus had, within a year of taking Kern on in 1903, placed some of his songs in two British musicals playing in the United States, Leslie Stuart's *The Silver Slipper* and Walter Slaughter's *An English Daisy*, and seen him contributing over half the numbers for a third, Herbert Darnley's *Mr. Wix of Wickham*, when it opened in New York. In 1905 two Herbert Haines scores from Britain, *The Catch of the Season* and *The Babes and the Baron*, also enjoyed Kern interpolations in New York. Kern's routine job at Harms for several years appears to have been song-plugging in the shop and rehearsal accompaniment for shows; the published music and trips to London will have been by-products.

This pattern continued for several years. Kern and his work were exposed to London musical theater practitioners whose names would thenceforward be linked with his. On his 1906 London trip they included George Grossmith, P. G. Wodehouse, W. H. Berry, Frank Tours, Seymour Hicks, and probably Lionel Monckton. His 1905 song with 1906 lyrics by Wodehouse, "Mr. Chamberlain," has been singled out as a first collaboration and for its topical guying of that ubiquitous politician, but it does neither composer nor author much credit, though Kern certainly captures the music hall strut in his lumbering 6/8 conceit with its extended upbeat phrasing (56-7|1-35--|--)* in the refrain. Many of the shows he saw or wrote for in London then traveled to Broadway; *The Little Cherub*, *The White Chrysanthemum*, *The Orchid*, *The Dairymaids*, *Lady Madcap* (retitled *My Lady's Maid* in New York), and *The Spring Chicken* were all on the West End stage in 1905–6, and all arrived in the United States in 1906–7 with a Kern song or two interpolated. Some of these fed back to England: "The Subway Express" from *Fascinating Flora* was reissued in Britain as "Bakerloo" to mark the opening of the Bakerloo Line. Kern also began to contribute to homegrown American musicals on Broadway, including Ludwig Englander's *The Rich Mr. Hoggenheimer* (1906), Kerker's *Fascinating Flora* (1907), and W. T. Francis's *Fluffy Ruffles* (1908). He also wrote single songs for a number of straight plays in New York ("Won't You Have a Little Feather?" for J. M. Barrie's *Peter Pan and* "Eastern Moon" for *The Morals of Marcus*, both Frohman productions), including, rather later, a fascinating Arthur Pinero play about musical comedy, *The "Mind the Paint" Girl* (1912).[18]

English musicals continued to be imported, and Kern continued to contribute to them—to *The Girls of Gottenberg* (Caryll/Monckton) in 1908, *Kitty Grey* (Augustus Barratt) in 1909, *King of Cadonia* (Sidney Jones), and *Our Miss Gibbs* (Monckton/Caryll) in 1910. But when *The Merry Widow* opened in New York on 21 October 1907 British dominance of Broadway began to decline, and from then until the United States entered the First World War, Kern's interpolations as often as not graced a Continental European score. Beginning with *A Waltz Dream* (Oscar Straus) in 1908, over the next eight years Kern contributed numbers to more than a dozen German-language operettas in their anglophone reincarnations, including *A Polish Wedding*, Leo Fall's *The Dollar Princess* (1909), *The Siren* (1911), *The Doll Girl*, and *Lieber Augustin* (as *Miss Caprice*, both 1913), Emmerich Kálmán's *Ein Herbstmanoever* (*The Gay Hussars*, also 1909) and *Zsuzsi Kisasszony* (*Miss Springtime*, 1916), Carl Ziehrer's *Liebeswalzer* (*The Kiss Waltz*, 1911), Richard Heuberger's *The Opera Ball* (1911), Henrik Berény's *The Girl from Montmartre* (1912), Viktor Jacobi's *Leányvásár* (*The Marriage Market*, 1913), and Edmund Eysler's *Der Frauenfresser* (*The Woman Haters*, 1912) and *The Laughing Husband* (1914). This last afforded Kern his first real hit, the song

* See Editorial Method.

"You're Here and I'm Here," which then got interpolated into five or six other shows and remained his best-seller into the 1920s.[19]

Not all of these operettas were new—*The Opera Ball* dated from 1898—but those that were had begun in some cases, like their British counterparts (compare *The Girl from Utah*), to exhibit American settings or references, doubtless with one eye on Broadway: *The Marriage Market*, for example, is in the cowboy genre. The other eye remained firmly on central European local color, from prince to peasant. The significance, function, and extent of Kern's interpolations are beyond the scope of this study and are fully dealt with by Randall.[20] But "You're Here and I'm Here" makes it abundantly clear that they might wield the stamp of naturalization, for it is an out-and-out ragtime song, one of Kern's most catchy and exuberant, with word-setting—meaning, here, the addition of lyrics, by the underrated Harry B. Smith—to match. This apart, we can see that his first professional decade associated Kern with the work of nearly all the European light opera and musical comedy composers active in the early years of the twentieth century, Franz Lehár, Edward German, and the French school being the major exceptions. Their names appear above, though Kern was also closely associated with others, most significantly Paul Rubens.

Yet although this linked him to both British and Continental traditions, as far as we know he never went to Vienna, Berlin, or Budapest to familiarize himself with a show or its creators, whereas he continued visiting London. He was probably there for the first half of 1908 and, after his father's death, for a spell later the same year and again for the first half of 1909. There were music-publishing arrangements to be agreed upon between the three firms T. B. Harms, Francis, Day and Hunter, and Ascherberg, Hopwood and Crew on these trips, and by 1910 he was being described as general manager for Harms.[21] But Kern was not just the businessman in England, for he continued to cultivate British friends and colleagues, especially in the theater. And in 1909, following the unsatisfactory pursuit of an American leading lady, Edith Kelly, in 1908, he cemented the anglophile predisposition of a lifetime upon meeting Eva Leale while on a Thames boating trip with friends at her father's pub, the Swan, in Walton-on-Thames, a riverside town within the London conurbation.

The Swan, next to the towpath though not a flashy river pub, still looks much as it did in Kern's day and honors his name on the menu and walls. He would have been pleased at this, for it takes no special insight to appreciate how clearly and beautifully Kern's music speaks the river's pastoral language: his is a Home Counties art, more attuned perhaps to the gentle, lazy Thames than to the Mississippi or even the Hudson, though he was inspired by all three. He found Eva when the Edwardian age of leisure was at its height and the river with its punts and boaters and striped blazers refulgently endorsed British confidence and well-being, which Kern exploited by transferring them to America when the West End could no longer innocently celebrate the here and now after 1914.[22] There is a lasting monument to all this in several of his most sumptuous melodies—"Drift With Me," "Go, Little Boat," "Weeping Willow Tree"—as well as the final scene of *Three Sisters*; *mutatis mutandis*, there is a counterpart of sorts in the plots of *Very Good Eddie* and *The Night Boat* if not in the symbolism of "Ol' Man River." Frohman, the producer who gave Kern so many of his early opportunities, though never a complete show, would have understood: his own monument stands only a few yards from the River Thames at one of its most idyllic spots, Marlow, where he had made a second home.

The wedding was an Anglican one and took place on 25 October 1910 at St Mary's old church, Walton. By Eva's own reckoning it was not a comfortable marriage—Ewen's account of its early days can have come from no one else. Kern was too self-absorbed and dogmatic to do much to help it, Eva too shy and insecure to steer the household and the relationship with grace and diplomacy. There will have been numerous resentments on either side, probably chalked up rather than fought out, and a certain repertoire of display and behavior stemming from them. They had only the one child, Betty, eight years into the marriage, and she was spoiled and neglected by turns, destructive in her own early relationships, and quite possibly part model for the character Sally in *Till the Clouds Roll By*. Yet the Kerns were married for thirty-five years, never raised a scandal, featured in many respects as an item (increasingly in later years), and were eventually buried together despite Eva's having remarried after Kern's death, her second husband a much younger gay singer called George Byron. And it would be wrong to think of Eva as cold: Bennett describes her as being overcome with emotion at what must have been the reconciliation scene in *Three Sisters*.[23]

After a honeymoon in London, the Kerns departed for the United States, which Eva had never seen, and until 1912, when they moved to West 92nd Street, she had to live in Kern's bachelor apartment. Only nineteen, she was terrified of her new environment, and with Kern's parents dead, her own three thousand miles away, and her husband master of his self-contained professional world, she had no elders to guide or support her. Yet, as we have

Fig. 1.1. Jerome and Eva Kern.

seen, she was determined to further Kern's career. This she did in New York and was not one to look back, accepting the States as her new home and preferring it once she had acclimatized. The Kerns possibly did not visit Britain for eleven years.

First Triumphs

Almost immediately after his marriage, Kern's creative opportunities broadened. However many songs and however much quality and success he had hitherto contributed to a show—and *Fluffy Ruffles*, *The Rich Mr. Hoggenheimer*, and *King of Cadonia* each contained no fewer than eight Kern songs—he had not since the days of *Uncle Tom's Cabin* been involved in the actual creation of a musical theater narrative.[24] That began to change with *La belle Paree*, half of a double bill opening the Shuberts' new Winter Garden Theatre on 20 March 1911.[25] Prefaced by a tragic Chinese opera, *Bow Sing*, by Manuel Klein, *La belle Paree* must have been the more substantial part of the evening's entertainment, since it consisted of two acts, eleven scenes, and twenty-five or more musical numbers. Only seven of the songs for this madcap revue were by Kern, however, the rest of the music being by his English friend Frank Tours.

The following year, again for the Shuberts, he was given his first opportunity to write a complete score: *The Red Petticoat* (Daly's Theatre, 13 November 1912), a substantial, three-act one. Set among the contemporary gold miners of Nevada, this was an ambitious attempt at a musical comedy western (the first?), with book and lyrics by Rida Johnson Young and Paul West. Young was fresh from her triumph as librettist for Herbert's *Naughty Marietta* (1910), which lent the show class, but also from her failure with a non-musical play, the "farcical melodrama" *Next*, refashioned for *The Red Petticoat*, which gave it generic problems. The implied connection with David Belasco's pioneering stage realism in *The Girl of the Golden West*, first as a straight play (1905) and then as Giacomo Puccini's opera, the first ever commissioned by the Met, in 1910, was important. The national spotlight was on the appropriate vernacular setting and musical genre for works in the American lyric theater.[26]

Indeed, for a while Kern's problem was the attempt to marry light operatic pretensions in the music with farce and burlesque in the scripts, and this applies to both *The Red Petticoat* and his next complete score, *Oh, I Say!* (Casino, 30 October 1913), yet another Shubert production. Kern's music for this "farce with musical interruptions," as the *New York Times* called *Oh, I Say!*, is much trimmer than that for *The Red Petticoat*, but it still revels in fancy numbers—a scena, two *terzettes*, a trio, a duo, a duet, a dance duet, a climactic *quintette-bouffe*, and (until scrapped) a sung duel scene—in addition to three acts' worth of the opening choruses and finales which he was now, at last, in a position to compose and which would remain a staple of his musical theater scores until the mid-1920s. Modest simplicity came with two-act consolidation in Kern's next two scores, *90 in the Shade* (Knickerbocker Theatre, 25 January) and *Nobody Home* (Princess Theatre, 20 April), which premiered within three months of each other in 1915. Here Kern was billed as the shows' composer, but in both he again shared space with others. *Nobody Home* was a reworking by Guy Bolton of Rubens's 1905 London show *Mr. Popple (of Ippleton)*, and as farce it reined in Kern's musical ambition. In fact interpolation seemed to guarantee equal and no doubt easier success, at least with *The Girl from Utah* (Knickerbocker Theatre, 24 August 1914); after this had been running in New York for a while the Sidney Jones score sported a new overture consisting entirely of Kern's tunes, of which he wrote seven for the show. One of them was "They Didn't Believe Me," which the British statesman David Lloyd George, soon to become prime minister, called "the most haunting and inspiring melody I have ever heard" when he witnessed it sung by Grossmith in *To-night's the Night* in London the following year. Bordman points out that "'They Didn't Believe Me' is generally regarded as the first 4/4 love ballad to become the principal song in a Broadway musical."[27]

But by 1915 Kern had arrived and was staking his claim on the musical as an American product; this obliged him to forge ahead regardless. Shortly before *Oh, I Say!* opened he had explained and lamented the interpolator's position to the press, which in September 1913 was not only according him exposure as a "native song writer giv[ing] foreign composers' scores new brilliancy" but even, though probably at the behest of a press agency, dubbing him "America's leading song writer," at which one newspaper demurred. Political feeling was by now thoroughly anti-German, and Kern benefited from this when Alan Dale, preferring his music for *The Doll Girl* to Leo Fall's, pointed out that he "was not made in Germany."[28]

Kern was also ensuring his preeminence and creating his myths in other ways. In 1913 he cofounded, with Herbert, Berlin, and others, the American Society of Composers, Authors and Publishers (ASCAP) to protect composers' royalties. He served on ASCAP's board from 1924 to 1929 and again from 1932 until 1942. Also around 1913, he probably gave up accompanying musical theater rehearsals for good, since that was a task which went hand in hand with the symbiotic roles of interpolator and music publisher's representative, and he was moving into a more authoritative position than either. He was working closely with Broadway's best lyricist, Harry B. Smith, who seems to have introduced him to the book auctions that eventually made him almost as famous an antiquarian collector as he was a theater composer, and whose wife helped him understand the essence of musical theater style as "the odor of sachet."[29] Certain leading ladies were associated with his work, including Florenz Ziegfeld's wife, Billie Burke, but most notably Julia Sanderson, who had been singing his songs on stage since 1907 but made a particular hit of Kern's "Honeymoon Lane" in *The Sunshine Girl* (Rubens, 1913) and the following year starred in *The Girl from Utah*. Most important, Kern was on the verge of team ventures with four practitioners about to clinch the identity of American musical comedy, with Kern as its musical epitome: the producers Elisabeth Marbury and Ray Comstock, and the writers Guy Bolton and P. G. Wodehouse. Together they would create what are known as the Princess Theatre shows. Ironically, but crucially in terms of generic flavor, there was a strong admixture of Englishness in this lineup, what with Kern's background, Bolton's parentage and early upbringing, and Wodehouse's style and nationality. At an unconscious level this may have contributed to their being perceived as "one of Broadway's little aristocracies," as Bennett described them.[30]

Nobody Home was the first of the Princess shows, produced two years after the new theater, a very small one (299 seats), had opened and failed in its initial repertoire of one-act plays by unknown authors. Bolton had been brought together with Kern as librettist for *90 in the Shade*. Where Wodehouse first fitted in is less clear: he probably met Bolton at the opening night party for *90 in the Shade*, but the account in *Bring on the Girls* transferring the occasion to *Very Good Eddie*, though factually impossible, makes memorable reading.[31]

Very Good Eddie had a book by Bolton and Philip Bartholomae based on a farce by the latter, and lyrics by Schuyler Greene and Herbert Reynolds. It was the second Princess show produced by Comstock and Marbury and opened in New York on 23 December 1915. But the first two shows to be created by the "trio of musical fame, / Bolton and Wodehouse and Kern: / Better than anyone else you can name," as they were versified, supposedly by George S. Kaufman,[32] arrived in New York over a year later when, after the customary out-of-town tryouts, *Have a Heart* opened at the Liberty Theatre on 11 January and *Oh, Boy!* at the Princess on 22 February 1917, only six weeks apart.

Thus *Oh, Boy!* was their first Princess show as a triumvirate. It was also their best. "Simplicity and good taste indelibly marked 'Oh Boy' . . . and . . . Lee Shubert . . . said that up to then, 'O.B.' was the best thing ever produced," Kern wrote to Hammerstein years later.[33] In fact their only other one was *Oh, Lady! Lady!!* (1 February 1918), which suggests that too much has been made of this particular configuration. Yet the configuration helped set up many variants. Kern worked again with Wodehouse and Bolton at different theaters on *Leave It to Jane* (Longacre Theatre, 28 August 1917) and *Sitting Pretty* (Fulton Theatre, 8 April 1924), with Wodehouse and Grossmith in a different country on *The Cabaret Girl* and *The Beauty Prize* (Winter Garden Theatre, London, 19 September 1922 and 5 September 1923), with Bolton but without Wodehouse on *Zip, Goes a Million* (Worcester Theatre, Worcester, Massachusetts, 8 December 1919), *Sally* (New Amsterdam

Fig. 1.2. Jerome Kern around the time of the Princess Theatre shows.
Copyright Getty Images.

Theatre, 21 December 1920), and *Blue Eyes* (Piccadilly Theatre, London,
27 April 1928), and with them both on songs for shows not predominantly his
own—two Kálmán imports (*Miss Springtime*, already mentioned, and *The
Riviera Girl*, from *Die Csárdásfürstin*, 1917) and a Ziegfeld revue, *Miss 1917*.
Bolton and Wodehouse also did a good deal of musical theater work with
other composers, most importantly *Oh, Kay!* with George and Ira Gershwin
(1926).

Astoundingly, Kern was also active on other creative fronts in 1917, his
annus mirabilis.[34] *Love o' Mike*, another distinctive Shubert musical (and
another Marbury production), premiered in New York on 15 January (Shu-

bert Theatre), between *Have a Heart* and *Oh, Boy!* and only four days after the former, with lyrics by Smith, a book by two youngsters, Smith's son Sydney and his friend Augustus Thomas, and a prologue with a musical number more innovative and sumptuous than anything in the Princess shows. Still two more musical comedy scores by Kern were completed and put on the stage before the end of 1917: *Toot-Toot!* and *Head Over Heels*, though neither reached New York until 1918 (both at the George M. Cohan Theatre, on 11 March and 29 August). Both these shows had books by Edgar Allan Woolf, as did Kern's fourth 1918 musical, *Rock-a-Bye Baby* (Astor Theatre, 22 May). Woolf was a "longtime vaudeville sketchwriter" from a theatrical family and played a small but important part in Kern's development, loosening him up from the rectitude of Bolton and Wodehouse.[35]

Eight complete shows in two years was a rate of output never surpassed by Kern, and probably not by anyone else. Yet he remained scarcely less productive well into the 1920s, and between 1919 and 1925 was partnered by a writer of book and lyrics with whom he created more stage shows than with any other person except Bolton: Anne Caldwell, sole or part author of *She's a Good Fellow* (Globe Theatre, 5 May 1919), *The Night Boat* (Liberty Theatre, 2 February 1920), *Hitchy Koo: 1920* (New Amsterdam Theatre, 19 October 1920, lyrics only), *Good Morning, Dearie* (Globe Theatre, 1 November 1921), *The Bunch and Judy* (Globe Theatre, 28 November 1922), *Stepping Stones* (Globe Theatre, 6 November 1923), *The City Chap* (Liberty Theatre, 26 October 1925, lyrics only) and *Criss-Cross* (Globe Theatre, 12 October 1926). The fact that five of these shows were at the same theater suggests a loyal audience and customized product.[36] But Caldwell lacked Wodehouse's fame, versatility, and style and has attracted virtually no attention, her musical comedies remaining by far the least known part of Kern's output. They sustained him nevertheless for the best part of a decade in his prime, with no serious falling off in song quality from his first peak at the age of thirty.

That same decade saw Kern achieve fame, wealth, and the personality traits of legend. Early in 1916 he and Eva had moved out of Manhattan to Bronxville, and there, the following year, they had a house built at Cedar Knolls which would remain their home for two decades, until the permanent move to Hollywood. Dreyfus lived nearby, and many collaborators worked or stayed at the Kern house, "The Nuts," enjoying or enduring the hospitality, the grounds, and the eccentricities, which might include midnight automobile drives, sheep on the lawn, and unduly demanding dogs and cats around the house. The antiquarian book collection grew. With

Fig. 1.3. Kern (far left), Irving Berlin (far right), Oscar Hammerstein I (at the piano), and other composers, 1916.

some of the songs of *Rock-a-Bye Baby* Kern began calling a refrain a "bur-then" (though there is an isolated precedent in "Bungalow in Quogue" from *The Riviera Girl*). Two Actors' Fund benefits at the New York Hippodrome organized by ASCAP in the spring of 1916, at which he joined twelve other piano-playing popular composers on stage, kept Kern favorably in the public eye (see fig. 1.3).[37] All in all, apart from the minor setback of *Zip, Goes a Million*, too flawed to reach Broadway, and a fallow period late in 1918, Kern had little to worry about except perhaps growing hubris, which served him ill when in 1922 a court case for plagiarism of the ostinato bass of the song "Dardanella" in "Ka-lu-a" was brought by the music publisher Fred Fisher, and Kern failed to defend himself successfully. By then he was nearing forty and had become something of a martinet, his character fixed in positive and negative ways of which instances would be told and retold over the years. He was, along with Berlin, the foremost living American songwriter and quite possibly at that point the one generating the greatest income. Certainly he was preeminent as a mentor of style, if not of encouragement, for the young. (Gershwin, the rehearsal pianist for *Miss 1917* and *Rock-a-Bye Baby*, may have been "awed to be working for his idol" but would not take his advice. "I am thinking of writing a show . . . in spite of what J. K. told me," he wrote to a friend some months after working on *Rock-a-Bye Baby*.) Gilbert Seldes based *The 7 Lively Arts*, a book published in 1924, partly on the premise that "some of Jerome Kern's songs in the *Princess* shows were lovelier than any number of operatic airs."[38] But it is Rodgers, in his autobiography, who best sums up what Kern's achievement between 1915 and 1920 meant for American musical history:

> It was at the Standard [Theatre] that I saw my first Jerome Kern musical, *Very Good Eddie* . . . the Kern score . . . captivated me and made me a Kern worshiper. The sound of a Jerome Kern tune was not ragtime; nor did it have any of the Middle European inflections of Victor Herbert. It was all his own—the first truly American theatre music—and it pointed the way I wanted to be led. . . . I must have seen *Very Good Eddie* at least a half dozen times, and even lesser-known Kern, such as *Have a Heart* and *Love o' Mike*, enticed me back more than once . . . [The Princess shows] were intimate and uncluttered and tried to deal in a humorous way with modern, everyday characters. They were certainly different—and far more appealing to me—from the overblown operettas . . . that dominated the Broadway scene . . . Kern's orchestral arranger for most of these early shows was Frank Sadler [*sic*]. Here again was something new. Sadler used comparatively few musicians, and his work was contrapuntal and delicate, so that the sound

emanating from the orchestra pit was very much in the nature of chamber music. The lyrics floated out with clarity, and there was good humor as well as sentiment in the use of instruments. Actually, I was watching and listening to the beginning of a new form of musical theatre in this country. Somehow I knew it and wanted desperately to be a part of it.[39]

Interlude: Kern the Composer

Rodgers included Kern's orchestrator, Frank Saddler, in his tribute to taste, novelty, and style in the Princess shows. Saddler was demonstrably the Jim Hessler of *Till the Clouds Roll By,* for draft scripts have the character named Frank Hostler.[40] In *Till the Clouds Roll By* Kern takes "Ka-lu-a" to Hessler, and the frustrated symphonist demonstrates how it should be orchestrated. "You've got to start the melody off with your strings, divisi," he expostulates, offering a classically gruff morsel of technical voyeurism. Such biopics inevitably show the raw, impulsive idea being worked upon by collaborators, from lyricists and musical mentors up to the corporate forces of music director, orchestrator, and producer in the theater or film studio. For how much of a composition was Kern actually responsible, then?

Kern the composer worked with a piano, pencil (or pen), and paper and with lyricists, librettists, and orchestrators. He could write quickly and apparently completed fourteen songs for *Leave It to Jane* in six or seven days in 1917, though, as exemplified below, he was painstaking over details. A perfectly serviceable pianist, he acted as a department store song-plugger with his first employer, as Marie Dressler's accompanist for a while with his second, and intermittently as Broadway rehearsal accompanist for shows to which he might contribute the odd number. "In those days he played the piano quite well," Bolton said of his earlier years, and although Edna Ferber's perception in 1927 was that "he didn't play the piano particularly well," surviving recordings from 1937 and 1940 demonstrate at least a sure, legato touch, even if rhythm and steady tempo are another matter. Though wary of doing so, he composed at least partly at the piano, and Hammerstein testified to having "heard him wrestle with a modulation for hours, take off his shirt and work in his undershirt, the sweat pouring off him," adding, "He won't let go of a musical problem until he licks it."[41]

The modulations were part of an impeccable voice-leading technique, demonstrable in his nearly every bar, of which example 4.2 is a prime instance, so complex in its strategy yet simple and winning in its effect that it might easily have been the sudoriferous creation Hammerstein witnessed (not least because it comes from *Sweet Adeline*, much of which was written in Hammerstein's presence on Kern's yacht). He knew what harmonies and part-writing he wanted, therefore, and sketched them precisely wherever necessary. Figure 1.4 shows Kern's pencil sketch for the title song of *Sitting Pretty*, its verse and refrain ("Burthen") drafted on small leaves of landscape music paper. Tempo, time signatures, walking bass notes, and accidentals are all precisely indicated (even if the half-diminished chord in bar 15 of the refrain is given a B natural rather than C flat), and although Kern does not generally feel it necessary to indicate the "oompah" afterbeats in the accompaniment, he does so when they might otherwise be omitted (verse, bars 6 and 8), and writes careful inner parts where harmonic persuasion or motivic working is of the essence (verse, 2/2 section; refrain, bars 4–9, 13–16, and bars 25–26 for rhythmic as well as harmonic detail). There are in fact three holograph layers of sketching present, differentiated by black, green, and blue pencil. The black clearly came first, in the form of a wordless refrain tune as melody and bass, with inner detail only at bars 15–16 in the right hand. The chords, Wodehouse's "wrong" lyrics, still in Kern's hand, and bass runs were added in green, as was the key signature for the verse. The verse itself was added only at the third, blue stage, as were the pagination, the double bar and indication "Burthen" above it, and the alto filigree work at bars 4–9 and 21–22 of the refrain.

A stemma of sources for musicals has been constructed by Graham Wood. It shows how all subsequent musical documents can be traced back to a composer's sketch such as figure 1.4, and from this stems the piano/vocal score in manuscript fair copy, which will have been used by copyists to make professional (rehearsal) and copyright deposit copies, perhaps also by the orchestrator as source for his orchestral score (the partitur). A holograph fair copy of many, perhaps most, of Kern's songs, including "Sitting Pretty," does not survive. This makes for a good deal of creative space between the sketch and the professional manuscript copy of "Sitting Pretty," which shows the song close to its published state. A four-bar introduction and a whole new middle section have been added, the accompaniment has been filled out, the lyrics are entirely different from those added to the sketch, and there are two crucial melodic alterations: B naturals instead of B flats in bars 9 and 11 of the refrain, and the brilliant touch of retrograding notes 2 to 4 of the refrain, possibly to make it sound less like the fourth movement of Claude Debussy's *Petite Suite*.[42] But in the absence of a holograph fair copy the question arises as to whether Kern or an arranger supplied the introduction

Fig. 1.4. "Sitting Pretty" (sketch).

and penned (or penciled) those crucial improvements and the full inner-part detail. Authorship of supplementary passages is certainly an issue with which much of Kern's film music is concerned, and in the theater music such apparently minor details as first endings can have a major impact on the effect of a song and are therefore authorially significant. The catchy first ending of "Bright Lights" from *Have a Heart* is a case in point.

On the issue of who wrote out a fair copy it is difficult to generalize. Most of the full working piano/vocal copy of *Oh, I Say!* appears to be in Kern's hand, and it was probably later in his career, when he had become "the Great God Kern," that he had the confidence to let an arranger act as amanuensis and realize his sketches. For it appears from Bennett's testimony that Bennett did do this. Having been summoned back to New York from Paris in 1926 to get started with Kern on *Show Boat*, he writes that he "took down some of Jerry's songs [for the show] from his performance at the piano" in order to generate or possess authorized material for orchestration or arrangement (for example, into dance sequences). He would not have had to were a piano/vocal fair copy already in existence. Bennett is even more specific on what happened the following year when work on *Show Boat* resumed; it confirms both the possibility that Bennett was filling out parts (depending on the range of detail indicated by "sketches") and the certainty that Kern had already precisely determined the continuity: "We worked in his living room in Bronxville, where he sat at the piano and played from his sketches, handing them over page by page. On the first day he gave me the entire opening Act One. It involved the song 'Make-believe' and yards and yards of music, both vocal and instrumental. I took home the great bundle of material and spent many hours writing out the voice parts and arranging the whole thing for piano and voices. . . . When we started work on the second workday I brought in the vocal score of the entire Opening in a carefully prepared ink copy, as is usual, and, also as usual, a few indications as to what instruments in the orchestra would play certain phrases."

Again, when "Why Do I Love You?" was added to *Show Boat* during tryouts in Pittsburgh, Bennett waited outside Kern's hotel room listening to endless experimentation with its five-note motif at the piano. Eventually, Bennett relates, Kern made up his mind on paper, "handed me his sketch then and there and I made a quick arrangement of it for voice and piano. So far no words, so a copy was sent to Oscar Hammerstein's room for words to be born." In this case speed was of the essence, and with all those concerned holed up on the spot it hardly mattered who wrote out what: they could corporately approve, adjust, or abandon it in the theater in little more than forty-eight hours. Bennett's account affords a precise chronology: the music was composed (sketched) on Monday morning, Bennett wrote out a draft that afternoon, a copy was made of it (or of Kern's sketch?) for Hammerstein, who provided first a joke lyric and then the real one that evening, a dance routine was devised in rehearsal on Tuesday morning, Bennett and his copyist worked through the rest of Tuesday and into Wednesday on the orchestration and parts, the latter were then distributed to the players for a twenty-minute orchestral run-through, and "Why Do I Love You?" was first performed at the Wednesday matinee. Bennett does not say whether he got any sleep on the Tuesday night after creating his thirty-one extant pages of full score for the number.[43]

Thus while there is little if any evidence for material being published under Kern's name without his approval or sight, and plenty that he exercised maximum control and could be very particular with musical details, it remains uncertain exactly what Kern wrote out himself and what was done under instruction by his copyist or his orchestrator, with or without the free hand to act as arranger. Pending more exhaustive comparison of manuscripts from throughout his career, the question must remain open. Bennett certainly originated many a fair copy in Kern's middle years. But a contrasting late case in point, the theme "Two Dachshunds" from *Centennial Summer*, suggests a third party. As preserved in manuscript (fig. 1.5), this seems to be in Kern's pencil hand as far as the title lettering is concerned, and the "Jerome Kern" and "Lively" superscriptions are very similar to his print style (he also had a cursive one). But what of the musical hand? It is standard for full copies of Kern's late music, occasionally applied over a rubbed-out original, and to complicate matters is used for both full pencil drafts and ink fair copies. But it also appears much earlier, crucially in a copy of "Where's the Girl for Me?" (1915) signed "arr. for piano by Chas. Miller." Miller, almost entirely behind the scenes, was Kern's long-term assistant and his amanuensis at T. B. Harms from at least this date. He remained associated with Kern in California in the 1940s (as of course did Bennett). Miller wrote out the music of "Two Dachshunds," and while this leaves us unsure as to whether the careful dynamics, phrasing, accents, and orchestral indications were Kern's or the studio's, it implies through Miller's authorial silence that the notes themselves were composed by Kern. The exact meaning of "the notes themselves"—octave doublings, grace notes, chord voicings?—we shall probably never know.[44]

Fig. 1.5. "Two Dachshunds."

Bennett's orchestration of "Sitting Pretty" offers further consideration of where Kern's responsibilities ended and his began. For the vocal portions he follows pretty religiously the published piano/vocal score, by this point in the production process a de facto authorized, canonic document, adding only octave doublings, sustaining of "oompah" accompaniment harmonies, and a few redistributed lines. In the dance break he comes into his own with a chattering countermelody that forms a highlight of the show, indeed of the period. This will surely have been Bennett's invention (ex. 1.2). What else was, in the second half of Kern's career, is a moot point. Bennett liked to play cat and mouse with Kern's capability, praising him one minute for being "rather better schooled than the majority . . . very sensitive to harmony and orchestral color . . . very conscious of the basses and harmonies under his tunes," undermining his authorship of fills, countermelodies, and background music the next with the comment, "some of the counter-melodies . . . were completely his invention"—some, not all. Bennett says he wrote the fills in the refrain of "Ol' Man River" (I have more to say about this in chapter 3). He points out that he wrote one of the two simultaneous melodies— "it was a simple strain, light-hearted and sort of Tyrolean, and the melody that went with it was more sustained and romantic"—"at the end of Act I in *Very Warm for May*"; he probably means *Music in the Air* (though by way of *Men of the Sky*). In *The Broadway Sound* he implies that he composed the "Waltz in Swing Time" with no musical input at all from Kern, though it is not quite what he told Bordman. This is no big deal in such a routine piece, part musical medley. The exact musical relationship between the two men can probably never be unraveled, and Bennett was both ambivalent and involved enough to have left a rather tantalizing record on the one hand and composed two tributes to Kern on the other.[45] Where Kern's finale sketch and Bennett's fair copy both survive, however, one can be precise about the division of labor: see the act 1 finale of *Dear Sir*.[46]

Whatever the distribution of musical labor on a stage or film product, Kern was musically literate enough for most professional purposes, although Bennett found him patchy in his intellectual grasp. "He studied, and he learned," and at times had "penetrating thoughts on symphonic compositions." At other times, Bennett claimed, he would say something and "I just went off into a corner and buried my head." The crucial thing to keep in mind is that Kern's lifelong job was the provision of songs for voice and piano, more particularly the creation of tunes as refrains preceded by more con-

Ex. 1.2. Sitting Pretty (dance break), orchestral score by Robert Russell Bennett.

versational melodies as prefatory verse sections. His piano accompaniments were nearly always written so as to include the melody line; his refrains, standard for his time, were in the thirty-two-bar Tin Pan Alley format, the most common forms being ABAB and AABA but with many an artful variant and with much depending on what happens at the four-bar, not the eight-bar, level, as Gerald Mast recognized and Randall, who calls it the thematic substructure, has explained. Kern's early songs often show what preceded this standardization—more tuneful verses, shorter refrains vying for memorability rather than commanding it. At bottom, his genius consists in two things; first, how he continued to create fresh, neat, fulfilling tunes within such limitations, and second, how he placed them, strung them together, interrupted them, and offset them with other material for dramatic purposes, and often with considerable dramatic ambition. Unlike his younger contemporaries, he showed a marked preference for the ABAB or ABAC rather than the AABA option. Wood has shown how in Richard Rodgers and Lorenz Hart the AABA form tends to be associated with the young lovers, ABAB/C with more formal, retrospective, or nostalgic contexts; this needs testing for Kern and would probably hold.[47]

Kern's idiom changed and developed a good deal as he grew older, but there is a stylistic norm nonetheless. One of his first satisfying, really characteristic songs is "Not Yet," first heard and published as "You're the Only Girl He Loves," an interpolation into Jean Gilbert's Berlin operetta *A Polish Wedding* (1910) when it transferred to New York in 1912. Kern revised it for the first act of *Oh, Lady! Lady!!* in 1918, where it acquired the later title and a new set of lyrics, by Wodehouse.[48] The refrain (ex. 1.3) has the standard thirty-two bars, but constructed as $A^8A_1{}^8B^8C^8$ (superscript numerals indicating the number of bars in each section) it is an amalgam of the two most common forms, containing both the midway dominant cadence of ABAB and the B-section "release" (with a lovely Kern sequence) of AABA. Tonally it is simple and standard. Kern is certainly capable of harmonic sleight of hand, including some spectacular enharmonic shifts in his later songs, but here he accomplishes all he needs in a cycle-of-5ths manner, chords V and I variously prefaced by [minor] ii, [major] II and a $^6_4$ prolonged by a diminished 7th at bar 29, though with the odd touch of subtlety as at bars 12 to 14, where vi in the dominant, A major, leads not to ii above the B bass but to the momentary second inversion of a premature V. Such ambiguity often needs accommodating where bass notes oscillating between the root and 5th of a chord are concerned, and Kern does it well.

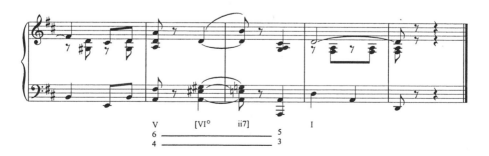

Ex. 1.3. Not Yet (refrain).

The accompaniment pattern is one of the basic three inherited from nineteenth-century social dance forms by composers for the popular musical theater: 2/4 march, most durably characterized as polka (quickstep, two-step toward the end of the century) or its faster version, the galop; 3/4 waltz; and *contredanse* or, again, quickstep march in 6/8. All three utilize "oom-pah" accompaniments consisting of bass note followed by inner-part harmonic afterbeats. Kern wrote plenty of waltzes, not his best melodies on the whole, and too few 6/8 marches, at which he excelled. His staple is the duple-time song, and "Not Yet" represents its first maturity, when it is still cast in 2/4. Later he wrote his "Broadway strolls" in 2/2, and with several songs from *Love o' Mike* (1917) as apparently the first of these to be published (though "A Woman's Heart" in *Oh, I Say!* [1913] is an unpublished precedent) it is interesting to speculate on why the transformation of meter occurred, with its smoother, more svelte implications of character and the "oompah" throbs more blended in to the right-hand accompaniment. (In fact the accompaniment of "You're the Only Girl He Loves" still has the "pah"s of bars 5 and 6 in the left hand; in "Not Yet" they have been transferred to the right.) The answer would appear to concern a mixture of changing vocal performance practice, changing social dance, and the changing, more "sacralized" cultural meanings of song in musical comedy. Be that as it may, for the moment the point is that already in 1912 Kern's melody is transforming his nineteenth-century models. For an explanation of how, we should turn to the words.

George Hobart's lyrics for the refrain of "You're the Only Girl He Loves" are as follows:

> Does he snuggle up beside you,
> With the lovelight in his eyes?
> Does he slip his arm around you?
> And fill the air with sighs?
> Do you both when no-one's near you
> Behave like cooing turtle doves?
> If he seals such bliss with a kiss like this,
> You're the only girl he loves!

Most of this could have been set by Offenbach or Sullivan as patter-song *couplets* to continuous melodic eighth notes starting with a two-eighth note upbeat (the traditional *bourrée* pattern), though a syllable is missing at the start of the fourth line (implying syncopation), line 6 is difficult, and lines

7 and 8 suggest a witty flurry of additional sixteenth notes *à la rataplan* (French military rat-a-tat rhythms) before the end-stopped "loves."

It is quite likely that Hobart wrote his words first and expected some such rhythmic pattern from Kern. On the other hand, Hobart's job elsewhere in *A Polish Wedding* was presumably to translate the German operetta lyrics into similarly vernacular English, so he would have been used to adding words to preexistent melodies. Indeed, Hammerstein claimed that the craze for translated foreign operettas in New York following *The Merry Widow*'s success in 1907 was one of the reasons a new generation of lyricists was schooled in letting the music be composed first, the norm on Broadway thereafter.[49]

However it came about, Kern's melody is strikingly broader than a patter-song treatment of the text—twice as long, in fact, for the older norm outlined above would have lasted only sixteen bars. Its unhurried, poised assurance can only be described as chic, the word that best sums up what Kern achieved stylistically in his first period of maturity, that of the 1910s. Beginning with a long note on the downbeat and then a tied one helps to achieve this, but still more does the fact that each of the refrain's four melodic periods, of two lyric lines each, stops two bars short of its eight-bar span (the F sharp at the beginning of bar 7 is a long melody note; likewise the E in bar 15) and indeed approaches this point with long notes and some strikingly slow harmony (see bars 21–22). These melodic cadences leave room for the instrumental fills that were becoming an integral part of the Broadway sound. One such fill, in the bass, appears here (bars 7–8, 15–16), provides motivic substance, and is developed into the delightfully eccentric bass figure accompanying the B-section sequence, dutifully respected in Saddler's orchestration and audible on bassoon in the song's *Oh, Lady! Lady!!* incarnation. It is quite possible, however, that Saddler wrote the fill himself—Bennett would have said so, since more than once he referred to Saddler dreaming up "some whimsical bass progression" in the Princess scores, and the surviving piano/vocal fair copy is in Saddler's pencil hand, not Kern's.[50] The sequence itself, whether or not the bass came from Kern, is craftily inexact, as are many of Kern's, as though he had been studying fugue with its tradition of "tonal" answers.

All in all, Kern's melodies in this period begin to sound more like chorale tunes than sidewalk burlesques, a vital shift in cultural meaning that helped sacralize the American musical just at the time when Europe, embroiled in an unspeakable war, was in no position to sacralize anything. As such they draw on the best European traditions—long-limbed phrases from English musical comedy and comic opera, sententiousness and solid harmony from Germany, quirky, contained, elegant rhythms from France. Important to the German and perhaps the English influence is often an underlying sense of sadness (more than sentimentality), certainly present in "Not Yet," and noted by Bennett, who said Kern had observed a tear in the eye of the hard-bitten musical director Gus Salzer when he played through "Same Sort of Girl" (1914) and came to the downward octave near the end of a perfectly carefree ragtime refrain.[51] Wit inheres in the sanctified sadness when it is combined with secular desire; "The Old Town" from *Hitchy Koo: 1920*, with the simplest ABAB refrain possible and virtually a hymn in double common meter, is a perfect example. Central to the French influence in "Not Yet" are the short notes, countering the long, tied ones (and to be complemented by the fills), in bars 2 and 10, and, more important, the phase shift in the final period. The shift begins (bar 24) with a two eighth-note upbeat continuing on over the barline with two more, downbeat, eighth notes and gives the defining, innocent esprit to the melody as a whole. It does this through the casual inflection of the two downbeat eighth notes (|353-|--, insouciantly followed up two bars later with an expanded interval (|363-|--). Something of this easy confidence is also present in the downward 6th at bar 15, landing the melody on the dominant of the new key rather than the tonic. As for the words, whether or not they were added to the tune or vice versa, they make the most of this musical added value. "Snuggle up" is sung cozily to sixteenth notes while "lovelight in his eyes" enjoys a long romantic gaze, "fill the air with sighs" indulges in the downward 6th, and the "cooing" matches its pair of o's and pair of doves with a pair of quarter notes; the wit of those phase-shifted eighth notes in the last period reflects and intensifies the wordplay (and lip-play) of "bliss" / "kiss" / "this" and their sibilant adjuncts "seals" and "such." Hobart's lyrics are better than Wodehouse's surprisingly clumsy later set, though Wodehouse points up the sequence with his "near us" / "hear us" parallelism and seems to recognize the last period's phase shift by abandoning the *w*'s that have saturated the beginnings of words (and therefore the vocal character) hitherto.

Characterizing the composer through his verse sections is less easy. They tend to be more discursive than the refrains, less memorable as wholes, but contain passages of heart-stopping beauty, as in "Land Where the Good Songs Go" and "First Rose of Summer." They can be full of one- or two-bar ditties (snatches of catchy, attractive melody) and therefore rather like individual lines or exchanges of speech, which indeed they often are when involving two characters fresh from spoken dialogue. Refrains by contrast are like miniature dramas, tightly packaged around a single idea, verbal and musical.[52] Some verses are virtually ballads in their own right, stemming from the drawing-room tradition and emotionally self-sufficient without more jovial release. The refrain is then a proletarian consequent to its genteel antecedent, signaling broader social territory or, as in "Poor Prune" from *Leave It to Jane*, the tough, independent present as opposed to a secure family past. When, on the other hand, verses negotiate the space between the speech of dialogue and the enchantment of song, the rhythm of vocal patter is more likely to suffice, with or without a recitative-like flexibility of phrasing and lightness of harmony. Or they may have more "applied" character than the refrain in order to stake out the musical and dramatic ground. This is the case with "You're the Only Girl He Loves," its verse based on a folk signifier, the drone bass quarter note and two eighth notes of time immemorial, here presumably conjuring up Poland as a couple exchange observations in a somewhat stylized courtship ritual that also involves episodic, 3rds-related key changes. (This verse is in the major key, but minor verses are common.) At thirty-two bars it is as long as the refrain, and it pulls the latter's focus. Six years later, in "Not Yet," Kern has the confidence to rely more on his refrain and opt for a quite different shorter verse of sixteen bars, one that is much more closely tied in to the refrain's musical character by saying just enough, in notes and (this time) perfectly honed words, to engage us with the cute, put-upon young lovers. After initial syncopation, its whole purpose is to release us, and their feelings, into those first long notes of the refrain, themselves a melodic inversion and rhythmic augmentation of the syncopation; it does so brilliantly in the last four bars with their modulation to the mediant (F sharp minor), jogging patter of continuous eighth notes and rhyme of "private" with "contrive it," the rhyme coming at the very last moment, delayed beyond expectation. Note that in the second stanza Wodehouse performatively sets up the chorus, so named in print, by referring to it—though in a different sense—the moment before it begins (ex. 1.4).

Kern's melodies, like his personality, could be disarmingly simple and direct and became more so as he got older. Example 1.5 (i) is a refrain tune from midcareer with a nursery innocence (and no American features); probably only the French could have established this kind of a model, and the rhythmic insouciance of bar 3 (compare ex. 1.4, bars 24–25) certainly comes from that country, as does its dramatic analogue, a Manhattan dress shop.

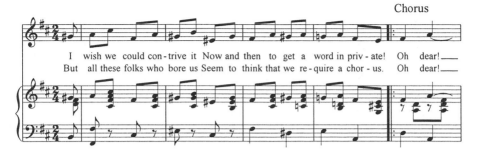

Ex. 1.4. Not Yet (end of verse).

The AABA form is utterly naked, yet even here the sequence in the B section starts with an unexpected scale inflection and is neatly adjusted to dovetail with the return. Example 1.5 (ii), written two or three years later, is equally un-American, rhythmically speaking, and equally ingenuous: it takes a brave composer to disguise the logic of continuation so little, for the less this is done the more weight the original proposition has to bear. There is considerable beauty in the tune's descent to î so early in its course (though the sequence which this involves is again almost imperceptibly adjusted) and even deeper feeling in its importunate rise back up to the dominant by long-line arpeggio rather than by scale (see the beams in ex. 1.5 [ii]). But the real stroke of genius is the inversion of a 6th to a 3rd four bars from the end. Two more 3rds reach the upper tonic and closure. Studying such melodies, one can see why Kern habitually chose to try their strength by picking the notes out without harmonic persuasion, and in the most unfeeling way possible (apparently at the piano with an eraser on the top of a pencil), like an engineer testing a product to destruction. He was conscious of their progressive logic, and in a 1916 interview described it as a matter of "musical plot."[53]

"Not Yet" shows the refrain becoming Kern's *modulor*, to echo the term used by Le Corbusier as a measure for architecture. In the classic American musical all other musical values and passages had to be calibrated around it, and it was Kern more than anyone who turned finding the right refrain for the right moment, and the right words for it, into a definitive procedure. This helps explain the presence of "trunk songs" throughout his working life—melodies he wished to rescue from failed or forgotten shows or unworkable spots for further dramatic use, always with the chance to win immortality. He reused a hundred or more of his own melodies, often more than once,

(i) Every Girl (*Good Morning, Dearie*)

(ii) What's the Use? (*Dear Sir*)

Ex. 1.5. Kern melodies.

and not all of these recurrences have been spotted by previous commentators. Mostly the process involved refrains, though verses resurfaced too, and a refrain could become a verse.

As we shall see, there are various ways in which refrains, and to a lesser extent verses, can not only be made dramatically meaningful but also turned into longer musical units in Kern's music; ways which change and develop as he grows older and involve cross-reference, reminiscence, fragmentation, concatenation, and occasionally simultaneous combination. The longer units may be in a scene of musical underscoring to spoken dialogue, with or without singing as well, and such scenes become emotionally important in the later shows and sometimes in the musical films. One can also find musical motifs of a shorter, less periodic nature than whole refrains or refrain periods; these are closer to the Wagnerian leitmotif in character and function, may constitute a tonally fluid harmonic progression or a mere snatch of melody (or bass) rather than a tune, and may appear in an introduction, an accompaniment figure, a fill, or a connecting passage. The long first scene of *Show Boat* is the locus classicus of Kern's armory of all these devices, Vallon's entrance occasioning perhaps his most Wagnerian motif (Chappell score, p. 37, presaged p. 12), though some of the earlier shows and most of the later ones exploit his skills equally well. Much of the music of such scenes being subliminal, however, and without the vocal continuity of opera, we are hardly dealing with composition as structure.

Where larger-term structure does enter the compositional process is in Kern's finales. What I shall refer to as his finaletto procedure consists of a more or less continuous passage of music, some of it sung, other parts underscoring to spoken dialogue or possibly dance, that incorporates refrains or parts of refrains from songs heard earlier in the act; it is his standard way of building a central musical pillar at the end of act 1 (or two such pillars at the ends of acts 1 and 2 in a three-act piece; in this case the act 2 finale would be the bigger). Since this process involves finding the appropriate dramatic contexts for tunes already heard, one might have thought that the librettist of a musical would have to know what those tunes would be when writing the book. The reverse may have been the case: Kern thought carefully about how a central finale would unfold, with all its dramatic complications and reverses, and then created and placed his act 1 numbers once he knew how they might recur. There is some evidence for this as his working method or at least his precompositional state of mind; when Hammerstein first met Kern in 1924 he observed how Kern helped plan a show: "He and Otto [Harbach] and I discussed a plot they had already hit upon before my entrance into the collaboration. Jerry stuck to the high spots of the show. He didn't care what came in between. Otto and I could worry about that. He wanted to talk only about the big stuff and his talk developed it and made it bigger. He didn't play any music. It was all story and showmanship that day." Although collaborators might agree in advance on certain spots or titles for songs early on—surviving playscripts often indicate these—it was customary on Broadway for a book to be written first and its freestanding songs added later. A comment by Hammerstein during the writing of *Sweet Adeline* bears this out: "When I have finished the dialogue of the play I will come home. Then I will have to start on the songs with Mr. Kern."[54]

It is easy to see how one of Kern's first-act finales works in practice, and that of *Oh, Lady! Lady!!* may be taken as typical. It contains "a mixed continuum of new choral music and partial reprises of the act's earlier songs," referring back to four or possibly five of the six act 1 numbers (not counting the opening chorus); I have described the process more fully elsewhere.[55] What is less easy to grasp is how librettist, lyricist, and composer actually put such a finale together, especially when collaboration was not always in situ. Grossmith's autobiography gives the fullest account of a working method, though it by no means clarifies it. For *The Cabaret Girl* (1922), he and Wodehouse, the Englishmen responsible for the words of this transatlantic product, took the opportunity to write them on the boat to America:

> Our plan was to confer on the story and scenes during our morning walks on deck, to write in the afternoon and relax in the evening—perhaps a final conference before retiring. Kern undertook to conjure up some melodies pending our arrival . . . Our work proceeded admirably . . . Arriving in New York, no time was lost in getting to work . . . Wodehouse and I proceeded straight to Kern's house at Bronxville where we were to be his guests. In little over a week the composer's task was complete or sufficiently complete. That is to say that such lyrics, chiefly concerted numbers and finales, as "PG" and I had completed or mapped out on the outward journey, he set to music, and such airs as he had already devised we allotted to the situations, and supplied with "dummy" lyrics, marking metres and accents, to be converted into the finished articles on the homeward trip.
>
> We had to be content with fiddle or piano copies, sufficient for preliminary rehearsal. Kern would bring the completed score to London himself a few weeks later. Back went Plum and I with our bits and pieces, his immaculately typed script, my pencilled scrawls and myriads of odd sheets of music paper covered with notes and hieroglyphics and the make-shift poetry:

"To-dáy it is our hóliday, it ís our holidāy
"We merrily síng, we merrily síng
"It is our hōl-ī-dāy (3 long notes)
"In the chírrupy sŷrupy month of Máy.
(repeat 8 bars)[56]

The most frustrating thing about this account is that it does not seem possible to match the dummy lyric with anything in the score of *The Cabaret Girl* (or, for that matter, with anything in *The Beauty Prize*, Kern's other postwar collaboration with Grossmith). Other comments, however, are suggestive. "Conjure up" will have left open the possibility not just of new melodies fitting whatever Kern already knew of the show's setting, characters, plot and, most important, flavor, but of old melodies that might be pressed into service as well. And "fiddle . . . copies" implies earlier usage, unless Grossmith means melody leadsheet sketches. But where dramatic continuity was vital—or, conversely, melopoetic wit might be unimportant, as in choral sections—the compositional procedure clearly involved Kern in setting to music preexistent words. Nevertheless, study of the "Wishing Well Scene" of *Dear Sir* (1924), equivalent to a finaletto in technique, suggests a different process. The scene is present, complete from the dramatic point of view, in an early script, and at the very end a sung refrain of "What's the Use?" followed after Laddie's exit by an instrumental reprise of "I Want to Be There" are specified.[57] (These two songs had already been agreed upon for the show, then.) *"The [offstage] music is playing,"* states the opening stage direction, but it was up to Kern to shape the continuous underscoring into five or six song references within a total of twelve musical sections, including the two from the original script. This involves a certain amount of intermittent singing as well as spoken dialogue, and overall not a single line of the original draft script is retained. Since the sung and spoken lines have to reflect the songs' original settings, lyrics, and sequence, one imagines Kern got the musical structure into place first, using the original script as his guide to the discursive and emotional content of the scene and including a diegetic reference to the dance music (which the couple now respond to), and then the authors came up with the new words. (*Diegetic* means as actually heard by the characters.)

The reprise finaletto is a kind of mirror image of the medley overture standard in musicals, if not in earlier comic operas (for Sullivan's and Johann Strauss's overtures, although utilizing tunes to be heard later in the show, are built into a sonata form).[58] Kern did not invent it, however. It is found in cursory form in Gilbert and Sullivan's act 2 finales, that for *HMS Pinafore*, for example, reprising parts of no fewer than five numbers. Oscar Straus's *Ein Walzertraum* (Vienna, 1907) contains an act 1 finale very much in the Kern mold, with its pantomimicry and snatches of tunes already expounded. Kern knew this score, for he contributed three interpolations when it played in New York in 1908. But in general Kern's procedure, which fixed a Broadway mold, is a more obviously commercial solution to musical continuity (because it hammers home songs) than the traditional operatic finale, which it nevertheless emulates with its ceremonial start, sudden interruptions or shifts of key for dramatic complications, introspective moments of misgiving or recollection, and rollicking or melodramatic close. Its connection with opera is particularly noticeable in the act 1 finaletto of *Head Over Heels*, where instrumental doubling of vocal lines is abandoned for several passages, presumably because the characters are Italian (and hence more freely demonstrative)—members of a troupe of acrobats. But the operatic finale tradition (its early peak act 2 of Mozart's *The Marriage of Figaro*) set store by new material, not reprises, and Johann Strauss's approach had been the opposite of Kern's: "It is impossible that the main themes of the finale appear already in the numbers coming *before* the finale—what musical stimulus would the closing number then have—on which the main success of the operetta depends?" Strauss wrote to his librettist during composition of *Der Zigeunerbaron* in 1885, though he granted that a theme might be repeated *within* the finale.[59] Kern by contrast never ceased to balance the exploitation of a song with the aspirations of musical composition.

The *Show Boat* Decade

Frank Saddler orchestrated Kern's very first complete show, *The Red Petticoat*, although earlier manuscripts in the Library of Congress date his association with Kern back to 1908, possibly 1906.[60] He subsequently orchestrated most, possibly all, of Kern's complete scores until his sudden death in 1921. Was he Kern's musical mentor to the extent depicted in *Till the Clouds Roll By*? Possibly not, though he was certainly a serious composer at heart, like most of the great Broadway orchestrators, with a one-act opera for the Met up his sleeve in his final years. He was twenty years older than Kern and had received "a sternly classical training in Germany." And in his correspondence with Kern he did initiate him into the mysteries of advanced chromatic harmony to help Kern "in his struggle with moving picture music" in 1912, whatever that may have meant. Despite this, it was a lighthearted, symbiotic relationship between genius songwriter and professional technician. It was also domestic and intimate—one unidentified Kern holograph carries a message to Saddler ending, "There is a flat box of Tomato seedlings waiting for you here."[61]

Rodgers was not the only one to attribute part of Kern's successful "branding" to Saddler, whose inventiveness included his favorite damping of piano strings in various ways to produce "mandolin attachment," "newspaper mute," and "banjo pedal" effects. Saddler himself did all he could to credit Kern, possibly at a temporary low point, with their joint success: "I had used method until with the tremendous amount of work which came my way it began to sound all alike. Then in sheer desperation, and as a matter of necessity, I began to let the tunes and the individuality of the composer work out their own way. From that period on I was really successful. . . . when I go and listen to a set of Jerome Kern orchestrations, it is like entering a new world, where you float unhampered by unnecessary pyrotechnics in a sea of beautiful sounds. You can pat yourself on the back for this, as it is in reality more Jerome Kern than Frank Saddler: In fact it *is* Jerome Kern expressed through the technique of Frank Saddler." But another of Saddler's letters to Kern makes it clear how carefully he rethought his task with each new show. It refers to *Zip, Goes a Million:*

> I have set the instrumentation for the next Princess show, subject of course to your approval. It will call for 18 men, but I think they can stand this, considering that they had twenty in their last failure. On a separate sheet I am sending you a complete list of the eighteen men and a few remarks as to their capabilities and duties. I realize that in one particular, but in one particular only, I will have to do a little "dodging" and that is the "um-pa." By omitting both second violins and violas, I have nothing (apparently) for my after time but the Harp or Piano, or the pizzicato of the Celli. These I shall use of course in moderation and the reason I mentioned in parenthesis, (apparently) is because I am going to spend a lot of time on the drum part and that means that I must have one of the best drummers in the city. By rhythmic motion of my parts and a careful manipulation of the drum part—always pp—I hope to get a new kind of after beat which, while rhythmical to the very limit of tapping feet, will yet be novel and interesting.[62]

The extra sheet does list the orchestra: four violins, four cellos ("all to be real Cellists"), one double bass; percussion: upright piano with mandolin attachment, drums (one small drum, one trap drum, one triangle, one large, one small Indian Drum, one large, one small "Wood Drum with light sticks," one set of "steel Bells"). "Wood and Reeds" consist of one flute (interchangeable with piccolo), one cor anglais, two basset horns [sic]. The brass is two trumpets with mutes. "*And* Harp." "Note: Drummer to report on day of reading rehearsal one half hour in advance of the hour set for the orchestra call and arrange and prepare his traps according to the wishes of the Composer or the Arranger."

This is a far cry from the standard operetta orchestra and as challenging in its commitment to a specialized, relatively small lineup as it is imaginative in its possibilities. (It appears that Saddler did not get his basset horns, however, settling in the wind for flute, two clarinets, and two bassoons instead.)[63] Yet if Saddler was the man who gave Broadway its musical color, it was Bennett who sealed its musical glamour, duly transferred to Hollywood. Saddler's own protégé was Maurice De Packh, but although De Packh did work with Kern on *Criss-Cross* and later in Hollywood, after one or two shows (*Good Morning, Dearie*, possibly *The Bunch and Judy*) orchestrated by Harms's house arranger, Stephen Jones, it was the young Bennett who filled Saddler's position by rescuing *Stepping Stones* from Kern's own scoring. (According to Bennett, however, Kern had attempted only sixteen bars.) Possibly this was why he later chose a tune from this show, "Once in a Blue Moon," for his Variations on a Theme by Jerome Kern. Bennett went on to orchestrate much of *Sitting Pretty* and handled virtually every subsequent Broadway show by Kern, plus *Blue Eyes* and *Three Sisters* (for which he was required to work in England) and several of the film scores. Once again, here was an intimate, respectful, and hugely important relationship, but this time, as already suggested, never quite without jealousy between Bennett the self-confessed musical snob and Kern the melodic wizard. Bennett testifies to this fully and fairly in his autobiography.

Bennett reached Broadway at the time when the American musical was becoming a thing of glory and stardom, and he was the right man to help give it its concomitant musical sheen. Yet his work can sound surprisingly old-fashioned, and he admitted that he was slow in grasping the "three-trumpet sound" that began to revolutionize musicals with the advent of swing around 1930. Kern began to represent conservatism even earlier, after turning the corner into the 1920s. He resisted jazz and dance-band arrangements, for which Dorothy Parker had thanked him in 1918: "I love the soothing quiet— the absence of revolver shots, and jazz orchestration, and 'scenic' effects," she wrote in a celebrated eulogy to the Princess shows, "and oh, how I do like

Jerome Kern's music—those nice, soft, polite little tunes that always make me wish I'd been a better girl."[64] He was also now writing less obviously for and about the young, contemporary urban couple on the traditional Anglo-American axis but incorporating exoticism of one type or another—musicals about childhood, the American past, the exoticized American present (urban crime, ethnic ghettos, jazz haunts), the "Ruritanian" central European hinterland, the glorified American girl, and exceptional performing talent. This last feature was an important change: if older musicals had featured star turns and unmotivated vaudeville routines, they were now beginning to be *about* stars and theatrical traditions.

In this at least Kern was up-to-date. Spectacular revue was flourishing as a showcase for many of these cultural topics, and with it came a new constellation of big names and influences that performed the change. The most important where Kern was concerned were the producers Flo Ziegfeld and Charles Dillingham; the dancing stars Fred and Adele Astaire and Ziegfeld's mistress Marilyn Miller; the acrobatic, quick-change comedian Fred Stone and his family; two Continental masters of operetta now resident in the United States, Rudolf Friml and Sigmund Romberg, who helped shape the more adventure-bound, geographically extreme, romantic cast of their librettists' books; and the librettists in question, Harbach and Hammerstein, whom Kern first met in or around 1924. Above all, the silent cinema was conveying, to unexampled numbers of people, spectacle, physical humor, a close spectator gaze that could now be returned by fragile beauties, and melodrama, all with an ease, effectiveness, and ability to astound that no genre had ever matched. The stage had no option but to compete with it.

Kern's work in the 1920s encompassed all of these people and ideas, though paradoxically his occasional song contributions to revues came to an end as the decade began (those for *Hitchy Koo: 1920* were his last). Ziegfeld more or less commanded him to compose *Sally* for Miller, the first real sex goddess and source of Marilyn Monroe's adopted name. And Ziegfeld was the only producer who could have mounted *Show Boat* in 1927. Dillingham was the producer behind all the Globe Theatre shows, of which *Good Morning, Dearie* included a Chinatown scene, *The Bunch and Judy* featured the Astaires, *Stepping Stones* showcased the Stones, including Fred's daughter Dorothy in a triumphant debut, and *Criss-Cross* was a follow-up for *Stepping Stones*. *Sunny* (New Amsterdam Theatre, 22 September 1925) was a second musical for Miller though now under Dillingham's aegis, *Sweet Adeline* for Helen Morgan, who had starred in *Show Boat*. *Sitting Pretty* should have been for the Duncan Sisters. *Lucky* (New Amsterdam Theatre, 22 March 1927) included Paul Whiteman and his band, though not much music by Kern. *Show Boat*, with its "million-dollar title" as Kern called it,[65] fused romanticism, melodrama, and the past with star turns and a glorification of entertainment values following on from those of *Sunny* with its circus heroine. Only *Dear Sir* (Times Square Theatre, 23 September 1924) and *The City Chap* seem to have perpetuated a less hyperbolic approach to musical comedy, *Dear Sir* actually having been written by two newcomers, the lyricist Howard Dietz and the librettist Edgar Selwyn, and *The City Chap* by James Montgomery. Kern's more fashionable work for Broadway might have continued indefinitely but for the stock market crash of October 1929 and subsequent economic depression. As it was, the star system remained buoyant in Hollywood after this date, and it was there that Kern would continue serving it.

Hinging musicals on stars meant longer runs and greater production risks in terms of a star's unavailability, illness, or failure to please. More spectacular values meant higher costs. *Sally* benefited from this when it turned out to be the most successful Broadway musical ever up to that point. But Kern was beginning to have failures too—not only *Zip, Goes a Million*, but *The Bunch and Judy, Dear Sir*, and *Lucky*, which lasted two months or less in New York (*Dear Sir* only two weeks). *Sitting Pretty* was a *succès d'estime*. Outwardly his life carried on much as before, financially more than cushioned for the risks. Yet if Kern was not yet facing serious competition from younger composers, Gershwin, Rodgers, and Porter were beginning to creep up on him and would soon have outdistanced him had he not achieved something extraordinary in 1927: *Show Boat*.

Show Boat (Ziegfeld Theatre, 27 December 1927) is sui generis, and as such to be considered later, but symptomatic of a growing desire in Kern to initiate and control his productions, to the eventual extent of attempting to direct *Roberta* himself. In his prime at the age of forty-one, with *Show Boat* he propelled a musical from inception to production with his own vision. Something similar would happen with *Sweet Adeline* (Hammerstein's Theatre, 3 September 1929), Kern's dream "of people on old-fashioned bicycles, wheeling around while carrying Japanese lanterns" its concrete starting point once he and Hammerstein had decided to write another show for Morgan.[66] For *Show Boat*'s production Kern was entirely at the mercy of Ziegfeld, but the eighteen months that elapsed between the idea and its fulfillment had more to do with finishing the libretto and the score than with finding the money; at a fundamental level Kern and Hammerstein were in no hurry.

DuBose Heyward's *Porgy* and Edna Ferber's *Show Boat* were two novels published in 1925–26 that, immediately seized upon by composers, would have an enormous impact on the development of the American musical theater. Both were written by formidably patrician whites and dealt with the historical wound of the black South, which suggests a cultural moment of responsibility as well as of nostalgia and mythmaking. *Show Boat*, the novel, was an instantaneous success. Kern was soon reading it and became determined to make it into a musical; in fact, he and Hammerstein were already busy with their adaptation before Kern was introduced to Ferber by Alexander Woollcott at the opening night of *Criss-Cross* in October 1926. Ferber needed persuasion to grant the rights, but contracts and press releases were flowing by the end of the year, though another passed before *Show Boat* opened.

Ewen points out that "few American stage productions before or since boasted so many song hits that subsequently became popular classics: not merely . . . 'Ol' Man River,' 'Why Do I Love You?,' and 'Bill,' but also . . . 'Make Believe,' 'Can't Help Lovin' Dat Man,' and 'You Are Love.'" *Show Boat*'s stature was recognized from the start, well before the New York opening. "Flo Ziegfeld's 'Show Boat' sets new musical standard" was the *Philadelphia Public Ledger*'s review headline.[67] Yet it is a curious hybrid, musically old-fashioned in many respects, its first act grossly overextended, its second with very little musical substance, and withal nearly as full of old common-law tunes as of Kern's new ones. It was the first musical to be based on a romantic novel, almost the first to be set in the American past, but like most subsequent treatments of a third-person prose original it trivializes much of the heartache and brutality in Ferber's narrative. At the same time it convincingly combines tripping chorus girls with oppressed Negroes old enough to have been slaves, classic escapist love scenes with the portrayal of apartheid, alcoholism, and desertion. Its first chord is a shocking triad of A minor, its first word "Niggers."

In the London production of *Show Boat*, Kern's 1906 success "How'd You Like to Spoon With Me?" was used in the Trocadero scene, again conducted by Herman Finck and again produced by Alfred Butt. This sealed more than two decades of affectionate association with the capital, which led Kern to write a series of shows for London in the 1920s. The seeds of these lay in the four songs, two recycled, he had contributed to *Theodore and*

Co. (Gaiety Theatre, London, 19 September 1916), all with lyrics by Clifford Grey, who would later supply more for *Sally*. (The show's main composer, Ivor Novello, was doubtless running out of time, having lost his score in a taxi and having to rewrite it.) One of them, "Three Hundred and Sixty-five Days," became the hit of the show and was recorded by Leslie Henson and Davy Burnaby as originally sung.[68] Grossmith was coproducer and joint author of the book and would have been in the cast alongside Henson and Burnaby had he not gone on active war service. These three leading comics dominated a strain of postwar comedy in Britain, their various outlets including not just a long-lasting concert party on stage and radio known as The Co-Optimists but a whole series of American musicals at the Winter Garden Theatre, analogous up to a point with the Princess Theatre shows. The Co-Optimists had six members (five players plus a pianist), were formed in 1921, and could well have been in Grossmith's mind as casting for the cabaret troupe in *The Cabaret Girl*. Though they did not appear, Henson and Grossmith joined forces with Dorothy Dickson and Heather Thatcher to star in several consecutive Winter Garden musicals (four, in Thatcher's case) produced annually by Grossmith and Pat Malone.[69] Three of them had scores by Kern: *Sally*, which opened on 10 September 1921, *The Cabaret Girl* (19 September 1922) and *The Beauty Prize* (5 September 1923). The fourth, *Primrose* of 1924, was by the young Gershwin, who promptly pensioned off Grossmith, its producer, from the cast, helping to oust the silly-ass leading man as a type, probably not before time, because he wanted someone who could sing. Grossmith's attempt at "They Didn't Believe Me" as performed in *To-night's the Night*, recorded in 1915, demonstrates that he couldn't.

The Kern scores at the Winter Garden were not his first sole billing in London, for *Very Good Eddie* had been produced there in 1918 and *Oh, Boy!* (as *Oh Joy!*) in 1919, but they defined the new postwar relationship between American creativity and British consumption where musical theater was concerned. The young Noël Coward clearly wanted to be a part of this and wrote a libretto for Kern, *Tamaran*, in 1923, perhaps hoping it would be Kern's fourth Winter Garden show. Only two songs came of it, and Coward and Kern never collaborated again, though "The Last Time I Saw Paris" was apparently written for Coward in 1940, and his recording of it could be regarded as definitive.[70]

Kern's reengagement with London in the 1920s ended on a high note in 1926–28, when *Sunny* and *Show Boat* successfully transferred to the West

End and he wrote an original operetta, *Blue Eyes*, for the opening of the new Piccadilly Theatre. All three productions included stars—Jack Buchanan, the missing link between Grossmith and Fred Astaire, in *Sunny*, Paul Robeson, for whom the role of Joe had been written but who had not played it in New York, in *Show Boat*, and Evelyn Laye in *Blue Eyes*—and all three generated fine original cast recordings, those of *Show Boat* advertised as "Actually recorded in Drury Lane Theatre." *Blue Eyes* is unique in Kern's output: a historical operetta set in Scotland and London at the time of the rebellion of 1745. Bonny Prince Charlie, "Butcher" Cumberland, David Garrick, and Dr. Johnson all appear, and the whole enterprise has the flavor of Edward German. Bolton wrote the unwieldy book, Graham John the lyrics, Kern some remarkably fine music, including the original version of "You're Devastating" (*Roberta*) as "Do I Do Wrong?" Yet *Blue Eyes*, despite playing an important role in Kern's development (see chapter 3), confirms that both Bolton and Great Britain were losing touch with the way musicals were developing: "In the later 1930s . . . a series of four (the last four) musical comedies at the Gaiety . . . were written by Bolton. What is depressing about that fact is that Bolton's American period had essentially ended with the 1920s. In the aftermath of the Wall Street crash, American musical comedies became more serious and satirical. Bolton (and his clones) kept writing the same plot, unimaginative management kept presenting it and British audiences kept accepting it."[71] Kern had traveled to London with Eva for all his 1920s productions there, with the possible exception of *Sunny*, sometimes staying for months at a time. But he must instinctively have realized the truth of diverging traditions when, after his successful decade of S's—*Sally, Sunny, Sitting Pretty, Stepping Stones, Show Boat, Sweet Adeline*—he saw his future with H's: Hammerstein, Harbach, and Hollywood. It was no farther to Hollywood than to London from New York; like most of his colleagues, he simply substituted west for east as his second front, though it would be one final London enterprise that led him to settle in California.

Into the Depression

Kern never tried to repeat *Show Boat*. A fortnight after it opened in New York he and Eva sailed for England, staying there until the summer. Then, as Bordman points out, for the first time since Kern began working in musical theater an entire season (1928–29) passed with no new songs from him.

With *Show Boat* running in New York for 575 performances, on the road for the best part of a further year, and garnering financial rewards from its first (semisilent) film version once that was released in March 1929, he could afford to relax, to put it mildly. Yet that had hardly been Kern's style, and he must have been slowing down for other reasons too. There is no record of ill health for another five years, but Eva had had a nervous breakdown in 1927 and was evidently unhappy with the responsibilities attaching to her husband's priceless book collection, the gangster subplots of musical comedies belying the real dangers of criminal violence to those in her position. Kern sold the collection in January 1929, the auctions generating $1.75 million altogether amid great public interest and a published catalogue. A yacht was duly purchased, which Kern called the *Show Boat* and had christened by Ferber. It was used for winter trips to Florida, where he liked to gamble and socialize.[72] Otherwise the proceeds of the auction were invested, and they disappeared in the Wall Street crash later the same year.

Kern was also thinking hard about the kind of musical drama he wanted to write songs for in the future. The one serious journal article on him in his lifetime, which appeared in 1929, was also doing this: Robert Simon, its author, a close friend of the Russell Bennetts, suggested that "Kern seems to be at the turning point of his career. If he makes the transition from a sort of opera-comique . . . to 'leit opera' we may finally have opera which is thoroughly and indigenously American."[73] This was voicing a quest that has been going on ever since in the cultural battles between musicals and opera, and Kern certainly responded to it, though he did so at first by breaking into films.

While Saddler's letters suggest that Kern was working for silent film as early as 1912, his earliest known film music dates from 1916, when he wrote sixteen modular cues for a serial in twenty weekly installments entitled *Gloria's Romance*. Billie Burke starred in it and quite probably enlisted Kern's contribution. The film is lost but the music survives, and ten of the cues have been recorded; they are not top-notch Kern, though one hears many a pre-echo of later songs and is surprised to find a minor-key canon in the middle section of "Conflict." One of the cues, "Little Billie," was published as a piano fox-trot and recast the following year as "I'm Going to Find a Girl" in *Leave It to Jane*, with the uncharacteristic change of a head motif (from |55♯45|65↑21|7 to |55♯45|1565|7). *Jubilo*, a second silent film assignment (1919), used a song of that title adapted from Henry Clay Work's "Kingdom Coming" and also found in *She's a Good Fellow*.

Sally was turned into a silent film in 1925 for showing with Kern's music, and the 1929 *Show Boat* has already been mentioned, but it is only with the 1929 First National sound version of *Sally* with Miller that Kern's film career can be said to have begun in earnest. It respects the plot and captures Miller's allure and energy, especially in the astounding verve of the "Wild Rose" sequence, which survives in experimental color; but Hollywood, starting in this case as it meant to go on, showed little regard for musical authenticity in throwing out most of Kern's score in favor of four repeatedly used songs by Joe Burke and Al Dubin, good though they are.[74]

In following up *Sally* with *Sunny* the following year, however, First National had to reckon with Kern's presence, for he was on site composing his first original film musical: *Men of the Sky* (Kern wanted it to be called *Stolen Dreams*, to sustain his success with S's), with story, libretto, and lyrics by Harbach. Harbach wrote the outline in Palm Beach, Florida, early in 1930, where Kern's wintering pattern of the previous year, which had seen the creation of *Sweet Adeline*, was being repeated. The Kerns were in Hollywood from May 1930—they went from Florida by passenger liner, through the Panama Canal with the Bennetts—and Kern wrote the music for *Men of the Sky* in June and early July 1930.[75] Its filming took place between then and mid-September, and *Sunny* must have been filmed at the same time, on this occasion retaining most of Kern's score as well as much of the dialogue. No doubt he would have tried to insist on this, but he probably didn't have to since it was early days for Hollywood, still courting rather than exploiting composers. Kern's contract for *Men of the Sky* gave him much apparent power, including "no interpolation of dialogue and/or music, and no additions or omissions or deletions in any composition without the consent of Kern and Harbach"; "Kern and Harbach [are] to supervise rehearsals."[76]

Men of the Sky, starring Jack Whiting, who would again play the lead in a Kern musical with *Very Warm for May*, was unusually serious, a romantic spy story of the First World War ending in heroic sacrifice. Harbach and his ten-year-old son, Bill, appeared in it, Otto as the French major, Bill as a German messenger; but the film is lost.[77] Kern's score survives and will be scrutinized in a later chapter. It did him little good, however, for by June 1931, when *Men of the Sky* was released, the bottom had fallen out of the market for film musicals and the numbers were probably truncated: at sixty-eight minutes' running time and with "an attractive score" but "only one verse of two short theme songs . . . sung by the leads," a hatchet job on the songs sounds probable.[78] The film made next to no impact.

A certain amount of mystery surrounds Kern's first visit to Hollywood. The First National contract also refers to a film musical by Kern and possibly Hammerstein for Evelyn Laye, two other stories by Harbach, and the possibility of cross-fertilization with Hammerstein and Romberg, who were contracted with Warner, had been in Hollywood since late 1929, and were at work on their second film musical, *Children of Dreams*, at the same time as the *Men of the Sky* production. One title which repeatedly occurs in the archives is *Forbidden Melody*, though it is unclear whether it was at this stage an early one for *Men of the Sky* or already the plot that would become a Broadway musical by Romberg and Harbach in 1936.[79] Hollywood was closely intertwining lives and careers at this brief expansive point.

Whatever the deal between the four colleagues, it is clear that Harbach was the key figure in Kern's creative life in the early 1930s, for he was responsible for the libretto and lyrics of two important stage shows, *The Cat and the Fiddle* (Globe Theatre, 15 October 1931) and *Roberta* (New Amsterdam Theatre, 18 November 1933) and together with Kern dreamed up the plots of *The Cat and the Fiddle* and *Men of the Sky*. So little is known about Harbach as a person that he is difficult to sketch here, and being twelve years older than Kern he was already sixty when he wrote *Roberta*. Being also a quiet family man, he does not figure in the social narratives of the time. He was not personally close to Kern and told his son he could never feel comfortable with him. (Harbach was, however, close to Eva, who confided in him when considering remarriage.)[80] But, while allowing for precedent in *Dear Sir*, there is a definite new cast of feeling in his musicals, at its most ambitious in *Gentlemen Unafraid*, to do with expressing the anger and anguish of young people and their loyalties to each other, which is as empathetically idealistic in its way as anything expressed by Hammerstein. Harbach repeatedly warmed to a *Bildungsroman* plot, as we shall see, and bourgeois realism—"integration"—in the musical almost certainly owes more to him than to anyone else, since he profoundly shaped Hammerstein's thinking. All three men—Kern, Harbach, and Hammerstein—had children of their own born between 1918 and 1921 and therefore facing young adulthood as the 1930s rolled on, more than one of them in a highly turbulent frame of mind; one senses them drawing on this experience, not necessarily of their own offspring, for emotional portrayal in a way not applicable to earlier shows, though this kind of identification would weigh more heavily still in Rodgers and Hammerstein.

Hollywood encouraged more ideas than it could deliver, and as the Depression deepened the same applied to Broadway, where it became increasingly difficult to get a show produced and the great glorifiers were gone:
Ziegfeld died in 1932, Dillingham in 1934. The early 1930s are littered with
references to Kern projects which never materialized, most notoriously *Porgy*
with Al Jolson in blackface and a Marco Polo musical with Hammerstein
to be called *Golden Bells*. "Here is a story laid in China about an Italian and told by an Irishman. What kind of music are you going to write?"
Hammerstein asked about *Golden Bells*. "It'll be good Jewish music," Kern
replied.[81] But real care was taken over the musicals that did eventuate, especially *Music in the Air* (Alvin Theatre, 8 November 1932), which Hammerstein wrote slowly and carefully, having had his fingers burned with rushed
Hollywood screenplays. As for *The Cat and the Fiddle*, it shows the marked
influence of Hollywood techniques of fluidity and intimacy and as a "boudoir operetta" represents Kern's major step forward after *Show Boat*, though
some critics were reluctant to accept the substitution of Hollywood sentiment for Broadway wit in a libretto. *The Cat and the Fiddle* can disarm such
criticism because its wit inheres in the musical conflicts of the plot itself;
the same cannot be said of *Roberta*, more vulnerable to ponderousness.

As he approached fifty, Kern was almost by definition now working with
a generation of designers, choreographers, and producers younger than himself. Max Gordon, producer of *The Cat and the Fiddle*, *Roberta*, and *Very
Warm for May*, was one of these. Ralph Reader, dance arranger for *Three
Sisters*, was another, and reading the memoirs of these men, higher on self-
revelation than their elders would have been, one wonders whether Kern's
mixture of increasingly snappy temperament and mischievous humor was
fired by their own of visionary confidence and insecurity.[82] And was it in an
attempt to reclaim older, grander values that Kern and Hammerstein turned
one last time to London? Hammerstein had enjoyed something approaching
continuous occupancy of Drury Lane since 1925 with large-scale operettas,
including *Show Boat*, but *Three Sisters* (9 April 1934) was not well received
there and never traveled to Broadway, despite Kern's confident prediction
of "New York this autumn" two weeks into the run. Hollywood was continuing to release films of Kern's stage musicals in his absence, *The Cat and the
Fiddle* in early 1934, *Music in the Air* later that year (*Roberta*, *Sweet Adeline*,
and the best of the three films of *Show Boat* would follow in the next two
years), and when Hammerstein asked Kern where he was going next after the

demise of *Three Sisters*, he replied, "Hollywood. For good."[83] With Roose-velt's New Deal, the Warner Bros. musicals and Astaire and Rogers all in their second year, one can understand why.

The Hammersteins got there first, renting a house from June 1934. De-spite Kern's pronouncement, he and Eva were less sure of themselves and while staying the best part of a year from the summer of 1934 remained in a suite at the Beverly Wilshire Hotel. Kern was unwell, suffering from kidney stones and the anemia which had proved fatal to his father. One of the hap-piest moments of his life passed at the Beverly Wilshire, however: his fiftieth birthday, celebrated live on CBC radio by Alexander Woollcott in a surprise tribute from a number of Kern's singers (including Julia Sanderson) and cli-maxing with a knock on his hotel door from Irving Berlin, bearing flowers. Ewen's account of Eva's attempts to get Kern to stay home that day makes delightful reading, and one regrets that this moment was abandoned as the narrative frame for *Till the Clouds Roll By*, as had initially been intended and which would have lent the film the proper character. Another bright spot was meeting Dorothy Fields, Lew Fields's daughter, while working on the film of *Roberta* at RKO. This was after she had been called in to write the lyrics for Kern's new song for the film, "Lovely to Look At," in his ab-sence. It is an indication of his sway even in Hollywood that the entire studio was on tenterhooks until he had seen and approved them.[84] Fields, Kern's specified librettist for *Swing Time*, became his last great collaborator, a close friend among the others he made working with younger lyricists in his final period—Johnny Mercer, Leo Robin, E. Y. Harburg, and Ira Gershwin.

This Hollywood period was frustrating, for it culminated in Kern and Hammerstein writing four songs for an MGM musical for Jeanette Mac-Donald and Nelson Eddy, *Champagne and Orchids*, that was abandoned by the studio. Also for MGM, they wrote the song "Reckless" for the film of that name, starring Jean Harlow, while Kern provided one or two cues for a fine straight film, *The Flame Within*. His second assault on the West Coast thus having, like the first, added precious little to his stock, Kern and his wife returned to New York in the late spring, only to leave again for Hollywood almost immediately to work on RKO's *I Dream Too Much* starring Henry Fonda and Lili Pons, a fine, underrated film and one of two Kern musicals for the screen featuring opera singers, a fashion of the moment. The other was *When You're in Love* for Columbia, featuring Grace Moore and released early in 1937.

Frustrated or no, Kern was musically represented in no fewer than five films released in 1935: *The Flame Within, I Dream Too Much, Reckless, Roberta,* and *Sweet Adeline. Roberta* had been refashioned from the stage show to star Fred Astaire and Ginger Rogers as what had been the secondary couple, but *Swing Time* gave Kern his only chance to write a new score for the magic pair. It is generally considered one of the high points of his career and of their series, and one of its songs, "The Way You Look Tonight," gained him one of his two Academy Awards (the other being for "The Last Time I Saw Paris" in 1941). Nineteen thirty-six saw the release not only of *Swing Time* but also of Universal's second film version of *Show Boat,* this time in sound with Paul Robeson, the essential parts of Kern's stage score, and more, for he and Hammerstein wrote five new songs for it, though two are lost.

Following yet more traveling between New York and Los Angeles in the second half of 1935, it must at last have become clear to the Kerns, perhaps with reluctance, that they should move permanently to Hollywood, and the decision was made around mid-1936. By then Kern had signed yet more film contracts, to do songs for *High, Wide and Handsome* (Paramount) and *Riviera* (Universal), with another soon to follow (*Joy of Living* for RKO). As with lyricists and librettists, he liked to shop around, and no one studio ever monopolized him—he worked for them all. The Kerns had a house built in Beverly Hills at 917 North Whittier Drive, only a few streets away from the Gershwins and apparently modeled on Irene Dunne's.

One of the benefits of Kern's Hollywood period was that he could write repeatedly for singers who had successfully made the transition from the popular musical stage, where unamplified voices were always battling against the odds to serve the music, to the screen, where the microphone aided clear diction, phrasing, and beauty of tone and the availability of a star did not depend on the unpredictable length of a Broadway run. Kern was particularly comfortable with how Astaire and Dunne presented his songs without abusing the text. Dunne had sung for him as early as 1925 in the cast of *The City Chap,* but it was as Magnolia in the 1936 *Show Boat* film that she made her mark. After that she was the star of *High, Wide and Handsome* and *Joy of Living,* though he subsequently lost her to nonmusical roles. Kern needed to remain flexible in his Hollywood years, however, for Pons and Moore as opera singers, Rogers as a "belter," and Dunne as a more traditional singing actress represented three different vocal types. The young soprano

Deanna Durbin would offer him a fourth, classically pure and clean, when she starred in his penultimate film, *Can't Help Singing*, and one might add Rita Hayworth, mute because her "vocals" were dubbed by Nan Wynn, as a fifth in *You Were Never Lovelier* and *Cover Girl.*

Reflection: Character, Personality, and Musical Development

"A little bundle of creative energy (the words weigh more than he did)" is how Robert Russell Bennett described Jerome Kern, physically a small man "looking like a tough little bulldog" when in professionally pugnacious mood. Bennett, himself unusually tall and lanky, probably associated Kern's capacity for getting his own way, demanding top treatment, and not suffering fools gladly with his slight stature, though he was careful to stress both that this was a professional, not a social, manner and that Kern could be humane, quick to reconsider a position, and generous. If even Hammerstein felt obliged to describe Kern as "a man of medium height," he was probably sensitive about being short (about five feet four, according to Howard Dietz), though whether this meant sensitive about being Jewish is less suggestible, for "he was, in the traditional phrase of his kind, 'a Jew and proud of it,'" according to Kurt List.[85]

Kern was clearly a social animal, for a Broadway composer could achieve nothing without collaboration, and unlike Porter and Berlin he did not write his own lyrics. Yet he seems not to have needed the stability of a perennial collaborator. He was his own man, never afraid to make enemies; Hammerstein claimed, "He hits hard when he hits, hates hard when he hates, and bears grudges for years." He expected loyalty from others but felt no compunction to continue working with a collaborator if he felt like moving on to another one. After *The Cat and the Fiddle*, he did not even bother to sign off Max Gordon, who described Kern as "mercurial" and found this "a bitter blow"; it indicates that Kern regarded himself as the unquestioned master in any creative enterprise—a musical monster, in Mast's words. "Dreyfus said, 'Look out for him, he'll pick your brains and then he'll let you go,'" claimed Harbach. He had a temper and could be withering: "I have never been on the receiving end of one of these blasts, but I have seen others get it, and they have had my sympathy," Hammerstein noted.[86]

The other side of the coin was "the most winning smile in the world," as Ferber described it; infectious, sometimes helpless laughter and an enormous fund of inventive energy, childlike in its unpredictability (he was never slave to personal routine); and a tremendous sense of humor directed at himself as well as others, for as his quixotic dress sense underlined, he was confident enough not to stand on personal dignity (witness the flowing ties). To Ferber he was "a pixie-looking little man . . . partially eclipsed by large thick spectacles." Gordon echoed this and stressed Kern's sophistication— "clothes well tailored and immaculate . . . a *bon vivant* and lover of life . . . a picture of dignity and sedateness . . . regard[ing] taste and 'class' as virtues of the highest importance." Kern carried an aura of Europe with him, and even Harbach could refer to him as "[coming] over here as the great American Englishman" as though he were Wodehouse or Bolton. A recording of Kern's speaking voice, introducing the first broadcast performance of his *Portrait for Orchestra* in 1942, confirms this and delivers a shock to anyone expecting to hear the tones of a bumptious Jewish American on Broadway: this is the aural equivalent of Harris Tweed, slow, deep, and measured, with swallowed *r*'s à la New England and much à la Old, only the repeated "foist" (for "first") giving away the vernacular New Yorker. It would be pointless to say which of these two sounds, that of the East Side kid who wanted to fit in or the connoisseur of Europe who wanted to stand out, was the "real" Kern, but both were reflected in his songs as well as in his speech.[87]

Unlike Rodgers and Gershwin, Kern seems never to have suffered from depression or dissatisfaction with his personal life, though we know little about his frame of mind as a young man and have seen that the relatively early deaths of his parents affected him deeply. "He is positive about all things," Hammerstein said, and this remained true in his final years when longevity seemed unlikely. His confidence and determination were not always charitably construed—"I wouldn't put anything past him with that ego," Arthur Hammerstein wrote. Ambitious he certainly was, though precisely how, as a musician, is less easy to gauge. The world of Tin Pan Alley, Broadway, and then Hollywood was as much a business proposition as a cultural one, and Kern was immersed in it as a production system from an early age, never exploring any other. Whether regarded as a racket or a golden era, it did not prevent him from continuing to create beautiful, perfected songs and finding ingenious and affecting, indeed sublime, settings for them. Yet there is the implication in this that he remained all his life a song pedlar, eager to trade in the best, most expensive quality and maintain or set the guild standard but trading all the same: selling his wares, wanting a fair price, continuing to produce. When a new score was wanted, out came his folder of "trunk songs" rather like a color swatch. Kern was more overt about this than many, almost as though he reveled in his connection with traditionally Jewish trades and their dealings. The young Howard Dietz saw the folder on the piano in Bronxville in 1924; Kern's last one seems to survive, with its gilt metal corners and contents intact, in the Library of Congress.[88] Gershwin traded in trunk songs too, but Gershwin also spent ten years of his life thinking about, composing, and then orchestrating an opera whose piano/vocal score, at 550 pages, dwarfs the largest of Kern's. Kern's scores grew as he got older, but he never attempted anything comparable. Perfection and artistic truth in Kern always return ultimately to the small-scale artefact.

An understanding of Kern's musical development has accordingly to be set against the fidelity of style implied by the description of a typical song given earlier. He did perfect the art of transition in his longer musical scenes; he set up or superimposed short passages of ostinato or colorful harmonic character rather than simple periodic grammar; and he occasionally wrote vivid and accomplished spans of music bearing little relation to the Tin Pan Alley song and its restrictions, as in the "Nursery clock" introduction to act 1 of *Stepping Stones*. And when he did such things, he did them extraordinarily well, with a neatness absent in many a more ambitious composer. But by and large he was content to range within the confines of the thirty-two-bar song module and its traditional accessories.

The social and psychological implications of this have not been probed except in an overlooked article by Kurt List published in a Jewish periodical in 1947. List is hard on Kern's lack of aesthetic ambition and, while praising his focus on "sheer singing" in musical comedy and the "quality of unassuming friendliness" that his melodies purvey, concludes that "Kern remained the gentleman—perhaps even the prig—that his upbringing had made him." But decades ahead of critical fashion he also gives full recognition to strengths he sees stemming from Kern's position as a well-integrated American Jew licensed to trade in genteel song, including "dramatic themes in which . . . the female as victim" achieves "such . . . impact in the one or two songs assigned to her that she seems to carry the whole deeper meaning of the show." He links this achievement with the "favorite theme of Western ghetto tales—the story of the Jewish girl falling in love with the Gentile"—and recognizes that in *Show Boat* the song of the Negro (both Julie's and Joe's) becomes the song of the Jew, and that Magnolia is the girl who "marries out." "Without Julie, Gershwin's Bess would have been impossible," he adds.[89]

Kern was taught the business of song, both in a musical and commercial sense, probably the business of harmony, and the business of the theater, again in both its artistic and commercial meanings. He was almost certainly never taught large-scale musical structure and could not orchestrate—two essential composer's disciplines alien to him. His musical wholeness stems instead from acute awareness of the technical and emotional strength of a song refrain both on its own and in its placing in a show or film—through contrast with other songs, susceptibility to "routining," efficaciousness of reprise, and so on. Structure for him is therefore a matter of large-scale contrasts and unities *in theatrical terms,* music the marker, not the measure, of such qualities. Important, too, for understanding Kern is the myth of the theatrical turn (in his case the song) as the hit, the trick, the wow, the fix, the stunt—Anglo-Saxon monosyllables denoting a thoroughly masculinized view of entertainment production as instant power in the era of similar values in journalism and business deals. Kern, perhaps more than his fellow Broadway masters other than George M. Cohan and Irving Berlin, was embedded in this world as a young man to the extent that he never broke from it entirely and remained at its service as song interpolator a good deal longer than his apprenticeship required.

There are musical aspirations beyond this, particularly in *The Cat and the Fiddle* and *Music in the Air,* but in general the process of development in Kern was one of keeping his style up-to-date or, conversely, resistant to fashion, reflecting cultural changes only insofar as they did not undermine his true voice and medium once he had found them. The concentration of technical and hence emotional expression was part of this, and it was Stephen Sondheim who in a 1957 sleeve note claimed that Kern's melodies became more and more smooth as he got older, eventually achieving aerodynamic lines rather as aircraft bodies eventually arrived at a cigar shape (though the observation about aeroplanes was Antoine de Saint-Exupéry's). This was true of all American popular song during the period of Kern's activity, which as it happens was almost exactly that of developing human flight in America from Kitty Hawk to the postwar airliner; but it is particularly noticeable in Kern.

His earliest songs are characterized by endorsement of a standard nineteenth-century inheritance, greater weight on the verse, and a shorter refrain than in the mature songs. Ragtime features are used, but patter and tripping dotted-note rhythms limit the degree of drive. This is exceeded around 1913–14 in songs hallmarking two invaluable personal trademarks: ragtime superi-

Ex. 1.6. Honeymoon Lane (refrain).

ority and lyrical breadth. The outstanding example of the latter is "They Didn't Believe Me," although it still shows the influence of Leslie Stuart's long "strolling" songs in the six-note dotted upbeat of its verse, the wistful modulation to the mediant in the middle of a long refrain, and the balletic but verbally awkward little triplet figure at the words "and I cert'nly am goin' to tell them." Of the former, "Honeymoon Lane" is a good instance, though "ragtime" is not quite the right word for its idiom, almost entirely a matter of melodic cross-rhythm (groupings of three against a duple-time accompaniment) rather than offbeat syncopation, found more in "The Ragtime Restaurant" and sometimes in later songs. Thus in "Honeymoon Lane" (refrain, ex. 1.6) the verbal meter, including that of the title, can be dactylic in an equal-note way although the musical meter is duple, not triple. It is this casual energy of vernacular speech rhythms, truly "ragged," in relation to musical decorum that gives Kern's early classics their American quality, and he never abandoned it. The music of the Princess shows highlights these two trademarks, though few songs fuse them, "Ain't It a Grand and Glorious Feeling" being one of the best exceptions.

The dactylic formation continues in use through the 1920s and into the 1930s, but the cross-rhythm is yet more casual, indeed elegant, implying the fox-trot ballroom glide. The single example in the first eight bars of "Why Do I Love You?," at the words "happy as we," pulling up short of the end of the period with poise rather than the need to drive on, is typical, as is its notation in 2/2 rather than 2/4, encouraging smoothness rather than hurry. (There are earlier examples of this, however: see "And I Am All Alone," from *Have a Heart.*) Further streamlining takes place as the 1920s give way to the thirties and Hollywood takes effect, with its intimate singing and emotional expression to match. The opening of the refrain of "Ev'ry Little While" (1930) is indicative (ex. 1.7): the harmonic motion is now slow, enhanced by savored

Ex. 1.7. Ev'ry Little While (refrain).

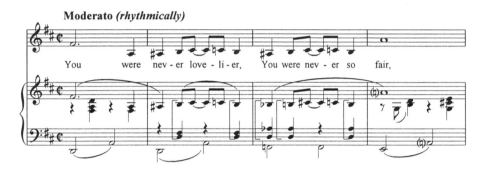

Ex. 1.8. You Were Never Lovelier (refrain).

appoggiaturas and a first inversion, the accompaniment leaves out beats and elides the functions of bass note and chord, and passing dissonances make the melody sit more casually on the harmonies (see the B flat at the end of the first phrase). What it does not demonstrate is the sumptuous chromaticism also found in Kern's late, "Hollywood" period. The start of the refrain of "You Were Never Lovelier" is a magnificent example of this, somewhat *Tristan*-esque in spirit and with the cross-rhythmic glide still flourishing (ex. 1.8).

Superimposed on these shortened and simplified hemlines, as it were, came a succession of ethnic influences, mostly African-American. Ragtime was an integral part of Kern's style more or less from the start. Jazz and then swing he resisted, too set in his ways to welcome or learn them. The song "Can the Cabaret" from *Have a Heart* wished "they'd . . . send the jazz band far away" as early as 1916–17. Kern actually forbad dance-band exploitation of his *Sitting Pretty* songs in 1924 because of its straitjacketing of tempo and texture: each carries the note "The right to make arrangements [of] or otherwise reproduce this composition is expressly reserved," presumably aimed at recordings and broadcasts. Twelve years later he could not satisfy Astaire's need for contemporary swing dance numbers in *Swing Time*, and three years after that, "High Up in Harlem" moved even farther away from him aesthetically. Yet even here Kern was perfectly capable of providing a basic song module that rhythm could turn hot, and "Katy-did" is virtually a burlesque (in the striptease sense) from as early as 1912. Furthermore, he did exploit the blues, both its subdominants with flattened 7th (spotted by Carl Engel as signaling a revolution in American popular music in "The Magic Melody" of 1915) and in the 1920s its march accompaniment of throbbing chords, simultaneously combining the "oom" and the "pah," which makes "Can't Help Lovin' Dat Man" irresistible in its build.[90] Finally, quarter-note triplets in all their smoothness were added to *alla breve* meter once Latin American music became known and fashionable around 1930. The end of the refrain of "Ev'ry Little While" dissolves into them.

Final Years

Kern knew he faced uncertain health when he moved to Hollywood. Bordman speculates that he began to adopt a more carpe diem approach to life because of this, but also recognizes that Hollywood songwriters had little alternative. They were paid for a relatively small amount of music, four or five songs per film, might see it rejected or inappropriately used, and had so little say in the production process that there was scarcely any point in attending rehearsals and shooting. Even Kern must have been subject to this, and accordingly made the most of his social life with the Gershwins, Romberg, Dorothy Fields, Dorothy Hammerstein, and younger songwriting colleagues such as Harry Warren, Harold Arlen, and Jule Styne. Country clubs, miniature golf, gambling, auctions, a collection of silverware, dinner parties, and the new game of Monopoly occupied a good deal of time both before and after his serious illness.

This occurred only a month or so after taking up residence on Whittier Drive. Moving house, one of the most stressful of human activities, was not helped in Kern's case when he discovered that the soundboard of his Blüthner grand piano had been wrecked by the movers. In March he suffered a heart attack with the possible complication of a mild cerebral hemorrhage or stroke. The Hammersteins sailed back from England immediately to be with him and Eva. Medical science of the day was able to return Kern to more or less full capacity in due course but insisted on keeping him a long while in lonely and inactive confinement. Even though pronounced out of danger in May, he was not told of George Gershwin's death in July, though he guessed the worst from a radio broadcast.

That same month he resumed work on the *Joy of Living* songs, and although not a good film it was at least released (in May 1938) with his music intact—at one point during his convalescence the studio had considered doing so without his songs. It is striking that for five years after his illness he did almost no more film work but turned again to the stage and for the first time to the concert hall. His own joy of living was certainly conscious of borrowed time from 1937 onward, and he wanted to make the most of his composing faculties in the years remaining; he may also have been aware or persuaded that writing for Hollywood was negatively stressful rather than positively exciting. Yet his creative imagination nevertheless remained fired by film: "For a long time now I have dreamed of combining a cartoon with a musical play," he wrote to Hammerstein about a particularly zany plot for a medium he considered "the most diverting branch of films."[91]

Kern turned down an offer of writing the songs for the MGM film of *The Wizard of Oz* because he was busy with a new stage musical, *Gentlemen Unafraid*, for the St. Louis Municipal Opera, where it premiered on 3 June 1938. This was based on a story sold to Hollywood by its author, Edward Boykin, but not used for any film. Predictably, therefore, Hollywood and the stage were beginning to draw a little closer together, though that would never happen to obvious mutual advantage. Los Angeles hosted a short stage revival of *Roberta* in June 1938, and Kern's next (and last) stage musical, *Very Warm for May* (Alvin Theatre, New York, 17 November 1939), not only had its genesis on the West Coast, where Hammerstein and Kern planned it during the spring of 1939 (Hammerstein returning East to write the script), but was intended to open there too, partly because Kern's health would not permit him a summer rehearsal period in steamy New York. Gordon's account of its production suggests all too clearly, however, the depredations on common sense and quality wrought by the new era of routine air travel:

May [1939] flew. I cleared my desk of various bits of unfinished business. Oscar Hammerstein told me excitedly that the musical on which he and Kern were working was going well. I said I would listen to the score when I saw Jerry on the Coast. I continued my missionary work [with television] for NBC [in New York] . . . [back in Hollywood] I found time to listen to Kern's score for what was to be *Very Warm for May* and loved it . . . According to our schedule, the filming [of another project] . . . would be over no later than the first week in October. Then I could turn my thoughts to casting the musical, open it in Hollywood around Christmas, and tour it eastward to Broadway. Simple. Only it did not work out that way.

Kern decided he preferred a fall production on Broadway, when the theatre season was getting under way. I was agreeable, though it meant that any casting done in the East would have to be done without me. Still, this did not appear to be too much cause for concern. There was the telephone for consultation. In an emergency I could always fly. I knew all the actors of any quality on Broadway and, certainly, I had the utmost respect for Hammerstein's good sense, perspective and experience. [But shooting the film took longer than planned] . . . Consequently, I did not catch up with *Very Warm for May* until shortly before Wilmington, first stop on the pre-Broadway tour. When I did, I knew we were in trouble.[92]

The failure of *Very Warm for May*, two months into the European war, spelled the end of Kern's Broadway career. On one level he did not know this, and more than one other stage musical was announced from him in the early 1940s (though not *Oklahoma!*, at which he demurred when Hammerstein suggested it). On another, one can read into his 1938–39 correspondence with Hammerstein and the *Oklahoma!* reaction the mindset of a man by now too wedded to Hollywood routines and intrigues to adjust to new leaps of faith on the stage. He accomplished little in the two tense years leading up to the U.S. entry into the Second World War. His daughter's first marriage ended in divorce before she had reached the age of twenty-two in 1940. Two mediocre films were released, a second version of *Sunny* (RKO, June 1941) and *One Night in the Tropics* (Universal, December 1940), the latter making stars of Abbott and Costello, using the songs for the abandoned *Riviera*, and starring Allan Jones, a fine tenor, who had been heard in *Reckless* and played Ravenal in the 1936 *Show Boat* film. On the instrumental front, some string quartet arrangements of Kern's songs were issued on record, but his *Scenario for Orchestra*, premiered by Artur Rodzinski and the Cleveland Orchestra on 23 October 1941, was no more than a rhapsody on the *Show Boat* themes.

Kern, who traveled to New York for the Carnegie Hall performance of his *Scenario* in November 1941, took his elevation to concert hall status seriously, but the *Portrait for Orchestra: Mark Twain* of 1942, one of several patriotic works (including Copland's *Lincoln Portrait*) commissioned from André Kostelanetz, adds little to his stature beyond a delicious polka (see ex. 1.1), though it does not disgrace him either. His real achievement in his final years was his last four film scores, containing some of his most heartfelt, memorable tunes, showcased in the main by fresh young stars. This was his war work, though he also paid tributes to a fallen France, a struggling England, and a heroic Russia in three single songs ("The Last Time I Saw Paris," "Forever and a Day," and "And Russia Is Her Name") and prefaced the score of *Scenario for Orchestra* with lines from a speech by Churchill about "the British Empire and the United States . . . together," no doubt flattered that Churchill had quoted from "Ol' Man River" in the same speech.[93]

All four of the final films are patriotic in one way or another, two set in the American past, a third in the military service present, the fourth a "good neighbor" depiction of Argentina by way of the usual backhanded cultural compliments. The Argentinian film came first—*You Were Never Lovelier* (Columbia, released in December 1942), starring Hayworth, Astaire, and Adolphe Menjou as a follow-up to Hayworth and Astaire's *You'll Never Get Rich*, which had a score by Porter. Hayworth was also in *Cover Girl* (March 1944), again from Columbia but this time in color, along with Gene Kelly and Phil Silvers. Kelly lent extraordinary vibrancy to this, the best of the late Kern films, and although his actual singing does little for the songs, the dance routines and underscoring have a new luster. The same can be said for Ira Gershwin's lyrics.

Johnny Mercer wrote the lyrics for *You Were Never Lovelier*, but for *Can't Help Singing* (Universal, 25 December 1944), the last of his films he will have seen, Kern worked with "Yip" Harburg on a buoyant, witty set of songs and incidental music in a production as close as he could hope to get to the innocence, color, and vivacity of the best Broadway shows; there is a sense here of Kern's milieu coming full circle even while it responds, rather obviously, to the runaway success of *Oklahoma!* in its tone and setting. Kern knew he was competing with Rodgers from here on, however much he might try to deny it by exclaiming, "Condescending music" upon borrowing the *Oklahoma!* sheet music he had spotted on Ira Gershwin's piano.[94] But it was with a recent film, *Meet Me in St. Louis*, that *Centennial Summer* (20th Century–Fox, July 1946) had to compete. About yet another commemorative world's fair, the Chicago one having featured in *Show Boat*, it missed its mark by shortchanging the songs: singing stars were lacking, routining truncated. Despite problems with his lyricist, Leo Robin, in whom Kern lacked confidence and who was supplemented by Harburg and Hammerstein, "Up With the Lark" and some incidental numbers were still a delight; yet Kern had been dead for eight months by the time of the film's release.

Kern's last two and a half years brought certain rewards, notably a grandson, Steven (born June 1943), from Betty and her second husband, the bandleader Artie Shaw, and membership in the National Institute of Arts and Letters, to which Kern was elected late in 1944. They must have brought frustration when an MGM film of *Very Warm for May*, *Broadway Rhythm* (1944), was scarcely based on it at all and pointedly eschewed all of Kern's music, including two specially written songs, except "All the Things You Are," by now a standard. A mixture of reward and frustration was the Jerome Kern Cavalcade film, released as *Till the Clouds Roll By*, to which Kern gave permission provided the episodes were fictitious. Warren drove him to the MGM studios for some of the recording sessions and was sad to hear Kern say he disliked the way the songs were being routined but had given up trying to influence Hollywood production values. He wanted to be back on Broadway, and Hammerstein made that possible in mid-1945 when he enlisted Kern as coproducer for a revival of *Show Boat* and as composer (with Fields as lyricist and librettist) for *Annie Get Your Gun*, which he and Rodgers were producing. Kern wrote his last stage song, "Nobody Else But Me," for *Show Boat* that autumn, and he was talking about moving back East when he and Eva visited New York for planning sessions on *Show Boat* in early November.

A busy weekend ensued. Kern made a point of visiting his parents' graves and was tired by the Sunday evening. The following morning, 5 November, he collapsed on the street in Manhattan with a cerebral hemorrhage while shopping alone for antiques. Lacking easy means of identification, the medical services first took him to the City Hospital on Welfare Island, where he was put in a ward of derelicts who nevertheless honored the celebrity in their midst with silence and space once his identity was known. Kern regained sufficient consciousness to recognize friends, but only intermittently and briefly, and the long vigil over the next six days, during which he was moved to Doctors' Hospital, must have proved disheartening for Eva, Dorothy Fields, and Hammerstein, who stayed by him. At the end Hammerstein tried singing "I've Told Ev'ry Little Star'" in his ear, but the telling varies as to whether or not he saw the flicker of an eyelid. Kern died on 11 November, aged sixty. The clock he had drawn on one of his *Centennial*

Summer manuscripts earlier that year with a single hand pointing to 6 had stopped.

Two months later the *Show Boat* revival opened, successful if not triumphant. At around the same time, Hammerstein took aside the fifteen-year-old Sondheim for a long, tough afternoon's tutorial in how to write for the musical theater. He must have passed on a good deal that he had learned with Kern. Kern's creative lineage would continue.

CHAPTER 2

Kern and Musical Comedy

The Plot Formula

IF PEOPLE MARRIED WHOM THEIR PARENTS WANTED THEM TO, HAD no romantic past, remained faithful and happy when young and older, could wait to get betrothed until they were financially independent, and were not smitten with entertainers, there would be no musical comedy plots. As it is, the male leads in Kern's earlier musicals prove themselves incapable of two or more of these desiderata and get into three hours' worth of trouble on the stage as a result. We sympathize with them for it because they are young and attractive and have excellent prospects if they can sort themselves out or because they represent economic and family stability and must be approved as procreators of the human race.

As such, they are subjects of a type of dramatic comedy which is above all topical, set in the home society and in the present. Home society generally means New York and its affluent hinterland, the very milieu of the Broadway audience itself in these years. (That is not true today, when so many Broadway denizens are tourists; in Kern's day Paris was the equivalent city, and it is striking that his one show set there, the early narrative revue *La belle Paree*, explores a far wider range of social, economic, and ethnic types than inhabit the musical comedy plots.) Of Kern's forty or so stage musicals, over two-thirds conform more or less to this type, if one allows Britain as the home society in the shows written for London, and, until *Show Boat* shatters the mold, every single one of them from *La belle Paree* onward is set in the present. After that, contemporaneity returns for half the remainder. Even the two fairy-tale musicals for Fred Stone, *Stepping Stones* and *Criss-Cross*, include topical references, radio in the former, an aviator in the latter.[1]

Topicality was a theater tradition that in Kern's period emphasized up-to-dateness and its attendant technology, particularly mobility, usually though not necessarily as a status marker. One show, *Toot-Toot!*, takes place entirely on the railway, and another, *The City Chap*, has two train scenes. Two other shows, *The Beauty Prize* and *Sunny*, are partly set on ocean liners crossing from England to America and two more, *Very Good Eddie* and *The Night Boat*, on pleasure boats or riverboats until with *Show Boat* the river theater becomes a symbol of past traditions rather than the latest idea. A car breakdown propels the plot of *Rock-a-Bye Baby*, though the bright young things in the act 1 opening of *Sitting Pretty* consider a motoring jaunt old hat and arrive by horse and carriage for a lark. Current issues are highlighted: in *Love o' Mike* a British army captain in the United States is the dubious hero, at a time when Europe but not America was at war, and once America has joined the Allies *Toot-Toot!* presents its leading man in the process of joining up. *Toot-Toot!* and *Head Over Heels* also forewarn their audiences of Prohibition, a major element in the plot mechanics of many a 1920s musical comedy. In *The Night Boat* the mother-in-law gets drunk on fruit containing liquor and a Hudson River boat captain is Scottish seemingly for the sole purpose of incorporating a criminal partiality to spirits. In *The City Chap* a drugstore, where alcohol can be legally sold by prescription, does good business by dispensing it more freely, not least to the town's hypocritical bank manager. New fashions are reflected—ship's games, mah-jongg, and a beauty prize in the show of that title in 1923, cabaret with similar eponymity the year before, Florida as a place for wintering (act 3 of *The Beauty Prize* and act 2 of *Sitting Pretty* take place on wealthy estates there), the ongoing New York dance craze in *Nobody Home* and *Head Over Heels*. The mirror had long been held up to shopping in English musical comedies, and the first scenes of *Have a Heart* and *Good Morning, Dearie* are respectively set in a department store and a dressmaker's shop, with characters to match and interact, from smart proprietors to elevator boy and serving girls.

But musical comedy plots reflect social change as well as social stability. The social mobility possible in a department store is one thing, ethnic admixture another. While more or less the entire cast of a typical show from the Princess period (*Oh, Boy!*, *Oh, Lady! Lady!!*, *Leave It to Jane*) represents white, Anglo-Saxon, Protestant, East Coast Americans, it is *Sally*, coming after World War I, that portrays an American immigrant, not the first of

Fig. 2.1. Musical comedy as chic — the Greenwich Village rooftop setting of
act 2 of *Oh, Lady! Lady!!* in a design by Claude Bragdon for a 1920
production.
Source: *Theatre Arts Monthly* 8 (1924), 512.

Kern's shows to do so but giving the lead and the first depicting immigration as a political or economic necessity. Here the exiled Duke Constan-
tine of Czechogovinia is washing dishes in New York; later, *Roberta* has an
exiled Russian princess as a dressmaker's assistant in Paris (but marrying an
American). Chinatown, an Italian gangster, and a French couturier feature
in *Good Morning, Dearie. Sunny* has the Swiss heroine stowing away to be
with the man of her dreams in the States, and while this is for reasons of romance rather than national displacement, much is made of her impending
immigration problems: "You are really in a very serious situation," Sue emphasizes. *Head Over Heels* had earlier featured an Italian acrobat similarly
coming to the States on romantic business, staying, and again underestimat-
ing American law.[2] For Broadway, emigration in the opposite direction does
not work: the heroine of *The Bunch and Judy* is not accepted into Scottish society and marries an American instead, though the American mother's marriage to an Englishman in *Three Sisters* had been happy. Except for *Lucky*,

which concerns a poor Ceylonese pearl diver betrothed to a rich American and suffering prejudice which is eventually overcome, this is about as far as it goes with multiculturalism until *Show Boat* signals a partial change of genre to melodrama and can thereby introduce blacks and miscegenation as shock tactics. Jews and gays are never more than implicit in the entire Kern oeuvre, and then not until his later films and last stage shows in the 1930s.

Three issues of plot mechanics inform virtually every musical comedy plot in Kern's output: marriage, mistaken identity, and money. Often all three are worked out in terms of accommodation (or not) between classes, nationalities, and lifestyles, since true, sustaining relationships have to be discovered in these terms, with errors demonstrated as a warning or a yardstick for true love. They are the same three issues found in *The Marriage of Figaro*, for musical theater plots did not vary much over the centuries while the comic tradition lasted in opera and its more vernacular progeny. Plots demand such mechanical complications, contrivances the audience will have difficulty in keeping up with and solved like a mathematical equation often at the very last minute and in the shortest possible time before the curtain. Personal disguise affects most of the Kern musical comedies. In *Very Good Eddie* the newlyweds have to pretend to swap partners; Jackson the butler assumes serial disguises in *Love o' Mike*; in *Oh, Boy!* the ingenue gets mistaken for the hero's fiancée and tries to pass herself off as the Quaker aunt; *Oh, Lady! Lady!!*'s Fainting Fanny is a burglar pretending to be an old flame; a philanderer in *Toot-Toot!* turns out to be a clergyman; not one but three babies suffer parental misattribution in *Rock-a-Bye Baby*; two entire families quickly swap places in act 3 of *The Night Boat*. Also in *The Night Boat*, two boat captains called Bob White inconveniently face each other, as do two vicars in the act 2 finale of *The Cabaret Girl*; twins cause misunderstandings in *Sitting Pretty*. Fred Stone adopted innumerable disguises in *Stepping Stones* and *Criss-Cross*. Male-to-female drag was in marginal taste in musical comedy and features only in *She's a Good Fellow* and for the oversized Pilbeam in *Blue Eyes*, though female-to-male cross-dressing is an altogether more titillating aspect of the plot of *Blue Eyes* when the heroine begins to be undressed as a wounded soldier boy. Thieves and their detectives masquerade by obvious necessity in *Sitting Pretty* and *Good Morning, Dearie* as well as *Oh, Lady! Lady!!* So does the villain in the Fred Stone musicals. There are not one but two detectives on different missions in *Have a Heart* and *Sitting Pretty*.

Money can change hands and fortunes with equally revelatory swiftness and efficacy. Confidence men and gamblers are a peculiarly American symbol for this and duly found as flawed heroes in *Show Boat* (Gaylord Ravenal) and *The Red Petticoat* (Jack Warner), but also in the English *Three Sisters*, its first act set at the Epsom Derby in which a stalwart policeman loses his life's savings at the hands of a petty crook. All these shows, however, play for higher emotional stakes than the classic musical comedies, in which the focus of financial plotting is more likely an inheritance or dowry (*Zip, Goes a Million* its apogee—the hero will inherit seven million dollars if he can spend one million in a day), counterfeit bills (*Have a Heart*), the unwise lavishing of gifts on a paramour (the pearls in *Oh, I Say!*, the ring in *Head Over Heels*), or a deal that has been made (wealthy Hiram Bolton's promise of his son to the rival college in *Leave It to Jane*), and sometimes a theft in conjunction with one of these (a train robbery in *Toot-Toot!*). In the plot type that began with *The Merry Widow*, wealth and glamour are a major factor of allurement in musical comedy but so also is true love; therefore it is crucial that the leading men prove they knew nothing about inheriting a fortune or even a major talent when they fell for the heroine. In *The Beauty Prize* both partners are rich but disguise the fact from each other. *The City Chap* has both its leads settle for a life of small-town industry in the wake of parental bankruptcy. In *90 in the Shade* the heiress rejects her eligible and mercenary suitors. The woman is, however, classically permitted to woo a financially resourceful man; his problem is securing both the fortune and the girl when one seems to preclude the other (*Oh, Boy!*, *The Cabaret Girl*). Nevertheless, there is an increasing sense after the First World War that wealth and social elevation will not in themselves bring the heroine happiness (in *Dear Sir* she is determined not to be bought for her looks and wants to set up in business).

Financial transactions are specific, performative, and instantaneous, which is why they keep a plot in motion. Stub Talmadge, for example, owes Flora Wiggins, his landlady, eighteen dollars' rent at the beginning of *Leave It to Jane* and must clear the debt both to get her off his matrimonial tail and in order to marry Bessie, for which he needs to be solvent. Every now and then, in a running gag, he pays Flora fifty cents or so; toward the end of act 2 she reminds him that the debt stands at $13.25. Meanwhile, Bolton has bet Talmadge a thousand dollars ten to one that Atwater College will not beat Bingham at football, a safe bet considering his son Billy is on the Bingham team. But Atwater persuade Billy to play for them, and they win.

Stub knows this will get Billy disinherited, which is par for the moral course with a secondary comic but allows him to win his thousand dollars, pay off the rent, and give the rest to Bessie for safekeeping (which he needs). Jane proves her love for Billy by accepting him as he goes to work for his father in lieu of a fortune. Flora proves mercenary (her speech intended as Irish?), and Stub's rueful accounting is maintained till the end:

> STUB: Here's five—ten—fifteen! (*Gives her money*) You just keep the one-seventy-five and buy yourself a nice sable wrap, a Rolls Royce and a titled husband.
>
> FLORA (*taking money, and drawing herself up proudly*): Mr. Talmadge, although Ma-mah and I take boarders, we are ladies.
>
> STUB: Certainly. No argument about that.
>
> . . .
>
> FLORA: And we ask charity of no one. I onct [wunst] thought you was a gentleman.
>
> *She stands up toward gate C.*
>
> BESSIE: Gee! You've insulted her.
>
> STUB: Yes. But she kept the one-seventy-five.[3]

Flora is nevertheless accepted by the trainer McGowan, and they make the third marrying couple. Items of property often change hands with equal adroitness, and it really is not possible to tell what has been happening to the pickpocketed necklace at the end of act 2 of *Oh, Lady! Lady!!* from the script alone.

Marital happiness is always the goal of a musical comedy plot, for one, two, three, or four couples (eight in *Love o' Mike*, virtually the entire cast). In the words of Billy, who sings "Niagara Falls" in *Good Morning, Dearie*, "Every play I see finishes[,] I am sure, / Just as the groom and bride go side by side upon their wedding tour." But there are important differences between Kern's earlier and later musical comedies. At first the emphasis is on parity of social standing within the leading couple, their difference more a matter of virginal innocence for the bride, the lack of it in the bridegroom creating the threat that has to be removed by the end of the show by neutralizing an old flame (true of *Oh, I Say!*, *Nobody Home*, *Very Good Eddie* and *Oh, Lady! Lady!!*). But there needs to be a bedroom in a bedroom farce (though with Kern they are, strictly speaking, lobby farces), which is why in several of the earlier shows, where farce carries the pace, the leads are already married, or think they are, and on their way to their honeymoon, true of *Very Good Eddie* and *Oh, Boy!* (and the Gershwins' *Oh, Kay!*, very much in the same mold). In *Oh, Lady! Lady!!* the marriage ceremony is halted in the act 1 finale, and it takes the whole of act 2 to retrieve the situation. In these shows the couples look beyond the wedding moment to the honeymoon (occasioning honeymoon inn, isle, land, and lane songs from Kern, all in the decade 1913–23), but generally no farther.

Around 1917 two new strands of marital plot develop. One of these is the romantic comedy of second chances, again initiated by *The Merry Widow* and doubtless given new impetus by the carnage and social disruption of the war. *Have a Heart* is premised on a second honeymoon intended to help rescue a failing marriage, treating the issue in a way which makes it emotionally remarkable, an "uncharacteristically lush . . . and very romantic" score, as McGlinn observes.[4] The leads' marriage is also foundering in *The Night Boat* and *Rock-a-Bye Baby*. A different type of second chance comes when the heroine settles for someone other than the man she thought she loved and had lost in act 1; this is the case in *Head Over Heels* and *Sunny*, though the girl-loses-boy emotional suspense of a musical comedy involves doubt along the way in any case, and it is often a near, even arbitrary thing as to who will end up with whom in the last few pages of script. As if to prove the point, different solutions to the marital equation are worked out in different versions of the book of *Very Good Eddie*, *Sunny*, and *Sweet Adeline*. If this seems to make nonsense of the romantic ideal, mistaken identity can be equally questioning of it but all part and parcel of the human comedy, in which ultimately it is mutual will that triumphs over appearances (and sustains marriage).

With the emergence of the divorce or desertion plot, however, a layer of pathos is added to the musical which was not there before. This was an understandable development in America given the precociousness of its divorce culture and the different state laws (which fueled standing jokes about Reno); but it was not necessarily a negative one. Stanley Cavell has examined one particular manifestation of it, "the Hollywood comedy of remarriage" in which a couple reunite after divorce, finds it rich and rewarding, and moreover uses it to explain why money and marriage are linked symbols of happiness:

> The comedy of remarriage is, because of its emphasis on the heroine, more intimately related to Old Comedy than to New . . . the drive of its plot is not to get the central pair together, but to get them *back* together . . . the genre of remarriage is an inheritor of the preoccupations and discoveries

of Shakespearean romantic comedy . . . The economic issues . . . are invariably tropes for spiritual issues. (Which is not to deny that they can be interpreted the other way around too . . .) The comedy of remarriage does not look upon marriage as does either French farce or Restoration comedy. [Instead, it is about] the miracle of change . . . [about] dismantling the doll house. . . . The quarrel, the conversation of love, takes lavish expenditures of time, exclusive, jealous time; and since time is money, it requires a way to understand where the (man's) money comes from to support so luxurious a leisure. The pair is attractive, their wishes are human, their happiness would make us happy. So it seems that a criterion is being proposed for the success or happiness of a society, namely that it is happy to the extent that it provides conditions that permit conversations of this character, or a moral equivalent of them, between its citizens.[5]

The opulence of a musical comedy—its dance, song, orchestra, decor, costumes, chorus—renders the genre peculiarly fit to symbolize this abundance and thrusts the musical into a key position for cementing genre.

Have a Heart anticipates the "comedy of remarriage" rather remarkably, though the leading couple stops just short of divorce, as does the secondary one in *Toot-Toot!* Although there are plenty of divorce jokes in the first scene of *Head Over Heels*, set in a New York lawyers' office, *The Bunch and Judy* would appear to be Kern's first actual divorce musical, its narrative weight prepared for in the play-within-the-play, "Love will find a way," a *fête galante* tragedy of romantic jealousy. *Sunny* treats the theme more ironically, but with bittersweet intensity: by the end of act 1 Sunny is married but loves the best man. The ceremony was only a convenience to get her into the States— hence the song "When We Get Our Divorce" at the start of act 2—but the man of her dreams is unavailable. By the time of *Show Boat* the depiction of marital afterlife has the support of the novel itself, for Ferber ended her equivalent of act 1 with the sentence, "And so they lived h——and so they lived . . . ever after."[6] The marriage in the musical's act 1 finale is a prelude to Ravenal's desertion of Magnolia in act 2, ominously foreshadowed by Parthy's revelation that he is a murderer, a classic interruption signaling an impediment not to the wedding itself but to future happiness. It is worse still in *Three Sisters*, with Gypsy deserting Mary on their wedding day at the crux of the plot.

The other new type of marital plot that develops in the 1920s is the Cinderella narrative. Here a poor girl achieves happiness through elevation to wealth and fame commensurate with her beauty or talent. It had been the backbone of the Edwardian musical comedy in Britain, but again one can see why it suited postwar American audiences, for this was the period in which immigrants were making good as never before, having arrived in huge waves as never before in the two or three decades up to 1920. *Sally* was Kern's flagship show of this type, flanked on Broadway by *Irene* and *Mary* from other authors. *Good Morning, Dearie* follows it up, as do the Fred Stone shows in a different way. *Sitting Pretty*, like *Sally* and indeed *Head Over Heels*, involves the social elevation of orphans (meaning foundlings) but tempers the myth by having one of the twins (a nice reason for using them) eventually partner a reformed criminal; the other gets the heir. *Sunny* is also Cinderella tempered (she settles for the ordinary guy), and *Dear Sir* Cinderella reversed when the independent girl is made to pose as a maid by her prince. But the small-town girl gets the (would-be) big-city boy in *The City Chap*, the poor pearl diver the rich American in *Lucky*, and the beer-garden waitress fame in the theater in *Sweet Adeline*. All of these heroines undergo a great transformation, Magnolia included, during the course of the evening; it is the theme of virtually all of Kern's 1920s shows, and it lends his music its added breadth.

One further topical theme can be traced through the Kern musical comedies, and that is the changing world of entertainment itself with its romantic appeal, true or false, for leading characters. Glamorous actresses are already financially resourceful women with their own luxury apartments in the farces *Oh, I Say!* and *Nobody Home*. The butler in *Love o' Mike* is infatuated with silent films in general, Henry in *Have a Heart* with one movie star in particular. Leaving aside the college footballers in *Leave It to Jane*, *Toot-Toot!* features Isadora Duncan–type dancers, and, as we have seen, *Head Over Heels* and *Sunny* are about gymnastic performers whose bodies are the objects of the leading men's and the audience's gaze. *Sally* includes an entire diegetic ballet for its star, the "Butterfly Ballet" composed by Victor Herbert. The equation of stardom and divorce with financial gain (and the power of the press) permeates *Head Over Heels* and is nicely summed up in a single exchange:

> MRS. MONTAGUE (*angrily*): In the two weeks you had to arrange this affair couldn't you find me an artiste not connected with some scandal?
> SQUIBBS: No mam—not in two weeks.[7]

By the time of *Show Boat*, *Blue Eyes*, and *Sweet Adeline*, on the other hand, the stage is a metaphor for romance, adventure, fulfillment, struggle, disappointment, and personal truth and illusion themselves. Actors, dancers, and singers need diegetic music, but eventually, with *The Cat and the Fiddle*, Kern tackles a composer as his subject: two composers, in fact. Since *The Cat and the Fiddle* is also about desertion and reconciliation, it will prove the climax of Kern's engagement with musical comedy.

P. G. Wodehouse and Social Comedy

The British connections of the "trio of musical fame" were noted in chapter 1, and it is indeed curious that Wodehouse, his prose, plots, settings, characters and even his personal appearance epitomizing Englishness for countless admirers today, should have done so much to help create the American musical. Anthony Quinton, in a passage quoted below, is right to draw attention to the Anglo-American mix of characters in Wodehouse, who in his prose outlets, that is, magazine columns and stories leading to the novels, was writing at first more for an American readership than a British one. But it is bootless to look for the two nations' structural interaction in Kern's musical comedies. With the exception of *The Beauty Prize*, a transatlantic romance, and *Love o' Mike*, in which the British lead is challenged as an impostor in American society, the alien characters are incidental (Harry Zona in *The Cabaret Girl*, the English milord in *Roberta*), though Wendell Wendell does represent an English threat to Sunny's American happiness and Vernon Popple's brother the necessary (English) buffoon in *Nobody Home*. This may be because, unlike the novel, the musical played on separate national stages, and in the 1920s it was more realistic for Kern, Wodehouse, Bolton, and Grossmith, all of them with personal links to both countries, to move backward and forward across the Atlantic than to expect their audiences to do so mentally. Indicative of this distinction between novel and musical is the fact that *Sitting Pretty*, its characters entirely American, was elaborated by Wodehouse into a transatlantic story in his novel *Bill the Conqueror*, which appeared later the same year (1924). Wodehouse and Bolton did script musical comedies of Anglo-American interaction, but they came later, when Broadway and subsequently Hollywood were invaded by English stars, and were created for composers other than Kern: Gershwin in *Oh, Kay!* (starring Gertrude Lawrence), Porter abortively in *Anything Goes*, and Gershwin again in *A Damsel in Distress*, the 1937 RKO film of Wodehouse's 1919 novel. However, it is difficult at this distance to disentangle American from English ways of speaking in the earlier Wodehouse, for Broadway inherited a good deal of the latter (including English accents, as early song recordings testify), and a character like Briggs the butler in *Oh, Boy!* is not yet an American as opposed to an English type. His demeanor and syntax seem to come from within the sound of Bow bells:

> BRIGGS *(left of table leaning over it)*: Actin' very strange 'e was last night. Had a look about 'im like my poor Uncle Joe 'ad the day he swallowed the rat poison.

Compare Mrs. Lovett in *Sweeney Todd*:

> MRS. LOVETT: It was me poor Albert's chair, it was. Sat in it all day long he did, after his leg give out from the dropsy.[8]

A word of caution here about authorship. Bolton and Wodehouse always shared credit for book and lyrics when working together, but it is generally believed that Bolton wrote most of the dialogue and never the lyrics, which are attributed to Wodehouse alone in the published sheet music. Nevertheless, plenty of dialogue from their musical comedies was reused in the novels based on them, which makes one wonder how much of Wodehouse's direct speech in the novels was actually written by Bolton. The following is an extract from a longer instance of reuse, first as it appears in *Oh, Lady! Lady!!*:

> MOLLY: Oh, don't pay any attention to mother, she's always having presentiments.
> MRS. FARRINGDON: Now see here Molly, I had a similar feeling regarding the marriage of my sister-in-law, to a young man named John Porter. I said—"I feel this wedding will never take place," and I was right. Porter was arrested on a charge of bigamy as he was entering the church.
> WILLOUGHBY: I assure you, Mrs. Farringdon, that as far as I am concerned I can scarcely tell one woman from another.
> MRS. F: Why, that's precisely what John Porter said when they asked him why he had married six different girls—but don't let me put a damper on the general gaiety. Marriage is a lottery—and alimony's a gambling debt.

and second, nine years later in Wodehouse's novel *The Small Bachelor*, based on the musical:

> "What are you hinting?" demanded Molly.
> "I am not hinting," replied Mrs. Waddington with dignity. "I am saying. And what I am saying is this. Do not come to *me* for sympathy if this Finch of yours turns out to have the sort of moral code which you might expect in

one who deliberately and of his own free will goes and lives near Washington Square. I say again, that I have a presentiment that this marriage will never take place. I had a similar presentiment regarding the wedding of my sister-in-law and a young man named John Porter. I said, 'I feel that this wedding will never take place.' And events proved me right. John Porter, at the very moment when he was about to enter the church, was arrested on a charge of bigamy."

George uttered protesting noises.

"But my morals are above reproach."

"So you say."

"I assure you that, as far as women are concerned, I can scarcely tell one from another."

"Precisely," replied Mrs. Waddington, "what John Porter said when they asked him why he had married six different girls."

Harrison Beamish looked at his watch.[9]

The differences are instructive, the prose more polished in the novel, a more statuesque mother arising from it, whereas on the stage her physical presence could tell, and a more frigidly burlesque confrontation through the loss of the connectives "Oh," "Now," and "Why" to begin speeches, which soften the musical comedy characters in lieu of a narrator's detached manipulation of them. Two-fifths of the more complex novel have passed before we get to this point, only five pages in the play script, which is not exactly in accordance with Wodehouse's own observations about the rewriting but makes his point.[10] Indirect speech in the novels can take the place of the multiple viewpoints, in terms of mood and response, indeed humor, created by music, setting, and movement on the stage; the first-act finale of *Oh, Lady! Lady!!* is a good case in point, described in the novel not at first but at second hand by the butler—he claims not to have eavesdropped on the events himself but to have heard them from "one of the lower servants." And both Wodehouse's own observations in his novels and those of their characters frequently demonstrate the same figurative cast of mind that arises from the development of a list of examples in song lyrics. Here is one such list on a favorite Wodehouse theme, that of the self-made man:

> Henry Ford and Charlie Schwab
> Once were hunting for a job
> And Heinz began his life without a pickle.
> —Henry, in "You Can't Keep a Good Man Down"
>   from *Have a Heart*

Look at Pierpont Morgan and Henry Ford and Selfridge and all of them—
they don't do the work themselves. They just sit and let other people do it
for them. That's what shows they are such great men.—Felicia Sheridan, in
Bill the Conqueror

Wodehouse reveled in his connection with musicals, and he and his
team incorporated frequent reflexive ploys. One of the chorus girls in *Oh,
Boy!*, in a miasma of punning nomenclature which runs to Shiela Ryve and
Inna Ford, is named Miss Annie Olde-Knight, referring to the Kern song
"Any Old Night" of 1914. *Bill the Conqueror*, based on *Sitting Pretty*, refers
to Kern songs when it digresses, "Those who make the nation's songs (so
much more admirable than its laws) advise us to look for the silver lining, to
seek the Blue Bird, to put all our troubles in a great big box and sit on the lid
and grin. Alice Coker had been unable to follow this counsel." *Bill the Conqueror* also reuses the names of characters from *The Cabaret Girl* ("Flick,"
Mr. Paradene) and anticipates one, Pilbeam, found in Bolton's *Blue Eyes*. It
contains plenty of actual dialogue from *Sitting Pretty*, and the plot includes
the burglary of a rich man's library precisely matching items in Kern's (which
cannot have pleased Eva).[11] *The Adventures of Sally* (1922) was dedicated to
Grossmith at the time of *The Cabaret Girl* because "we had a lot of fun writing the thing together. Not a reproach or a nasty look from start to finish."
As a wealthy young American composer of musical comedies who successfully courts an English beauty, the hero of the novel *A Damsel in Distress*
(though not of its film), George Bevan, is surely modeled on Kern even if
the character himself is more like Gershwin (who had not yet achieved transatlantic fame) and pointedly unlike the autocrat Kern increasingly became:
"He hasn't let success give him a swelled head . . . he's just the same as he was
when I first knew him, when he was just hanging around Broadway, looking out for a chance to be allowed to slip a couple of interpolated numbers
into any old show that came along. Yes . . . he's an ace." *A Damsel in Distress*, written immediately after the early peak of Wodehouse's involvement
with Bolton and Kern, is full of such references and glories in the world of
Broadway and West End musical comedy: George's inamorata signs herself
"The Girl in the Cab"; Lord Marshmoreton reminisces about the old days
when Meyer Lutz was resident composer at the Gaiety Theatre (George has
never heard of him); George's nine shows are described in backstage economic detail by the chorus girl Billie and seem to echo Kern's eight of the
previous two years; a reference to a song by George "about Granny dancing

Fig. 2.2. P. G. Wodehouse, Guy Bolton, Ray Comstock, and Jerome Kern.

the shimmy" foreshadows Wodehouse's actual song with Kern about this in *The Beauty Prize*, "Non-stop Dancing."[12]

A Wodehouse novel, then, may share references and material with a Kern musical comedy. Where does that leave the narrative whole, with its apparently inconsequential characters, settings, and humor? Still today triumphant in the novels, which remain paperback staples, in the musical comedies it has long been pronounced superseded. But whether an injustice of history or a moral lesson about genre, this verdict belies the fact that the social and comic formulae of the novels apply equally to the shows, for musical comedy was only the latest of a number of media that set about balancing and foiling characters and their motivations with gleeful means that can be traced back to Menander's "new comedy," a series of plays from classical Greece. Comic novels and farces perpetuated new comedy, as Quinton explains:

The fundamental structure of comedy . . . begins with a young person who is frustrated by parental, or at any rate elderly, obstruction. The action consists in the outwitting or exposure of the obstructing character or characters. In this the hero is frequently assisted by some skillful trickster who makes up for the lack of combative resources entailed by the hero's essential innocence. In the end the society of the narrative reaches a more ideal condition, closer to the desires of ordinary, reasonable people than the artificially regulated state of affairs maintained earlier by the obstructive seniors . . . Others of the sympathetic youthful innocents of Wodehouse's fiction are heavily encumbered with parental authority, buttressed in the English cases by titles and status, in the American ones by large quantities of money and habits of asperity undiluted by considerations of good manners . . .

The tradition of the *Tractatus Coislinianus* picks out four main character types as proper to comedy. These are the impostors (both conscious and hypocritical and unconscious and self-deluded), the self-depreciators, the buffoons and the boors . . . In Wodehouse, as in life, it is not always easy to draw the line between the hypocrite and the self-deceiver, the conscious and the unconscious impostor. By and large, the more socially established or English heavy characters are the more self-deluding, the more self-made or American ones the more hypocritical. That is wholly intelligible. Those who have had to work deliberately for the position in which they can interfere with the desires of others are more likely to maintain the public display of that position with conscious artifice than those who have grown up with their status as part of their apparent natural endowment.[13]

It is easy enough to apply this critique to the Princess musicals, for example, *Oh, Boy!* and *Oh, Lady! Lady!!* Both George and Lou Ellen and Willoughby and Molly, the respective leading couples of these shows, are "heavily encumbered with parental authority," which Mrs. Farringdon in *Oh, Lady! Lady!!*, having buried two husbands, is more than capable of representing single-handed; in *Oh, Boy!* Lou Ellen's parents comprise the interrogatory Mrs. Carter and the Judge, an impostor because of his drunken flirtation with the ingenue Jacky, as is George's disapproving Quaker aunt when she gets drunk (see fig. 2.3 for a list of *Oh, Boy!*'s characters). The leading man's trickster sidekick is in both cases more of a hindrance than a help and thereby complicates the plot: Jim through having thrown a bachelor party in George's apartment without respect for (or even knowledge of) George's new matrimonial status, Hale, Willoughby's best man, when he gets Fainting Fanny to impersonate an old girlfriend. Both (Hale as best man) represent the freedom the hero must renounce for marriage, but themselves also marry by the end of the show, as the second-couple comedy buffoons whose emotional tribulations we take less seriously than those of the leading couple but who nevertheless interact with them: both, in these cases, when their women pose a residual or incipient threat to the hero's proper partner. Fanny, as professional pickpocket, is another impostor, though she renounces her ways in *Oh, Lady! Lady!!* and marries the valet Hudgins, equivalent of Briggs in *Oh, Boy!*, who along with the policeman Sims represents the boors. (There is no space in the musical comedies for Wodehouse's fantastic self-depreciators such as Garroway the poet cop and Sigsbee H. Waddington, cowboy *manqué*, both found in *The Small Bachelor*.)

Quinton sees Wodehouse's humor as a combination of farce (people behaving mechanically) and burlesque (grandiose mockery, including "exaggerated imitations of the conversational idioms of . . . rich aunts, American millionaires and so forth").[14] With romance added, the mixture is reflected in the musical comedies. If for the tenderness and still more the emotional violence of romance one has to read between the lines in Wodehouse's novels, music can and does provide ample quantities of the former and at least a hint of the latter in the classic Kern songs, rueful and nearly always sad beneath their idyllic credo—"Till the Clouds Roll By," "You Never Knew About Me," "Bill," "Land Where the Good Songs Go," "Drift With Me," and so on. Burlesque inhabits the drunken Quaker aunt, the Judge making a grab for his purloined speech, the doom-laden pronouncements of Mrs. Farringdon, the elegant and nostalgic conversations (and, in another show, songs) about prison life in Sing Sing, Sims's infatuation with Lou Ellen's pajamas, and Hudgins's romance with Fanny, whom he persuades to go straight.

Farce is the basic genre of the earlier Kern musicals. The object of the hero is a mechanical one: he must get married, or remain married in some cases, including that of *Oh, Boy!* This has two concomitants. The first is a foil to his romantic determination and weaves much of the texture of the play as a series of running gags on matrimony and monogamy. They range from the typical presence of the chorus girls in the opening number (and in act 1 of *Oh, Boy!* they keep returning to add to George's problems) to the jokes that pepper the script and were judiciously recycled from one to another. In *Oh, Boy!* George himself shows insecurity about marriage before he has spoken a dozen words:

LOU ELLEN: Don't be so nervous, dear.
GEORGE: I can't help it.

LOU ELLEN: You seemed quite self-possessed until the middle of the cere-
   mony.
GEORGE: I was all right until I heard the minister say "Wilt thou, George,"
   and then I did—
LOU ELLEN: Did what?
GEORGE: Wilted.

His nervousness is Mrs. Farringdon's cynicism, expressed equally soon
after the start of *Oh, Lady! Lady!!*:

ELSIE: Well, she knows she's getting a good husband.
MRS. F: My dear, there's no such thing; what women call a *good* man is only
   a careful one.

Minor characters can be planted so as to take the idealism out of love and
courtship and keep the audience titillated as well as amused. This particular
exchange recurs in *Oh, Kay!* eight years later:

GEORGE: My wife wouldn't lie, Constable.
SIMS: No?
GEORGE: She has too much honor.
SIMS: Too much on her? If she had much less on her she'd be pinched.[15]

The second classic concomitant to the hero's matrimonial aim is that he
has to hide or pretend something and is forced to act more and more "mechanically" as a result, periodically with the additional burden of knowing
that a person is secreted behind one of the doors of the stage set, preferably
a bedroom (Lou Ellen or Jacky at five different points in act 1 of *Oh, Boy!*,
Fanny and May in act 2 of *Oh, Lady! Lady!!*), or a betrayer could arrive at
any moment (Fanny in the act 1 finale of *Oh, Lady! Lady!!*, the Quaker aunt
in *Oh, Boy!*). The much put-upon George in *Oh, Boy!* is subject to an increasingly fraught tissue of lies and other pressures in his bid to protect first
his state of elopement and then the fugitive Jacky: there are about twenty
of these pressure points in an ever more convoluted act 1. First he and Lou
Ellen must pretend they are not yet married, because of the aunt's telegram
of concern; then he has to hide her in the bedroom when he realizes Jim
and a bevy of his girls are on the premises. During his first encounter with
Jim, in quick succession he temporizes about whom he was talking to, signals Lou Ellen away as she appears at the door, is told he may get evicted,
hides Lou Ellen's slippers, and gets chatted up by the girls, with the risk of
Lou Ellen seeing this if she reappears. After a respite as the subplot between

Jacky and Jim gets under way, George's second nexus of woes begins, when he can't bring himself to throw Jacky out because of an obligation to Jim and then has, first, to prevaricate to her about Lou Ellen's pajamas and then to pass her off as his wife to the constable; this lands him in further extremity when he admits he has never seen her bare back and when pressed says he's only been married one day. By this point the deceptions have gone so far that he has told a truth, though Jacky admires it and the attendant marriage certificate as inveterate falsehoods. His third round of deception begins with Jacky now in the bedroom and the Judge appearing on the scene. First he says the Judge can't go in because he's got explosive chemicals in there; next he has to explain the returning girls as friends of Jim, and why he was expecting to get evicted (all truthfully though implausibly to the Judge); finally he not only has to pass off the emerging Jacky as the Quaker aunt but simultaneously convey to Jacky, who knows nothing about the aunt, that she is no longer acting his wife. This involves frantically trying to cover up two of Jacky's slips, on the second occasion unwittingly helping to get the Judge off the hook. Finally, as the curtain comes down, he is about to compromise himself by assisting Jacky, still wearing the pajamas, to get into a dress in the woods on their way to the country club.

Dramatic Segmentation and Music

Farcical plots have to be immaculately worked out, which Wodehouse knew from his stage experience and practiced in his novels, whose methods have frequently been compared with those of musical comedy. Wodehouse himself said that his idea of a novel was "making a sort of musical comedy without music," and David Jasen goes so far as to maintain that "all of the Wodehouse plots can be broken down into their components of acts, chorus numbers, duets and solos. The dialogue is crisp and concise, the entrances and exits are carefully prepared and vividly executed." Possibly true, but in the novels he offers frequent respite from plot mechanics with whimsical asides on the part of the third-person narrator as well as his reliably paced and blended descriptions of the characters as they are introduced. Lyrics are Wodehouse's equivalent in the musical comedies, though he is not beyond putting affectionate humor into his stage directions. The following prefaces the act 2 opening chorus of *The Cabaret Girl* and surely comes from Wodehouse's pen, not Grossmith's: "*Enter in frock coats and top hats a bevy of* BUSINESS MEN. *The 2.15 from Liverpool Street is just in. All the trains to Wool-*

lam Chersey—change at Broxbourne—are good, but this is perhaps the best, and they exude happiness. They are met by their wives and children."[16] This is exceptional, but the point is that both songs and such passages in the prose of novels need careful handling in terms of congruity (they relax the action without breaking the mood); above all, they need careful placing. In order to show how the music is placed in one of the Bolton, Wodehouse, and Kern comedies, I must address dramatic segmentation.

There is only one stage set for the first act of *Oh, Boy!*, but that does not mean that its action passes in an undifferentiated way. Like that of all conventional plays, it can be segmented into relatively small units that accomplish something particular, normally in terms of an exchange between two or more characters that establishes a topic, facts, or a relationship or dynamic between them, however momentary. An entrance or an exit normally signals a new segment unless part of a cumulative curve of effect or more or less incidental (like the movements of Briggs the valet in act 1, though not act 2, of *Oh, Boy!*).[17]

Oh, Boy!'s first act (fig. 2.3) can be divided into twenty-one such segments. They are between one and five typed pages in length and average three and a half. In each, two or more characters are present, with a buildup of numbers of people on stage toward the climax of the act until at the very end everyone leaves for the country club except George and Jacky. The act is divided into two scenes, with the passing of a night between them, but can be subdivided further into sections which are groupings of segments; there are four of these, the last itself subdivided by the onset of the musical finale, and each is shorter than the one before (29, 22, 14, 6, and 4.5 pages) as the pace increases. The first section establishes the relationship between and immediate circumstances of George and Lou Ellen. The second introduces the subplot with Jacky's sudden arrival through the window. The third, the morning after, brings some respite but also the Judge into the action and functions as housekeeping for the strands of plot and preparation for the accumulation of characters and their pressure not just on George but on the Judge as well in the fourth section, which begins with the entrance of Mrs. Carter and Lou Ellen, the latter absent since the first. Ironically, in this fourth section, where George's difficulties climax, all the characters are present except his "helper," Jim, and the Quaker aunt who caused the problem in the first place.

The archetypal formula of the musical comedy scene (that is, segment) has been summarized as dialogue, song, dance. Spoken prose leads into sung

Characters

Juveniles

Leading couple
G   George
LE Lou Ellen

Secondary couple
J   Jim
Jy Jacky, an actress

Chorus
Gl Girls
By Boys
P   Polly, a flapper

Seniors

Ju   Judge Carter, Lou Ellen's father
Mrs Mrs Carter, Lou Ellen's mother
[Q   Miss Budd, George's Quaker aunt]

Comic functionaries
B   Briggs, George's valet
S   Sims, the policeman

Musical numbers, Act I

i) Let's make a night of it
ii) You never knew about me
iii) A package of seeds
iv) An old fashioned wife
v) A pal like you
vi) Till the clouds roll by
vii) A little bit of ribbon
[r = reprise]

Segment	Characters present	Musical numbers	Performers	Section / Scene
1	J Gl / By / P	i) i)r	Gl / By	**Section 1** (29 pp.) — **Scene 1** — **ACT I**
2	G / LE	ii)	G / LE	
3	J / [B]¹ / Gl	iii)	J Gl	
4	G / LE			
5	J G / [Gl P B]			
6	LE / Gl	iv)	LE / Gl	
7	G J / 2Gl			
8	G / LE	iv)r	LE	
9	J / Jy			**Section 2** (22 pp.)
10	J / S			
11	J / Jy	v)	J / Jy	
12	Jy / G	ii)r	G	
13	Jy / G / S	vi)	G / Jy	
14	Ju / G / B			**Section 3** (14 pp.) — **Scene 2**
15	Gl / [G B P]	vii)	Gl	
16	G B / [Jy]			
17	G / J / Jy			
18	G LE [B] / Mrs P Gl / [By]			**Section 4** (6 pp.)
19	G LE Jy / Mrs P / Gl By		+	
20	ditto / Mrs P Gl / By Jy Ju	i)r / melodrama / ii)r / i)r /?v)r FINALE	Jy Gl By // Jy G Gl / LE / Gl By	4.5 pp.
21	G / Jy			

¹ Square brackets indicate partial presence

Fig. 2.3. *Oh, Boy!* segmentation, act 1.

poetry, a more bodily as well as more stylized means of expression; unsung music, more corporeal still, follows, giving a kind of sawtooth wave pattern of expressive idealism (frequently, of eroticism) when this formula is repeated several times in succession. Several of the act 1 segments in *Oh, Boy!* follow it, though as elsewhere in Kern's musical comedies, the dance may be integrated into the song or there may be a further sung refrain after it. The single songs in segments 2, 3, 6, 8, 13, and 15 come at the end of the segment in question, and in addition to the numbers involving the chorus (in segments 1, 3, 6, 15, and 20), which naturally highlight choreographed or at least organized stage movement, "A Pal Like You," Jim and Jacky's number, concludes with a couple dance.

Not a great deal of music graces act 1 of *Oh, Boy!*, but it probably accounts for about half of the running time by the clock. The basic pattern is no more than one song per segment, and with only seven songs in the act the average is clearly much less, for although there are seven reprises as well, three or four of these are placed end to end in the finale. Bolton stressed the need to get the spread right. The segments without music (these would be book scenes in later musicals, where the curtain might come down ten times within one act) keep the play moving after three opening numbers in quick succession and, equally obviously, occur when someone is secreted behind a door and tension is high; this does not, however, preclude music in scene 2, when "A Little Bit of Ribbon" punctuates the long dialogue buildup to Jacky's entrance from the bedroom and the musical finale. The act 1 finale itself is decidedly undeveloped compared with Kern's longer ones and much simpler than that of *Oh, Lady! Lady!!*, though it is difficult to be certain of its dimensions in the face of mismatched script and score and some missing music.[18]

The songs, like the individuals and their motivations that they help articulate, have to foil and balance each other and at the same time lend the show its overall character, its "odor of sachet." (See ex. 2.1 for the refrain incipits of the seven musical numbers.) Key relations, however, have no meaning in musical comedies such as this, and songs were frequently transposed to suit performers. By default, the large number of songs in E flat major, favorite key of church-hall pianists, does emphasize the old-fashioned coziness, sometimes sanctimoniousness, of this score, for that is what George and Lou Ellen's wished-for idyll represents, and when the D major songs are added to their number, a *doh*-to-*doh* octave at around the same pitch does seem a recurrent opening gambit. Instructive here is the original cast recording of "You Never Knew About Me," unbelievably slow and *rubato* in refrain as well as verse, like a deathly organ voluntary and replete with simpering instrumental *portamento* in the introduction and interlude.[19] Yet this is in keeping with the music, which carefully avoids Tin Pan Alley formal repeats and in its sentimentality contrasts all the more deliciously with George's impending tribulations, as does the virginal piety of Lou Ellen.

Certainly the large number of songs in duple or quadruple time, combined with Kern's fondness for sequence, here in full flower, creates a churchiness and solidity to the musical idiom, even in the syncopated numbers. Again, though, a contemporary recording, this time not with Tom Powers as George but a real tenor, James Harrod, illuminates character: "Till the Clouds Roll By" goes at a brisk, strict-tempo allegretto, the only way Saddler's delicious raindrop orchestration can be fully effective. One wonders therefore whether this duet with the "wrong" woman (Jacky) hasn't cast just a little too much doubt on George's marital destiny by contrast with "You Never Knew About Me." At least it demonstrates that he badly needs a bit of a challenge. Jim, as the more athletic, dancing male lead, also has his duet with Jacky, "A Pal Like You," as well as his earlier solo with the girls, "A Package of Seeds." Both are characterized by the half-time cakewalk rhythm (see the first complete bars of ex. 2.1 [iii] and [v]) that relates him and his cocky kind to the minstrelsy idiom. This is one of four stage traditions represented by the act 1 songs. Another is the parlor gentility already witnessed in "You Never Knew About Me" and, on a coy note, in "A Little Bit of Ribbon," its confidential patter redolent of Gilbert and Sullivan. (Kern could excel at this genre: "Thirteen Collar" from *Very Good Eddie* is delicious.) The third stage tradition in evidence is that of the balletic chorus girl. The girls are kept both visible and audible as much as possible, and their dotted-note parading in the opening chorus has remained a musical theater staple (compare "One" from *A Chorus Line*); it also underlies Jacky's act 2 number with the girls, "Rolled Into One," in which they trip around fantasizing about partners at "the op'ra," "a musical show" and "the races / And other lively places." The second melodic phrase of "A Little Bit of Ribbon" (to the words "And a little bit of silk that clings" in ex. 2.1 [vii]) seems to remember the line "Are there any more at home like you?" from Leslie Stuart's "Tell Me, Pretty Maiden," the *fons et origo* of girls' production numbers. Finally, we have only one triple-time number in act 1, Lou Ellen's "An Old Fashioned Wife," and no compound time except in one of the verse sections of the opening chorus. Even allowing for the duplicity, so to speak, of the

(i) Let's Make a Night of It

[Con brio]

He can't be here at all, If he were near at all He'd have heard the noise.

(ii) You Never Knew About Me

Moderato semplice

I nev-er knew a-bout you, dear, And you nev-er knew a-bout me.

(iii) A Package of Seeds

Marcia

If I'd a gar-den where girl-ies would grow,

(iv) An Old Fashioned Wife

Poco allegretto e grazioso

I want to be a good lit-tle wife In the good

old fash - ioned   way.

(v) A Pal Like You

Moderato

Doz-ens   and doz-ens   of girls I   have met,

p - mf

(vi) Till the Clouds Roll By

Allegretto

Oh, the   rain_____   comes a pit-ter,   pat - ter,_____

p - mf

(vii) A Little Bit of Ribbon

Moderato

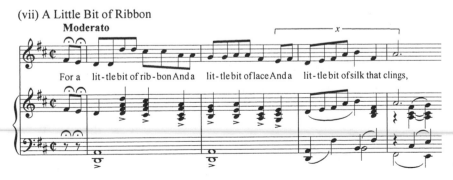

For a   lit-tle bit of rib-bon And a   lit-tle bit of lace And a   lit-tle bit of silk that clings,

Ex. 2.1. *Oh, Boy!* act 1 refrains.

period, this is atypical—*Oh, Lady! Lady!!* is not quite as extreme in its metrical preferences and *Have a Heart* has three sumptuous waltzes in act 1, while making something of a point of them. There is no triple or compound time in act 2 of *Oh, Boy!* except for a reprise of "An Old Fashioned Wife" (as "Oh, Daddy, Please"). Even then, "An Old Fashioned Wife" is more a minuet than a waltz, and the stage directions specify "a minuet courtesy with each girl in turn" in the instrumental break after Lou Ellen's third refrain.[20] Together with the suggestion of gavotte phrasing in "Till the Clouds Roll By," this defines the fourth stylistic world of *Oh, Boy!*'s music, that of antique quaintness and courtesy, a local habitation of the innocence pervading all the Princess shows and indeed Kern's musical language of this entire period. With this recognized, we can see the point of Saddler's harpsichord orchestrations, their first classic example the sixteenth note figuration in *Very Good Eddie*'s "Babes in the Wood."

Act 1, then, contains, without counting the finale, one duet each for the two "right" couples and one for the leading "wrong" one (George and Jacky), the latter balanced by a solo each for the other two youngsters (Jim and Lou Ellen), both with the girls. The chorus has two numbers to itself, though "A Little Bit of Ribbon" includes solos for Jane, one of the ensemble, played by Marion Davies in the original production. George has a short solo, "The Letter Song" in segment 12, by way of a reprise of "You Never Knew About Me." The other leading character is Jacky, playing opposite him for a good deal of the show despite not being his destined partner, and she has more music than anyone: two numbers close to each other in section 2, the leading musical role in the first-act finale, and a big number as well as participation in two others in act 2. Listening to Anna Wheaton's 1919 recordings of "Rolled Into One" and "Till the Clouds Roll By," one can hear why—she brings out the fun and creates an aura. Nevertheless, various musical balancing acts take place across the show overall in order to keep the four leads afloat— a number for Lou Ellen and the chorus boys, "Words are Not Needed," in act 2 complementing Jim's earlier one with the girls; an act 2 opening number for Jim, "Land Where the Good Songs Go," following his absence from the first-act finale; two act 2 duets for the "right" couples, "Nesting Time in Flatbush" for Jackie and Jim, "Oh, Daddy, Please" for George and Lou Ellen, though the latter, which was cut, was only a reprise and in any case more of a trio, for it included the Judge; and one further trio to counteract all the duets, "Flubby Dub," for Jim, Jacky and George.

This account is based on a musical snapshot of *Oh, Boy!* Inevitably, as was true of most of the earlier Kern shows, numbers were slotted in and out during the tryouts, New York production run, subsequent tour, and London production. Bordman gives details of these, and Day prints the lyrics. They included "The First Day of May," "Be a Little Sunbeam," "Ain't It a Grand and Glorious Feeling," "The Bachelor," "Koo-la-loo," "When the Orchestra Is Playing Your Favorite Dance," "Why Can't They Hand It to Me?," and Dorothy Dickson's dance speciality. In London, "Wedding Bells" was added for George, Jim, and the Judge. The one that would have changed the balance was "The First Day of May," an eighth song for act 1 and, as a rollicking trio, a contrast to all the romantic duets. It was sung by George, Jacky, and Jim and placed in segment 17, breaking the musical silence of that portion of the act.

The musical principle of this more or less typical if modest musical comedy is variety and balance rather than unity through repetition and transformation, though reprises share the ongoing space with new material and have their particular moment in the act 1 finale. Admittedly, "Land Where the Good Songs Go," yet another number in E flat major, distills the essence of the genteel, wistful act 1 numbers in a remarkable way when it opens act 2, while remaining a completely fresh (and very beautiful) song in its own right, though it was not written for *Oh, Boy!* But "leit opera" is nowhere on the horizon except for one tiny but telling instance when "A Pal Like You" is introduced with the head motif of "You Never Knew About Me": both couples have found their predestined mates. Nor is there any compunction to "integrate" music and drama, either by rendering the songs subliminal or by presenting them as diegetic numbers (for none of the characters is actually heard as a singing entertainer, however close Jacky gets to this through being an actress). The drama is a spoken farce with sung and danced interludes. Kern was in no hurry to change this formula, and *Sitting Pretty* works in much the same way seven years on. It does make for some transparent cues for songs, however:

GEORGE: Life's too complicated. I wish we were back in the Golden Age.
JACKY: Or the Bronze Age.
JIM: Or the Stone Age. I'm strong for the Stone Age. Think, Jacky—you would be the seductive tanglefoot, and I would be Flubbydub, your burly champion.
JACKY: My great big—cave-man.

MUSIC CUE: *Start Introduction to*
"Flubby-Dub [the caveman]"[21]

To a later generation this sort of thing was anathema.

Language and Music

The secrets of Wodehouse's prose have been analyzed. His rhythmic flux, especially in dialogue, is important: "Join the right-hand line ends with a pencil . . . and a page of Wodehouse conversation takes on a seismographic design," Basil Boothroyd has observed. This was a principle of the Broadway musical comedy book too, short lines and snappy ripostes being at a particular premium. By contrast, Kern's British shows indulge in noticeably longer speeches. But it is also a flux of syntax and vocabulary. Robert Hall has accounted for this in an article which is particularly useful because it submits prose to style analysis comparable with that of musicologists. Wodehouse's "peculiar effectiveness as a comic writer," he explains, "consists especially in his skillful alternation of a SB [stylistic background] of narration with frequent SC's [stylistic contexts] and SD's [stylistic devices] with a rapid, kaleidoscopically varying stylistic rhythm." His general background is high style, "what Usborne calls . . . 'copper-plate Augustan,' exemplified at its most impressive in the speech of Jeeves, but in evidence throughout Wodehouse's narrations. Against this SB, informal usage stands out, especially in conversations. . . . a number of informal non-standard varieties [of English] serve as sources for SD's, particularly British and American peculiarities." Wodehouse's mastery lies in "the rate at which incongruous [style] elements are introduced," and Hall points out that "in humor . . . the stylistic rhythm is much more rapid" than in serious, epic, or tragic writing, and "the more discrepancy there is between the SD's and their context and background, the greater is the humor."[22]

Bolton's humor, with or without Wodehouse contributing to it, achieves something similar in much of the dialogue of a good farce such as *Oh, Boy!*, and in this particular case is at its architectural peak at the emergence of the Quaker aunt as played by Jacky, schizophrenically adjusting her vocabulary and demeanor as she goes along at the crux of both act 1 and act 2:

> SIMS (*Enters L2E and stands by arch L*): About that py-jammis pattern —
> GEORGE: It's coming! It's coming!
> LOU ELLEN (*Wonderingly*): Pajama pattern?

JACKY: Thee shalt have it. I promise thee.

SIMS: Eh? How's that?

JACKY *(Going over to* SIMS*)*: I will even give thy good wife mine if thee wilt only beat it.[23]

If here the stylistic background is "normal" conversation, the immediate stylistic contexts are supposedly Quaker English ("I promise thee") colliding with Sims's New York vernacular, and Jacky's abrupt "beat it" is a stylistic device that caps them with its sudden, end-stopped incongruity.

Lyrics superimposed on vernacular music, and Wodehouse's in particular, offer still richer scope for delight in such effects, already hinted at in the discussion of "Not Yet" in chapter 1. The overriding principle is avoidance of redundancy: this means rhythmic and linguistic variety in the verbal phrases, but still more, verbal phrasing that parallels the musical phrasing only up to a point. Yes, rhymes and repeated verbal phrasing have to accompany a melodic sequence, but only to the point of confirmation: beyond that, surprise is needed. This is true of each medium, music and words, on its own, where something such as a sequence is concerned; when the media combine, they can keep the brain guessing about a squared number of possible outcomes.

Take the verse of "Moon Song" from *Oh, Lady! Lady!!* (ex. 2.2). It begins with a romantic and leisurely musical sequence. Wodehouse's first line is comparably and congruently poetic, with its "Oh," its *s* and *v* alliteration patterns ("silvery," "shimmering," "see," "shining," "above") and its determination to cram every possible word to do with the moon into a single phrase. But once beyond it, he completely rejects "poesy" for a conversational address that reads like prose because of its varied phrase lengths and tricks of addressivity—contractions, colloquial clichés, much use of "you," a sudden question and its insistent exclamation, and various qualifiers and changes of syntactical position: "I've something to tell you. Between you and me, I'm in love! Yes, there's no concealing, old friend, I'm fairly knocked flat: How, how in the world is it all going to end? Tell me that! You've seen quite a number of lovers, no doubt, moon, in your day. True love is a thing that you know all about, people say. But, still I'm willing to bet, though love's in your line, you never in all your existence have met love like mine!"[24] This could be Bertie Wooster expostulating to a confidant in a bar or a sports car. Printed and read thus, one scarcely spots the rhymes, certainly not the musical periodicity, and would never guess that the passage as a whole is split

Oh,   sil - ver - y shim - mer - ing moon that I   see   shin - ing a - bove,
You've seen quite a num - ber of   lov - ers, no doubt, moon, in your day.

I've some - thing to tell you. Be - tween you and me,____ I'm in love!
True love is   a   thing that you all know a - bout,____ Peo - ple say.

Yes, there's no con - ceal - ing, old friend,   I'm   fair - ly knocked flat:
But, still__ I'm will - ing to   bet,   Though love's in   your line,

How, how in the world is it   all going to end? Tell me that!
You   nev - er in all your ex - ist - ence have met Love like mine!

Ex. 2.2. Moon Song (verse).

down the middle where the music of the verse repeats in its entirety (with
the first refrain in between). It is not a perfect lyric—no lyric ever is—and
"How" has to be repeated to match the music. But it has the flow, the colloquial reassurance, and the confidentiality that were Wodehouse's legacy to
the musical theater, an invaluable legacy because it brought the songs right
up close to people's ears.

If we assume that Kern had already fixed his melody before the words
were added, and would not have altered it for Wodehouse, then certain tricks
of Kern's become prompts for Wodehouse. In fact one suspects that he did
alter it a little, though the fused melopoetic effect (of verbal and melodic
fulfillment registering simultaneously) is the thing, however it was arrived
at. The first melodic peak is d^2 on "shim[mering]," subsiding with a second
on c^2 which Wodehouse parallels with "shin[ing]." But Kern avoids melodic
redundancy over a long (four-bar) sequential consequent by altering its last
four notes. This means that the last note is no longer a tone lower, like the
rest of the sequence, but two steps below. Wodehouse can thereby retain
the exact parallelism of rhyme ("-bove" / "love") at this point without over-
predictability. But the more important effect is that Kern has altered the

preceding beat more radically, from three notes to two and from stepwise motion to a little fanfare figure outlining an E minor triad that lies casually aslant the tonic harmony. Wodehouse congruently catches his protagonist's breath by pulling her up short before trumpeting the exciting news: "I'm in love!" Two unequal phrases have filled the space of the earlier single one.[25]

In the next phrase the slang of "I'm fairly knocked flat" pulls strongly and effectively against the elegance of the melody, which continues to refer to its opening motif in a process of "good continuation." In fact the melody is already on the antecedent of another sequence, and despite some melodic disguise (d^1 on the first "How" in place of a^1) its consequent, basically a 4th higher, is rhythmically regular for the first bar and a half, at which point we expect the rhyme "end" ("How, how in the world will it end?" would fit perfectly) for "friend." We do not yet get it, this time in a joint surprise sprung by composer and lyricist when they both extend the phrase by three notes and syllables, the d^2 on "end" coming a half-bar too late. Kern has rounded off the four-bar phrase here with a three-note cell that vaguely echoes that of "I'm in love" but is slightly more abrupt because of the change to a 4/4 time signature; Wodehouse seems to grasp this nuance when he issues his peremptory "Tell me that!"[26] Second time around, however, Wodehouse rides out this last four-bar period with one long, unpunctuated clause, which rather than go over old interpretative ground now reminds us by contrast of its growth from the very first period of the melody, which in the second stanza Wodehouse has similarly set to a complete grammatical clause beginning with "You [have]," though not on this occasion without parentheses. The second half of his second stanza is broader still than this, for the four bars preceding that final period are also dependent on it, "But . . . I'm willing to bet . . . [that] you never . . . have met love like mine!" being the overall sense and lasting eight bars. To summarize, although Kern's melody, despite subtleties along the way, is basically a matter of four four-bar periods all based on the same idea and then all repeated exactly for the second stanza, Wodehouse sets no two of them in the first stanza to the same syntactic formula, and having therefore found four different phrasings for the first stanza, proceeds to find two more (one of eight bars) for the second. Nor is the second period constructed the same way both times.

Other songs show this verbal flux more as a matter of vocabulary than phrasing, but the musical concomitant in that case tends to be rhythm — perhaps this was what Otto Harbach had in mind on the musical front when he testified to "the way [Kern] could take those English melodies and give them a twist and make them palatable for this country."[27] There is a perennially fruitful trade-off between slang or casual inflections in the words and syncopation or cross-rhythm in the music. Coming as it does hard on the heels of the ragtime crazes of the early twentieth century and the triumph of the American vernacular in popular song lyrics, this procedure is neither surprising nor unique to Wodehouse, but Wodehouse exploits it with unique poise and effortless wit.

The refrain of "Ain't It a Grand and Glorious Feeling" furnishes a fine example (ex. 2.3). "A grand and a glorious feeling" is orotund language (and the "breakfast gong" implies a classy lifestyle for the person speaking it) but is set to syncopation and then triple-time cross-rhythm on the word "glorious" (creating a glorious feeling indeed). "Ain't" has already got the comment off to a slangy start, again with attendant cross-rhythm. The equal-note, steady rhythm of "when the world is fair and bright" counterbalances this with a musical gravity more appropriate to the somewhat poetic phrase "fair and bright." "Till you go to bed at night," on the other hand, although replicating that same rhythm, injects a streak of vulgarity into both lyrics and music, through "go to bed" in the one medium, the downward octave and chromatic infill on "bed" (with its own juicy chord) in the other. This is also true of the quarter notes at the end of the refrain, blaring out repeated high Es as a |--3-|3-3-|1 (as opposed to |3-2-|1) cadence, involving as it does a dogged dominant 13th. Wodehouse's analogue for this, "the world's all right!" captures its spirit perfectly with its verb contraction and blunt but assertive "all right." Part of the effect of these four-bar clauses, in both words and music, is how abruptly and how soon they end, with not a word or a note strictly more than is necessary and with a firm periodic downbeat in the melody, a strong Anglo-Saxon rhyme ("bright" / "night" / "right") in the lyrics. This contrasts strongly with the tumbling abundance of notes and syllables in the syncopated first four bars and ties in with the observation about chorale-like melody in chapter 1. The instrumental fills for which such melody leaves room (see ex. 2.3) act like laughter in response to the wit. Compare, too, Wodehouse's prose, in which a babble of colloquial monologue can be pulled up short by an elegant authorial observation:

"Not a bad idea, your coming too," he admitted. "Quite likely fellow may turn nasty. Then you could sit on his head while I kicked him in the slats. Only way with these birds. Treat 'em rough."
Bill was cold to this outline of policy.[28]

Ain't it a grand___ and a glor - i - ous feel - ling, When the world is fair and

bright!_____ When noth - ing's gone wrong___ from the break - fast

gong, Till you go to bed at night.___ When you're a - ble to say,___ as you're

hit - ting the hay,___ "This is the end___ of a per - fect day!"___

Ain't it a grand and a glor - i - ous feel - ing, When you feel the world's all right!___

Ex. 2.3. Ain't It a Grand and Glorious Feeling (refrain).

The C section of this ABCA refrain, meanwhile, has taken a different tack: Kern's music, by substituting a genteel throbbing pattern for the "oompah" accompaniment and pursuing a most delicate sequence that passes through minor keys, superimposes a sophisticated shade of feeling on the ever-continuing ragtime rhythms. Wodehouse's equivalent is to introduce poetic quotation, a genteel habit, and the elegant phrase "able to say," while retaining slang ("hitting the hay") and making his quotation a vulgar one, for "the end of a perfect day" appears to refer to a popular song published the previous year, "When Grandma Sings the Songs She Loved at the End of a Perfect Day."

"Ain't It a Grand and Glorious Feeling" is a thoroughly standard type of ragtime song for Kern and for its decade, and Wodehouse's techniques were common to others. Where he stands head and shoulders above his contemporaries in such songs is in the domestic specificity of his references. "I'd have let you feed my rabbit / Till the thing became a habit" is an unforgettable instance from a different type of number; on the ragtime front "The First Day of May" glories in this capability, as a song about moving house. The springtime season "brings the peas on"; "there's no place like home" because "the place is filled with packing cases"; the movers "do jiu-jitsu with the Steinway" (a sore point with Kern in retrospect); "They've smashed Aunt Minnie's bureau," and "the maid is all a-twitter / 'Cause the dog got sore and bit her."[29] Its unrelenting concrete immediacy is perfect.

Wodehouse could be romantic, humane, and serious in his lyrics as well as in his novels, though he is not given credit for this because of his wit. Like Ira Gershwin's, his recognition of heartache is distilled into epigram, but a glance at the *Have a Heart* lyrics shows that it is there. His plain expression of a second chance at marriage (in "The Road That Lies Before") may not be as original as his figurative humor, but when sung to the music it proves extraordinarily touching:

> The road that lies before
> Is dark and hard to see.
>
> What though we missed it once
> We did not understand
> Better today we know the way,
> So let us set out hand in hand.

And the vulnerability of the secondary couple, embarking for the first rather than the second time on a lifelong commitment, is perfectly expressed when in "You Said Something" the woman sings, "Girls much prettier you will meet by the score. / Will you regret you never met them before?"

The directness of that question, with its assonant bisyllables ("regret," "never," "before"), is astonishing; its emotional effect when heard with Kern's music, syncopated as ever but with a magical contrary-motion progression from $I^{\flat\substack{6\\5}}$ to $I^{\flat\substack{4\\3}}$ in the bass, is on the surface routine; underneath, heart-rending.

Musical Comedy Scores of the Princess Era

La belle Paree was subtitled "a jumble of jollity," which in a different way could apply to *The Red Petticoat* as well. Kern's first score for a show with any degree of generic discipline was *Oh, I Say!*, and as already mentioned he supplied it on the basis of something rather more ambitious than a mixed bag of punctuating songs plus reprise finales and leisurely opening choruses. Paradoxically this would be his way of learning that he could have greater impact in his earlier function, that of interpolator, when the reviews singled out "The Old Clarinet" as its best song—the only one not by him. In farce, a musical number is obliged to stop the show in both senses of the phrase, and Kern henceforward had to negotiate rather more carefully his desire to convey the drama through music.

The act 1 trio of *Oh, I Say!* (not its preceding *terzette*, which was published as "I Know and She Knows") demonstrates the problem, for it is cast as a sung waltz sequence, with continuous sections across a number of changes of key, and five separate tunes. Yet there is nothing in the conversation between Sidonie, Henri, and Marcel to suggest that they should be waltzing or listening to a ball here; only their on-the-spot embarrassment at what Henri has just had to fabricate (that he, not Marcel, Sidonie's ex-lover, is getting married) would seem to justify setting this moment to music. The act 3 "Quintette-bouffe," an intermezzo of some charm nearly a hundred bars long, freezes the action less awkwardly and is on a par with the musical structuring of quite a lengthy part of the act 1 opening, which wanders conversationally through seven or eight contrasting sections before the need for any spoken dialogue is felt. This opening sets up a more leisurely, tableau-like approach to musical comedy than the Princess shows will sustain (though they too have their opening numbers), yet it survives as late as the first scene of *Show Boat.*

In some respects *Oh, I Say!* is one of a pair with *Have a Heart*, for despite the Parisian setting this is very much a Viennese operetta in musical glitter and sentiment. There are plenty of waltz numbers, seven at the most generous count. *Have a Heart* quotes Lehár's "'Gold and Silver' Waltz" and Johann Strauss's *Die Fledermaus* in "Look in His Eyes," written in fact for an earlier Viennese operetta, *Lieber Augustin*; in *Oh, I Say!* there are echoes of German's *Tom Jones* ("For tonight") in the act 1 trio and of Hanna's entrance in *The Merry Widow* as the act 1 curtain goes up. The suave, smooth refrain of "Each Pearl a Thought" is used like the *Merry Widow* waltz as a romantic signature tune in the act 1 finale and as part of the act 3 finale medley. At the same time, both the first- and second-act finales culminate in a spirited new tune, which as we have seen is a European, not an American, feature. Both are memorable, and both indicate Kern's mastery of the quickstep gaiety needed for such a spot. Two recurrent polka motifs are used to underline the social frivolity — x in example 1.1 is one of them, a dotted-note figure (|5.43-|5.43-|6.54-|↑1) the other. Both can be seen in "I Know and She Knows." Kern thought well enough of this score to reuse two of its most lyrical numbers, "Alone at Last" and "I Can't Forget Your Eyes," in much later shows of high profile (the former reappeared as "In Love" in *Blue Eyes*, the latter as "Sunshine" in *Sunny*, as well as in *Criss-Cross* as "In Araby With You"). But its best song, "A Woman's Heart," never resurfaced.[30]

Kern's next three scores are less easy to assess. *90 in the Shade* cannot be reconstructed in the absence of a script, and as with *Nobody Home*, virtually none of its music beyond the individually published songs survives, with the exception of the act 2 opening.[31] All of the published songs of *90 in the Shade* were reused later, as were one or two from *Nobody Home* and *Very Good Eddie*, and *Very Good Eddie* suffered importations from a good many other Kern shows when revived in the 1970s. With so many songs coming and going, getting a clear picture of each score is difficult in retrospect. *90 in the Shade*, its exotic setting and mix of characters harking back to the Edwardian musical comedy and *Florodora*, will have had, like *Oh, I Say!*, style elements relatively distant from Tin Pan Alley, to judge from the exquisite music box miniature "Peter Pan" (which was reused in *Have a Heart*) and "Where's the Boy / Girl for Me?" (it was published separately for both genders), which is more solid than most popular songs and includes a "symphonically" contrasting middle section. *Nobody Home* and *Very Good Eddie* share certain other features, however, particularly if one takes into the equation Rubens's 1905 *Mr. Popple (of Ippleton)*, on which the script of *Nobody Home* was based while the songs were replaced. In fact *Mr. Popple* also replicates *Oh, I Say!*'s type of farce in which a glamorous actress or her servants rent out her empty apartment only to find it filling up with her admirers and, separately, their uninvolved wives. In *Mr. Popple* there are two older married men chasing the star, and one of the wives is forever bullying the other. This was simplified to the one couple (Mr. and Mrs. d'Amorini) in *Nobody Home* but brings the two married couples of *Very Good Eddie* to mind, with the statuesque Georgina dragging the minuscule Eddie "by the hand behind her / Like a captive minnow on a dangling hook."

Rubens's score for *Mr. Popple* was a modest compendium of neat, chic, tuneful, freestanding songs; there were seemingly no finales or extended passages of music. One can see the Princess ethos stemming from this, and Rubens spoke about trying to achieve something similar.[32] *Nobody Home* has its English touches, including a waltz song, "In Arcady," reminiscent of the setting of those words in the opening chorus of *The Arcadians* (1909), and two British characters, the "soldier dancer" Vernon Popple, based in New York, where the action takes place, and his rustic brother Freddy, visiting from England. In the Rubens original, set in England, the lead was a young barrister called Norman Popple. The change of given name and retention of national origin are transparent topical references to the phenomenally popular Vernon Castle, who with his wife was rapidly transforming young bourgeois America into a social dance culture.[33] This would never have stuck without a new type of insidiousness in popular music, triumphantly building on ragtime, on a speeded-up, vulgarized version of the tripping dotted rhythms previously associated with quadrilles and chorus girls, and on reflexivity in the lyrics—tunes that describe themselves and the irresistible effects of music. Irving Berlin's "Alexander's Ragtime Band" is the model for all that follows, Gershwin's "Fascinating Rhythm" and Kern's own "Little Tune, Go Away" later classics of the genre. Kern, using his Alley credentials to produce a type of novelty song for *Nobody Home* and *Very Good Eddie* that would sustain him long thereafter, drew freely on "Alexander's Ragtime Band."

There are four songs about frantic dancing in these two shows: "The Magic Melody," "The Chaplin Walk," and "That Peculiar Tune" in *Nobody Home* and "I've Got to Dance" in *Very Good Eddie*. Two more, "At That San Francisco Fair" and "Any Old Night" in *Nobody Home*, also address themselves to consumer crazes, the latter with the message that it's better to stay at home "with a wonderful girl." All four draw attention to their own characteristics—"Just see them syncopating Chaplin's walk," that song's lyrics urge, with quickstep cross-rhythm on the last two words. "Come on, take a chance, and we'll dance to the syncopated melody," exhorts "The Magic Melody" to the subdominant with flattened 7th noted by Engel. This signals the turn to African-American harmony as well as rhythm, and the verse of "That Peculiar Tune" showcases the same chord just after the lines "A harmless syncopated melody, / A tricky little blend of harmony." Neither of these songs exploits the blue 3rd melodically, however: it took a third "social whirl" song of 1915, "Society," from *Cousin Lucy*, for Kern to do that. Then it was perhaps by accident, as an appoggiatura both downward to $\hat{2}$ in the refrain and upwards as $\sharp\hat{2}$ to $\hat{3}$ in the accompaniment of the verse, without any suggestion of black music or feeling as topic, though the effect is unmistakably bluesy. *Cousin Lucy* starred the female impersonator Julian Eltinge, and like "Katy-did," "Society" makes one wonder whether "extreme vaudeville"—the style of white burlesque in these cases—was historically responsible for some of the musical razzmatazz more traditionally associated with African-American influence.

But the best of these fashion songs by far is "I've Got to Dance." Its introduction is like an old-fashioned ballerina tiptoeing onto the stage, but when the dotted notes combine with a heavy "oompah" accompaniment and syncopation, the display is altogether more Dionysian and communal, implying that in the audience not only feet will tap but bodies will want to start moving. There is a stroke of genius when the tune stops for a single downbeat before the renewed command "Get up and walk," words just reminiscent enough of the Gospel to sound blasphemous, their music, with its cheeky upward 6th, all the more lovable for momentary piety. The reflexive modulation later on is outrageous rather than bluesy, but Kern recovers from it with what in his later output will become seasoned deftness. Rubens has been left far behind here, though the number for which *Very Good Eddie* is best remembered, "Babes in the Wood," reestablishes European values, pointing the way forward to *Oh, Boy!*'s decorum, and it should not be forgotten that ragtime rhythms were sung by bel canto women in Kern's day: Julia James's 1916 recording of "That 'Come Hither' Look" from *Theodore and Co.*, imbued with operatic tone, emotion, and freedom, demonstrates the kind of interpretation that must have been expected for similar songs such as "Another Little Girl" from *Nobody Home*. Such singing makes the harmonies all the more persuasive, if at the expense of the rhythm.[34]

Nevertheless, there are too many ragtime songs in *Very Good Eddie*. When Kern falls prey not just to the rhythms of "Waiting for the Robert E. Lee," but also to its actual melodic shapes in the show's opening number, "We're On Our Way," he begins to sound ephemeral rather than topical. Yet *Very Good Eddie*'s topicality lends one crucial feature to his ongoing development, and that is the absorption of the Charlie Chaplin figure, merely a song's correlative in *Nobody Home*, into the plot and meaning of the whole. Eddie, the put-upon "little man" of farce, might not have resonated without Chaplin's stardom, the Chaplin who in his prime was "the quaint representative of those millions of the poor who may be found in all our great cities and who seem to be for ever fighting hopefully a losing battle with Fate."[35] "Thirteen Collar," with burlesque weariness in its dotted rhythms and defeat in its affectionate chromatics, is the perfect theme music for Chaplin. Already sympathy for the loser, and very soon for the bewildered immigrant, becomes part of the American sound and style, a particular slant on youth's oppression by age, a new take on the traditional dandy lead, and in the Princess ethos an equation of the little show with the little, ordinary person.

Love o' Mike and *Have a Heart* come next and offer something more expansive and romantic within the topical formula. This is where the dramatic aims of the Princess team first elicit musical mastery from Kern, and two examples stand out, one in each show: the Prologue to *Love o' Mike* and the act 1 finale to *Have a Heart*. Both help convey dramatic conceptions or moments of breadth with a tableau element, which is what musical comedy needed at this juncture if it was to furnish Kern with opportunities for musical expansiveness. But there was another vehicle for expansiveness with which Kern was involved at this time, spectacular revue. It was undoubtedly revue that nurtured key aspects of his musical vision when for a large theater such as Abraham Erlanger's New Amsterdam, home of the Kálmán *Miss Springtime* (though an operetta, not a revue) or for Ziegfeld and Dillingham's *Miss 1917* at the Century Theatre, he could compose such songs as "My Castle in the Air," "Go, Little Boat," and "Land Where the Good Songs Go." All three are gems, all three enjoy lyrics by Wodehouse that leave humor behind and affect the heart, and Wilder praised "My Castle in the Air" for having, for the first time in his opinion, a verse by Kern written, "in a manner of speaking, at the same sitting as the chorus." If glorifying the American girl meant sanctifying her, then smooth, unhurried, richly harmonized melody had an important sacralizing role to play, and Kern, with his strong basses and textures amenable to sustained inner parts, was the person to provide it. As if to prove the point, the refrain in the 1917 recording of "My Castle in the Air" by its original artist, George MacFarlane, enjoys a continuous inner-part countermelody on cellos and horn, a distinct step on the road to the Broadway sound of later decades.[36] The bell-like ostinato of the refrain of "Land Where the Good Songs Go" has a similarly broadening effect, also exploited in "You Found Me and I Found You" from *Oh, Lady! Lady!!*, "The First Rose of Summer," and "Teacher—Teacher" from *She's a Good Fellow*. So does the art-song serenade figure of "Go, Little Boat," presaging that of "Smoke Gets in Your Eyes." "Go, Little Boat"'s wordless coda similarly foreshadows the coloratura and enharmonics of "All the Things You Are," and there are impressionist harmonies in the verses of both "Go, Little Boat" and "Land Where the Good Songs Go," though why another of the *Miss 1917* songs, "We're Crooks," should have ended with the *Tristan* chord is something of a mystery.

Love o' Mike concerns a British army captain, Lord Michael Kildare, who is guest at a country house party while invalided out of frontline duties on a secret armaments assignment to the United States. All the girls fall for him, but aristocratic modesty prevents him from demonstrating how he lives up to their heroic requirements until, at the end, his award of the VC is announced. In between, a good deal of farcical complication ensues when in order to win the hand of Vivian, one of the girls, with the aid of the crooked butler he pretends to have rescued a woman and her children from a fire. Unfortunately, a disgruntled suitor was the real rescuer. The musical's opening scene, the Prologue, must owe something to the *tableau vivant* topic of revue and was devised as a splendid example of having one's cake and eating it too, for Marbury wanted to luxuriate in her six girls (the house party debutantes) undressing for bed but challenge her middle-class audiences to find it smart, seemly, integral, and even educational, as a press release had the chutzpah to insist:

> [The girls'] haste in their undoing, which may seem a trifle early in the course of a musical play, you immediately find justified by the programme, which says that this prologue is in a boudoir, at a fashionable country resort, at two oclock in the morning. . . . the undressing scene is probably the politest undressing scene that has been staged . . . It is positively Arcadian in its guileless simplicity, although perhaps the same cannot be said of the lacy complications that fall from the forms of Miss Gabriel Grey and Miss Gysie Dale . . . This scene was rehearsed at greater length and pains than any other scene in the play . . . So when Miss Grey and Miss Dale start the gowns a-falling soon after the play begins, they make a positive art of casting their raiment. Miss Grey stands right up straight and lets her frock fall from her as though she were a little statue at its unveiling. Miss Dale and the others who jump into bed were all specially rehearsed . . . Said one well-known society matron who saw "Love o' Mike" several times during its long run in New York: "My daughter tears an evening gown every time she steps out of one. . . . I shall insist that she see this play. These are thing[s] every girl should know before it is too late." [37]

This was guaranteed to attract an audience, and Kern gave the scene his most ravishing music yet, Arcadian indeed. It begins with the bustling Prelude, an instrumental piece quite unlike his songs, reused in *Men of the Sky* and *Music in the Air* and a perfect curtain-raiser, almost neoclassical in the manner of Richard Strauss. As its subdominant trio, a one-step (it becomes the song "Don't Tempt Me") is heard on a piano offstage at the house party, followed by a waltz version of "Home, Sweet Home" which makes the butler cry while burgling Molly's bedroom. He hides in the closet as six girls enter and prepare for bed. This is quite some opening, and "Drift With Me," first heard hummed offstage by the chorus boys and only at the end of the scene sung by the girls, is equal to it, taking its antique cue as something between a serenade and a lullaby from the ukelele plucked by one of the girls, Peggy (played by the young Peggy Wood). Saddler's orchestration is original enough in its combination of instruments for the show as a whole — note the two bassoons, absence of clarinets, trumpets in A, two pianos, six violins, and two viola parts. It comes into its own here with both pianos as well as the trumpet muted in different ways, the violins hocketing *arco* and *pizzicato*, and a good deal of pentatonic filigree work to represent the ukelele's Edenic contribution (ex. 2.4). Since the song is supposed to be from a current opera (or operetta?), Kern gives it an unusually poetic verse, with almost constant sixteenth note accompaniment motion but syncopation too, in the original classic ragtime combination here forming a link between that art and a Bach allemande, then a broad refrain in 2/2 which feels longer than its twenty-two bars because it repeats no section and is spun out as pure cantilena with bold contouring in the upward arpeggios. A good deal of the number's attraction comes from the 7–6 suspensions of the verse (see the fifth complete bar of ex. 2.4, first viola and first trumpet parts), which recur in the refrain.

In some respects this song sets the model for the creamy smoothness of Kern's 2/2 refrains, and there are two other *alla breve* numbers in *Love o' Mike* ("It Wasn't My Fault" and "We'll See"), plus a third, "It Can't Be Done," notated in 2/2 though without the two-in-a-bar feeling. None of them is half as good as "Drift With Me," however, and *Love o' Mike*'s problem is that it has set up a rich texture in this first scene which it cannot sustain, musically or dramatically. Particularly far-fetched farce takes over, as do novelty songs of one sort or another. Of these, "Moo Cow" was a hit, but thankfully not published; "The Baby Vampire" works well enough but is essentially burlesque, complete with trick harmonies; "Hoot Mon" tacks Scottishness onto standard novelty rag features. As usual, many songs came and went while the show was in production, but one of those discarded, "Who Cares?," is a gem, a waltz that looks forward to the sumptuousness of *Have a Heart*, for it has learned from Lehár the seductiveness of diatonic appoggiaturas over very slow-moving harmonies. Moreover, it notates its effect of erotic rubato in meters changing every bar from 3/4 to 2/4 to 3/8 and back to 3/4. Its first six bars are on the tonic, the next four on the dominant — compare "Wie die Blumen im Lenze erblüh'n," from *The Merry Widow*. This was too good to bury, and resurfaced in *Good Morning, Dearie*. There, if the overture was Kern's work, its chromatics and seamless countermelody make it Kern's first great waltz (ex. 2.5), though it never reappears in this form in the score; instead it is transformed into a simple 2/4 as the show's title song.[38]

Ex. 2.4. Drift With Me, orchestral score by Frank Saddler.

Ex. 2.5. Good Morning, Dearie (waltz).

Love o' Mike has an extended first-act finaletto, but it is largely a matter of instrumental march sections (two of its themes reused in *Sunny*'s opening circus music) with spoken dialogue over them. The "Strike the lyre" choral homage, echoed by the girls' cast-off cynics as "Strike the liar!" when Mike Kildare, the British war hero, is unmasked, may not have worked on the stage as a pun set to music. *Have a Heart*'s act 1 finale, on the other hand, is Kern's first characteristic reprise finaletto and works perfectly, all sung save for a few spoken words over held notes. It begins with new material, a minor-key waltz demonic enough to set the pace of excitement about the absconding primary couple. This leads neatly into the fourth couple's reprise of "I'm So Busy" as they implore Lizzie, who had first sung it, to do something about the elopement. Such reprises work best when the words can be repeated verbatim with new significance or changed to topical effect, as when they turn Quaker in the *Oh, Boy!* first-act finale; here minimal change is required, from "Lizzie, Lizzie, / I'm so busy, / Don't know what to do" to "Lizzie, Lizzie, / Quick, get busy, / Tell us what to do." As an adroit sequel the beginning of the refrain's final C section is changed from |5-♯4|5-3|6--|↓2- to |5-♯4|5-3|6--|↓♯1--| and repeated up a tone sequentially as |6-♯5|6-♯4|7--|↓♯2--|, which the words enact as "His game we must be balking, / Don't let's stand here talking," followed by a fifteen-bar dominant pedal as the chorus turn on Henry, the elevator boy, expecting him to do something. He responds in self-defense with the first sixteen bars of "Have a Heart," originally sung by the male lead Schoonmaker with a quite different contextual meaning of the title words and quite different ensuing lyrics. The chorus repeat this a minor 3rd higher and take the refrain almost to its end, as with "I'm So Busy" notching the first four bars of its final eight-bar strain (here an A₁) a tone higher in sequence before settling into another dominant pedal (this time on C, not G). The new lyrics, as Henry temporizes, are splendid, not a note of the refrain lost or delayed as the following plays out:

HENRY: Don't imagine that I'm shirking
But the darn thing isn't working
The machinery has got all tangled up.
(The elevator sticks on its way down. Rises again until it is half way between top and bottom at door. Door opens[;] Henry's head is seen as he crouches on the floor of elevator and looks out. He is hammering on an iron plate with a hammer and a monkey wrench.)
ALL: What has happened to the elevator?
Golly! Has its stuck?

And all the while it's getting later,
What a rotten bit of luck.

Henry shouts, "Going up," but held sixteenth notes fanning downward chro-matically indicate that the elevator droops while permitting excited spoken conversation, Owen calling from the elevator, "Quick! Look out of the win-dow. Can you see them?" "Yes," shout the chorus and describe their automo-bile departure by launching into a *contrafactum* of Schoonmaker's earlier song of sadness, "And I Am All Alone," the words changed from "I see you there" to "We see them there / Just as they used to be . . . The motor hums a merry bridal tune / As they begin their second honeymoon." This time the whole of the final section of the thirty-two-bar refrain is developed into a dominant pedal (once more on C) before sixteen bars of it are repeated one last time as a solo, in A major before a quiet instrumental coda (based on the refrain's three-note upbeat) for the curtain. This tonally circular tune lends itself to modular splicing, which is cleverly applied here: the second half of the chorus's third period is a 4th higher than it should be (leading to the pedal), and the solo half-refrain fuses its first eight and last eight bars. The only flaws in the musical and lyric succession are perhaps too many domi-nant pedals and a questionable motivation for the final solo, unattributed in the score but indicated in the script as belonging to Peggy, the female lead, which makes little sense.

This finaletto may not reprise as many tunes as that of *Oh, Lady! Lady!!,* but it sustains and caps a splendid first act whose plot has been steadily accel-erating. Immediately before the finale Schoonmaker has accidentally sat on the row of buzzers on his executive desk, and this has brought a male voice quartet, a series of shop girls, and Henry as fire officer to his service in farci-cal succession just as he is grabbing Dolly Brabazon in order to retrieve some incriminating letters and is seen in this posture by his wife's snooping aunt. *Have a Heart,* with its star comic in the young Henry—originally played by Billy Van, who recorded his act 2 number "Napoleon"—is swift and lean, would play perfectly well on the stage today with no change of script, and is perhaps the best of the Princess-era shows. Unlike *Love o' Mike,* it blends romance and farce in a smooth and sophisticated manner, and its music and lyrics are equal to both genres. The triumph of Wodehouse's limitless encores for such songs as "Napoleon," "It's a Sure, Sure Sign," and "Polly Be-lieved in Preparedness" contrasts with musical suavity of one sort or another in the romantic waltz "The Road That Lies Before," the glamorous yet sad fox-trot "And I Am All Alone," the whimsical introduction to "They All Look Alike," and a number of fresh 2/4 tunes such as "Bright Lights" and "I'm Here, Little Girls, I'm Here." "I'm Here, Little Girls, I'm Here" is distinctly similar to Gershwin's Broadway marches of the 1920s. Most important, "The Road That Lies Before" in act 1 is not just a song but a musical scene of romance of the sort developed later in *Dear Sir* and *Show Boat* all the way through to *Gentlemen Unafraid*. Its introduction quotes "Have a Heart"; a verse leads to a reprise of "And I Am All Alone," part sung, part spoken by Schoonmaker and his wife, Peggy, as he gives her back her tokens, and they realize they are still in love. The melody of "The Road That Lies Before" is then heard instrumentally (its first use in the show except in the overture) as they kiss: music, as subliminal underscoring that represents emotional action, here changes the course of the drama, acknowledged when Peggy then sings the tune, in 2/4 against the 3/4 "oompah" accompaniment as a sort of hesitation waltz that embraces 3/4 as she gains the confidence to try again with their relationship. Dialogue follows as the waltz continues instrumentally, helping them to make up their minds about a fresh start; the curve of the scene is complete as the music fades out, a curve that had been set up in an earlier dramatic segment when the couple first confronted each other at an emotional temperature surprisingly volatile for a 1917 musical comedy, with a distinct foretaste of *Private Lives*.

Woolf and Caldwell

The Princess shows were followed for some years by a bewilderingly mixed bag of musicals. Yet there is generic continuity of a sort, for first Kern wrote three scores for Edgar Allan Woolf farces, then he teamed up with Anne Caldwell and explored a new range of topicality in music. Moreover, the Princess model still resonates in the second of the shows with Woolf, *Rock-a-Bye Baby*; its characters could almost be the babes in the wood after a year or two of marriage but not yet with children, the focus of *Rock-a-Bye Baby*'s plot. Accordingly his songs explore new forms of tenderness, while harking back to *Have a Heart* with its similar themes of loneliness and distrust and consolidating the flavor of *Oh, Boy!*'s "sanctified" songs, notably in "The Kettle Song," with a particularly lovely verse, and "There's No Better Use for Time than Kissing," both in the inevitable E flat major. Lullabies are obligatory in this score, "Lullaby" itself being more waltzlike but also more delicate than Kern's regular waltzes. "Not You" has been suggested as a possible model for Gershwin's "Someone to Watch Over Me," since its "bur-then" shares an opening melodic contour with Gershwin's verse, both songs exploit gentle parallel 4ths, and Gershwin was rehearsal pianist for *Rock-a-Bye Baby*. Although "Just a Little Line" from *She's a Good Fellow* has a similar head motif, the point is plausible. Two other *Rock-a-Bye Baby* songs evoke early childhood, "My Boy" and "Nursery Fanfare" ("My Own Light Infantry"). "Nursery Fanfare" is disappointing, not quite the miniature gem one would hope for from Kern and be granted five years later in "The Nurs-ery Clock." Bordman is probably right to resist the "mawkish" "My Boy," but it allows Kern to progress toward his 1930s style—compare "Ev'ry Little While," echoing more than one aspect of this song's phraseology, which in-cludes early use of quarter-note triplets though not yet a full thirty-two bars of such a low-rise refrain. All this gentleness is counteracted by a new fox-trot brashness in "One, Two, Three" (again catalytic for Gershwin?).

The *New York Times* confidently proclaimed Kern's score for *Rock-a-Bye Baby* "his best, undoubtedly, since 'Oh, Boy!'" Other shows following the Princess years may yet prove similarly praiseworthy, at least for their music. There is delightful élan in the opening number of *Head Over Heels* (ex. 2.6), and Kern's style frankly benefited from this loosening up, though nothing quite matches it later in the score. The corollary in *Toot-Toot!*, however, was a coarsening of the dramatic fabric into a rambling, inconsequential farce set on a train, with humor and plotting far less stylish than those of Bolton and Wodehouse. The comedy exploits two objects of oppression in a single exchange as early as page two:

> SHAW: I guess this is the station man. *(To Porter)* Say, Rastus, one moment—
> Do you—
> PORTER *(Angry at Shaw, and looking at bundles, crosses R)*: No emigrant
> trains—only on Tuesdays and Thursdays.

and *Head Over Heels* depicts the Italian acrobats as vain, pugnacious, noisy, mercenary, and short. Woolf's reliance on stock gags was criticized in the *New York Times* review of *Toot-Toot!* Yet the clergyman wanting a fling, the secondary couple hot from their divorce party and bound for Reno and sepa-ration, and the arty Greek dancers furnish the carnivalesque *Toot-Toot!*, like *Head Over Heels*, with timely musical liberation: Kern includes richer tex-tures and a more colorful variety of effect than in the Princess shows. "Quar-rel and Part," a divorce number, includes some brittle surprises, including a tonic minor ending; "Runaway Colts" is a refreshingly hearty 6/8; "It's All

Greek to Me," its instrumental opening on cor anglais sporting 2/4, 5/8, and 3/8 bars in succession, has a lush refrain with an octave countermelody working its way up through the accompaniment over ten bars; "Girlie" is a more stylish, modern waltz than Kern had previously written; and the "Smoking Song" has a welcome opulence as well as a refrain head motif echoing that of "Runaway Colts". What is lacking is an overall focus: *Toot-Toot!* presents the army seriously, with four soldier numbers interspersed among the other songs, yet only two of them, "Ev'ry Girl in All America" and "Yankee Doodle on the Line," are by Kern, his authority evidently taking second place to surefire effect in a wartime show. Nor is he up to the task in these songs, and *Toot-Toot!* is no *Yip! Yip! Yaphank*. To keep the comedy going, it takes Marjorie almost to the end of the play to accept the message the audience is intended to hear, after her frustration at not finding a minister to join her to Harry has climaxed with the leading characters being robbed and left on the track:

> HARRY: By a fast all night hike I can catch the next train for New York to join my regiment. Marjorie, I must be on my way.
> MARJORIE: All right, dear, I'll go with you.
> HARRY: But, girlie, your little feet would fail you — Now, come be brave and *smile* as you let me go.
> (MRS. WELLINGTON *re-enters up L*)
> MARJORIE: I see — you're right. Millions of women have been brave and I can be too. The country's need comes first, Harry. *You must go at once.* Good bye and good luck!
> (HARRY *kisses her ardently. Tears himself away and rushes off up* R. MARJORIE *sways and* MRS. WELLINGTON *goes to her. Music stops*)
> MRS. WELLINGTON (*Comfortingly*): Come, dear, brace up. I'm proud of you. Come, it's moments like this that make women of us all. I'd send my Jimmie, too, but he'd only take up room.[39]

The songs for *Zip, Goes a Million* (not a Woolf show) consolidate the richer textures and fuller detail of *Toot-Toot!* but remain unmemorable. Those for *Head Over Heels* are slightly more individual and reflect Woolf's carnival atmosphere. "The Big Show" has a circus richness, with twiddly brass-band fills and relaxed, warm harmonies, and if others have associated Bohemian polkas with circus or acrobatic music, so does Kern, in the verses of "Moments of the Dance" and "Head Over Heels." He also reminds us of Mitzi's Italian identity, however, with a suitably Mediterranean tendency toward parallel 3rds in "I Was Lonely" (split, not duplicated, between voice

Ex. 2.6. *Head Over Heels*, opening.

and piano, a feature also found in *Rock-a-Bye Baby*) and the recycled "Let Us Build a Little Nest" as well as the effervescent act 1 opening number.

These are old-fashioned signifiers; the most obvious features of Kern's work with Anne Caldwell, by contrast, are its tokens of up-to-dateness, particularly in terms of dance. The problem is the dramatic equivalent of this, for because of the social leveling of war, the postwar dancing craze embraced a wider and lower class spectrum than applied to Wodehouse and Bolton's Princess show types, and this is not necessarily evident in Caldwell's scripts. *The Night Boat*, a flatly ridiculous farce, seems to acknowledge this by exploiting alienation techniques: a bizarre chorus of "plot demonstrators" appears on two occasions, explaining the action (apparently in music) for latecomers and then pointing the moral. Caldwell seems to have been at home in the world of revue, where such techniques might be at a premium—they are engagingly exploited in "Moon of Love," written by Kern and Caldwell for *Hitchy Koo: 1920* and a spoof into whose romantic refrain are inserted cynical dotted-note fills by the chorus girls: "Oh what the deuce do you suppose we care to hear the silly stuff you have to spill about the moon?" they sing. But it is difficult to imagine how *The Night Boat* could center such material, though Seldes liked it.[40] The Scottish numbers, "I Love the Lassies" and "Left All Alone Again Blues," create a gratuitous, music hall exoticism (were they thinking of Harry Lauder?), "Left All Alone Again Blues" not even recognizable as Scottish in its published form because the "Bluebells of Scotland" countermelody, which runs throughout, is absent, an extraordinary omission. "The Bluebells of Scotland" is, of course, a standard thirty-two-bar AABA song, making nonsense of the tendency to think of the form as American. The Hudson River setting occasions no "odor of sachet," though "The Lorelei" is à propos the musical's theme, and there are vaguely referential songs in "I'd Like a Lighthouse," recycled from "Honeymoon Land" in *Toot-Toot!*, "Rip van Winkle and His Little Men," and "Good Night Boat," all disappointing numbers. True feeling is reserved for the "Bob White" number, a tender waltz of reconciliation, its "hook" the mocking chirp of that name by a bird in a garden. Dramatic assessment of *She's a Good Fellow* and *The Bunch and Judy* is impossible without access to scripts, but reviews suggest no great cogency.

There are, however, two musical developments in the *Night Boat* songs, traceable earlier in *She's a Good Fellow* and unmissable in quite a few other Caldwell numbers. One is a more emphatic emphasis on triple eighth note cross-rhythm, noticeable in "Whose Baby Are You?" from *The Night Boat*. At the line "Who'll own your smile as you walk down the aisle with him?," not only does the tune skip into 3/8 against the 2/4 meter but so does the accompaniment, with accents, rather than maintain the "oompah"s: the Charleston is on the horizon. "Happy Wedding Day" from *She's a Good Fellow* also behaves this way. The other development, an important one for Kern, is that he begins to utilize blues features beyond the subdominant with flattened 7th and the blue 3rd already noted.

First the shimmy and the blues and then the Charleston were the key tokens in dance and song of 1920s frivolity, liberation, and malaise. The frivolity might be manic, as in "Ginger Town" (supposed to be in Jamaica) from *She's a Good Fellow*, with its secondary rag, cakewalk syncopations, and crazy chromatic linkage at the words "Where the rivers shimmy shiver." But in general, heavier, more insistent, coarser rhythmic textures than ragtime and the "trot" dances were involved, in line with a scoring in dance halls that was less orchestral (a jazz sound, based on brass, "reeds," and "rhythm section") and soon to be amplified, live or over the radio. Theater orchestration changed slowly, but Kern's textures did not stand still. One should

not ignore the meaning of this. The new sounds and dance movements signaled a more overtly, aggressively sexual age, which musical comedy sooner
or later had to accommodate: an age more accepting of female sexuality
in particular, for the slow, loose amble of the shimmy and the blues linked
white women for the first time with the enviable capabilities of southern
blacks, whose "relaxed movements [had] long been a stylistic trait . . . coun-
tering the deliberate stiffness of European styles."[41] Some of Kern's work
with Caldwell suggests the change, leading as it does to *Show Boat* with
its story's consequences of sexual alliance (the half-caste Julie; a daughter
for Magnolia and Ravenal), even if only *Show Boat* fully articulates it and
applies it to the past through the lens of the present.

Although "Shimmy With Me," from *The Cabaret Girl* and reused as "He
Is the Type" in *The City Chap*, is Kern's most overt acknowledgment of the
postwar dance craze, numerous other songs evoke its world. Kern associates
shimmying and the blues with simultaneous melodies not only in "Shimmy
With Me" but also in "Left All Alone Again Blues," as noted above, and
"Blue Danube Blues" from *Good Morning, Dearie*, presumably to epitomize the jazzing of genteel culture when an old-fashioned tune combines
with a modern one. Several songs in *The Night Boat* have passages of throbbing repeated chords against a series of eighth notes in the melody, often
in the form of repeated notes or oscillating steps, but with the fourth tied
to the first of the next group within the bar. The B and B_1 sections of the
refrain of "A Heart for Sale" exhibit these features, and there are traces of
them in "Good Night Boat." "Funny Little Something" from *Head Over
Heels* seems to presage the trend, in this case with strong signposts in the
lyrics' syntax and vocabulary, such lines as "Something 'bout you honey"
reappearing in Kern probably for the first time since the blackface of *La
belle Paree*. More significantly, blues topics come together in "The Bull-frog
Patrol" from *She's a Good Fellow*. All sorts of new style markers appear here,
beginning with performance practice, for it was sung in the show by the
Duncan Sisters in a speciality appearance. Their definitive 1922 recording of
the song stresses southern accents and, in the lower of the two sisters' parts,
something associated with them (through the tradition of "coon-shouting"):
chest-voice singing, employed throughout and particularly noticeable when
the sisters are duetting because of its lack of vibrato. The tempo is slow, re-
lentlessly plodding, "oom"s often without their "pah"s (so that the cakewalk
motif |75–6 is heard without intersection), the refrains cumulative; the tex-
ture is burlesque in places, as when the tune appears in the bass with yet

another |-656|5 E flat major ostinato above it. The harmony of both strains (there is no verse/refrain structure; two tunes are heard separately and then superimposed) is that of the twelve-bar blues, though extended to sixteen measures: I I IV I V I [V I]. The lyrics also have the blues' three strains in each section, though the last is repeated (to make four, rather than repeat the first of two to make three).[42]

The circle of references here is African-American, in topics appropriated, as usual, by whites. A patrol, of which "The Bull-frog Patrol" is a perfect example, was "a march with a crescendo-decrescendo dynamic contour"; Kern would utilize it again, though with only the crescendo, in "Can't Help Lovin' Dat Man" and several later blues-influenced numbers, and outside the black context in "The Pergola Patrol." It was a favorite stage topic, for "from the time of the Civil War . . . comic portrayals of supposedly inept black soldiers were a staple of the minstrel stage"; *Hayfoot, Strawfoot*'s very title owes something to it, as does that show's genius for cumulative ensembles.[43] But where Kern's blues style comes really out into the open is in three other Caldwell songs. The first is "Bring 'Em Back" from *Hitchy Koo: 1920*. This was reused as "Dahomey" in *Show Boat* but heavily revised, without its verse and blues stomp, which in "Bring 'Em Back" includes a persistent dissonance formation in the accompanying chords, for instance, 1#4513 as the tonic chording. The second is "'Have You Forgotten Me?' Blues" in *The Bunch and Judy*, marked "à la patrol." The quarter-note chords, or at least bass notes, never let up, clearly signifying marching as well as the pulse of blue feeling, and on the last word of the title line's last reiteration the harmony moves flatward not, this time, to IV$^{\flat7}$, but to the more extreme and expressive flattened submediant, ($^{\flat}$VI$^{\flat9}_{\flat7}$). This is the chord that later appears on the word "lovin'" in "Can't Help Lovin' Dat Man." The third is "Sympathetic Someone" in *The City Chap*, rich in progressive features if not particularly appealing. Its lyrics set up the bright and then the dark side of 1920s youth:

> *[Verse]* Happy boys and girls around I see.
> What can be wrong with me?
> Merry young dancers throng there;
> Maybe I don't belong there.
> Other girls have lots of lovely things,
> Chums and pals, frocks and rings.
> How could they know I long for
> Something that friendship brings:
> Just a

[Refrain] Sympathetic someone
Who will ring true when I'm blue.

The verse jogs along not only with the tripping dotted notes of yore—compare "What a pretty bevy!" in *Show Boat*—but with a much more *moderne* tenor line in the accompaniment, its half-note upward suspensions a kind of species counterpoint for the approaching age of *deco*. The refrain plunges into a heavy pseudo-blues with the repeated chords strummed across 10ths and unusually sidelong harmony: the four initial bars of dominant 13th go directly to four on the flat 7th degree. Not until the nineteenth bar is a root position tonic reached, and it is undermined by the addition of a jazzy flattened 7th in the song's final bar.

This was about as modern as Kern would get in the 1920s, and, the magnificence of "Can't Help Lovin' Dat Man" aside, it hardly sounds natural to him. Yet in one of his scores for Caldwell, *Good Morning, Dearie,* he provided a feast of rhythmic numbers within a dance-culture plot almost without reference to the blues, instead latching onto the tinkling novelty pianism of Gershwin, Zez Confrey, and Billy Mayerl, which provides him with the vitality he needs and suits him better as an outgrowth of his dotted-note schottisches. It is a fine score and includes a number of significant developments as well as highly memorable tunes (two have already been quoted), with little residue of the Princess style except insofar as *Have a Heart* was red-blooded. One new feature is the joining of two consecutive songs, "Rose-Marie" and "Didn't You Believe?" with underscoring to the connecting dialogue, as Ethan Mordden observes—a love scene in the musical making. Another is transition music, which continues between the first two scenes of act 1 as the curtain comes down on the *modiste*'s shop and goes up some bars later on Chinatown. Appropriately, it is the waltz motif for "Way down town we go, / All the way down town" (3/4 |3--|5--|↓1.11|-76|7--|1--|2), a fine one whose third and fifth to seventh bars can be spotted in example 2.7 (see the accents), that effects the transformation into would-be Chinese music. The Chinatown setting must have been a shallow backdrop, for a "Coolie Dance" with Tiller Girls immediately plays against it before the scene changes again to the interior of the Hell's Bells dance hall. This is Caldwell and Kern "slummin' it," as the lyrics for "Way Down Town" put it and the stage directions for the new scene indicate: *"At opening three Touch Couples are dancing, and Cutey, a professional dancer, is sitting at the table with Gimpy, eating ice-cream. The Chink is seen walking about as if to see that people are*

Ex. 2.7. *Good Morning, Dearie,* transformation music.

waited upon, etc. Cokey Dan is standing behind Gimpy and Cutey smoking a cigarette" — and as if to prove it, another musical innovation is a fight scene in the act 1 finale, which reduces the role of singing and turns the music into a short development section based on the head motifs of "Easy Pickin's," "Rose-Marie," and the French sailors' scena ("When the Guns Are Booming"), all appropriate because the gangster, Chesty, had sung "Easy Pickin's," is now fighting with Billy over the heroine Rose-Marie, and the sailors join in. However different an underworld this is from Wodehouse's, it is not yet *West Side Story: "comedy stuff with gun,"* the stage directions indicate, before *"general rough-house fight as the curtain falls."* [44]

The head motifs in *Good Morning, Dearie* show Kern's melodic inspiration running high, and it is a forward-looking score because he exploits to the full their memorability and pliability, based as these are on a single melodic-rhythmic gesture with pointed harmonies, often a dominant or diatonic 7th or a progression involving an inversion. In other words, he is drawing closer to the post-Wagnerian world of Puccini. Around two-thirds of the music for act 1 is in the form of extended vocal and instrumental numbers, many involving one or more of these motifs, as opposed to simple verse-and-refrain songs. It includes an extended finaletto for scene 1. Only in certain respects do Kern and Caldwell fare less well. The enforced gaiety of dotted-rhythm dancing, its songs including the latest fashion dance, a "Toddle," becomes tiresome. So does the ethnic stereotyping, "Melican Papa" being to song what such lingo as "Me had plortnat blissiness!" is to dialogue, matters made no better just because, as of old, the character perpetrating these tropes is not really Chinese. "Sing Song Girl" is this idiom's lowest point. Most dubious, however, is this:

> CHESTY: Citronella—I'll kill the Wop!
> MME BOMPARD: That's not his name—that's a piece I want the band to play
> —Citronella—(She moves away from Chesty who sees Steve with hand-kerchief)
> (Band plays No. 8B, the first eight bars of vamp and melody of "Dardanella," repeated)[45]

In other words, if the Tams-Witmark script and manuscript score represent the original version of Good Morning, Dearie, Kern knew perfectly well he was quoting "Dardanella" when he incorporated the vamp into "Ka-lu-a," which appears in the next act (curiously, with the vamp now renotated, though in the published piano/vocal score it appears exactly as in "Dardanella"). No. 8B was excised from the published piano/vocal score of Good Morning, Dearie. Was this a crucial piece of evidence the court never found?

Scores for the 1920s

Kern's two most durable musical comedies between Oh, Lady! Lady!! and Show Boat were Sally and Sunny. Easily confused, starting with their titles, they were both written for Marilyn Miller, both filmed with her in the early days of sound, and both focused on the female lead as a performer in ways which drew the script away from farce as a genre toward romance yet, paradoxically, closer to vaudeville in some respects. The vaudeville slant came with the emphasis on diegetic performance and a new, prosperous era's two commercial imperatives, spectacle and participation. Spectacle meant bigger production numbers, ever stronger spotlighting of the star, and/or more scene changes, and scenes could now follow each other rather like vaudeville acts, the curtain down between them; revue encouraged this. Participation was a matter of hit songs to be danced or at least listened to, often while eating or drinking, via the radio, pianola, gramophone, or live dance band. The songs were still sung at home, as they always had been, and sheet music continued to outsell gramophone records, but the balance was rapidly swinging away from active musical participation toward passive or at least—when dancing—silent consumption. Songs accordingly had to be ever more catchy, memorable, and satisfying without the aid of voice or fingers on the keys. Many song arrangements for records and radio, and all piano rolls, did away with the voice altogether or reversed refrain and verse, tucking the latter into the middle reaches where a single vocal refrain might also be heard. And dance bands began appearing in musicals, on or below the stage. *Sunny* had George Olsen's band on stage in New York.

These developments had two overlapping effects on Kern's scores, amply demonstrated in those for *Sally* and *Sunny*, and one on his songs. The songs themselves were more and more subject to a short, repeated gesture as the refrain's building block. The tendency can be spotted in Kern as early as "Some Party" in *She's a Good Fellow* (the refrain begins with repetition in the words—"Some party, / Some peachy party"—to the 2/4 motif |5--|35--|-564|35) and "Girls in the Sea" from *Hitchy Koo: 1920*. *Sunny*, produced immediately after *No, No, Nanette* in New York, represents the apex of this style (or nadir, depending on one's point of view). The songs' foot-tapping insistence, so well caught on the preelectrical dance band recordings of the day with their incessantly stomping tubas and heavy rhythm sections (however far from the theater orchestration this was), required enormous energy from the stage performers. Grossmith discovered as much, to his cost, in *No, No, Nanette*, in which he starred in London with Binnie Hale and Joseph Coyne (Hale was also in the London *Sunny*, along with Jack Buchanan and Claude Hulbert): "Never did actors have to work so hard as in this play," he wrote. "It was only by dint of exercising every power I possessed that I managed to keep at all up to Coyne's level. Our clothes were soaking wet after each act from sheer exertion."[46]

As for the scores as a whole, the first effect on them was a great number of reprises, the second more instrumental music. The proportion of instrumental music in *Sally* is remarkable: 54 of the 132 pages of the published piano/vocal score, which represents 41 percent. *Sunny* is less extreme, but still, 26 percent of the score is instrumental. Compare this with *Have a Heart*, only 6 of whose 98 pages, or 6 percent, are nonvocal. More of the incidentals were being printed in the scores by the 1920s, so it is not possible from this figure alone to ascertain the full extent of *Have a Heart*'s underscoring and dance music, but the very fact of publication is symptomatic of greater need for musical repetition and continuity. Instrumental music was required for the many dance sequences, since Miller was a dancer. Most of the songs in both shows, especially *Sally*, lead into dance refrains, and songs are now transforming themselves metrically in the process—this happens with "Dancing Time" in *The Cabaret Girl*, and "Look for the Silver Lining" becomes a fox-trot, with dotted rhythms and much melodic elaboration, then a one-step, in the dance break after it has been sung in act 1 of *Sally*. This is a process of jazzing up, which Kern tried to prevent four years later with *Sitting Pretty*. Many of the straight song reprises are instrumental too. They are increasingly used to cover scene changes, which is certainly applicable to *Sunny*, though *Sally* has only five scenes altogether, one in each of the first two acts, three in the last. Refrain repetitions also underscore dialogue and action or simply act as extra choruses in big production numbers. The result is a smaller number of tunes plugged an increasing number of times. The "Wild Rose" refrain is printed out, mostly complete, a total of nine times in *Sally*, while *Sunny* subjects "Two Little Bluebirds" to five renditions, "Sunny" to seven, "D'Ye Love Me?," a particularly nauseous melody, to ten, and "Who?" to fourteen. No wonder Hammerstein hated the show.

If one includes the two-and-a-quarter-bar-long first note of "Who?," all five songs are based on short, repetitive motifs. Even more insistent is the cross-rhythmic motif in the London *Sunny*'s "I've Looked for Trouble," simultaneously used in *Criss-Cross* as "You Will—Won't You?" with tongue-twisting words to match the wrong-footing notes. All these songs are in 2/4 once "D'Ye Love Me?" has transformed itself from its initial Swiss yodel (a kind of *Ländler*), though "You Will—Won't You?" renotated "I've Looked for Trouble" in cut time, and all except the folksy "D'Ye Love Me?" emphasize the sixth degree of the scale, part of the casual approach to melodic responsibility brought by jazz. Melodic repetition no longer by eloquent sequence but at the same pitch over changing harmonies, or shifting only marginally up and down (compare "Tea for Two"), is another feature of some of these melodies, most notably "Two Little Bluebirds" and "D'Ye Love Me?" The latter is thereby in especial need of the aptly named "release" when it comes, and it redeems the tune with a touch of mastery. Such repetition is another feature applicable to jazz, soon to be developed as the riff.

Aside from these songs' robustness as dance band hits, based on perfectly sound structuring of both music and lyrics, the best, certainly the most *composed*, music in both *Sally* and *Sunny*, but particularly *Sunny*, tends to be the least-known numbers, including the finales. *Sunny*'s wedding march, retained in the film, is a gem, and as with some of the less incidental music in *Blue Eyes* and *Sweet Adeline*, one wishes Kern had found a more extended role for it. In fact all the wedding music of *Sunny* is inspired. It begins, after lengthy book scenes in which the marriage of convenience is agreed on, with a trio for Sunny, Jim, and Tom, "It Won't Mean a Thing." In contrast with

Oh, I Say!, here Kern manages to find the occasion for a genuinely expansive operatic tableau, the score's centerpiece, and in ironic retrospect the spiritual opposite of its title. There is nothing at all of the jazz age here, but rather an emulation in miniature of *Der Rosenkavalier* or *Die Meistersinger*, especially in the emotional wind-down after Sunny has hit her top A: real singers are needed (probably the reason it was cut, though restored in London). The following number, "The Wedding Knell," proves one of Kern's rare 6/8s in the trio, a fine rollicking tune a little like "Whoop-de-oodle-do!" in *The Cabaret Girl*, and after "Two Little Bluebirds" the act 1 finale begins. This includes substantial recapitulations of both "It Won't Mean a Thing" and "The Wedding Knell" before it launches into the elegant refrain of "Dream a Dream," surely the prototype of Kern's late songs, although it has only sixteen bars. Like "Bill" in the first-act finale of *Oh, Lady! Lady!!*, this song's ghost survives without its embodiment, which was cut from earlier in the first act. As published separately, it becomes clear it had a double refrain, the two halves then combined in counterpoint—hence the modest length.[47] The refrain culminates in an even higher top note for Sunny before her passionate embrace of the best man, which brings its shocked response from the guests and a couple of fragmentary reprises as the curtain falls.

All this is balanced by the hunt music in act 2. Its first installment is "The Chase," an intriguing set piece for Sunny's faked accident, described by the chorus in music as it happens offstage. One guesses that Hammerstein or Harbach wrote the words first, for a galloping poem rather in the manner of John Masefield's *Reynard the Fox* is provided. Kern sets it to music as a kind of ABA scherzo using themes from "The Arrow," a Kern composition from as early as 1905, to which is appended a rhapsodic romance for the chorus, with Tom as Sunny carried onstage. Comparable in some ways with the longer "Derby Day" in *Three Sisters*, this gets right away from refrain structures, though a half-chorus of "Who?" is tacked on the end—and is not necessarily banal, for it conveys the onlookers' anger at her deception. One or two songs intervene, of which "I Might Grow Fond of You," apparently written for the London production, is one of *Sunny*'s best dance band numbers, then the second installment of hunt music takes place. A "house that Jack built" hunting song for male quartet, which Jack Buchanan made into a perennial comic routine that was released as a film short, is followed by the hunt ball, a chorus number of that name resurrecting some of the dash of "Wild Rose" from *Sally*'s party scene.[48]

But *Sally* is a disappointing score and includes nothing by Kern comparable with *Sunny*'s set pieces: Herbert wrote the "Butterfly Ballet." Kern's waltzes, rarely his strongest suit, sound tired, in "The Schnitza-Komisski" little more than a vehicle for endless stanzas of comic lyrics. Act 3 contains no new song. "Look for the Silver Lining" became a classic, but *Oh, Boy!*'s hymnlike songs sound fresher. Nevertheless, "You Can't Keep a Good Girl Down," in which Sally compares herself with Joan of Arc, is a new departure for Kern, a blend of quickstep patter and imperial march lightly achieved, the verse being marked "In the manner of a toy march." He accomplished something comparable with the title song of *Stepping Stones* two years later, another fine but neglected number from that show. "Whip-poor-Will," salvaged from *Zip, Goes a Million*, has that real rarity, a minor-key refrain. There are only four or five in Kern's entire output, though minor-key verses are relatively common; and even this one goes into the tonic major halfway through. Generally Kern reserved the minor for dance or instrumental sections redolent of central Europe or somewhere further east, and with the exiled Grand Duke of Czechogovinia a leading character and the heroine posing as a Russian ballerina, it is hardly surprising that the instrumental Czardas in the act 2 finale is another of several further usages in *Sally*. This finale is one of Kern's best and demonstrates that even for a show subject to dubious production values—the vaudeville restaurant routines in act 1 are interminable—he could by 1920 produce something with flair, ending both act 1 and act 2 on notes of considerable glamour (pathetic in the latter case) for the star. The act 1 finale is short but in its anticipation of the party manages to reprise "On With the Dance" in four different ways, following this with partial reprises of "You Can't Keep a Good Girl Down," "Look for the Silver Lining," and Sally's entrance music before concluding most effectively with the "toy trumpets" fanfare that had introduced "You Can't Keep a Good Girl Down." The act 2 finale sees the Cinderella Sally unmasked as an impostor and, like its first-act precursor, has reached a durable formula for achieving its emotional flux through a mixture of sung, danced, and underscored reprises. Songs built on short motives can assist this in an almost Wagnerian way, as is the case here with "Wild Rose," its long notes avoiding conflict with the dialogue above and malleable to different tonal destinations and starting points (see p. 110 of the published score). This facilitates short sections, and there are fourteen altogether here, though only four of them are sung and a couple more danced. The "Wild Rose" motif inhabits four separate (and separated) sections, another indication of its symphonic pretensions; altogether six previously heard numbers are referred to, though there are two passages that could be additional references to material that was otherwise lost to the production.

Since *Sally* and *Sunny* both played in London and *Sally* instigated the run of annual Kern musicals at its Winter Garden Theatre, it makes sense to give brief consideration here to his two other British musical comedies, *The Cabaret Girl* and *The Beauty Prize*. Both copied *Sally* in their casts, as we have seen, and in the format of two substantial acts (the second-act finale being the show's climax) followed by a third that ran to seed in set pieces and, in the case of *The Cabaret Girl*, several short scenes including diegetic performance. *The Beauty Prize* lacks freshness in both plot and music, and one can see why Gershwin was brought in to rejuvenate the Winter Garden series in 1924. Act 1 attempts a new flavor by experimenting with 3/4 usage beyond the waltz, in polonaise and mazurka. The second-act finale is intricate and cleverly wrought, as by now we expect from Kern. It includes a sly quote from "They Didn't Believe Me" as a character tells a lie. But the best moments of *The Beauty Prize* turn up elsewhere. "You Can't Make Love by Wireless" was rewritten as "Bow Belles" for *Blue Eyes*, and "Moon Love" became one of the versions of "Sunshine" in *Sunny*.

The Cabaret Girl, however, is full of good music and a tighter attempt at composition than Kern had yet achieved. After a rather labored series of opening numbers, things liven up with the entrance of the cabaret troupe, though before this, "Journey's End" has set down a pastoral marker as a study in parallel 6ths and 3rds (ex. 2.8), its title a quote from Shakespeare, its introduction canonic (creating the 6ths). This is something Kern could not have done on Broadway, as was proved when "Journey's End" lost its 3rds, 6ths, and distinctiveness in separately published form for *The City Chap*. Those intervals are again highlighted in the next *Cabaret Girl* number, "Whoop-de-oodle-do!," which is in the same key, D major. The follow-up to this is the remarkable act 2 opening, "The Pergola Patrol," once more a D major pastoral with fugal opening, which exploits an uninterrupted drone bass for nearly 150 bars in alternating tonic major and minor sections. It subsequently became "Is This Not a Lovely Spot?" in *Sitting Pretty*. After this tableau, the "Opening Scene" of Jim and Marilynn is cast as a sectional reprise number, and the refrain of the following song, "Shimmy With Me," is on second hearing fitted in counterpoint with that of "Journey's End"; this continues for all thirty-two bars. A suite of three highly characterized numbers follows by way of compensating variety. The musical pillar at the end of act 2 corresponding to "The Pergola Patrol" at its beginning is a finale which at sixteen pages of score is possibly Kern's longest (that of *The Beauty Prize* has fifteen). Perhaps only here does he approximate a Gilbert and Sullivan finale in musical scope, for he permits lengthier reprises than normal and includes important new material as well. One new tune becomes "London, Dear Old London" in act 3. The charade of the two vicars, highly Gilbertian, proves extremely funny when the second is explained in Wodehouse's lyrics, to the "Pergola Patrol" music:

> JIM: Most towns, I own,
> Have one vicar, one alone.
> GRIPPS: But in this place
> They engage 'em by the brace.
> It may seem odd I know at first, but there, well there it is.
> JIM: Two vicars tend our little flock and in their care it is.
> GRIPPS: Sin thus becomes the very rarest of all rarities.
> CHORUS *(Tutti. Religioso):* Oh! is this not
> A model spot.

Altogether, act 2 can be heard as an essay in musical development, though as usual act 3 operates on the principle of a rapidly diminishing perspective.

   Dramaturgically *The Cabaret Girl*, like *The Beauty Prize*, is loose, conservative, and unoriginal, still trading on Grossmith's aging dandy types and youthful leads interesting more for their class, money, and physical allure than for any demonstration of character. But in *Dear Sir* the following year, the Broadway show that took the place of Kern's third Winter Garden one for London, Kern helped rescue musical comedy from the outmoded routines of farce, while keeping it deliberately within the same social tradition. Thus Dorothy, the heroine, is first appreciated for her glamour, Laddie is the conventional man-about-town surrounded by chorus girls (he could be Jim in *Oh, Boy!*), Bloxom, played by Walter Catlett, the Grossmith-style older comic, and the plot and subplot hinge on money and gifts. In a scene remarkable for its anticipation of *Oklahoma!*, Dorothy auctions herself as a maid for a week at a charity fair and is bid for by two explosively angry suitors. Because neither lead has yet had the chance to show integrity, mistrust of motives keeps the members of the love triangle more hateful than loving of each other, and the book accordingly emotional, until wrong pledges have

If you just take heart And make a start, That's all there is to do.

Ex. 2.8. Journey's End.

been made out of spite and it is seemingly too late for amends—hence the regretful "Wishing Well Scene," a real breakthrough in Kern's development. Laddie's character trajectory in *Dear Sir* stems from that of Danilo in *The Merry Widow.* This is a world away from the mechanically complex plot surfaces of the Princess shows, far closer to being a prototype of the Fred Astaire/Ginger Rogers musical films, including *Swing Time,* whose "Never Gonna Dance" is the emotional equivalent of the "Wishing Well Scene." Best of all, *Dear Sir* is full of gorgeous, silky music, Kern's new, smoother style the analogue to much greater emphasis on continuity of feeling, brooding or fiery, in the characters. "Weeping Willow Tree," a serenade, comprises a broad ABA span more like a slow movement than a popular song (Kern labeled it "Canzonetta"), and the refrain of "I Want to Be There" is a model of the new, slower harmonic pace in a 2/2 song. Kern has also refined his waltzes into something more French and delicate, less of a vehicle for verbal comedy—witness the verse of "I Want to Be There" and the waltz fashioned from *Toot-Toot!*'s "Girlie." All these tunes recur in the "Wishing

Well Scene," as does the most poignant of all, "What's the Use?," flippant and carnivalesque in act 1 but now played softly to a countermelody sung by Laddie, who is at the end of his emotional tether. At last Kern the composer is exploring romanticism, and doing so with a tact and finesse that will carry him from musical comedy into its various fusions with operetta in his subsequent works for stage and screen.

CHAPTER 3

Kern the Romantic: Three Shows

Not Operetta

THERE IS ALWAYS A TRADE-OFF BETWEEN WIT AND MUSICALITY IN the singing theater and its film equivalent, a contract favoring music at the expense of wit in most opera after Rossini and wit at the expense of music, especially singing, in most musical comedy before Rodgers and Hammerstein. In Kern's day, at first the leading men could not really sing but were dandy comics, while their female partners warbled away with impeccable voice production and, no doubt, posture but little sense of youthful spirit or warmth (Dot Temple sounds about fifty-five and a deadpan prude in the 1919 *Oh Joy!* recordings). With the "Cinderella" musical comedy arrived the alluring female dancer as heroine. Now it was the woman who could not sing properly, and the limits of both Marilyn Miller's and Dorothy Dickson's vocal abilities in the title role of *Sally* are repeatedly evident in their period recordings: one can hear why Kern wanted to veto Dickson for the part.[1] To complete the turnaround, Dickson was paired with an all too vocally impressive Blair Farquar, the baritone Gregory Stroud, in the London production of *Sally*. But in the 1920s Kern was writing long, smooth cantilenas—indeed had been, in some of his best songs, ever since "They Didn't Believe Me"—that, however well trimmed for singing actors, actresses, and dancers with their confined tessituras, short phrases, and carefully placed vowels, demanded uniformly excellent singers and orchestral playing if they were to achieve maximum emotional effect. This applies to the music of *Dear Sir*, which certainly did not receive these attentions in 1924. Oscar Shaw played

Laddie, and of Genevieve Tobin in the role of Dorothy the *New York Times* wrote, "The inadequacy of her voice must be apparent to even the great-hearted many."[2]

By 1924 Kern deserved, and wanted, a better musical return on his investment than musical comedy's conditions could offer him. Bordman recounts a sad anecdote about the tribulations of *Dear Sir:* "Kern's feeling about the music was revealed in a dramatic moment that Goodman's publicist, Marian Spitzer Thompson, could still recall vividly more than half a century after the event. Frustrated by [Max] Bendix's inability to properly phrase the longer musical lines Kern was employing, the composer stood on the street outside the theatre helplessly reduced to tears. He finally demanded that Goodman replace Bendix with a conductor capable of handling the more difficult, progressive material. Gus Salzer was rushed in."[3]

The musical answer would have been operetta, but there the social comedy at whose service Kern had so successfully placed himself over more than a decade, even in his finalettos, had little place according to the traditions of the day; and Kern had burned his fingers with generic muddle in *The Red Petticoat.* Nevertheless, in 1924 operetta was a force he had to reckon with as much as he had to reckon with jazz at the other end of the entertainment spectrum. It was the year of Victor Herbert's death, probably the year of his first meeting with Otto Harbach and Oscar Hammerstein, and the year of the phenomenal success of *Rose Marie* and *The Student Prince.* Kern may have been reluctant to venture into too exotic territory at this juncture, though *Lucky* would suggest otherwise, or reluctant to challenge Romberg and Friml on their more European ground (both had been born in central Europe, Friml indeed in Kern's ancestral Bohemia), even though the superiority of his music to theirs must have been as evident to him as it is to us. But it is surely significant that his most obvious opportunity to follow up the romantic lyricism of *Dear Sir* came four years later in a project for which he revived three of its best tunes, "All Lanes Must Reach a Turning," "What's the Use?," and the central section of "Weeping Willow Tree"—that is, *Blue Eyes,* Kern's only true operetta, which he wrote for London, not New York, as a historical costume drama.

Ethan Mordden wittily if inaccurately sums up the differences between 1920s musical comedy and operetta by laying down a series of pat markers for the latter, including "a harp in the pit rather than musical comedy's piano."[4] A harp *Blue Eyes* certainly has, at least on record, in the second refrain of the title song as sung by Geoffrey Gwyther and Evelyn Laye in their original cast recording with the Piccadilly Theatre Orchestra and the musical's conductor, Kennedy Russell. This and the other two Kern numbers from the show that the cast recorded, "Do I Do Wrong?" and "Back to the Heather," must be among the best performances, musically speaking, Kern's songs ever received: extremely flexible, lyrical playing and singing, sustained and shapely lines, and pure tone, all dying qualities on the musical stage. His harmony and melody gain immeasurably in strength from this treatment, and one would give anything for a complete period recording of *Blue Eyes*. Not only the three melodies salvaged from *Dear Sir* were top-notch Kern, but much else of the score besides, including "Do I Do Wrong?," which was reused as "You're Devastating" in *Roberta*.

Yet Gwyther and Laye would not have been the right actors for a Broadway musical, and the unamplified theater never did find a musical formula that smoothed out all the generic differences between spoken and sung allure. Rodgers and Hammerstein would come closest to it. Film tackled but only exacerbated the problem when it began investing in romantic operetta, fending off as much of the disjunction as was necessary through its various illusional techniques while making stars of Jeanette MacDonald and Nelson Eddy. Did Kern ever try to promote *Blue Eyes* for them and for the screen? One would like to know, while bearing in mind, first, that his film for them, *Champagne and Orchids*, was abandoned by the studio probably for good reasons, and second, that Hammerstein's career with film operetta was disastrous—the whole genre was a miasma of "'picture operas' full of musical bad taste," as Max Dreyfus felt obliged to tell him after seeing *Maytime* in 1937.[5] There was, however, as noted in chapter 1, talk of a Kern/Hammerstein film with Laye.

The horizons and documentation in sound of *Blue Eyes*, then, must remain a small, isolated musical high point, a tantalizing glimpse of paths Kern never pursued wholesale. He continued for the rest of his career to make compromises between dramatic and musical possibilities, both on the stage and, more and more as the focus of his work shifted, in the film studio. He began to aspire on both fronts, which is what changed with *Dear Sir*, and this shaped the rest of his output along more romantic lines than hitherto, while necessitating a different generic contract for each new project, starting with *Show Boat*. Yet much of this musical romanticism will have been an inevitable rather than a strategic broadening of his musical language, and several times he made comments showing how he guarded against its luring him toward operetta; he was eternally wary of swinging the male balance too far in favor of singers. "Operetta ain't my dish," he reminded Hammerstein, and to prove it he consistently took a radical line on the casting of Ravenal for the 1936 *Show Boat* film and its stage revival in the 1940s. He was not keen on Allan Jones, and in 1942 wrote to Hammerstein, "The whole truth of the matter is that Ravenal should never have been played by a singer. Not only are singers lousy actors congenitally, but the better Ravenal sings, the less one believes in his having to resort to pawning *the* ring and *the* walking stick." The following year he went further: "About Ravenal . . . We have never had a good one yet, and until Clark Gable plays it and cuts out all the music except 'Make Believe' in the convent scene, I suppose we never shall." This is a staunchly masculinist approach to musical drama, very much of its time and place, and credit has to be given to Hammerstein for moving beyond it with Curly, the singing cowboy. Kern was more comfortable with a male singer when safely exoticized, not only in *Blue Eyes* but most notably with Paul Robeson as Joe in *Show Boat* (though Robeson was not in the initial New York production). With women he would continue to discover rich opportunities for vocal beauty, and Peggy Wood, Mary Ellis, Irene Dunne, and Deanna Durbin each did a good deal to add musical value to Kern's romantic later style.[6]

Sitting *Pretty, Show Boat* and *The Cat and the Fiddle*, three shows I want to discuss here, represent, respectively, Kern's established musical comedy world, his bid for grandeur, and his retreat into something still novel and integral but more manageable and pregnant with future possibilities. At the same time all three shows are positioned at cultural pressure points. *Sitting Pretty* was contemporaneous with Gershwin's endorsement by the concert hall, when jazz, "serious," and light music were having to renegotiate their relationships with each other. *Show Boat* arrived at the same time as sound film, the implications of which I consider in chapter 5. And *The Cat and the Fiddle* reflected that new medium's independent handling of sung drama, after several years of imitating Broadway, in the genre known as boudoir operetta. Kern makes enormous strides forward across these three shows, as will be seen. At the same time each has a romantic core that is satisfying in its own terms and need not be seen as either progressive or conservative. Only *Show Boat* is canonic, of course, but at the same time is the most flawed of the three musicals. *Sitting Pretty* enjoys the only "critical edition" recording of a Kern show other than that of *Show Boat* and has been singled out here for that reason. Like *Show Boat* but unlike *Sitting Pretty, The Cat and the*

Fiddle can be studied in published piano/vocal score, though all three works suffer from hopelessly rare or unpublished scripts.

Sitting Pretty—Genesis

Sitting Pretty was the last of Kern's collaborations with Wodehouse, though he worked again with Bolton on *Blue Eyes* and the early scripts for Kern's screen biography. The team was happy to be "the old firm back together at last," and the producers would announce it as "The Seventh of Their Series of the Princess Musical Comedies." The sheet music was labeled as being "'by Bolton, Wodehouse and Kern,' much as if it had been by Gilbert and Sullivan," as Bordman points out.

Sitting Pretty's initial impetus was a commission for Bolton from the producer Sam Harris to write a musical comedy for the Duncan Sisters, "two small girls who created the impression of being about twelve years old," sang "in close harmony and . . . were . . . terrific," with music by Irving Berlin. Bolton invited Wodehouse to join him in creating the book. Berlin would supply his own lyrics, supplemented with a few by Wodehouse as though by special favor (a note of patronage on Berlin's part sounds throughout accounts of this). In the summer or autumn of 1921 Bolton discussed the show with the Duncan Sisters in London, where they were appearing in *Pins and Needles*, and proceeded to write or at least plan the libretto "in Plum's study in Onslow Square"; at the same time, the authors' account implies, Wodehouse also composed the lyrics for "Tulip Time in Sing Sing" in the knowledge that his characteristic vein of crooks' sentimental humor would have full scope in the story they had decided upon: "Its central figures were two sisters in an orphan asylum, one of whom was adopted by a wealthy old man whose passion was Eugenics. He had already adopted a boy, and it was his aim to marry these two, not knowing that Horace, the boy, was in partnership with an amiable burglar named Uncle Joe, who insinuated him into rich houses to prepare the way for him by leaving doors and windows open."

Work with Bolton on *Sitting Pretty* continued in New York during the late autumn of 1922. But pinning down Berlin and Harris, busy with their *Music Box Revue* series, and the Duncan Sisters proved difficult. The producers wanted to delay the show until the following October, but by the summer of 1923 it became clear that the Duncan Sisters would be unavailable, for rather than wait, they had opened on the West Coast in a show of their own called *Topsy and Eva* in July, and it was quickly proving a hit. With the sisters out of the picture, Berlin lost faith in the project and withdrew. Kern, surveying it with Wodehouse in London where they were stationed for *Beauty Prize* rehearsals in August 1923, offered himself as composer instead, and Comstock, with Morris Gest, took over as producer. Bolton "crossed to England and settled down to fit the numbers Plum and Jerry were writing into the *Sitting Pretty* book." Casting must have been done in early winter, when Queenie Smith was free of her previous engagement, the musical *Helen of Troy*, which closed in New York on 1 December 1923.[7]

Smith, who went on to appear in further musicals, including *Tip-Toes* and *Street Singer*, was one of two strong female leads replacing the Duncan Sisters. (She can be savored as Ellie in the 1936 *Show Boat* film.) She played the tough sister, Dixie Tolliver. Gertrude Bryan was her genteel twin, May. But although the Duncan Sisters were not twins, unlike the Dolly Sisters, who took over the roles for the post-Broadway tour, Bryan and Smith as a pair made for the first of two problems in *Sitting Pretty*, as Kern pointed out in a letter nine years later: "*Sitting Pretty*[,] as you know, flopped because the amusing complications due to the unrecognisability of twin sisters aborted, chiefly on account of the stupidity of casting for the girls, supposed to look exactly alike, Gertrude Bryan and Queenie Smith. Ignoring their racial differences, their linear measurements differed about eighteen inches." Wodehouse and Bolton's own explanation of failure is somewhat disingenuous in not acknowledging this. They merely observed that "charming Gertrude Bryan and clever Queenie Smith, brilliant individually, were not a team. When they met, when they performed together, the electric spark was missing, and the play was so written that these were the vital spots"—whereas in effect a whole layer of farce is missing from the plot, the only mistaken identity with any mechanical impetus being Jo's.[8]

Bryan came back from retirement, where "she had picked up some haughty airs that would cause backstage difficulties, particularly after the youngster brought in to play her sister walked off with the notices," and soon after the New York opening she was replaced. May's inamorato, Bill Pennington, was played by Rudolph Cameron, not known for his musical roles, while the adolescent crook Horace was Dwight Frye, familiar as The Son in the original New York production of Luigi Pirandello's *Six Characters in Search of an Author* but not in musicals.[9] George E. Mack, who would go on to play Senator Robert E. Lyons in *Of Thee I Sing* and *Let 'Em Eat Cake*, was Pennington senior, the well-known Frank McIntyre Uncle Jo, the first to be cast. The only veteran of Kern shows was Eugene Revere, who had been in the cast of *Have a Heart, Miss 1917*, and *The Bunch and Judy*. He played Bill's sidekick Judson Waters. It was too loose and unmusical an ensemble for comfort. No cast recordings were made—indeed no recordings at all—so we cannot hear how the songs sounded in 1924.

The genesis of *Sitting Pretty* was complicated at the eleventh hour by another, parallel script by Wodehouse and Bolton, *Pat* ("a rotten title"). This was in some respects a prototype of *Sunny*, a Wild West musical—its first act takes place outside a circus in Montana—drafted in the autumn of 1922 for Ziegfeld on the basis of a "Marilyn Miller type" heroine, with Jack Donahue as leading man and Charles King his partner, and similarly shelved by its producer. A letter from Wodehouse to his stepdaughter Leonora, dated 4 February 1924, explains what happened: "We were going along nicely casting *Sitting Pretty* for Ray, when Jack Donahue (Marilyn Miller's long time partner) suddenly called up and said he thought *Pat*, the other piece, a corker and wanted to play in it. So Ray instantly switched *Sitting Pretty* and started to cast *Pat*. Two weeks into rehearsal their director died. And as for the piece, it knocked it cold. We tried three other directors and couldn't get them, and now we have switched back to *Sitting Pretty* again and are trying to cast that . . . The nuisance is that *Pat* is complete, with all the lyrics done, and half the *Sitting Pretty* lyrics have to be written." This seems an extraordinarily late production hiatus for a show that opened on 23 March at the Shubert Theatre in Detroit before moving into the Fulton Theatre (much bigger than the Princess) in New York on 8 April. And since *Sitting Pretty* and *Pat* share about half their songs, it raises major questions of precedence. Most likely, where songs were shared between the two scripts (*Pat*'s script survives, complete with lyrics and dated 23 February 1924, in the Library of Congress), the music had been written or, in the case of trunk songs and reusage, chosen for *Sitting Pretty*. But one wonders whether any of it originated later during the weeks in which *Pat* was the active production. Which versions of the lyrics came first, those for *Pat* or for *Sitting Pretty*, is indeterminable where they were written to preexistent tunes, though "A Year from Today" so clearly fits *Pat*, in which act 3 is set one year later, and not *Sitting Pretty*, in which act 2 is set only six months later, that its provenance would seem clear. Complete lyrics for *Pat*'s opening number are of the sort that suggest Kern would have added the music afterward; whether he got that far is not known. The lyrics of another first-act song, "Back East," strikingly anticipate Lorenz Hart's for "Way Out West" in *Babes in Arms*:

I want to be . . .
Back East where
Taxis are hooting,
Boot-leggers booting,
Crap-shooters shooting,
Cuties patooting:
I want to inhale God's wonderful air
As it blows clean and sweet through Longacre Square:

Do they fit any known Kern melody?

The music of *Sitting Pretty* furnishes the most accessible, perhaps simply the best, example of Kern's "odor of sachet" desideratum, which John Mc-Glinn, the score's latter-day exponent, sums up perfectly: "[Kern] often talked about the need for a score to have a particular tone, a style unique to itself. In this he echoes Verdi and his particular care for the *tinta*, the color of each of his operas. In *Sitting Pretty* we can hear Kern . . . beginning to give each score a sense of emotional unity (thematic and motivic unity was not to come until *Show Boat*). What particular flavor, then, did Kern find for this score? For me, it's a sense of yearning for an unobtainable ideal, the melancholy of unfulfilled longing. All the major characters have a song (or duet) in which they long for a state of bliss that doesn't exist in the real world—or even in their fairy-tale stage world." He also points out that since "the dichotomy between the frivolity of the book and the richness of the score" is a crucial part of the formula, "a moment of distilled sweetness can pierce the heart. Such is the power of this gentle, silly little show."[10]

Sitting Pretty—Overture and Act 1

Kern's orchestrators, Russell Bennett, assisted by Max Steiner and Hilding Anderson, exploit *Sitting Pretty*'s "particular flavor" with frequent use of cor anglais, a brass section of two trumpets and two horns (no trombone), harp, and three violin parts (though this is common).[11] The very first notes of the overture evoke a special world. They begin a melody heard nowhere else in the show (unless from a cut, lost song—no surviving lyrics seem to match it), a tune deeply etched with nostalgia and Victorian echoes—of Stephen Foster, Sankey and Moody, and, in Bennett's orchestration (two trumpets in parallel 3rds, entirely unaccompanied on the initial upbeat), of Salvation Army cornettists in the gloaming. The German 6th at the end of the third two-bar phrase—a diminished 7th second time around—underlines the sad

Ex. 3.1. *Sitting Pretty*, Overture.

air of parlor gentility and bygone days, a mood entirely appropriate to the yearning of the orphan girls for a family that drives the plot and its musical counterparts. Kern had sounded old-fashioned before, for example, in *Gloria's Romance*, but this is a bolder, surer bid for countercultural character. No sketches survive for this tune, and the *tutti* counterpoint on second statement, somewhat Dvořák-like, is probably Bennett's.

"The Enchanted Train" follows, for, according to McGlinn, Kern conceived of the overture as "a little symphonic poem entitled 'A Journey Southward,' depicting a train ride from New York to Florida." The train effects, escaping steam in a two-bar string glissando followed by the arrival bell on harp, lead not to a glorious restatement of "The Enchanted Train" but to the sad overture tune with its same opening notes ($\hat{3}\hat{4}\hat{5}$)—the end of the train journey as emotional frustration. One imagines the splicing of the first half of the overture tune with the second of "Worries" to have been Kern's proposition. Its sequal, bittersweet indeed, comes when the two tunes, "Worries" with added descant in 3rds, subsequently combine in almost Mahlerian counterpoint (see the consecutive 5ths in ex. 3.1) whose authorship remains uncertain given that when this moment returns in the act 1 finaletto the overture tune is omitted, true to Kern's sketch. The first four bars of "A Year from Today" lead to the "weird unresolved chord" that concludes the overture, built up by the strings in 3rds as far as $^{\sharp}\hat{4}$ and picked out on harp played "at the ends of the strings!," sounding like something from Benjamin Britten.[12]

The act 1 curtain rises on the garden of Mr. Pennington's country house, separated by a wall from the Middleboro Orphanage. The New York program began with "The Charity Class," which is lost, while two opening production numbers survive. Both are good. The original one began with a waltz for the (female) orphans who had scrambled over the wall to pick flowers and led via a posthorn call to the 6/8 entry of the rest of the chorus as a coaching crowd of bright young things led by Judson Waters, driving Bill to his assignment with his rich uncle, William Pennington. This was the start of a scene which, minus the orphans, was immediately reused by Wodehouse in *Bill the Conqueror,* in which Judson's arrival, separate from Bill's, is even more dramatic:

> Roberts, the butler, agreeably relaxed in his pantry over a cigar and a tale of desert love, was startled out of his tranquillity by the sound of a loud metallic crash, appearing to proceed from the drive immediately in front of the house. Laying down cigar and book, he bounded out to investigate.
>
> It was not remarkable that there had been a certain amount of noise. Hard by one of the Colonial pillars which the architect had tacked on to Mr. Paradene's residence to make it more interesting lay the wreckage of a red two-seater car, and from the ruins of this there was now extricating itself a long figure in a dust-coat, revealed a moment later as a young man of homely appearance with a prominent, arched nose and plaintive green eyes.
>
> "Hallo," said this young man, spitting out gravel.
>
> Roberts gazed at him in speechless astonishment. The wreck of the two-seater was such a very comprehensive wreck that it seemed hardly possible that any recent occupant of it could still be in one piece.
>
> "Had a bit of a smash," said the young man.[13]

The original act 1 opening will surely have been the pair of songs listed by Bordman as "Roses Are Nodding" and "Coaching," but the lyrics for the former are—or were—lost, and McGlinn was forced to record this section without voices.[14]

This opening is the more attractive of the two musically, with its *Casse-Noisette* feel in the delicate B flat major introduction, its emotional foretaste of *Show Boat*'s "Convent Scene" in the plagal oscillations of the school bell, and its touch of Gershwin in the middle reaches of the "Coaching" section. But, as mentioned in chapter 2, its replacement, "Is This Not a Lovely Spot?," was "The Pergola Patrol" from *The Cabaret Girl* (somewhat shortened, and with some—not all—of its lyrics rewritten), and this is wittier, more atmospheric, and certainly more unusual. Its introduction and coda are a perfect representation of the forced sanctimoniousness of the orphans' existence and, presumably, appearance, but genuinely touching, too, as they must be. It also serves to introduce more of the characters—Mr. Pennington, his nephew Bill, Bill's sidekick Judson Waters and girlfriend Babe La Marr, and a chorus of gardeners as well as the orphans and the coaching party, though Russell Warner's (reconstituted) orchestration misses the patrol effect of the original's *fff* midpoint. Wodehouse revels in some virtuosic lyrics on a favorite theme when Mr. Pennington, battling nature like Lord Marshmoreton in *A Damsel in Distress*, says to the gardeners, "I see my roses have been nibbled by greenfly, and I'd suggest you go and mix some arsenic or cyanide and squirt it over them before the creatures try and hide!"—perfect casual prose when presented like this, but perfect comic verse too with its triple rhyme.

A short dialogue segment establishes Bill's indigence and Babe's gold-digging. She quotes Edward FitzGerald's *Rubáiyyát of Omar Khayyám* at him to deflate his romantic idealism, but this misfires when he says he would not even want a book of verses, a jug of wine, and a loaf of bread: "You Alone Would Do." Her riposte in the song (which was cut), a colloquial discussion of Omar Khayyám's philosophy, augurs ill for their marital agreement. Note that the show's title song was originally sketched with these refrain lyrics: "A jug of wine / Beneath the bough is fine / For those inclined that way" (see fig. 1.4). Was "Sitting Pretty" originally intended for this spot, therefore? "You Alone Would Do" is hardly a great Kern song, though the chugging wind fills, carefully specified in Kern's sketch, help keep momentum going, leading to a dance after two stanzas, while the use here of an almost continuous presence of cor anglais rather than oboe undercuts this plaintively in Bennett's orchestration.

May and Dixie enter, trespassing. Dixie is the naughty twin, May (called Angel in Kern's sketches) the good girl whom Dixie constantly gets into trouble. Mrs. Wagstaff, matron of the orphanage and butt of *faux pas* from both Dixie and Bill, would for this reason like to send Dixie away, but the two girls are at this stage inseparable and both dream of being adopted; ironically it will be May who goes away at the end of act 1. Bill says a good word for them, and they tell him their troubles. The orphanage being a school, Wodehouse and Bolton once again put the subtext of the classics to work:

MAY: Yes, I wish Pandora had never opened that box.
BILL: Pandora?
MAY: Haven't you ever heard of Pandora?
BILL: I've heard of Dumb Dora.
DIXIE: Guess you must have been badly educated.[15]

Ex. 3.2. Worries.

This is the cue for "Worries," sung by the three of them. Its initial motoric accompaniment pattern, carefully sketched by Kern, furthers another of the show's subtexts, that of railway travel as emblem of the personal journey. Did the production make something of this in the dance break which follows the two stanzas? Again, Bennett's orchestration seems to encourage the image in its use of side drum, stopped and open horns (the fine upward scale probably his, not Kern's), and lonesome piccolo dying away at the end.[16] Here is one of Kern's most endearing verses, because its thirty-two bars arrive at the dominant then defer the refrain with a further bout of melodic inspiration (omitted in the dance break), to which Wodehouse sets the sound of plain spoken prose, again demonstrating the advantages of letting the music be written first (ex. 3.2). The infectious locomotion of this song and its break "finds the button" for the show and seals our interest in and attraction toward its main characters.

The ensuing segment, most of which was reused word for word in *Bill the Conqueror*, does the opposite by burlesquing the unmarried Pennington's nauseous relatives, a bunch of spongers assembled at his command only to be told they have been disinherited in the interests of eugenics: he has instead adopted a boy "with a splendid physique, a wonderful character, and a perfect disposition . . . My slogan is 'Fewer and better Penningtons!'" All except Bill leave in disgust; Bill decides he needs "a jug of wine" after all, and the section closes with a brief reprise of "Is This Not a Lovely Spot?" as the butler reels off the names of available whiskies.[17]

Horace's age is *Sitting Pretty*'s other problem. When his minder Uncle Jo signals a new section by coming surreptitiously onto the scene—as played by McIntyre this would have been a star moment—the difference in age, status, and girth between the two must be great (Horace makes disparaging remarks about Jo's stomach: McIntyre was enormous). Horace is treated with the contempt deserved by a pubescent or even prepubescent horror; an immemorial Wodehouse type, he appears as such in *Bill the Conqueror*. At the same time, he gives Jo as good as he gets, tough little criminal, prematurely adult, that he is. He should be much younger than Bill. Yet he and Bill will pair off with twin sisters. Bluntly, the problem as to whether he should be in short or long trousers on the stage seems insoluble. His music fits the latter, his comic status the former.

Comedy comes into its own with this extended segment, expertly written and full of traditional business with a stolen cuckoo clock in Jo's bag that won't keep quiet, plus the usual references to prison:

(Clock goes "Cuckoo, cuckoo!")
JO: You see? It's broken! And I got it as a present for Cousin Phoebe's coming
    out party.
HORACE: What do you mean, "coming out party?"—She ain't no debutante.
JO: No, but she comes out of Elmira next Tuesday.[18]

Jo masquerades as Horace's new tutor, Professor Appleby. After getting rid of Pennington, included so that Jo can discover the awful truth that Horace will be abstracted from the gang when Pennington marries him off to an adopted daughter-in-law from the orphanage, he and Horace are joined by Judson, addicted to big-game hunting stories, for no other dramatic reason than to set up a low-comedy song for the three of them, "Bongo on the Congo." With endless encores, it was one of Wodehouse's greatest lyric hits and admired by the young Ira Gershwin.[19] Musically no great shakes, it does its job as a burlesque soft-shoe schottische, the same kind of vaudeville perennial as Sondheim's "Everybody Ought to Have a Maid" and the first song in the show to have been orchestrated by Max Steiner, whose style seems bolder than Bennett's. Kern's sketch proves his point about self-sufficient melodic strength, for he includes few inner-part indications and virtually no harmony, yet even the verse's tricky modulations could hardly have been misconstrued.

Horace, left on his own at the end of the song, encounters Dixie, who enters eating a cookie she has baked herself. Horace's appetite as a growing lad having been mentioned in the preceding segment, food forms the eager topic of conversation between them, and almost immediately Horace has his eye on Dixie as his adopted partner. Dixie's guide has been *Mrs. Rorer's Cook Book*, which naturally leads to a duet on the topic, "Mr. and Mrs. Rorer," establishing their mutual need for domestic fidelity. It is treated affectionately but signals a crying emotional hunger in them both underneath the material negotiations, neatly summed up in Wodehouse's closing lyrics, however politically incorrect: "And there'd be no divorce today / If only wives would act the way / That kind Missis Rorer used to do!" Kindness being a vanishing quality in modern life, he implies, its absence has turned Horace criminal and Dixie recalcitrant. Once again, a spiritual journey seems hinted at in the verse's locomotive figure, the song relaxing into a 6/8 jog-trot by having its even-note $\flat\hat{6}$-$\hat{5}$ opening bars massaged into the *iné-gale* $\sharp\hat{6}$-$\hat{5}$ appoggiaturas of the refrain, which is orchestrated by Bennett with Sullivanesque diplomacy, the chattering clarinet parts in particular. Kern, whose sketch specifies the figure and its treatment, was drawing on a long tradition of contented two-steps here, and British listeners will be reminded of "Oh! Mr. Porter." At the same time, a frequent musical theater syndrome, that of implanted orientalism, is at work in the song, for the counterpart of the $\flat\hat{6}$-$\hat{5}$ opening comes in the *minore* "Dance eccentrique" (Kern's term). Not for the only time in his output one wonders whether Kern was reusing old material with blatant disregard for orientalist origins, which can have no dramatic justification here.

Horace exits, and further mistaken identity lands Dixie in further trouble when, mistaking him for a servant, she bad-mouths Pennington to his face. This leaves him in a particularly uncharitable mood toward Bill, who is told to go away and get a job. Babe hears this and throws him over for Judson. Bill, alone on the stage, bewails his fate in "There Isn't One Girl." As a mournful, self-indulgent soliloquy this song represents every student's idea of musical theater expression but a dangerous and difficult resource that Kern and Wodehouse use sparingly. Written for *Pat*, it was never published. It is *Sitting Pretty*'s blues number, building on a stance Kern had developed in the Caldwell shows and sporting the usual throbbing accompaniment and strategic dominants. ($^{\flat}$VI$^{\flat 7}$ leads first time around back to V-I, second time to $^{\flat}$II, both reconverging on VI$^{9}_{7}$.) Its lyrics surely influenced Ira Gershwin's "But Not for Me" from *Girl Crazy*, though, unlike Gershwin, Wodehouse builds self-mockery into Bill's overall topic, thereby keeping musical comedy unsentimental:

> I needn't put oil on the old latchkey,
> For no one cares if I get home at three!

—lines that were expanded for a comic speech by Judson in *Bill the Conqueror.*

The sentiment comes in the ensuing dialogue, begun, before a sung reprise, with underscoring comprising a verse and refrain of the song on strings (not yet a multisong reprise scene, therefore). Here May, having overheard Bill's lament, shows sympathy by believing in him. This helps him believe in himself, and he promises to prove his worthiness by returning rich. She promises to help him spend his first million; thus their union is sealed. Their duet, "A Year from Today," follows, very much heir to the *Oh, Boy!* songs in its candor and a model of daring ABAB$_1$ simplicity. It is difficult to explain why such lines as "Bees in the clover will hum this refrain[:] / Winter is over and spring's here again!" and their melody with its VI-ii-V-I reharmonization should be touching rather than hackneyed in their effect. Kern knew he had something unusually delicate in this song, its *volkstümlich* artlessness not a far cry from Schubert's, and marked it "à l'antique"; Bennett knew so, too, and once again employed cor anglais throughout, mostly on the melody.

Jo and Horace take the stage again for further comic business when the real Professor Appleby, ancient and deaf, arrives and has to be speedily dispatched. The purpose of Horace's further appearance is to show how well ensconsed Jo is and how little chance of going straight Horace therefore has. This comes home to roost when Mrs. Wagstaff parades the orphan girls across the stage. Horace, who can manage only a brief word with Dixie, tries to warn her of his real social status: "Listen, little pal. Some day folks'll say things about me but you—you'll think back to a moment when Horace Pennington showed you his heart." She doesn't understand and doubts his true feelings, a blatant cue, via May, for the obligatory "coon" song and dance about cheering oneself up when blue, "Shufflin' Sam." After the previous two songs, such animation is sorely needed, though even in "A Year from Today" the accompaniment ostinato (|56555|) had helped maintain some sense of locomotion.[20]

So far we have had a duet for each of the principal couples (Horace and Dixie, Bill and May), two trios (one for Bill plus the twins, the other for the three male picaresques), a solo for Bill, and a duet for him and Babe, but nothing for the twins on their own, which the Duncan Sisters would surely have needed prior to act 2. It is odd that "Shufflin' Sam" does not fulfill this function before their separation in the act 1 finale, given its blackface and patrol qualities—in *Pat* it was to have been sung by two men, Plug and Jed, as one of the circus-girl Pat's old songs, she no doubt a "coon shouter." Probably Bryan's voice and persona were not up to it, though the stage directions do suggest that she and Dixie dance together before exiting. Perhaps the Dolly Sisters duetted the number on tour: Bennett's dance band orchestration for them survives and includes a Charleston refrain in the encore, but the convention of omitting voice parts from Broadway full scores precludes our knowing for sure. "Shufflin' Sam" is well suited to the locomotive subtext of *Sitting Pretty*, for although no explicit "choo-choo" imagery is invoked, the very word "shufflin'" invites biomechanical dancing in that imitative tradition. The whole song is a genre piece of rural Americana, which by 1924 could embrace a rich web of associations—the steam whistle introduction (a whole-tone one in the published song, different from the major/minor Doppler effect heard in the orchestration); the skidding brass triplet fills in the verse before the machinery of the song gets fully under way; the "Kingdom Coming" quotation in the first-time bars; the two references to Dvořák's *New World Symphony* in Bennett's orchestration; the upward-scale countermelody (compare "Worries") scored just like a banjo (two low clarinets and bassoon in unison with pizzicato cello) in the dance break's B section; and the lonely, exotic fade-out to the dance break on oboe as though receding into Indian territory.

Having eight musical numbers interspersed with dialogue scenes ranging between two and nine pages in length, the course of act 1 of *Sitting Pretty* has run very much along the classic lines of *Oh, Boy!*; only the nine-page comic segment between Jo, Horace, and Judson indicated the more star- and vaudeville-oriented dramatic capacity of the 1920s. The act 1 finale is equally classic as a reprise finaletto, close to that of *Have a Heart* in construction and effect. In traditional manner, it follows the previous number almost immediately so that music is by now the driving force, and only a brief comedy scene with Jo, impersonating Appleby, separates the two. Dixie is elevated to leading character by doing her first good deeds: owning up as Pennington's insulter when he thinks it was May and insisting that May take the adoption opportunity. This accompanies the initial underscoring. The finale reprises, in the following order, parts of "Just Wait," "Mr. and Mrs. Rorer," "Just Wait" again, the verse of "Worries," "A Year from Today" (complete), the plagal passage from the original "Opening," "Mr. and Mrs. Rorer" again, "Coaching," "There Isn't One Girl" (almost complete), the refrain of "Worries," and finally the first four bars of "A Year from Today" exactly as at the end of the overture. The major solos are for May and Bill, with Horace and Dixie not far behind. Not all sections are sung, but the singing is more continuous as the finale progresses. "Just Wait," in the form of residual underscoring, requires explanation, duly offered by McGlinn: it "was written as the big comedy number for act One . . . 'Bongo on the Congo' (originally in act Two) was brought forward to replace it"—a pity in some ways, for it is a fetching number with a particularly delicate verse with touches of schottische, beautifully scored by Bennett; perhaps it proved too difficult for the men involved with its rapid interactive patter.[21] There is some psychological subtlety in the use of this and other underscoring— "Just Wait" accompanies the tension induced by the question of which girl will get adopted and therefore, from Horace's point of view, "come and grab you," to quote his lyrics, and Dixie puts her "Worries" behind her in a more magnanimous sense than in the song when she sacrifices herself to May's future.

Kern's compositional intentions for the finaletto were sketched with absolute clarity. McGlinn's recording follows them exactly, with the possible exception of duetting the last half of "A Year from Today" between May and Dixie, marked for Dixie alone by Kern. Two variants arose, however: "Coaching" and Bill's reprise of "There Isn't One Girl" do not appear in the available script, and at some point, presumably after the opening number substitution, the sections from "Coaching" onward were replaced by parts of "Is This Not a Lovely Spot?" (with convoluted modulations that reappear in the entr'acte) and a refrain of "Shufflin' Sam" with which to end, for Bennett's orchestrations for these survive. The general technique was to add as little new material as possible—only the four bars of two-part invention that open the finale and ten bars of $\frac{6}{4}$ extension to "Worries" before its refrain's sung reprise—and to juxtapose songs by modulating onto a $\frac{6}{4}$ (as in *Have a Heart*), which happens three times, the last as Bill's climactic A flat tonic on the word "me!" becomes the 3rd of an E major $\frac{6}{4}$ underpinning "Worries." The dramatic corollary is the traditional one from operetta of everyone preparing to go somewhere as the act ends: Judson and his yuppies back to town, Bill to find a job, Dixie and the girls back to the orphanage, May and Horace to Florida on Pennington's yacht, Jo to Wanamaker's to do some "shop-lifting . . . Shopping, I mean, shopping."[22] The emotional corollary is unusually poignant, involving separation for both the main couples: the Britten-like harp notes from the overture are now Dixie's tears as she breaks down in midrefrain, the sad personification of partial reprise as the curtain falls.

Sitting Pretty—Act 2

After an entr'acte labeled "Interlude," which juxtaposes more reprises, act 2 opens with May's coming-out party in the Hispanic courtyard of Pennington's Florida home. This maintains the air of old-fashioned regret since it is a fancy-dress ball with the empress Eugénie's period as theme. The opening number's lyrics do the same job as had the overture's preludial tune when they refer to "Ancient tunes . . . tinkling soft and low." So do its melodies, cast as though it were a three-section quadrille in the sequence 4/4 bourrée, 6/8 contredanse, and 2/4 polka (at a pinch, all *l'istesso tempo*) as prelude to a more extended waltz, more engaging than Kern's waltz songs because its melodic line was not required to be sung and could be more sinuous.[23] The waltz denotes that the characters who sang the quadrille are still dancing offstage, and it accompanies a rather labored dialogue scene between Babe, present as Judson's partner, and Pennington as various famous personages of circa 1860 flit by. These climax with the Empress (played by no named character), who gets a solo spot of "Go, Little Boat" from *Miss 1917*, recast as "Days Gone By." It needs and in 1924 presumably had a real singer, its top Gs (top B flat in the coda) the culmination of *Sitting Pretty*'s musical yearning and in this context something of a precursor of "All the Things You Are" in *Very Warm for May*.[24]

Bill turns up at the party. In a book scene structured to culminate in his reunion with May, he reencounters Babe, proves to his uncle he has made good, for he is now a detective, and asks the butler how May is faring. May has already been described as appreciative of Pennington, a reference planted so as to prepare us for Horace's impending gratitude toward his adoptive father, who is proving less than the ogre he seemed in act 1; Dixie is working for a dressmaker in New York. The show's waltz song, "All You Need Is a Girl," is sung by Bill and May when he thanks her for believing in him—it made all the difference. As waltz songs go, it is somewhat routine.

But it is helped by its harmonic flavor, its wide melodic range, its revolving final phrase (foreshadowing "Can't Help Singing"), and Steiner's glittering orchestration, which is much more Lehár-like in its use of glockenspiel and rich wind stippling than Bennett's style with its puritan reticence. Steiner, after all, was born into the Viennese operetta tradition.

Jo and Horace then plan the evening's big jewel theft, after which they— or at least Jo—will naturally abandon Pennington. Jo says he needs to be armed and to justify carrying a gun will masquerade as a conjuror, which he practices in incompetent comic business with teacups. But Horace wants to go straight, explaining, "He's been takin' me to the theatre and I see it doesn't pay to be a crook . . . crooks that don't reform always come to a bad end." This is the cue for "Tulip Time in Sing Sing" as Jo, every inch the sentimental criminal, reminisces about his time there. All of Jo's appearances have hinged on a running gag substituting prison or criminal references for civil ones, and here they culminate in a mock-Victorian ballad sustaining prison as a metaphor for the congeniality of college life. Such incongruity lies at the heart of Wodehouse's humor; what has scarcely been observed, however, is its ironic applicability to his own future: a decade and a half later he himself was imprisoned in a series of Nazi war camps and seems almost to have enjoyed an experience that was like being back at public school.

Anderson orchestrated "Tulip Time in Sing Sing" and perhaps added the published introduction (there is a different one in a rehearsal copy), whose chromatic first two bars sound more like Frederick Delius than Kern in his wind scoring. Musically a functional rather than an inspired number— Kern's sketch is nothing more than a leadsheet—the release of its AA_1BA_2 refrain nevertheless sounds modern, not archaic, distinctly foreshadowing Warren's "You're Getting to Be a Habit With Me," though the song's final line, "Of that dear old-fashioned prison of mine," sets the seal on the show's motif of nostalgia when it mawkishly duplicates the melody on solo trumpet, an aural link with the overture's opening. The song is followed by Dixie's reappearance, and as the sisters are reunited Dixie explains how she was so miserable without May that she went to work for a company with an outlet in Florida and managed to get sent there. She doesn't want to spoil May's society chances, but May proposes fitting her out for the party. Dixie insists it should be incognito. Witness here the fudged dramatic intention: is she supposed to be an identical twin? It would seem not, despite Pennington's confusion in act 1 and again slightly later in act 2. After all, Horace and Bill have to fall for individual appearance as well as personality. At last the sisters sing a proper duet, "On a Desert Island With You," as they wish everyone else away.

This is the first of four expansive, romantic numbers, three of them duets, that bring the show to a lyrical culmination by resolving its dramatic tensions. Thus, though one of these numbers, the title song, was cut, there is no "act 2 problem" of diminishing musical perspectives in *Sitting Pretty*, a fact worth bearing in mind when considering the generic shift away from musical comedy that *Show Boat* represents. Of the ten songs that were published, five came from each act. "On a Desert Island With You," like "Ka-lu-a," reflects the 1920s faux-Hawaiian song craze with its finger-picking accompaniment figure (worked out by Kern himself) and lazy quarter-note triplets, an early use of these in an American popular song, foreshadowing their more widespread Latin American connotations in the next decade and beyond. The sickly sweet atmosphere demands parallel 3rds, but it is not clear whether Smith and Bryan sang them on stage. The lower vocal part was added for publication. The song's dance break, whose choreography must have included some primitivism to judge from the drumbeats, begins with a rare, open-throated orchestral tutti, its brass chording one of the few reminders in this show that radio dance halls and, a little later, Hollywood are to determine the sounds of the future.

The script begins to falter a little after this, for Horace and Dixie's reunion follows but leads straight into criminal plotting by Jo and Horace with no indication of how the segments pivot. Bill then encounters Jane, a colleague from the same detective agency being employed by Pennington to keep an eye on the jewelry, and as Jane exits May enters. Apparently Bill has told Pennington he is in love with her and Pennington has told May. But these communications make no sense when it becomes clear that May is still expecting to have to marry Horace, at which point the scene develops into an extended piece of comic business as Bill and May, with Jo present, declare their love to offstage interjections by Horace barking like a dog to signal Jo the all-clear. Eventually, as they fantasize about their first home, a "little place all smothered in mortgages," they manage to get rid of Jo and launch into the second star song of act 2, "The Enchanted Train," a Wodehouse classic of commuter bliss full of the names of Long Island Rail Road stations. Bennett scored most of it, though the final encore with steam whistle effect is Steiner's. Here the locomotive imagery is at last made manifest (and Kern specified the chugging fills), though again not without some sense of sadness, clear from the lonely monodic introduction played on cor anglais, a brilliant *ranz des vaches* touch that merges urban pastoral with traditional solitude. Cute though the song may be, the emotional undercurrent is of an orphan's desperate craving for a home, and Kern's B section (the refrain form is ABAB$_1$), the apogee of his classy approach to sequence and positively Elgarian with its falling 7ths, reflects this perfectly.

Horace and Dixie's romance will take longer to resolve—they are really the main couple—and the longest book scene, ten pages, accordingly follows, much of it with physical comedy. Silly girls preparing for the bathing party conveniently tell Jo where they are going to leave their jewelry; Jane encounters Jo and Horace in a segment of extended double bluff, Horace continuing to harp reflexively on plays about reformed thieves as he becomes more and more uneasy about the impending robbery; Pennington discovers Dixie and persuades her to leave so as not to disgrace her sister—

> PENNINGTON: "I wouldn't do nothing"—don't you see you can't even speak correctly?
> DIXIE: I'd learn. I love May so much that if it lays in my power—
> PENNINGTON: Lies.
> DIXIE: I mean every word I say.

—and Horace makes her cry by being so nice to her before having to rush off at Jo's dog bark, leaving her alone with her childhood fantasy of dancing with her shadow in the moonlight. This is the emotional apex of the show, and Horace's disarming exit speech ("What are we after all but puppets dancing at the bidding of a remorseless fate?") does not so much undercut as underline it by casting himself and Dixie as *commedia dell'arte* characters.[25] Dixie then becomes the lonely, serenading Pierrot and Columbine combined— one more step on the road to the Harlequin operetta that Kern had long wanted to compose. Kern supplies this moment with a ravishing musical number for Dixie and dinner-suited chorus boys, "Shadow of the Moon," which was also to have appeared in *Pat*. Its refrain, in his favorite ABAB$_1$ form, has a most beautiful sequence as the B section, its "tonal" consequent modified by only one note, which nevertheless makes all the difference. The slow harmonic unfolding of this sequence is matched by the parenthetic harmonic opening of the verse: after a guitarlike introduction apparently to an F major tonic, the verse begins, extraordinarily, on a first inversion of the chord of A flat major, which twice resolves directly to C major (the real key). This Tchaikovskian gesture—it shares the mood of diplomatically restrained passion found in *Eugene Onegin*—carries the verse toward the refrain in a single harmonic arc. Bennett is at home in this world, and the song contains some of his best orchestration for the show, especially in the filigree work on the diminished 7ths and sequence of the refrain in its dance break.[26] The song ends with a companion cadence to that at the end of the overture and act 1 finale, with harp and string harmonics picking out a ladder of 3rds, this time with flattened 7th but natural 11th and 13th.

"Shadow of the Moon" represents Dixie's nadir of self-esteem, as does what the by now thoroughly reluctant Horace is up to while she is singing it: helping Jo steal the guests' jewels. Yet both rise to deeds of good character immediately thereafter, Dixie by catching the thieves red-handed, insisting that Horace give her the jewels and promising not to implicate him, Horace in turn by sticking by her rather than Jo. Jo has no option but to sneak away apparently empty-handed, though we see him pocket the jewels before handing over their box. Horace's action having proved his resolution to go straight and start a new simple life away from the pretense of his position with Pennington, it takes only brief dialogue for Dixie to agree to join him in his no less domestic vision of happiness than that of Bill and May, more modest though it is. "All I want is to come home to our little shack and find you waiting on the porch and sit down in the old hickory rocker with you on my knee," he says, whereupon once again an endearing song hides and heals the great hunger for love and family life—real family life, not Pennington's travesty of it—that both characters must be feeling.[27] That song is "Sitting Pretty," whose loss ruined the score's integrity when it was cut before the New York opening apparently because Dwight Frye had a slight speech impediment and could not safely sing, "I want to sit, / Just sit and sit and sit." It is a redemptive moment when all the youngsters' pain melts away with the warmth of that first I$_4^6$ chord of the refrain, especially in the glorious dance break (see ex. 1.2), which nearly a decade before Fred Astaire first captured such things on film is one of the American musical theater's great, simple visions of pure joy. At last Dixie has truly banished her "Worries," a quote from that song linking refrain and interlude in "Sitting Pretty." Dixie enacts her occupation in the lyrics of the interlude, though curiously in the published song these are about secretarial typing rather than dressmaking.

After this, the quick wrap-up, in four pages of dialogue. But although musical completion has already been effected with "Sitting Pretty," dramatic tension has to be maintained until the last moment. Four or five complications come in quick succession: Jane apprehends Dixie with the jewel box and pronounces her the thief; the jewel box proves to be empty; Dixie is accused thereby of covering for the real thieves; May is about to be disinherited for supporting Dixie; Horace clears Dixie by producing the missing jewels; he clears himself in her eyes when Jo is caught trying to run away; and Pennington bows to "a splendid re-adjustment" of his "plan for starting a new race of Penningtons" when the double marriage is announced (this is presumably not ironic now that Bill is solvent).[28] One can puzzle over the finer points of motivation and logic here, but it works well enough. The "Finale Ultimo" follows, a concatenated reprise of three refrains. Steiner scored a refrain of "A Year from Today" as the exit music.

McGlinn's recording includes two appendices further to those already mentioned, the songs "All the World Is Dancing Mad" and "I'm Wise" minus their vocal parts, whose lyrics do not survive. Both make rather attractive light music miniatures in this state. Two further cut numbers, "Ladies Are Present," for Horace, Bill, and Dixie, and "A Romantic Man," for Horace and the female chorus, both from the second act, do not survive.

Introducing *Show Boat*

Critics and commentators wrote from the start that *Show Boat* was wonderful, special, unique, a solution to the problem of superficiality in musical comedy. "The greatest musical comedy of the American theater," David Ewen called it in 1953, drawing on the magic word "integrated" six lines later.[29] But few of them gave specific thought to the implications of genre in adapting a novel as a musical. This procedure has become such a commonplace that it is difficult to imagine a time when it was not standard practice. But the fact is that *Show Boat* was more or less the first musical to dramatize a novel.[30] The genesis of Rodgers and Hart's *A Connecticut Yankee* dates back further, but that show reached the stage only after *Show Boat's* adaptation had been put in hand, so Kern and Hammerstein were unlikely to have been copying it. Besides, Mark Twain's *A Connecticut Yankee in King Arthur's Court* is a satire, as burlesque (though an extremely black one) far more obviously congruent with the impossible world of musical comedy than Edna Ferber's *Show Boat*, a novel firmly in the realist tradition of Charles Dickens, Emile Zola, and, closer to home, Theodore Dreiser. Dreiser's *Sister Carrie* (1900) surely inspired the Chicago scenes of Magnolia's marriage to the gambler Ravenal, which are far more emotionally central to the novel than to the musical.

Opera had been setting novels to music for quite a while, however. Mention of Zola and realism calls to mind Alfred Bruneau; Puccini had set Henri Murger's *Scènes de la vie de bohème*; and long before that the historical novels of Walter Scott had furnished the plots of a number of works in the French, Italian, and British repertory. Frédéric d'Erlanger's operatic attempt at Thomas Hardy's *Tess of the d'Urbervilles* brings the comparison closer, Tess being, like Magnolia, a heroine of extraordinary fortitude in the face of passion, desertion, and social humiliation. Like *Show Boat* and indeed like many another opera and later musical, *Tess* also foreshortened the plot to an eyebrow-raising extent. This seems a problem endemic to the genre, for a novel can shade off into an epic ending. Ferber's *Show Boat* does this with a full-fledged portrayal of the middle-aged Magnolia, who is satisfied to return to the floating theater. She has inherited it after her mother's death at the age of eighty and resists her fashionable, successful (and loving) daughter's distaste for the old south, for Kim is about to go to Europe with her equally modern husband. A twentieth-century musical or opera, on the other hand, demanded a wrap-up far more closely related to its starting point, not least for reasons of musical recapitulation: the themes, musical as well as dramatic, had to be rounded up neatly, which tended to mean melodramatically or sentimentally, at the end. *Gypsy* perhaps avoids this, having more than a flickering structural resemblance to Ferber's *Show Boat* in its latter stages, but *Show Boat* the musical does not: Hammerstein has Ravenal and Magnolia reunited on the levee, Kim being still a little girl in the 1951 film. In the novel Magnolia never sees her husband again after he leaves her in Chicago, and he is dead long before the end. In the musical theater a leading man cannot just disappear. Herbie can do so in *Gypsy* precisely because he is not a leading man.

Apparently, then, Kern and Hammerstein were consciously or unconsciously moving toward opera in taking a novel as source in *Show Boat*; consciously, perhaps, if it is true that in the 1920s "the working classes attended movies much more often than theatre, which allowed theatre to move up in the social hierarchy." But in other respects, as Kern's later comments about Ravenal testify, they will have been equally determined to stay away from it, letting Ziegfeld's spectacular production values provide the scenic grandeur while keeping a very tight rein on expressive excess in libretto and music. Joe's singing of "Ol' Man River," a vision of poetic and musical catharsis—a hymn, in short—is a rare moment, possibly unique where Kern is concerned. In its performance all other theatrical values are subordinated to lyrical eloquence, for, unlike Julie's songs and the diegetic music of, say, *The Cat and the Fiddle,* Joe's self-expression has no effect on the plot. "The melody of OL' MAN RIVER was conceived immediately after my first hearing Paul Robeson's speaking voice," Kern later wrote. "It was in a preliminary tour of a play called BLACK BOY, performed in Mamaroneck, New York, and Robeson's organ-like tones are entitled to no small share of 'that thing called inspiration.'"[31] To hear speech and conceive musical breadth was operatic enough, but opera will indulge many such moments or sustain an entire evening's expression on that basis. *Show Boat* does not do this. What it does do is use memorable music and its adjuncts, dance, sustained dialogue, humor, melodramatic action, burlesque, to enhance a dramatic evocation of time and place couched in terms of the national pageant—a narrative display seen and heard as a "rhapsody of laughter and tears," as Al Dubin's lyrics in "Forty-Second Street" would later put it. Yet it accomplishes this without achieving any kind of artistic balance, at least in its stage version. "The proportions are outrageous," Lehman Engel pronounced.[32] Does this matter?

The musical theater literature is awash in discussion of *Show Boat.*[33] Miles Kreuger makes clear what was so special about *Show Boat* and prepares the way for Geoffrey Block's more analytical discussion of its position as the first American musical in the canon:

> The history of the American Musical Theatre, quite simply, is divided into two eras: everything before *Show Boat,* and everything after *Show Boat.* This seminal work revealed that a Broadway musical was free to embrace any kind of theme, however controversial, could deal with serious issues in a suitably mature fashion, could counterpoint light and cheerful scenes with those of human anguish, and yet never need to sacrifice popularity and a memorable, tuneful score.
>
> Further, Magnolia is the first protagonist in a Broadway musical to mature from a seventeen-year-old innocent to a strong, independent adult as do characters in novels or straight drama. *Show Boat* is also the first musical to present a black and white chorus singing together on a Broadway stage, a most daring venture (in a time of southern lynchings) for Ziegfeld, whose reputation had been established with light, escapist fare. *Show Boat* set a tone that allowed other revolutionary musicals to follow.[34]

All this is true, and Kreuger's point about Magnolia probably makes *Show Boat* the first *Bildungsroman* in the lyric theater. Yet the theme on which nearly all the *Show Boat* literature harps, as does the historiography of the

American musical in general—namely, that it was the first "integrated" musical and therefore heads the canon—has served certain agendas and ignored others. Here, therefore, I shall consider whether the loss of generic balance and clarity, of economy of organization and expression, inherent in the classic musical comedy has been truly compensated for by a sprawling, ambitious naturalism of a sort long dead in less bourgeois forms of theater; whether Kern (leaving aside Hammerstein) really regarded *Show Boat* as the musical theater's panacea when, as Ziegfeld reminded him, "you yourself told me you would not risk a dollar on it."[35]

These are not questions asked by most of *Show Boat*'s commentators. Neither do those commentators ask what specifically musical influences went into the score, clearly novel for Kern but not necessarily for the era taken broadly.[36] Instead, they typically adopt four or five critical themes: that with *Show Boat* the American musical reached its "first maturity"; that its first scene contained an unprecedented continuity of musical thought in terms of integrated songs, character motifs, and thematic transformation; that act 2 is potentially weak and its ending problematic; that racial issues are tackled directly, with sensitivity or punity; and that its production history and reception are a complex tale worth telling. All these questions will concern my account as well, for they are inescapable; it will not, however, be organized around them, but rather around *Show Boat* as a musical composition.

Show Boat—Overture and Scene 1

That opening A minor triad—this is with reference to the 1927 score: the 1946 overture is quite different—is a chilling sound as sustained by Bennett in close position on two trumpets and trombone without the two horns (woodwinds sustain open higher doublings; strings swipe at it in multiple-stop quarter notes, with timpani).[37] It begins an overture that, as a preview of the "Colored Blood Scene," as Kern's sketch calls it, for the greater part of its length foretells a story of tragic melodrama, decked out with fustian orchestration laid on in crude strokes as though for a restive silent film audience: ubiquitous banjo, clucking away like a chicken; blaring trumpets; tuba tapping out an ominous ostinato like Morse code. It is the perfect equivalent to Ferber's chapter 7 opening: "Julie was gone. Steve was gone. Tragedy had stalked into Magnolia's life; had cast its sable mantle over the *Cotton Blossom*."[38] And it masks the imagined opening of Julie's theme, which on

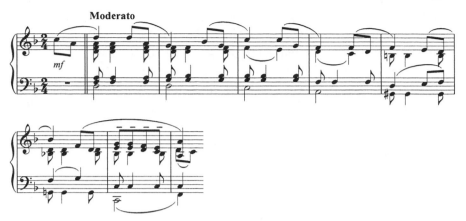

Ex. 3.3. Julie's theme.

its second appearance could almost be by Edward Elgar: this is certainly a
new bid for emotional depth on Kern's part (ex. 3.3), inspirational in its return to the opening triad (not shown in ex. 3.3) at its climax, a postromantic
modal touch that MGM could never bring itself to acknowledge in the 1951
film. The other inspired moment is when, after "Mis'ry's Comin' Aroun'"
has generated something of a development section, one of the cakewalk mo-
tifs (2/4: |555ᵇ3-4|5ᵇ354-|) is sung by an invisible voice—the image of a sing-
ing Negro across the plantation, a topic instantly recognizable but never so
similarly done, one imagines, as in Delius's *Appalachia* (1904). Can Kern
have known this piece?

Already the motivic transformations to which musicological commentators have habitually drawn attention are in evidence, making several songs
"musical anagrams" of each other, as Gerald Mast puts it.[39] The motif cited
above clearly relates to that of "Mis'ry's Comin' Aroun'" (|5-[5-]|22-12-|, from
the opening of act 1 scene 4, but cut both in 1927 and 1946) and to the
theme of "Ol' Man River" (|5-[5-]|61---|5-[5-]|32---|) as heard here, identical
to "Cotton Blossom" with its first phrase reversed (|1165-| and |5532-|). "Cap-
tain Andy" (|1566|) is a later variant of "Cotton Blossom," the name of his
boat.[40] The pentatonic emphasis on 1, 2, 3, 5, and 6 also generates Julie's
theme (53|6-63|2) and its psychological obverse, Ravenal's "I Drift Along
With My Fancy" (|[1-]|63|5), a connection made manifest at the very mo-
ment when Julie is forced to leave the boat (score, p. 111, bar 5).[41] Both are
characters in trouble with the local law. The second part of the overture

continues to pursue such relationships, for it picks up on the final 4th in Julie's theme and connects it by reversal with "Why Do I Love You?," introduced as a waltz but then played through as its cut-time refrain, its final note connecting back to "Mis'ry's Comin' Aroun'."

Act 1 opens with another Elgarian motif, the treble-and-bass counterpointed theme later associated with the sheriff, Vallon, when he enters halfway through the first scene. Again it bespeaks the crude melodramatic modules of silent film music and is marked "à la bombarde" (whatever that means). The operatic comparison would be with *Carmen* and its "fate" motif at the end of the overture, leading straight into the act 1 opening curtain. *Show Boat*'s opening curtain generates musical motion with a curious passage that could have been left over from a Chinatown scene but soon settles into an operatic opening number with the usual flirtatious choruses of men and women (in this case African-American). The men, stevedores, utter their shocking first word, "Niggers" ("Colored folks" by the time the score came to be printed), the women, courtesy of Hammerstein, cram into four bars of lyrics the maximum number of stereotypical references: "Coal black Rose or high brown Sal, / Dey all kin cook de sparrergrass an' chicken pie." The men's tune is a work song, which is indicated by the cross-rhythmic thumps of the accompaniment, but it is also a southern pastoral (the Mississippi is mentioned in bar two), and when Joe repeats it at the end of the scene as the verse of his "Ol' Man River" and, as before, a flat 7th is added but to a now *sostenuto* accompaniment (score, p. 58), we realize the uncanny resemblance to J. S. Bach's "Sheep May Safely Graze" (compare 2/4: |543354|3561| with |553553|5661|).[42] The middle section of this ternary tune, and indeed of "Ol' Man River," in the mediant, G sharp minor, is the women's, very much like a Dvořák folk trio with its parallel 3rds and 6ths and made even more so by the plaintive orchestral countermelody added to it in "Ol' Man River" (score, p. 57). Dvořák's pastoral Americanism did not affect just the symphonic repertoire, and Whiteman's recorded arrangement of "Ol' Man River" with Robeson in 1928 quotes "Going Home" in the introduction and elsewhere.[43]

"Cotton Blossom" forms a coda to this opening diegetic song but is subsequently used as a kind of refrain holding together this enormous opening scene, whose operatic resonances continue when the first individual character to enter after the noise of the opening proves to be a burlesque servant encumbered with various props, just like the Sacristan in *Tosca*. This is Queenie, and immediately we know that "Can't Help Lovin' Dat Man" is a song of her race, for as underscoring it accompanies her conversation with the villainous Pete, who wants to know where this "Nigger" obtained the brooch she is wearing, which he had given Julie. This single exchange and its music already define the harshness of race relations, the melodrama of passion (Pete is stuck on Julie), the unalterability of river life (Queenie is quite unfazed by Pete's rough questioning), and the symbolic role of diegetic music as personal possession which will be played out across the show.

The stevedores' tune and "Cotton Blossom" return, but a group of "mincing misses" brings the white female chorus onto the stage, closely followed by their male counterparts, the "town beaux." Ninety-six people were on stage by this point in the 1927 production. The mincing misses' 6/8 *scherzando* underscoring could almost be the *music* of *Tosca*'s Sacristan; the girls admire Julie's picture in the advertising frame that Steve, her husband, has set up during the opening song but soon turn to be admired by the beaux instead. At this point *Show Boat* reverts to operetta with a sprightly dotted-note schottische which echoes Gilbert and Sullivan: compare the bridesmaids' entrance in *Trial by Jury*. An expansive song in its own right, it indulges in a delicious semitone modulation in the spacious refrain from which Kern is reprieved from having to find a return, since that refrain is broken off by leading back into "Cotton Blossom." This climaxes on top A for the sopranos at the lines "Thrills and laughter, / Concert after," something of an ironic summary of *Show Boat*'s entire structural problem.

The disgruntled Pete steals Julie's picture from the frame and slinks off as Parthy's voice is heard, seeking her husband. Andy Hawks (half French, hence his *insouciance*) is captain of the showboat; his termagant wife, Parthenia Ann, a Massachusetts puritan, is Ferber's most vivid creation in the novel, horrifically grotesque in her *Schadenfreude* and quite indestructible, unlike her husband, who drowns in a storm. She makes a fortune out of the floating theater she despises and dies rich at eighty. The 1929 Universal film plays up her melodramatic creepiness as Magnolia's impossibly strict mother and shows her husband's death, but her comic side, while amply apparent in the novel, becomes her essence in the stage show, the first casualty of its musicalization. Her prim, pantomimic theme captures the fact that the only way her family can deal with her is to ignore her but reduces her to a cartoon, precluding demonstration of the very real similarity of determination between her and her daughter (and, still more, her granddaughter) that emerges during the course of the story. Neither can we witness the desperate battle of wills between her and Ravenal, which in the novel directly causes his desertion of Magnolia and Kim when she announces she is coming to see them in Chicago.

For all that, Parthy's theme does its mimic job with perfect, crisp economy and furthers the web of motivic relations by being a kind of perversion of Captain Andy's (hers: $|52\,{}^b311|$ — that is, in the minor; his: $|1566|$, major). As the bystanders begin to ask her about the troupe and about her daughter, we hear Magnolia's offstage piano practice, its rat-a-tat rhythm a graceful obverse of hers, though the theme — she is clearly trying to learn a simple Mozart sonata or something of the kind — comes from *The Beauty Prize*. This gives way to a snatch of diegetic march (not in the Chappell score but present in the Welk one) as Andy, something of a mascot for the young girls and clearly the source of his daughter's allure, arrives with his band, which has been in town advertising the show boat.[44] The girls sing "Captain Andy" as the latest refrain in this extended rondo — one hears it as a variant of "Cotton Blossom." Both tunes are used to separate the two episodes in which the show is previewed, first by Andy's descriptions and accompanying brief demonstrations of circus, gags, and pulchritude (this last the province of Julie, who appears with Steve, who scowls at Pete), second by an instrumental schottische daintly danced by Ellie and Frank. In the crowd Pete manages to challenge Julie about the brooch, and Steve fights him, to ten bars of *melos* and shrieking girls. Andy cleverly pretends it was just another preview and that they are really "just one big happy family!"[45] Like the post–Civil War society of which this show is the emblem, the dialogue that ensues after the crowd has dispersed makes it amply clear they are not, for Parthy spurns Julie, her daughter's best friend, and rows with Andy.

Melos, as Kern called underscoring to speech, comes triumphantly into its own in the next segment. Parthy has had the last word, the close of her theme like a slamming door as she exits, and the battered but unbowed Andy's theme follows as *pianissimo* underscoring, linking him with Ravenal — another river character and his future son-in-law — at the latter's first entrance when it pointedly turns into Ravenal's song, "Where's the Mate for Me?" In the long run this functions as his verse for "Make-believe." First heard here as underscoring, it was originally the refrain of the song "Morganatic Love," which Kern had written with Coward for *Tamaran* and which had been rewritten by Dietz as "A Merry Mormon Life" in *Dear Sir*; the subject of a carefree life may be common to all three, but the mood is changed utterly.[46] Ellie is taken with the handsome, dapper stranger but to no avail. Vallon's entrance music includes the dotted rhythm that will reappear in the refrain of "Make-believe"; it suggests Ravenal's restless yet relaxed life, whose essence he is obliged to rehearse with Vallon when the latter reminds him he can't stay long in town because of a previous incident. Left alone, Ravenal demonstrates both his indigence and his poise when he carefully re-lights a discarded cheroot and "once more his easy magnificent self . . . now soliloquizes languidly."[47] After one verse of "Where's the Mate for Me?" he hears and is amused by Magnolia's faltering piano playing, but it penetrates his subconscious all the same, for his song's central section, which follows prior to a repeat of the verse (if one may call it that), is based on it. His consciousness is struck much more bluntly, however, by Magnolia's sudden appearance, and he forgets to sing his last two words, which significantly were "for me." Hammerstein's stage direction reminds us that we, the audi-ence, must be equally struck by her: "(What a picture! A very young face and a fluffy dress all pink with flowers and everything—and she is becomingly shy—yet bold enough to return his gaze—and to speak first.)"[48]

Their conversation develops, underscored first by a beautiful new me-lodic period (see the score, p. 42, systems 1 and 2), then by Magnolia's piano theme as Ravenal discovers to his comic disappointment that it was she he had heard, then, with genuinely Wagnerian effect, by Parthy's theme as Magnolia thinks of her social transgression (even though her mother is no-where to be seen or heard) and says, "I must go now."[49] Next, Ravenal's verse is heard as he steers the situation toward his philosophy, and finally Vallon's theme at the mention of "seventy-five years," for Ravenal has just been re-minded by Vallon that he has only twenty-four hours. All this happens within two pages of score, minutely coordinated with brief or single dialogue ex-changes—but Kern had by this stage in his career learned to judge such things perfectly, not just in length but with suitably flexible melodies and joins in which rubato, phrasing, and the actors' speech might need mutual adjustment.

Ravenal has been feeling the need for a "mate." He has very little time to find one in this town, so it is understandable that Vallon's dotted rhythm introduces his crafty ploy for gaining immediate social access to the stage-struck young girl: "[Only] make believe we know each other," which as early as the first line of the song has become "Only make believe I love you." By compression of events and scenes, this anticipates rather precipitately the point in the novel at which Magnolia and Ravenal have both been enlisted into the acting troupe and are playing opposite one other with the inevita-bility that they should fall in love: "Their make-believe adventures as they lived them on the stage became real," Ferber writes.[50] But the teasing die-getic levels in and out of which the song moves are clever and satisfying. By the end of the refrain, Ravenal has confessed, "For, to tell the truth, I do [love you]." Then, as Magnolia "draws back" in response, he covers himself by revealing a further putative layer of playacting in his coda of apology in mannered waltz-style, suggesting that the whole performance, declaration and all, has been an old-fashioned charade. This reassures Magnolia, who completes the coda. And indeed the music is cast throughout in a sufficiently operetta-like style that both parties remain safely within the bounds of arti-fice by comparison with the "sincere" or at least direct expression implied by the preceding music in the scene and, even more, by Joe's heartfelt "Ol' Man River," which follows. But by the same token the song is unashamedly romantic. Performance practice should follow composition here, and it is instructive to hear just how pointedly the 1928 London performers, Edith Day and Howett Worster, observe Kern's instructions of "deliberato" over the quarter-note triplets and "molto rit." (*molto portamento*, too) over the se-quence "Couldn't you? couldn't I? couldn't we?," he even more than she.[51] Magnolia's verse—if Ravenal's "Where's the Mate for Me?" is also heard as a verse it is significant that they have different ones—is sandwiched between the two refrains, dance band style, but leads to a rambling *minore* interlude with further operetta-induced glimpses of central or eastern Europe (one thinks of Aleksandr Borodin) before the second refrain.

The role of those *deliberato* triplets in the repertoire of genteel courtship is made clear when they sound in the orchestra as Ravenal reaches up to kiss Magnolia's hand but remain suspended on a secondary dominant when he is interrupted by the return of Vallon: he has to report to the law. Thus Vallon's motif, representing harsh reality, frames "Make-believe" on both sides, and from here until the end of the scene the narrative lens is zooming back out to where it began, with the land, its community, and their constraints. Joe enters, and one might argue that another musical transformation is percep-tible, from the last three notes of the "Make-believe" coda (3/4 |5--|↑2--|1) to the first three of "Ol' Man River" (2/2 |5-61), which follow directly as under-scoring. Joe knows Ravenal for what he is; he also knows that his incipient philosophizing about destiny will be interrupted by Queenie, whose flour (for her legendary biscuits) he is carrying—hence "Can't Help Lovin' Dat Man" as underscoring while he sets down the flour in order to cogitate. Mag-nolia rushes off to tell Julie all about her beau, and, sure enough, before Joe can launch into "Ol' Man River" Queenie comes and nags him about the flour, in immemorial coon-show style. But he stands, or rather sits, his ground and links the stevedores' work song of the scene's opening with his own quieter occupation of whittling at a stick by turning the song into "Ol' Man River." There is nothing else quite like this in Kern's output, and apparently Hammerstein had to squeeze it out of him; he made the suggestion that their path could be eased if the "Cotton Blossom" motif was reused (inverted, in the event). But Kern had little option but to create a pseudo-spiritual when Ferber's text progressively invokes the genre. In chapter 4 she refers to "the mellow plaintive voices of Negroes singing on the levees and in cabin doorways" and forty pages later gives a complete notated musical example of "I Got a Robe," following it with not just a reference to "Go Down, Moses" (its title rhythm the same as that of "Ol' Man River") but a description of Joe singing it. In the novel it is Joe, not Julie, whom Magnolia imitates, and two spirituals (the same two), not the blues, that she sings in her Chicago audition. Luckily Ferber had left "Deep River" unmentioned, and Kern undoubtedly drew on this for the shape and feeling of "Ol' Man River." His source was most likely Harry T. Burleigh's arrangement of it, replete with "Ol' Man River"'s *arpeggiando* half notes in the accompaniment, the Dvořák-like *minore* middle section, and the higher-octave scale degree 3 as climax after this. Burleigh may also have strengthened Kern's idea of Robeson for the part of Joe and a statuesque performance for the song, for he was a well-known baritone soloist and sang in Kern's grandfather's synagogue for twenty-five years. Further *Show Boat* features relate closely to other well-known spiritual arrangements by Burleigh. The quick-slow-quick cakewalk syncopation motif is found in most of them, and "I Got a Robe," whose notation Ferber must have taken from Burleigh, includes the "Scotch snap" (|5-6̂1 in Kern) to the repeated word "Heav'n" and the cadential 2-1̂6̂|[5]1 melodic figure used as an orchestral sign-off in "Can't Help Lovin' Dat Man."

Or is "Ol' Man River" a shanty? Ferber describes river shanties, though with no suggestion that blacks sang them, and the central mediant reaches of Joe's work song have a hauling feeling, which stevedores would presumably have found useful, though not when endeavoring to "tote" a barge (a howler of Hammerstein's). One could also associate Joe's stick-whittling with scrimshaw. Joe is not a stevedore, however—at least, not for the six months of the year he is on the boat—and it is the chorus that sings "pull dat rope."[52]

Either way it is a wonderful tune, its range of a 13th, broad contours and phrasing, and sense of climax quite beyond what musical comedy had purveyed; this alone might well have set the American musical's aspirations in motion. There are several early recordings by the original creators of the role of Joe, Jules Bledsoe in New York, Paul Robeson in London. Bledsoe's (London, 1931) is powerful and theatrical despite its dance band elements, with a strong top G from him at the final cadence. Robeson's with the Whiteman band (New York, March 1928) is something of a travesty, whereas his 1928 performance with Finck and the original orchestration, sadly unavailable on CD, presents the song with a simplicity perhaps unmatched since, down a tone in B flat (Robeson's bottom Fs are magnificent).[53] Whether Robeson's 1932 recording more or less represents how "Ol' Man River" sounded in the New York stage revival of that year at the Casino Theatre, in which he played the role of Joe for the first time in the United States, is a moot point. Since it was part of what Kreuger calls "the very first American record album ever made from the score of a Broadway musical," which used only two singers from the stage production in its eight numbers, with "dreary," "pretentious" arrangements by Victor Young, it probably does not, though the song is sensitively handled apart from the end-of-phrase orchestral fills.

Those fills have never quite settled down; neither have certain of the song's harmonies. Bennett was not unduly complimentary about the song — or about *Show Boat* altogether, to judge from Kern's comments below and elsewhere:

> When [Kern] handed me his sketch it had no name and no lyric. It was thirty-two not wholly convincing measures that sounded to me like they wanted to be wanted. In the first place it starts with two harmonically powerful and self-reliant bars and then comes to a mud puddle and doesn't know where to put its feet for the next two. . . . the Muse of Music never spat at either Jerry or me for not finding the chords that should have been there. I found some rather nice fills for the ends of phrases and didn't worry about it until a few days later when I looked at it with Oscar Hammerstein's words written in. I didn't worry about it then either — just said to Jerry, "Gee, that's a great song!" Kern said, "You didn't say that when I gave it to you." He knew as well as I did that it wasn't a song at all until Oscar came in with the words.

(Hence Dorothy Hammerstein's insistence that Kern did *not* write "Ol' Man River"; he only wrote "Dum dum da da.")[54]

As can be seen in example 3.4 (i), and leaving aside the question of the rhythm in bar three (compare the refrain's final bars), Kern's sketch does indeed begin with strong harmony — too fussy, in the case of the first inversion in bar two. Bennett — it appears to be his hand — changed the reviled bars three and four to a more functional I-iib-I-vi chord sequence in his piano/vocal score, which is what appears in the separately published song (ex. 3.4 [ii]). But the engraver's copy (not shown in ex. 3.4) for the complete Chappell score, which follows it exactly, reverts to Kern's superior, lazily warm tonic oscillations with added 6th and second inversion on the weak beats. Concerning the fills, as can be seen from example 3.4, Kern had thought of a modal idea, but Bennett came up with something completely different. Again, this was used for the published song but not for the Chappell score, whose solution is different again and closer to Kern's original, though without the flat 7th.[55] The orchestral score, however, presents a fourth version, with dotted notes on the oboe; Finck's recording with Robeson uses this. Harmonically, the second beat of bar eleven ("dem dat plant 'em") is also at issue. Kern simply specified a dominant bass; Bennett changed this to chord vi, which is what is retained in the engraver's copy and Chappell score; but the orchestral version reverts to tonic with added 6th and G bass, surely the best sound. And do I detect ii^7b rather than IV in bar two on the McGlinn recording?

Some details, however, were not negotiable. The diminished-7th harmony and appoggiatura on "soon forgotten" appear in all versions from Kern's sketch onward; Hammerstein's delaying of his first refrain rhyme (with "cotton") until this moment was a stroke of genius which crystallizes the song's expression of centuries of heartache into two words and two chords.[56]

Repeated by the "colored male chorus" in four parts, if not the "male octette (double 4[tette])" Kern envisaged, "Ol' Man River" brings this extraordinary scene to the "big finish" specified by Kern in his sketch.[57] Musically, although not entirely continuous (there are short stretches of unaccompanied dialogue), it has set out, together with the overture, a lexicon of musical motifs, characterizations, moods, connections, and balancing forms sufficient to represent the span of feeling and potential for action inherent in *Show Boat*'s plot; indeed, the main emotional developments have already been shown. This is truly operatic—or one might say symphonic—thinking, but more than a quarter of the score has already passed (it will be 70 percent by the end of act 1), and it cannot be sustained over its whole length.

Show Boat—The Remainder of Act 1

Kern's cinematic technique of a fluid continuum of familiar motifs is already fully functional by the end of scene 1 and carries, for good or ill, many later moments, especially transitions, including that into the next scene, a

(i) Kern's ink sketch

(ii) Bennett's ink fair copy

Ex. 3.4. Ol' Man River.

shallow one set in *Cotton Blossom*'s pantry while the complex auditorium setting is prepared behind. Originally Magnolia described her encounter with Ravenal to Julie in yet a third verse to "Make-believe," an attractive waltz; its reprise in the miscegenation scene was never excised (Chappell score, pp. 108–09).[58] But the main business of the scene is to set down clues about Julie's race problem and establish her as stage mentor for Magnolia, in "Can't Help Lovin' Dat Man," the song only black people are supposed to know, as Queenie pointedly observes. Mordden explains its significance: "In this nineteenth-century America of strict racial segregation, black culture is so cut off from whiteland that Queenie grows suspicious when Julie knows a black song . . . real black music, unheard by whites"—not a work song, spiritual, or distant wordless voices, that is, but something secret, intimate, shared only between women (which makes its male violation in the Trocadero rehearsal all the more shocking). "Can't Help Lovin' Dat Man," Kern's best blues song by far, was where all the preparatory essays in the genre with Anne Caldwell had been leading. Kern casts the verse (and Hammerstein its lyrics) as a genuine twelve-bar blues: I-[II-V⁷]-I-I♭⁷-IV-iv-I-I-V⁷-V⁷-I-I, with a melodic flat 7th in the very first bar and acciaccatura representation of blue notes, including the 3rd, at the final cadence. The refrain, by contrast, is a classic AABA "lyric binary" with the dominant preparation as high point (literally, in terms of melodic apex). The stomping accompaniment helps the irresistible build of its routining as Magnolia learns how to shuffle. Everyone concerned with the production must surely have taken their cue from black shows of the period like *Shuffle Along*: this number, more than any jazz or "genuine" blues, explains in a stroke the mass appeal of black music in the 1920s. Something of the cast's infectious joy comes across from the still of its Drury Lane performance (fig. 3.1), as indeed it does on Finck's recording of the song with his choral sextet and the Drury Lane orchestra, though Marie Burke's English accent ("But when he comes beck") is painful. Helen Morgan's 1928 performance of "Can't Help Lovin' Dat Man," recorded with Ziegfeld's original conductor, Victor Baravalle, but inauthentic orchestration, is curiously innocent, demonstrating Julie's fragility in headvoice purity of tone but nothing of her sultriness. By 1932 Morgan was singing the song down a 3rd in C major with as many swoops and husky low notes as could be imagined. If she represents cultural change through singing, then it was swift indeed at this period. In fact the classic period recording of "Can't Help Lovin' Dat Man" is Tess Gardella's (1928; as Aunt Jemima she played Queenie in blackface)—the belt of a classic "coon shouter," cast

Fig. 3.1. "Can't Help Lovin' Dat Man" at Drury Lane in 1928.

in B flat major and accompanied by what the 1920s would have considered riotous jazz. It works perfectly.[59]

Scene 3 in 1927 was again played on a shallow stage and omitted entirely in the 1946 revival. Set outside a saloon, it makes Ravenal's gambling clear and builds up his mystique when Ellie again tries to flirt with him. Musically speaking it returns *Show Boat* to traditional genres with its two nondiegetic performances, one for Ellie to her lounging admirers, "Life on the Wicked Stage," the other for Ravenal singing of his *carpe diem* philosophy, "Till Good Luck Comes My Way." "Life on the Wicked Stage," musical comedy daintiness personified, has a verse absent from the Chappell score but published after 1946, when the song was transferred to the later box office scene. "Till Good Luck Comes My Way" shows Kern not entirely at ease with operetta bravado, as Ravenal's dashing masculinity is treated to various musical topics (for he has to impress the small-town chorus with his risk taking). A cavalry-march introduction is curiously followed by a strutting 2/4 allowing him some long notes; a couple of bars of throbbing 12/8, as though from grand opera, prepare his refrain, which seems to begin with its final phrase (deliberately expressing his loss and further anticipation of luck?) but neatly incorporates the coda of "Make-believe" later on; he rides

the chorus's coda with a final top B flat. Originally this song came first in
the scene, which had underscoring (recitative, in fact) from the start and
was followed by "Yes, Ma'am" for Ellie and girls, an early version of "Poor
Wet Fish" from *Sweet Adeline* (see chapter 4) but with a different refrain,
not as good. The scene's opening was about as close to opera as Kern would
get but correspondingly static; "one is amazed," McGlinn comments, "that
Kern and Hammerstein would attempt such a daring device, surely knowing
that it wouldn't survive more than a few performances. Such is the difference
between opera and musical comedy."[60] Overall, this scene in its various versions (including its omission) is the crucial point of evidence for Kern's and
Hammerstein's inability to sustain any particular genre as *Show Boat*'s act 1
proceeded.

Insofar as it too was cut from the 1927 production and not reinstated in
1946, the same might be said of the next new number, "I Would Like to Play
a Lover's Part," their most sprightly and, in musical comedy terms, attractive up to this point in the show. The miscegenation scene intervenes before
this, but it contains no new music—"Mis'ry's Comin' Aroun'" (which also
was cut in 1927, "the most grievous loss the score suffered") and its introductory underscoring have been heard in the overture, and beyond that it
is all piecemeal underscoring already heard in scenes 1 and 2.[61] The crucial melodrama of Julie's unmasking (she has been "passing" for white), of
Steve's sucking her blood as evidence of mixed blood in him too (with wit-
nesses, including the normally silent Windy), and of their decision to leave
the show boat is essentially unaccompanied. This is the first real book scene
in the show, though "Mis'ry's Comin' Aroun'" reappears in the orchestra to
prepare the actual moment of the knife cut and Vallon's reappearance to
arrest Julie, and Julie's theme ("On my back") accompanies Vallon's departure. Music returns for the scene's final segments, from Ravenal's enlistment
as an actor through Julie's final exit from the boat to the passionate stage kiss
between Ravenal and Magnolia. This entails a further refrain of "Ol' Man
River" from Joe, as he stands in an upper box like a Greek chorus—another
generic implication only intermittently sustained—and a further hearing of
the "Make-believe" coda as Ravenal plays out its implications in reverse, this
time courting for real.[62]

Perhaps *Show Boat* should have three acts, for we are already halfway
through the score, and a tight musical unity has been achieved but is now
broken off. "I Would Like to Play a Lover's Part" opens scene 5, one more
shallow one allowing the *Cotton Blossom* auditorium to be transformed from

rehearsal to performance space. The time is three weeks later, Ravenal and Magnolia now the darlings of the crowd as it queues for tickets at the boat's box office. Ellie sells them, to sales patter as interlude in this splendid song that has something of Gershwin's up-to-dateness. The ineffectual Frank tries to supplant Ravenal in the crowd's affections but is put down by both them and Ellie. The ensuing dialogue scene for this secondary, comic couple, humorously setting up the Backwoodsman's debut in a theater audience when Frank backs off from a showdown with him over Ellie, is by far the longest we have yet witnessed without any musical support, even though *Show Boat* was intended to maintain traditional proportions of traditional comic business. The segment ends with "I Might Fall Back on You," substituted for "I Would Like to Play a Lover's Part" but in turn wisely cut in 1946, for Ellie has already had one showcase in this act, and the song is undistinguished except for its quickstep cross-rhythm (later matched by that of "Why Do I Love You?" for the other young couple). Parthy and Andy then converse about Magnolia and Ravenal; this sets up Parthy's revelation of him as a murderer in the act 1 finale. Different scripts have different ways of ending this scene. "Queenie's Bally-hoo" is one of them: after a rather pointed dialogue cue about blacks having to sit in the balcony, she helps muster them into the audience with a "roll up!" turn offering in nondiegetic song the essentials of a melodramatic plot. Not all the vocal part is printed in all the published scores, but all the music is, including the passages of parallel minor triads, their sequence and modulatory resolution not as simple as might appear, for the juicier parts of the description.

After four or five foretastes of melodrama—the music of the overture, the rehearsal in scene 4, Steve and Julie's real-life trauma, and Queenie's and Captain Andy's previews to the crowd—at last the curtain goes up on an actual performance in front of a stage audience. *The Village Drunkard*, *East Lynne, Tempest and Sunshine*, and *The Parson's Bride* have all been mentioned or sampled; this peformance is *The Parson's Bride*.[63] Kern has already shown himself keen to enter the musical world of Victorian hand-me-downs, just as he will eagerly resurrect tunes not his own in act 2 of *Show Boat* and the overture of *Sweet Adeline*. The scripts specify various old chestnuts as Magnolia's piano accompaniments, chosen "for no reason," to the rehearsal of *The Parson's Bride* in scene 4, to which are added "Love's Old Sweet Song"—still quite new in 1890—in the orchestra (or "Hearts and Flowers" on violin) when we witness the actual performance.[64] To ensure a proper distance between our reception of the stage play and Hammerstein's and Ferber's story, things go hilariously wrong: Ellie trips on exit, a cow moos when a bell is referred to, the clock shows the wrong time, Andy makes an announcement to a member of the audience, and Frank ruins his villainous climax when, seeing the Backwoodsman in the audience aiming a gun at him, he mollifies rather than threatens Magnolia. The play has no place to go from here, and the Backwoodsman sheepishly withdraws as Andy brings down the curtain, announcing the "olio" (postplay concert) and/or acting out the remainder of the truncated play in a virtuosic comic turn, depending on which script is followed. Part of that olio is then witnessed by the show audience in front of the curtain while the scene is changed. In the published score it is Frank's "Villain's Dance." Or possibly "A Pack of Cards" was intended for this spot: if it was, and if it really is by Kern (the refrain is a polka, after all), its narrative would have had a grim relevance to the thoughts going through Parthy's mind after seeing her daughter and Ravenal embrace so fervently in *The Parson's Bride*.

Scene 7, on the upper boat deck by moonlight, begins with that archetypal romantic trope, the wordless singing of distant Negroes across the water. The song is "Ol' Man River," of course. Magnolia and Ravenal have engineered a tryst (the "love surge" from *Dear Sir* recurs as they meet), and he proposes to her—proposes that they get married the very next morning, in fact, while Parthy is away (ironically, doing detective work on Ravenal). Their main love duet naturally follows. Searching, one feels, rather desperately for inspiration, as indeed is Ravenal for agents of persuasion, Hammerstein originally cued in yet more local color:

> (*She turns away. Boy with Guitar sings off stage—high tenor*)
> RAVENAL: Listen . . . All over the world, under this same sky there are lovers
>   like you and me—and their love is the only thing that counts—Oh, come
>   Nola—answer me—never mind words—See that Creole girl in the boat
>   is kissing her serenader—Look at them—Nola—
> (*Pause for six to eight measures of vamp—Ravenal starts singing very softly*)[65]

"Creole" here implying Hispanic West Indian, the "Creole Love Song" was the consequent, fit for "any Shubert operetta of the period" and "more like Romberg than Kern," though perhaps more like Georges Bizet still, and with a most eloquent winding down from its climax in the refrain.[66] Its replacement with "You Are Love" was a wise move, although a "tempo di bolero" introduction (with the "Creole Love Song"'s vocalized coda) was retained, whence the song rather creakily moves toward waltz time in Ravenal's verse, its lyrics ("Like a lonely Punchinello") not among Hammerstein's best. "You Are Love" is certainly the emotional high point of *Show Boat* but not a great waltz song. And Kern was not keen on it. While its refrain starts with the cool sumptuousness of Lehár, a tendency in the later Kern toward cloying chromaticisms soon becomes apparent, first in the swooning melodic descents (compare "The Song Is You") and then in the cycle-of-5ths harmonies (notably at "Wonder of all the world"), though the originality of the form compensates for this when the second half of the refrain begins an octave higher than the first.

Scene 8, back on the levee beside the show boat the following morning, is a classic central finale—that is, a wedding is about to take place and halfway through the celebrations a character rushes onstage to announce an impediment. That character is Parthy, accompanied by Pete and Vallon, but when, on the augmented 6th antepenultimate chord of "Can't Help Lovin' Dat Man," she denounces Ravenal as a murderer, Vallon is forced to admit that he got off on self-defense. Andy admits that even he killed a man when he was nineteen, and this is too much for Parthy, who for the first time in her life faints. "Good! Now we can go on with the wedding!" is Andy's response. Intriguingly, the underscoring during his own revelation is "Make-believe," leaving us to wonder whether he made the story up on the spot or was indeed making believe all those years with Parthy by not telling her about it. As Kern's reprise finalettos go, this one is neither particularly developed nor particularly noteworthy. It begins with the customary new music (a gossip chorus for the village guests whom Andy has invited as good for business), reprises Magnolia's piano theme against distant bells for Andy's proclamation, offers a new waltz, "Happy the Day," for the chorus, with a good deal more *Schwung* than "You Are Love," and keeps the shuffle ethos to the fore with its reprise of "Can't Help Lovin' Dat Man" framing a buck-and-wing dance. The latter offers the cakewalk rhythm yet again. Resuming the journey to the church after Parthy's interruption, the crowd makes sure that prior to "You Are Love" as instrumental coda, "Can't Help Lovin' Dat Man" gets heard one more time.[67]

Show Boat—Act II

With only 30 percent of the score remaining, act 2 is highly problematic. Much of what follows its promising beginning, however powerful dramatically, is frankly musical kitsch, either by Kern or in the form of imported period songs complementing those for the act 1 melodramas. *The Play Pictorial* felt the need to comment on this at Drury Lane in 1928: "To an 'old timer' like myself it was strange to hear one of the waltz tunes of my youth being sung, but there it was, 'After the ball is over.'"[68] Ferber's novel has a similar structure of attenuated narrative as the years stretch out after the central climax of Magnolia's wedding, but the proportions are more balanced (ten chapters before, nine following).

It starts well enough, however, for the 1st Barker's ballyhoo inevitably reminds us of Queenie's (though the actual motif is different) and raises hopes of musical parallelisms across the acts. These are furthered when other barkers vie for attention in recitative: this is operatic writing similar to the rejected opening of act 1 scene 3. The setting is the World's Fair, a venue barely mentioned by Ferber. The Midway Plaisance setting, with the famous Ferris wheel in the background, makes for a fine dramatic portal, a production number concentrating as much color and abundance onto the stage as did act 1 scene 1. Not that the music itself is anything special, with its choral continuum, its generic 2/4s, and old-fashioned 3/8 (compare the opening of *Sally* as well as that of many an English comic opera)—until the refrain, "When the Sports of Gay Chicago," yanks the writing back to a modern showbiz focus with something of a jolt. The "Hootchy Kootchy Tune" is inserted for the oriental Fatima's dance, first of the many act 2 interpolations.[69]

Ravenal and Magnolia are living in Chicago; Parthy and Andy are visiting them. Originally this opening scene drew on the novel to explore some of the seriousness behind these appearances and circumstances when it included the brothel madam Hetty Chilson, meeting Ravenal, who is clearly familiar with her ladies, on the Plaisance and offering to lend him money when he loses badly on a race at the fair. His anticipation and concealed dejection framed, with nice irony, a segment in which Andy tried to show the barkers how to ballyhoo by exhibiting Parthy as "Sober Sue—try an' make her laugh!" This turned into a song, "Cheer Up!," eventually quarried instead for "I Might Fall Back on You." But later versions of the script simply have Ravenal win, which leads without irony into "Why Do I Love You?" One can see why Kern took such trouble over the melodic motif of this song (see chapter 1 for its genesis), for it is one of the show's hits—very much an act 2 counterpart to "Make-believe" in its candor—and has to bear virtually the entire burden of freshness and then repetition as the act 2 novelty.[70] The refrain is durable enough, with its classic "tonal answer" sequence in the B section, its single cross-rhythm, and a repetitive role for the head motif, and the tune can bear the six and a half statements it receives (one of them as a waltz), though higher praise eludes it. But after the second refrain, awash with banjo jollity and sung by the chorus, its meaning subtly changes. An *arioso* interlude shows Ravenal eager to return to his gambling—one can imagine with what result. "I'll come home as early as I can," he sings, to the tune of "Can't Help Lovin' Dat Man," whose original words were "He can come home as late as can be." The refrain returns, but he exits after singing the first two bars. Magnolia is left alone to continue blithely with "Why do you love me?" Yet, as in the novel, the anguish is more ours than hers: she accepts his "business," and they do still love each other. There is grimmer irony in Parthy and Andy singing those same words when their turn with the refrain comes.

The irony in the scene's remaining number, "Dahomey," is lighter and involves black people passing not for white but for black, since the "Colored chorus," which performs this song and dance, here demonstrates another level of "make-believe." Pretending to be a live ethnographic exhibit of Dahomeyans, they are really a group of New Yorkers dressed, or rather undressed, for the part and as keen to be "Back in old New York / Where your knife an' fork / Gently sink into juicy little chops what's made of pork!" as their onlookers (the "White chorus") are keen not to become a "spearful" for these savages, who are, in more senses than they realize, "acting vicious."

The next scene, set a decade later in a dingy Chicago boardinghouse, has nothing light about it and centers the act 2 narrative. Frank and Ellie, now variety artists at Chicago's Trocadero music hall (vaudeville being all the rage at this date), are looking for lodgings. Magnolia is about to be evicted because of Ravenal's gambling debts, and her pretense with her old friends gives way when his desertion letter is handed to her by the landlady's maid. The emotional crux of *Show Boat* but played entirely without music except for underscoring of "Why Do I Love You?" while Ellie reads the letter to Magnolia, it is at the same time another scene worthy of a *Cotton Blossom* melodrama and thereby balances the miscegenation drama of act 1. Simultaneous with this action and again highly pathetic, but this time with emotional release in music, scene 3 takes place at St. Agatha's Convent, where Ravenal is saying farewell to Kim.[71] Now it is "Make-believe" that is pressed into ironic service, as Kim, taken out of her class procession for a few moments, prompts her father to sing it to her once again as his panacea and her motto (and a fine panacea it has proved, Parthy would no doubt say). If this seems in dubious taste, the scene's musical hand-me-downs are more so.

"Captain Andy" is turned into a processional at the start and counterpointed clumsily with the "Te Deum" which the girls sing after a rather more tasteful "Alma Redemptoris Mater"—most of this is not in the Welk score, and the entire scene was evidently omitted from the Drury Lane production. Similar treatment is meted out to Magnolia's piano theme, which follows as part of the "Te Deum." The cello *melo* that underscores Kim's conversation with her father has musical integrity but feels stylistically out of place. Another operatic phantom, it could almost be from Jules Massenet.

Kern treats juxtapositions of taste and genre defiantly by running the music straight into the next scene with "The Washington Post." Originally, however, a further book scene intervened, closely based on the novel and tying up the business with Hetty Chilson when Magnolia discovers from whom Ravenal got his parting gift. This is where Julie was supposed to have reappeared, in Chilson's brothel. No doubt this was too strong for Ziegfeld, and her descent into alcoholism rather than prostitution was substituted.[72]

In the statutory scene 4 Julie sings "Bill," imported from *Oh, Lady! Lady!!*, in rehearsal atop a piano and must be credited with turning it into a torch song, which it never was, more by association of character and plot than through the lyrics, which do not fit the genre or her situation (deserted by Steve) at all. It is odd she was not given a blues, though it would have been anachronistic in a variety performance in 1904; but "Out There in an Orchard," which "Bill" replaced, would have had period veracity at the expense of emotional resonance with the 1927 show audience. "Bill" was the best compromise, for it suited Helen Morgan perfectly.[73] This scene is *about* music, and the later reaches of *Show Boat*, as the story's chronological shadows lengthen, take on the idea of music standing for the passing of time, mores, fashion, and ways of life. From the start it was a "backstage" musical, but vaudeville rather than melodrama takes over as the metaphor, just as urban survival takes over from rigid community values in the plot.

Originally Hammerstein had Magnolia audition a spiritual and then "the song Ravenal sang to her at the water-barrel"; this would have been the "Creole Love Song."[74] But the song in *Show Boat* that ended up emblematizing American history, from the slow rural south of the nineteenth century to the frantic urban north of the twentieth, was "Can't Help Lovin' Dat Man." Magnolia's faltering attempt at jazzing it up in the audition is one of the most memorable moments in the musical, even if it never quite rings stylistically true, perhaps because built as much around Frank's hoofing as Magnolia's singing. But the *Show Boat* scene is also about Julie, and her role is metaphorically fulfilled here far better than in the novel: by walking out on the show after recognizing Magnolia and her plight, she has not only taught Magnolia her song but handed her her act. This is a culturally transformative, and transformed, America in the making, the very sound of diasporic ingredients being thrown into the melting pot.

Scene 5 was another set-changer they could cut in 1946 and simply prepared Andy's appearance at the Trocadero, where in scene 6 on New Year's Eve 1904 he saves Magnolia's debut in front of a restive audience by giving her confidence midsong from the floor. The opening choral number to this scene, with its daring dominant-preparation curtain (it sounds like Jean Sibelius), was cut in rehearsal, though it soon resurfaced as "Long Live Our Nancy" in *Blue Eyes*. Daring it may be, but it would have introduced only a variety scene of old numbers ("Apache Dance," "Good Bye, My Lady Love," and "After the Ball") in which Kern's voice drops out completely, though his "How'd You Like to Spoon With Me?" replaced "Goodbye, My Lady Love" at some point in the Drury Lane run.[75] *Show Boat*'s integrity is no further helped when it leaps, straight from this musical mishmash, a further twenty-three years to 1927 (that is, the present) for scene 7. Yet another scene before the curtain, this comprises yet another reprise of "Ol' Man River," performed again by Joe, now aged (although curiously able to sing it a semitone higher), plus a new ballyhoo for the reinvented Queenie: "Hey, Feller!" This is a fine number, unmistakably like Gershwin in its oscillating imperfect cadences and its cross-rhythms (though the latter are speeded-up versions of "Niggers all work on the Mississippi"), and it does *Show Boat* a disservice it can ill afford by not appearing in the Chappell and Welk scores.

The problem with *Show Boat*'s ending stems from three factors. The first is its sheer compression, too much time, detail, and musical continuity having been expended on the early parts of the show. Neither Kern nor Hammerstein knew how to write an opera, in which all dramatic lines have to be radically simplified and distilled into purely musical spans in an epic plot. By contrast, the second act of *Show Boat* suggests frantic foreshortening at every turn. Magnolia the mature professional is never shown directly in action; this is also true of the novel, in which some of the same problems of proportion and sustainability are evident. The second factor is the very principle of adapting a musical from a novel, for, unlike certain operas, in which the characters have more self-sufficient musical scenes, musicals do not respond well to having too many of their leading characters killed or pensioned off before the end. The New Year's Eve scene could not have occurred in the novel because Andy was already dead; still less scene 8, in which Andy, now eighty-two, has met up by chance with Ravenal, now sixty-five, on his new *Cotton Blossom*. (The early script has Andy fall into the river and be fished out by Ravenal immediately prior to this, a blatant happy-ending version of the fate he meets with in the novel.) Ravenal's reunion with the sixty-year-old Magnolia rings sentimentally false, despite the irony of the Old Lady's innocent comments about their happy marriage; and his one last opportunity for a top B flat when he partially reprises "You Are Love" to himself the night before he meets her only draws attention to the fact. Hammerstein himself was never entirely happy with the scene, and one is likely to side with Parthy for once when she takes one surprised look at him in the early script and says to Andy, in Ravenal's presence, "You pick him to save you — the man that deserted your own daughter —." In the 1946 script they are kept well out of each other's way. Letting Andy lecture Ravenal on where he went wrong hardly compensates.[76]

The third and most important factor is the circumstantial mess of a final song for Kim. Played as a woman by the actress playing Magnolia, her quick change of costume necessitates the juggling of the final short scenes. Kim's influence on her family and surroundings as a successful 1920s actress is built into the script: "Hey, Feller!" is Queenie's response to having been given a flapper dress by her in the 1927 version, while in 1946 Parthy is the one modishly decked out by her granddaughter. But it was never securely built into the score.

Four songs were written for this culmination of the family saga. The first is the most integral, "It's Getting Hotter in the North," with modern jazz scoring (high improvisatory clarinets in particular) and Kern's blues features — flatward harmonies, a persistent four-beat stomp, insistent melodic repetition. Crucially, it is built on Magnolia's piano theme. McGlinn is very persuasive in his assessment of its importance: "It should come as a great shock to the audience to see Kim (and Parthy!) in flapper dresses, and to hear Kim belt out a raucous jazz number. This 'hot' music clashes violently with the rest of the score, and that is the point . . . life goes on. . . . Norma Terris, the original Magnolia, barely remembered it, recalling only that she didn't want to sing it. Kern should have insisted."[77] But it is a difficult number for the actress who has been playing Magnolia to sing (as McGlinn's recording demonstrates), it can become musically irritating, and one hesitates to burden *Show Boat* with its additional length. Nevertheless, it was what Kern meant, if a similar musical ploy at the end of *Music in the Air* is anything to go by. The second song was Norma Terris's substitute, "Kim's Imitations [of leading entertainers]," her vaudeville speciality, based on "Why Do I Love You?" Irene Dunne, who took over the role on the national tour, changed this to a "hot-jazz chorus of 'Why Do I Love You?,'" heard on the McGlinn recording. It follows "the way my mother used to sing it," as Kim explains to her audience—but all she does is sing it twice as fast (the jazz occurs in the dance break), and we have already heard this ploy once in act 2. Third came "Dance Away the Night," written for Drury Lane. This perhaps best captures the nonstop dancing spirit of the twenties but is incorrigibly European, an Eric Coates schottische of charm as well as vitality—Kern must have had *Blue Eyes* far more on his mind than *Show Boat* when he wrote it. Finck took it at a breathtaking pace on the 1928 recording, which it needs, but the words are impossible to sing and the dotted rhythms almost impossible to play at that speed; McGlinn, much slower, cherishes the detail but makes it sound more like a village-hall social than a flapper rave and has to speed up for the central section. Finally there is "Nobody Else But Me" for Jan Clayton to sing in the 1946 New York revival, the last Broadway song Kern composed. It includes enough of the dainty dotted rhythms of "Dance Away the Night" to suggest that that vision of Kim's essence corresponded more with Kern's ongoing imagination than "It's Getting Hotter in the North," while allowing for another extended dance break after the song, this time focusing on the Charleston. Yet none of these four songs stuck, and by the time of the 1962 script (and indeed the Welk score) the fifth ending was in place, in which Kim had no song at all and was "reduced to nothing more than a silhouette seen an instant before the final curtain."[78]

For the future, the meaning of *Show Boat* will change according to which of these five endings it adopts or which further alteration is made. It may choose the heartlessness of "It's Getting Hotter in the North," from which Kern's own sensibilities seem to bow out as author; or personify the vaudevillian aesthetic of "Thrills and laughter, / Concert after"; or continue to woo its audiences as an escapist musical with a happy ending. These three possibilities remain consonant with Hollywood's dictates, already looming large over the entire enterprise in 1927 and, as I argue in chapter 5, helping *Show Boat* find its most satisfying version. It may, on the other hand, prefer to retain the charm and vitality of Broadway or the West End as its culminating sound. But it will never mean a unified, balanced score in any one genre, be it operetta or musical comedy, still less a properly consolidated stage hybrid, which it took Kern several more years to produce.

The Cat and the Fiddle as Boudoir Operetta

Their first brush with Hollywood, with *Men of the Sky* in 1930, had a profound impact on Kern, Harbach, and Hammerstein. Hammerstein retired to lick his wounds and write for the stage more slowly and carefully; the result was *Music in the Air*. Kern and Harbach, having used a tune as the fulcrum of a spy plot in *Men of the Sky*, decided to return the principle to Broadway (where it had been nascent in "Can't Help Lovin' Dat Man" from *Show Boat*) and extend it so that an entire show would be based around diegetically motivated music; the result was *The Cat and the Fiddle*, their next collaboration and Kern's next musical after *Men of the Sky*. It had been Harbach's idea: "I said, 'I'm going to write a story in which the score will be fighting each other,'" he told his son.[79]

The young Max Gordon was fresh from success as producer of *The Band Wagon* when Kern, via Max Dreyfus, summoned him to Bronxville. After a lengthy dinner at Dreyfus's house, "one of those typical German repasts that seemed to go on for hours," Kern took Gordon aside and announced, "I am thinking . . . in terms of another musical which, like *Show Boat*, would attempt to explore new paths. I think the American public is ready to accept musical theatre that is more than routine claptrap. *Show Boat* has encouraged me to think that it is possible to work artistically and with greater integrity in the medium than may have been imagined. Otto has an idea for a musical that I think lends itself to serious treatment. You should know that we have been talking about eliminating chorus girls, production numbers and formal comedy routines. We are striving to make certain that there will be a strong motivation for the music throughout."[80] Kern and Harbach held to their vision, and the result was Kern's most perfect creation. His idea of an "integrated" musical, of "strong motivation for the music throughout," was not the operatic principle we have come to associate with the term through the Rodgers and Hammerstein shows, that is, characters soliloquizing their innermost thoughts or sharing intimate dialogue unaware that they are singing. Rather, he sought a plot and a treatment in which all the musical performances would be diegetic. "Musical performances" here means not just all the singing but some spectacular piano playing too, while excluding the pit underscoring, which remains subliminal. It was a principle Kern would perfect in *Music in the Air* (see chapter 4), and there are points at which it still seems gauche, far-fetched, and ambiguous in *The Cat and the Fiddle*; but it gives the show unity of structure and tone and an extraordinary dimension of wit and vitality, of genuine music theater in the sense of music being the actual protagonist, in the scenes with the two composers' pianos—the Dykstra/Greenblatt 2 *Pianos 4 Hands* sixty years before its time. It "may be the most integrated musical of all time," Mordden hazards, adding ruefully, "Can a musical be *too* integrated? . . . A full-out recording would . . . [be] an all but impossible task."

The British critics were peculiarly alert to this dimension of *The Cat and the Fiddle* and presumably to the fact that, although the Hollywood musical had already established itself on the same backstage terms—of avoiding all singing that was not "source music," realistic at least in principle—it was another matter to adopt them at twice the length and up to three times the number of songs in the live theater. Several comparisons with recent films were made: *Congress Dances*, René Clair's *Le Million*, Ernst Lubitsch's *The Love Parade* (this last also a song title in *The Cat and the Fiddle*). The London press thus gave thoughtful attention to what Kern and Harbach were trying to do, as well as generous pictorial coverage of Charles Cochran's production. "Here is a musical play of an entirely new sort . . . there is not a note sung or played that is not relevant to the action," one reviewer pronounced. E. A. Baughan of *The Era*, in a rather muddled piece, discussed the whole future of the musical and its relationship to opera, taking *The Cat and the Fiddle* as his starting point: "In 'The Cat and the Fiddle' the hero and heroine are composers, and what they sing is mainly the music they are supposed to be writing or have written. Naturally that does not solve the problem of making musical utterance the natural medium of expression . . . Would it not be possible . . . to treat a story in which the characters were not musicians with a fantasy which would make singing quite natural?" He seemed to want an operatic popular musical theater and would no doubt have been satisfied with Rodgers and Hammerstein, though the purpose of his focus on Kern and Harbach was to shame British composers into emulating them. Most important, the all-powerful James Agate adored *The Cat and the Fiddle* when it came to London five months after its Broadway opening, finding it "the high-water mark of the musical play." Harbach never forgot his praise, recalling it in his deathbed interviews with his son.[81]

The American reception had been less enthusiastic. Possibly the London production was simply superior, and it also seems likely that New York was unwilling to reconsider the necessity for the traditional carnival of elements in a musical: "It was too difficult. No jokes . . . no dancers. The thing didn't even have a dance director. It was put on just like a play," Harbach recalled, though he might have added that the Albertina Rasch Dancers appeared in the act 2 jazz "Phantasy," which began in front of the curtain with "eight girls in grotesque costumes of jazz band playing different instruments." There were practical difficulties, too, at least in the out-of-town tryout. Harbach testified to this, referring to the filmic continuity of underscoring that ties together the songs and their narrative recurrences: "That was the hardest night I ever spent in a theatre . . . Jerry had conceived the idea of writing a full score underneath the dialogue, so that you couldn't hear the dialogue at all on opening night in Philadelphia . . . We did have a row about it. I said, 'Jerry, there's no use in playing the book with that orchestral effect going on. You can't hear a word they're saying.' He said, 'What would you like to do, then? Let's throw it all out.' He was sore, naturally, because the score was the whole thing to him." Harbach also stated that a New York band had to be engaged for the Philadelphia opening: "So intricately was the score woven into the plot, that we couldn't use any [local] band because it would take too long [for them to master it]."[82]

There is an important point underlying this comment, which is that Kern had negotiated with the Musicians' Union for an expert, highly paid band for *The Cat and the Fiddle* below the minimum theater size of twenty. It was his first Broadway run scored for multi-instrument "reed" players— three, in this instance, named Benny, Milton, and Joe on Bennett's manu- scripts—rather than a semisymphonic complement of woodwind, the point being that saxophones came in threes (at least) and were taken up as dou- blings by standard woodwind players. *The Cat and the Fiddle* involving a "jazz" composer in the plot, it needed its saxophones, part of a lineup in- cluding flute, piccolo, oboe, cor anglais, clarinets and bass clarinet, three trumpets (the first Kern show with this triadic provision), trombone, two percussionists, three pianos (one player doubling on celesta), three violins, viola, cello and string bass doubling on tuba. It also needed the idea that the instrumentalists were individuals (they were listed by name as "soloists" in the program) because as minstrels they would reinforce the idea of the show as an essay in *commedia dell'arte*.[83]

As early as 1917 a published interview with Kern had announced, "Of course he is ambitious, and chief among his plans for the near future is the writing of a pantomime, similar to 'Pierrot the Prodigal.' 'I have the idea for it and the offer to produce it,' he says, 'and although the critics will prob- ably jump on me and tell me to go back to my musical comedy tunes I am going to go through with it.'"[84] *Pierrot the Prodigal* was a French pantomime with music on the story of the Prodigal Son which ran on Broadway in 1916–17. One surmises that Kern never composed such a work (though see chapter 4) but tried instead "to go through with it" with singing in the act 1 diegetic operetta of *The Bunch and Judy*, "Love Finds a Way," set among the nobility at the Venice carnival of around 1770 and actually a play-within-a-play-within-a-play as these characters mask tragically, very much as in *Pagliacci*. As we have seen, *commedia dell'arte* surfaces again momentarily in *Sitting Pretty*, but it was not until *The Cat and the Fiddle* that Kern successfully pursued his Harlequin operetta, where it appears as *The Passionate Pilgrim*, the new musical theater "play" in production in Brussels and composed by the serious, ambitious Rumanian composer Victor Florescu, hero of Kern's musical.

The Passionate Pilgrim, portions of whose music, instrumental and sung, we hear five times during the course of the action, sets the tone for *The Cat and the Fiddle*, more than can be said of Bruno's operetta in *Music in the Air*, and it is important to appreciate the background to that tone. Kern and Harbach wanted to write a musical about music, rather than about drama as in *Show Boat*: specifically, about the struggle between European classical and American popular music, timely to say the least in 1931, as embodied in the two composers, Victor and the young American woman he falls in love with, Shirley Sheridan. (If it seems daring that they should have depicted a female popular composer—clearly a kind of Kay Swift—think of the alternatives! In any case, Herbert's *The Only Girl* had featured a female composer as early as 1914.)

The Cat and the Fiddle is set in the present and the emphasis throughout, despite its opening on the crumbling quais of Brussels, is on up-to-dateness. For a Broadway audience in October 1931 one aspect of contemporaneity had to be reference to hard times. This is carefully built into the script and the plot, for Angie and Alec clearly need work in Europe, are living on a shoestring supported by Shirley (which is why she cannot afford to alienate the producer Daudet), and all three have left behind a dysfunctional America. Alec says of the night he first met his wife, "I'd delivered some bonds to a bank there [in Albany]—bonds were worth delivering in those days—guess I shouldn't have given up that job, Angie!" Shirley, for her part, admits to Daudet as he is preparing to seduce her that she comes from "just a typical [American] family. Mother is living with her second husband on Long Island and Father is now a clerk in a brokerage firm where he used to be Vice-president," which helps us understand her need for and attraction

Ex. 3.5. *The Passionate Pilgrim.*

toward the security he represents as well as her independence and courage in standing him up a few moments later.[85]

Shirley's music is up-to-date in the commercial manner of American popular music—hence the saxophones and "three trumpet sound" in the orchestra, which can be heard on an electrifying recording of the entr'acte by the original London theater band and its conductor, Hyam Greenbaum.[86] Yet a contrasting angular modernism for Victor's music would have alienated the Broadway audience and, more important, rendered it unsusceptible to commercial modification by Shirley once his defenses are down. It might also have positioned its starting point too close to jazz, which is Shirley's province. The solution was to present Victor's music as pastel neoclassicism of a highly Gallic cast. (Presumably the musical was placed in Brussels rather than Paris simply to avoid too hackneyed a setting, but most of the terms of reference, including frequent dialogue in French, proved interchangeable.) The salon style of Gabriel Fauré or Reynaldo Hahn is frequently invoked, as can be seen from example 3.5, the first music by Victor we hear in actual performance (it opens the portion of *The Passionate Pilgrim* witnessed at the end of act 1); it could be from a Fauré barcarolle. This abuts Kern's own idiom well enough, which although basically conservative offers elsewhere in the score the illusion of contemporaneity through odd touches such as the parallel triads for "The Crystal Candelabra" (a series of diegetic tinklings in the interstices of the phrases of "The Love Parade") and the momentary bitonality and jazzy riffs of Victor's nightmare fantasy.

The pastel neoclassicism is reflected in the art deco covers of the published songs and the Chappell piano/vocal score (see fig. 3.2). Sheet music covers were by the 1930s being recognized as part of the overall style package of a musical and were signed accordingly: this one is by "jorj" (Ben Jorj Harris), who also created the artwork for "Ev'ry Little While" and *The Cat and the Fiddle*'s idiomatic sequel, *Roberta*.[87] One of the reasons *The Cat and the Fiddle* was so well received in Britain will have been because this soft modernism (if it can be said to relate to modernism at all), affectionately rather than detachedly neoclassical, had for ten years or more been a staple of such scenic, graphic, and production designers as Rex Whistler, Nigel Playfair, and indeed C. B. Cochran. Agate understood this Gallic context and accordingly had no difficulty in linking *The Cat and the Fiddle*'s London production with the *fête galante* as well as with French film: "The atmosphere was that of Henri Murger with some slight infusion of the modern film, the old story of Pierrot and Pierette in the atmosphere of René Clair-de-lune. The scenery, a great deal of which had been painted on velvet in order to give depth to the shadows, was wholly delightful, and suggested with amusing discrepancy both Fragonard and Vlaminck."[88]

The show's links with American cinema are important, too, for it forms part of the canon of what has come to be known as "boudoir operetta," a genre contemporaneous with the Depression and epitomized by the four film musicals starring Maurice Chevalier and Jeanette MacDonald, *The Love Parade* (1929), *One Hour with You* (1931), *Love Me Tonight* (1932), and *The Merry Widow* (1934), three of them directed by Lubitsch, who invented the genre, the fourth, *Love Me Tonight*, by Rouben Mamoulian. It seems remarkable that *The Cat and the Fiddle*, itself filmed by MGM in 1933 with Ramon Novarro and MacDonald, appeared on stage after only the first of these classics. *Roberta*, surely a fifth, was filmed by RKO in 1935, but by then the Hays Code on film morality had been stringently enforced, and the genre shifted toward the all-American wholesomeness of Astaire and Rogers, which necessitated changing its plot emphasis. By contrast, boudoir operettas were appreciated "because they were concerned with glamorous people in glamorous locales far from the troubled shores of the United States, because they offered moviegoers something a bit spicier than the ordinary domestic product." In fact *The Cat and the Fiddle* is not quite the same, generically speaking, as the Lubitsch operettas because it lacks Chevalier's straight-to-camera soliloquizing, his ascertainable philanderings, his wealth or courting of wealth and class, the frothy morality, and

Fig. 3.2. *The Cat and the Fiddle*, sheet music cover art.

the double entendres, for "Nobody's Using It Now" from *The Love Parade* is of a different order of sexual innuendo from "She Didn't Say 'Yes,'" even though "she" admits she did not want "to travel all the way with him." In their place, Harbach offered passionate anger and jealousy from both leads, a more *verismo* social context (including violent swearing in French from both Odette and Victor), and an earnestness which critics found short on humor. Nevertheless, *The Cat and the Fiddle* shares with boudoir operettas its European locale, with places and events where you can drink, liberal use of the French language or at least a French accent, sophisticated bedroom politics without a trace of farce, classic jealousies with interlocking triangles, strong, determined heroines, picturesque scenes of city apartments, a brisk pace and concentrated period of action, a good deal of prurience on the part of secondary characters (which the audience is thereby invited to share), a fondness for eccentric cameo roles, and a general determination to make the music's contribution efficient, witty, and urbane. It was a little too risqué for the British censor, who insisted that "the words 'He's had her' . . . [be] omitted."[89] The British critics did not care, either, for the dressing room scene which builds toward the revelation that the flowers sent to Alec, clearly not above suspicion as he sprays himself with Angie's perfume, are from a male admirer. One after another objected to this.

The Cat and the Fiddle — The Story and Its Music

The plot of *The Cat and the Fiddle* concerns the test of fidelity and jealous misunderstanding that Victor and Shirley have to weather in order to mature and earn each other's trust and love. Unlike those in farce, the obstacles in this boudoir operetta are not mechanically imposed from the outside but boil down to whether Shirley has slept with the producer Daudet; everything hinges on this. Victor and Shirley meet—they are both studying at the conservatoire—and fall in love along the quais as Shirley's brother Alec, her self-appointed but ineffectual protector, is off looking for his wife, Angie. Alec and Angie, the comic couple, constantly bickering, are a hopeful popular dance team. Shirley has to go to Paris to visit her music publisher; she and Victor agree to write to each other, but Victor's absentminded colleague Biddlesby, who is translating his libretto into French, loses the letter from Shirley announcing a change of address, so further correspondence and the nascent romance fail. On her return, Shirley, together with Angie and Alec, by chance takes lodgings opposite Victor. Her music, though he doesn't know it is hers, drives him crazy while he is rehearsing *The Passion-ate Pilgrim* with his leading lady, Odette (a violin-playing Pierrot), who is jealous of his affections though she has an admirer in Major Chatterly. The producer Clément Daudet enters and tells Victor he cannot stage his play unless it is lightened: Shirley's tunes wafting across the courtyard are the sort of leavening he wants. Victor refuses to write trash, and Daudet declines to proceed with *The Passionate Pilgrim*, though Odette assures Victor that Chatterly liked what he heard and will reverse the decision, since she has influence with him and he is putting up the money.

In Shirley's apartment, a couple of days later, Daudet is about to arrive, having made enquiries about her. They play up to him because Alec and Angie need a break, and when Shirley admits to having written a personal torch song ("Try to Forget") he sees his chance to court her. An offer for the three of them with a generous royalty advance follows, Shirley to act as song interpolator for Victor's musical play, Angie and Alec to appear in it as a dance novelty. When Shirley is told by Daudet that Victor is infatuated with Odette she agrees to the deal, not knowing that Odette already sees she had better look elsewhere than Victor (for Biddlesby has told her about the un-known new woman). Act 1 concludes at the end of Victor's out-of-town try-out in Louvain, when Shirley, Alec, and Angie are brought on stage to begin rehearsing their interpolations immediately. Victor sees Shirley, and Odette tells him she is Daudet's new flame. Victor is hurt, and Shirley notices.

Act 2 begins shortly after this at the postperformance party in Daudet's apartment. Shirley, tired and emotional, is recuperating in the bedroom. The guests depart, leaving Daudet to the expected conquest. Shirley enters to find herself alone with Daudet. She makes it clear that she respects Vic-tor's work and would rather not tamper with it and manages to make her escape, under cover of one of her own songs on the gramophone, by invei-gling Daudet into the bedroom without her. The following morning Victor and Biddlesby are working on a new song when Shirley enters to apologize for the previous night's humiliation. The central love scene follows. It is cast in the form of Shirley's gently showing Victor how he can Americanize his tunes without violating them; they begin to work together. No sooner has she left—she makes him get back to his work—than Odette enters, certain that Shirley has slept with Daudet the previous night and in possession of the lyrics to one of her love songs, which Odette associates with Daudet. Victor, in a blind rage, forces her to leave, driven into a mad fantasy by the continuing sound of Shirley's piano.

Two weeks later, the Brussels opening of *The Passionate Pilgrim* is a triumph—everyone admits that the interpolations have improved it—but Victor has not been seen. Shirley acts disappointed but appears not to suspect new misunderstandings (this is a weak point in the plot). Daudet, in a further attempt to win her for himself, throws a supper party in her honor at the restaurant below her lodgings, during which Odette learns from Major Chatterly that she was mistaken about Shirley's virtue, and he learns that Odette had misled Victor. Victor, drunk on returning to his lodgings, appears at the table to sing bitterly some of his own Pierrot score, aimed at Shirley. He and Shirley argue: "I only did what I could to keep *your* play unchanged," she insists, but he implies she was unfaithful, whereupon Daudet forces Odette to tell Victor she had lied to him. A speedy reconciliation brings down the curtain.

The Cat and the Fiddle, whose published score perfectly matches the British Library script, offers the poise, balance, and achievement of a single authentic version which *Show Boat* lacked.[90] Its action takes place in four concentrated time periods: the opening scene on "a night in July," when Victor and Shirley meet; scenes 2–4 of act 1 when she returns from Paris four weeks later and Victor's Pierrot play is going into rehearsal; the end of act 1 and first four scenes of act 2 five weeks after this, at the Louvain premiere; and the remaining three scenes of act 2 two weeks later at the Brussels premiere. The music too is concentrated into substantial blocks of material, each one, and, more important, the cross-references between them, more fluid, continuous, and intricate in construction than anything yet accomplished by Kern.

The first of these blocks throws down a cinematic gauntlet from the opening of scene 1 on the quai with its nine pages of underscoring, diegetic vendors' ditties, and five or six orchestral motifs, which are all heard before a real song, the chansonnier Pompineau's "The Night Was Made for Love," makes its appearance. Even after this the music remains continuous for another eight pages, past the first rendition of "She Didn't Say 'Yes'" and almost to the end of the scene. This musical streetscape is stylistically much less sophisticated than Gershwin's *An American in Paris* but in some ways comparable to "Paris Awakes" from Gustave Charpentier's opera *Louise*, which also has its romantic street singer. It is complemented by seven further set pieces across the score, five of them, as already mentioned, portions of Victor's Pierrot operetta, the sixth the fugal piano duel that erupts after the rehearsal in his apartment and is reprised in the entr'acte (there was no overture), and the seventh the jazz "Phantasy" counterbalancing this in act 2. Interspersed with these set pieces and sometimes included within them (as in "She Didn't Say 'Yes'" and "The Night Was Made for Love") are the show's eight songs (ex. 3.6), most of them hit material: the two just mentioned, "The Love Parade," "The Breeze Kissed Your Hair," "Try to Forget," "A New Love Is Old," "One Moment Alone," and "Hh! Cha Cha!"; to these one might add Alec and Angie's dance, musically retained though vocally cut (as the song "Don't Ask Me Not to Sing") before reuse in *Roberta*. This is the same balance between foregrounded songs and subliminal, extended musical sections that would be found in most Hollywood musicals. *The Cat and the Fiddle* thereby straddles the stage and screen genres profitably, making it all the more regrettable that the MGM film adaptation changed so much. All five act 1 songs and part of the fugue find reasonable occasion for reprise in act 2, which also adds three new ones. Two of these, "A New Love Is Old" and "One Moment Alone," rewritten by Shirley from part of Victor's Pierrot music in act 1, cement exactly the intensity of feeling required to keep the act concentrated and directional. Only "Hh! Cha Cha!" is substandard, harmonically and melodically uninspired because for some reason it feels the need to run "Why Do I Love You?" from *Show Boat* in counterpoint the second time through.

The motivic material of *The Cat and the Fiddle* divides up neatly into a number of themes for the city and a somewhat larger number, roughly eight or nine each, for Shirley and Victor. Example 3.6 shows the main themes, though others appear and occasionally recur. Both the street music and Victor's themes, all of them except the first (his sad love motif) ostensibly from his own compositions, are noticeably Gallic. The "Love Parade" march, before its main theme, is reminiscent of the urchins' entrance in act 1 of *Carmen* and accompanies a comparable streetscape. Victor's themes are full of nonchalant *rataplan* rhythms—eighth notes in groups of two and four fluidly placed but never syncopated (see "The Breeze Kissed Your Hair" and the sixth and seventh bars of "Poor Pierrot"). When combined with a strong bass line and a quick, persistent offbeat eighth note accompaniment, as in "Poor Pierrot," these are pure Fauré (ex. 3.7). Victor's waltzes are also decidedly French, and when we first hear him at his piano these form a continuous stock of melodies, like a suite, with rhythmic founts far from the impoverished waltz-song patter Kern had frequently relied on in his earlier musicals; the hemiola of Pierrot's waltz (see ex. 3.6 [xix]) demonstrates the point. This is almost a resumption of the musical continuity attempted in

a) Brussels street themes

(i) (Street vendors)

(ii) (Dandy)

(iii) (The Night Was Made for Love, refrain)

(iv) (The Night Was Made for Love)

(v) (The Love Parade, march)

(vi) (The Love Parade)

b) Shirley's (and American) themes

(vii) (Shirley's love theme)

(viii) (She Didn't Say "Yes")

(ix) (Try to Forget, verse)

(x) (Shirley's blues)

(xi) (Shirley's novelty number)

(xii) (Try to Forget, refrain)

(xiii) (Alec and Angie's dance, refrain)

(xiv) (Alec and Angie's dance, verse)

(xv) (Hh! Cha Cha!)

c) Victor's (and Pierrot) themes

(xvi) (Victor's love theme)

(xvii) (Flirtation waltz)

(xviii) (One Moment Alone)

(xix) (Pierrot's waltz)

(xx) (Victor's piano waltz)

(xxi) (The Breeze Kissed Your Hair)

(xxii) (Fugue)

Ex. 3.6. *The Cat and the Fiddle*, themes.

act 1 of *Oh, I Say!*, and its later offspring includes the "Derby Day" music in *Three Sisters*.

Shirley's music has to be catchy, rhythmically infectious, and annoyingly insistent. This applies to all her themes except the first, heard initially when she enters in scene 1, which again is the only one not diegetic—that is, not a tune she is supposed to have written—and represents her capacity for love. It really belongs to them both as a couple, for she is the positive force in the relationship against Victor's more passive wistfulness represented by his own theme. As if to prove this, it enters Victor's consciousness and becomes the coda of his Pierrot song "The Breeze Kissed Your Hair," among his first music written after meeting her, where it proceeds to further music that had been in Victor's head when he met Shirley, the "Flirtation Waltz," his Pierrot song "One Moment Alone," and an earnest further waltz motif (score, pp. 67–69). Most of Shirley's tunes are syncopated and have striding or stomping piano accompaniments, in one case supporting a "novelty" style very much in the Zez Confrey/Billy Mayerl tradition (see ex. 3.6 [xi]). This is important because in act 2, at last beginning to make inroads into Victor's sensibility, she explains that modernizing his music (as with opening up his life to a partner, we are to understand) is not a matter of negating his integrity or having something alien imposed from the outside. "You could do it so easily yourself . . . it isn't a case of melody, but of rhythm and accent— here, take Pierrot's love song, for instance," she suggests, and transforms his "One Moment Alone" (see ex. 3.6 [xviii]), from *The Passionate Pilgrim*, into a typical Kern blues with melodic cross-rhythm and heavily accented stomp accompaniment (ex. 3.8).[91] Yet she too has been deepened by meeting him, for *her* first subsequent composition is "Try to Forget," probably the show's best tune and a perfect torch song for the soulful Peggy Wood, who sang and

Ex. 3.7. Poor Pierrot.

recorded it in London.[92] Here the music is really not much different from
Victor's except for its fox-trot *Luftpausen* (the rests in bars two and four of
ex. 3.6 [xii]), the slightest hint of cross-rhythm occasioned by the rest at the
beginning of bar three, which throws agogic weight onto the preceding note
("won't *you*"), and its shorter, more cellular phrases, all too encouraging of
Harbach's jejune lyrics, which are the weakest element of *The Cat and the
Fiddle* ("Your day dreams, / Your gay dreams, / Your glad dreams, / Your
mad dreams").

   As in his subsequent Hollywood musicals, it is Kern's popular tunes that
form *The Cat and the Fiddle*'s musical foreground. Those for Pompineau are
splendid, with a sprightly AABA format in "The Love Parade," though with a
good deal of prefatory march material. "The Night Was Made for Love," by
contrast, exhibits a novel form of initial four-bar melismatic refrain prefacing
the main thrust of the melody, a completely non-American, intimate cantilena of some harmonic beauty and rhythmic subtlety. The song is actually
sung in French the first time around, and the cantilena completes twelve
bars before leading back into the refrain.[93] It could afford to be musically dif-

Ex. 3.8. One Moment Alone.

ferent because the role of Pompineau was created by an opera singer, George Meader. "She Didn't Say 'Yes'" is equally unconventional in form, showing Kern in the second half of his career willing to foreshorten refrains just as he had been broadening them in his earlier years. Here, four-bar A and B sections are followed by A_1 in the submediant leading back to an unaltered B (reversing the more normal $ABAB_1$ formula) plus a throwaway four-bar A_1 as coda, making only twenty bars altogether and illustrating the tease of the lyrics, "So what did she do? / I leave it to you, / She did just what you'd do, too"—a thirties update of the gimmick of "Katy-did." In fact we never hear "She Didn't Say 'Yes'" sung complete, a crafty acknowledgment of the hit it could already have become through sheet music and record sales before the production even opened, just as in the story it is already a well-known tune of Shirley's and need therefore only be referred to, not presented fully. On its first appearance its first sixteen bars are shared by Shirley and Pompineau, already in his repertoire as it is; later in scene 1, Angie and Shirley trade it knowingly, stopping at bar twelve. The song's titled slot in the program comes in act 2 when Shirley places a recording of it on Daudet's gramophone after his party, but this is clearly an instrumental version, and she adds her own voice only in bar three and words only in bar five. (All three appearances have different words.) This is the only occasion on which we hear the teasing coda sung. Finally, in the act 2 denouement its first four bars are again sung by Pompineau, quietly to Victor as he observes Shirley's indecision about forgiving him. Here, for the only time, they have a *fête galante* mandolin accompaniment, another fusion of the two protagonists' idioms presaging the final outcome of their encounter. "A New Love Is Old" also shows old- and new-world styles beginning to merge in the narrative and old forms giving way to new in Kern's development. Its sixteen-bar refrain comes before the verse, which is more of a sixteen-bar B section within an ABA whole (hence the shorter refrain). Victor's song includes gentle but persistent melodic syncopation, embedded only in the B section as though he cannot yet bring himself to base a refrain on it or even write a verse/refrain song.

But unlike Hollywood, Broadway also enabled Kern to compose his own musical background in *The Cat and the Fiddle*, those subliminal parts of the score and the larger set pieces referred to earlier. The apex of the latter, as the show's very embodiment of "the score . . . fighting each other," is the battle between the two pianists halfway through act 1. It actually begins with Shirley's pop paraphrase of Edvard Grieg's "Morning," which Victor's well-trained mind transforms loosely into his fugue subject by retrograding the last three notes of Grieg's theme—precisely those he does *not* play when his piano corrects Shirley's through the open windows across the courtyard. (There is a bust of Grieg on Victor's piano. It too, like that of Wagner on Kern's, gets retrograded as Shirley's music insults it.) It is not a very good or a very real fugue, but it makes the musical point exultantly as no other ploy could have done at this moment in the drama. In A major, it comes in the course of things to a surprise pair of accented chords of G major that Shirley tries to correct harmonically to B minor, which indeed would have been more tonally acceptable, though the G major chord harmonizes part of the countersubject on a later appearance against Shirley's dominant pedal point. Shirley finds that the fugue's 1-2-3 motif is also that of her novelty number (see ex. 3.6 [xi]), and she appends this, with residual touches of Grieg, as the battle continues. Added to it in counterpoint are a vocalize by the convent girls across the way and Pompineau's "The Night Was Made for Love" sung ironically as he strolls by on this sunny morning.

Finally, to the Pierrot music. We first hear Victor's waltz suite, taking off from Pierrot's waltz of example 3.6 (xix) as he runs it through on his piano. In the next scene he is rehearsing the same passage with Odette, who plays the melody on her violin as Pierrot; but here it is sixteen bars longer and after a while abandons its earlier course (we do not hear ex. 3.6 [xx]) in order to lead to "One Moment Alone," sung in their love triangle by Pierrot, Harlequin, and Pierrette and in the rehearsal by Victor, Odette, and Constance; this appears to conclude that musical section of *The Passionate Pilgrim*. At the Louvain opening the music heard in the rehearsal is prefaced by a diegetic sung prologue utilizing Victor's fugue subject and presenting "Poor Pierrot," after which it proceeds similarly except that the lyrics—entirely in French—have been added (Biddlesby couldn't find them in the rehearsal) and "The Breeze Kissed Your Hair" is now inserted before "One Moment Alone" (Victor had only just composed it when they were rehearsing), though significantly without most of its appended love motifs. "One Moment Alone" is, however, extended further: it had been sixteen bars in rehearsal, thirty-two when Victor was singing and playing after the rehearsal, and now leads back after the thirty-two to an earlier part of Pierrot's waltz before continuing with a love motif he had sung before as its B section ("One word or two tenderly spoken"; compare pp. 70 and 107 of the score) and ending tragically with Pierrot's death, to music heard nowhere else.

Apart from a small section of the Prologue reprised by the guests at Daudet's party, the next rendition of the Pierrot music is when Shirley, in Victor's apartment, tries to persuade him to lighten its ending. First she realigns "One Moment Alone" from 6/8 to 2/2, as discussed above; this also sees "One word or two tenderly spoken" turned duple, as though Victor, being central European, had been too wedded to endless waltz sequences. Then the convent girls' vocalize intervenes once more, like a larger-scale episode in "One Moment Alone" in order to emphasize that that song's A-section return will now proceed differently—which it does, in a climactic duet passage ("But there's a hope eternal") that returns to 3/4 in a lingering, sumptuous cadence and to a motif first heard at their first meeting (*x* in ex. 3.9; compare pp. 23 and 148 in the score) as they sing it together in improvization. We never hear this in stage performance, but confirmation of its Brussels incorporation comes at the first-night dinner when Victor and Shirley sing it again to each other in reconciliation and to end the score both of *The Passionate Pilgrim* and *The Cat and the Fiddle*. One little extra touch has been added: the convent vocalize is now part of a longer coda. One suspects that a piece of diegetic music that has gone through so

Ex. 3.9. *The Cat and the Fiddle,* final duet.

many meticulous transformations and extensions could not have been accomplished without a firm knowledge of Wagner's similar techniques in the Prize Song of *Die Meistersinger*. And it is the final trio of *Der Rosenkavalier* that comes to mind in the "hope eternal" passage (ex. 3.9). Surely *The Cat and the Fiddle* deserves to be taken as seriously as anything by Kern when these works, all distances kept, are the correlatives.

CHAPTER 4

Mostly Hammerstein

The Memo, the Ambition

O SCAR HAMMERSTEIN IS OF INCALCULABLE IMPORTANCE TO THE history of the American musical—even to the history of America, for a recent critique of *Oklahoma!* calls it "a major work of popular art, developing a collective identity for the USA . . . at an important point in its modern history." But his contribution to the musical between *Show Boat* and *Oklahoma!* is virtually a critical blank, reflecting the gap in the Broadway canon between these two shows, both his. His celebrated New Year greeting in *Variety*, after the success of *Oklahoma!*, dwelt on his failures during those intervening years, and more than most theater and film practitioners he missed the mark as spectacularly as he hit it, his nadir coming perhaps with *Golden Dawn*, which it is difficult to conceive of having opened on Broadway only a month before *Show Boat*. How could such a giant of the lyric stage and screen be so variable?[1]

The simplest answer would seem to be that he lacked formative experience of the tight theatrical unities in either farce or melodrama. The same might be said of Harbach, with whom he collaborated so often and in a manner so undocumented (or at least unresearched) that for all we know they continually dragged each other down. Be that as it may, there is in Hammerstein on the one hand a singular avoidance of musical comedy plots' technical sleight-of-hand, and on the other a distance from *verismo*, the "well-made-play" ethos of a Belasco or a Pinero. One cannot imagine Hammerstein as the librettist for *Tosca*, partly because his overwhelming sympa-

thy for human beings seems to have prevented him from wanting to take
their actions to logical and heartless conclusions. He may have sensed this
and tackled *Carmen Jones*, his signpost to *Oklahoma!*, by way of redress in
1942.[2]

But throughout his uncanonical years he never lacked compensating
motivations and qualities, and even his most problematic work possesses a
defining richness, character, and thrust which we should now rehabilitate
within the long view for a number of reasons. First, those qualities did not
emerge without warning in *Oklahoma!* but were incubated over the preceding years. There is a scene in *High, Wide and Handsome* (1937) in which a
"kissing game" at a barn dance offers the villain, Red Scanlon, the chance
to kiss the heroine, Sally Watterson, lasciviously. The hero, Peter Cortlandt,
intervenes, and a fight breaks out, Grandma Cortlandt urging on her grandson without fear while Sally looks on in anguish. Peter is asked by the sheriff
to leave, but with a clear token of approval. This, of course, is Jud, Curly,
Aunt Eller, and Laurie at the box social and in the kangaroo court—and
Rouben Mamoulian directed both musicals. Second, the recipe for success
in one show may have caused failure in another when the ingredients mixed
less well. Hammerstein took great risks in presenting some of his preoccupa-
tions on the stage. Masculinity was one of them, triumphant in the farmers
and cowboys of *Oklahoma!* but disastrous in *Very Warm for May*, as we shall
see. Another was the sexual power relations between races and classes; this
won immediate and lasting bourgeois acceptance in *South Pacific* and *The
King and I* but has been subjected to a good deal of critical deconstruction
in recent years: one wonders whether in the longer term these shows will
be any safer for posterity than *Three Sisters*. Third, and most important, a
tight consortium of aesthetic ambition bound together Hammerstein, Harbach, and Kern (and Romberg?) over a period of many years. Together they
struggled with new visions for the deployment and meaning of music in the
commercial singing theater, and we cannot assume that a breakthrough attributed to Hammerstein did not originate with one of his partners.

A memo from Kern to Hammerstein offers strong and unexpected evidence on this last account. It is dated 19 May 1933, the date of *Music in the
Air*'s opening night in London. Kern was working on *Roberta* at the time,
or had just finished and was already in London to mull over possible new
projects with Hammerstein (they went to the Derby at Epsom two weeks
later):

Memo for Oscar Hammerstein

At such time as we are reaching in the air for ideas, form of musical play of any texture, viz. grave, gay, satirical, fanciful, sentimental, romantic or frivolous. Briefly, prepare a straight dramatic play, in which speech is presented in the usual way but thoughts are treated musically.

Unlike the O'Neill formula in "STRANGE INTERLUDE," instead of introducing the thought after the spoken line, the thoughts (musical) are reserved for the end of the spoken scene, then, by shrewd manipulation of lights, we retroact and produce the thoughts that induced the spoken scene, or accompanied, or even controverted it. To clarify, the concumnation[3] to be wished performed musically, might conceivably be in direct reverse of the episode as actually first performed.

This device seems to be an improvement over the static condition existent in "LE COQUE [sic] D'OR." It necessitates of course, a duplicate company, plus a group of singers.

These notes are entirely improvized without profound study and may of course, be shot full of holes. As now envisaged, the battery consists of the following: (1) Set of legitimate actors; (2) set of young lithe pantomimists, who play the characters in #1, not as we have seen them but as those in set #1 imagine themselves to be; (3) set of singers, amplifying the small but choice orchestra of virtuosi. The singing group performs from the orchestra pit entirely, unless of course, the action demands say, a building up of a climax in which the stage should be filled. A piece called "BARBARA" occurs to me, in which the beautiful spinster, living alone, yearned for a family of children. This defeated maternal ache preyed upon and finally turned her mind. Her idee fixe permeated her household. Her domestic staff indulged her and at given moments, the lights subtly change, accompanied by the sound of eerie music, and the children of her dreams appeared before us and went through the necessary action. When a resumption to normal balance was required, the lights change to the same mysterious music, and the routine life of the characters proceeded.

JK[4]

What Kern has in mind here is his old responsiveness to pantomime, for he refers to the Met's production of Nikolay Rimsky-Korsakov's *The Golden Cockerel,* performed annually in 1918–21 and 1924–28 and fondly remembered, which used pantomime dancers with singers at the side of the stage. Once again, though, he did not quite get his pantomime but set in motion new configurations of singing, dancing, and symbolic action that led to Hammerstein's later dream ballets, and in this respect the memo changes musical theater history.

Fig. 4.1. Jerome Kern, Oscar Hammerstein II, Liszt(?), and Wagner. Copyright Getty Images.

The idea of subconscious desire being in direct opposition to conscious behavior, or as Kern puts it, thought being opposed to speech, could have stemmed from his understanding of and admiration for Wagner but more likely was related to what he knew of Hammerstein's psyche. Hammerstein had come painfully to terms with marital failure and divorce, with the traffic between dreams and reality, and although he seems not to have availed himself of psychiatry, at least at that juncture, many others of his circle must have done so. The whole topic was in the air in the United States in the 1930s: it was a Freudian age. That the idea of a dream ballet, celebrated in *Oklahoma!* (though found earlier, for instance in *Babes in Arms*) and something of a musical theater cliché by the time of *West Side Story*, reflects this is no great revelation; what has not hitherto been suggested is that Kern played a crucial part in its development, an example, perhaps, of the "part of a theatre composer's job to create for himself the vehicle which he needs for his music," as Kurt Weill later put it.[5] Kern and Hammerstein almost immediately put the idea into action and pursued it in all three of their remaining stage shows. "Mary Dreams" in *Three Sisters* is well on the way to being a dream ballet, with a hero in tights surrounded by choreographed girls, and it was followed by similar conceptions in *Gentlemen Unafraid* and *Very Warm for May*.

It was part of the broader quest for musical meaning in the commercial theater that Kern, Harbach, and Hammerstein, but particularly Kern and Hammerstein, never ceased to pursue. One wonders whether Kern's memo was partly prompted by Baughan's London editorial on *The Cat and the Fiddle* and by Hollywood's fashion for backstage musicals on the assumption that for the general film public all singing had to be diegetic, lest any hint of an operatic aesthetic should alienate the masses. Not everyone approved of the development as transferred to the live theater, one critic lamenting that diegetic music "circumscribes the author's range, for the plot has necessarily to do with music and its makers."[6] Kern was reining in dancing, too. Eventually a performance practice would develop in which singing, dancing, and speaking were all accomplished by one set of "legitimate actors" who were themselves the "young lithe pantomimists." The closest Kern himself got to this was probably with Gene Kelly in *Cover Girl*, but Gypsy Hood in *Three Sisters* was an important precursor, and this show demands careful attention. Meanwhile, another approach to "the problem of making musical utterance the natural medium of expression," as Baughan had expressed it, was already attracting Hammerstein: the traditional dramatic soliloquy.

Operatic though it would inevitably feel, it plays an important role as early as 1929 in *Sweet Adeline*.

Sweet Adeline

Sweet Adeline is an intriguing mess, difficult to appreciate through scarcity and no clear precedence of source material. Its Broadway run in 1929–30 was cut short by the aftermath of the Wall Street crash: "Full of nostalgia and heavy with sentiment, it suddenly became an anachronism." This did not reflect its critical acclaim, and Richard Rodgers for one clearly admired the work. No London production followed, which meant that no piano/vocal score was published: it is the only one of Kern's filmed stage shows to lack one. Neither were there any obvious hit songs. The 1935 Warner Bros. film did not star Helen Morgan, for whom the show had been written, and even the stage audiences and critics seemed not to appreciate its connection with *Show Boat* through her. Only two recordings by a member of the cast were made during the 6½-month run, Morgan's of "Why Was I Born?" and "Don't Ever Leave Me."[7] Worst of all, the plot is unclear, for Hammerstein revised the script at some unknown date, leaving a confusion between versions and characters. Scenes were added and subtracted, numbers shifting position and slotting in and out, Addie's sister's name was variously Nellie or Jennie, and the men rotated around the girls in a bewildering nexus of three-letter identities as Tom, Jim, Dan, Sid, and Gus. In all the versions Adeline loses handsome Tom as the price of stardom and settles for one of the others, the heartbreak and reverses zigzagging through act 2 in a variety of vignettes and outcomes.

This does nothing for Hammerstein's reputation as the creator of the "act 2 problem," that of a plot and score running to seed in a surfeit of sentiment and sequel. Yet the musical interest and quality of *Sweet Adeline* are not in doubt, and its compositional aim is crystal clear in all these versions, more satisfying than that of *Show Boat* for one simple reason: a follow-through of musical coherence, amounting to symphonic focus, in act 2.

As noted in chapter 1, it was recognized at the time that Kern was at a musical crossroads in this, his first American composition after *Show Boat*. Yet as the 1933 memo demonstrates, he was never simply concerned to join up the music and make it into post-Wagnerian music drama, whether as singing in the folk manner of (the later) *Porgy and Bess* or as underscoring in the manner of film music, or even to compose music in new ways; rather, he wanted to find new, logically consistent and sustainable roles and meanings for music within a theatrical presentation. In short, music as the *subject* of *Sweet Adeline* places it firmly and properly between *Show Boat* and *The Cat and the Fiddle.*

This helps explain the use of 1890s popular tunes as *objets trouvés*, at first sight in direct contradiction to the symphonic urge. A musical comedy set in the past was still a novelty in 1929, and to compose songs as pastiches of a period style, as accomplished up to a point in *Oklahoma!* and then wholesale in such later musicals as *The Music Man* and *Follies*, might well have seemed strange to Kern, especially when the period and milieu under review were those of his own youth. What was he supposed to do—revert to his juvenile idiom? His solution was to offset the subliminal music of 1929's viewpoint on 1898 with actual tunes of the period. He had already done this in several numbers and scenes in *Show Boat*, not to mention the choral medleys of Scottish songs in *Blue Eyes*, college songs in *Leave It to Jane*, and various circus numbers in *Head Over Heels* that were routine items in his vaudeville era. The *bricolage* of quotation, borrowing, and cross-reference was a standard feature of American popular song and musical theater with its eternal bugle calls, snatches of Felix Mendelssohn's Wedding March, "Yankee Doodle" instrumental fills, and the like.[8] Kern had perpetrated his fair share of this, mostly in his earlier songs, and he ended up in court for it over "Kalu-a." To us, the culture of automatic quotation seems tiresome, but in the early twentieth century it was as much a fact of musical life on the stage as mother-in-law jokes were in stage humor.

Kern laid his cards on the table as early as the overture in *Sweet Adeline*, which consists of nine period tunes. And in one version of the script the curtain then goes up on a male voice chorus in Schmidt's Beer Garden in Hoboken singing the song "Sweet Adeline" itself. The tune does not seem to have been taken as the basis for any of Kern's own score, though the unidentified seventh theme in the overture shares the rhythm of its refrain. "A Hot Time in the Old Town Tonight" follows before we hear Kern's own first number, "Play Us a Polka, Dot."[9] Other borrowed melodies later in the show include "A Simple Little String" by Lionel Monckton, "Sweet Sixteen," "Pretty Jennie Lee," and whatever Irene Franklin, playing the coon-shouter role of Lulu Ward, chose to include, for she wrote some of her own material. (Kern himself seems to have supplied the music for "My Husband's First Wife.")

"Pretty Jennie Lee" is the most striking instance of extraneous material because it forms the verse of Kern's most symphonic number in the score, "Some Girl Is on Your Mind," explicitly modulating between external, diegetic performance and internal sublimation and allowing the contrast between the two musical styles involved to speak for itself. Or to put it another way, it shows how heard (diegetic) music can act powerfully on individuals' feelings and thoughts, transforming them into something symbolized by nondiegetic music of a very different kind, cast in this case as four soliloquies. The key to the style modulation is the blues, the great unlabeled theme of *Sweet Adeline*, insofar as the show's plot and star, Adeline, epitomize the birth of the torch singer, the girl who goes from innocence to womanhood and learns a vocal style to match, speaking in the process for a nation's experience of growing up (which is why the Spanish-American War is not an arbitrary background in *Sweet Adeline*).[10] This had also been the idea behind *Show Boat*, but it is more musically sustained in *Sweet Adeline* and culminates in this act 2 number. And we are not allowed to forget that Adeline is the daughter of an immigrant, for the "before" as well as the "after" punctuates the score with its periodic reprises and underscore reminiscences of "'Twas Not So Long Ago," sometimes sung in German as "Es war schon damals so." This tune represents Adeline's German father and his passing world and was labeled "Folk Song" in the opening night program. It frames the entire show with a border of innocence, as had "The Land of Let's Pretend" in *The Girl from Utah*. *Sweet Adeline* is a statement about German assimilation and its contribution to American culture (hence about Kern's and Hammerstein's own positions) and must surely have been influenced by *The Jazz Singer*.

It is entirely appropriate, then, that Kern, here as in *Show Boat*, should have adopted the mask of a black idiom to clothe an utterly white, indeed European, solidity of musical expression. In *Show Boat* he accomplished this in "Can't Help Lovin' Dat Man." In "Some Girl Is on Your Mind" and to a partial extent in "Don't Ever Leave Me" the blues similarly mean rich, unrelenting harmonies, the odd melodic flat 7th, 5th, or 3rd underpinned with some form of subdominant substitute, an unfolding and massively building line over a throbbing chordal accompaniment in 4/4, and a syncopated melody expressing its supposedly improvisatory freedom by emphasizing the notes of the tonic triad.[11] "Why Was I Born?" also emphasizes these scale degrees.

"Some Girl Is on Your Mind" is an extraordinary, wonderful number. Three gloomy men are in a saloon, and after listening to a fourth making a

fool of himself singing "Pretty Jennie Lee," the transition from this as verse
to the refrain—the song proper—occurs when one of them offers another
a drink. The musical corollary to this gesture is an added flat 7th that sets
off a bluesy chord sequence in recitative and prepares us for the unforgettable unfolding of a delicate blues line, melody and bass moving outward
from the initial tonic on the word "Why" held over more than a bar in a
kind of sublime sequel (with reversed emotion) to the trick in "Who?" of
only four years earlier. It is this unfolding, rich in suspended dissonance,
that lays down the symphonic claim, though the blues claim comes first, in
an initial A span of twelve bars phrased with a rhyme at bars 4 and 8 and a
third, two-bar line (the title) then repeated in blues fashion. The form developed from this statement is AABA, the eight-bar rising release very similar
to that of "Can't Help Lovin' Dat Man." The symphonic dimension consists
in the fact that when this expansive, forty-four-bar module is repeated (with
chorus), a series of countermelodies accompanies the three A sections: first,
"Pretty Jennie Lee," sung by several of the men, then, at the emotional peak,
eight bars of "Why Was I Born?," sung by Adeline observing them (ex. 4.1),
and finally four bars of the beautiful release of "Here Am I," sung again by
Addie, soaring musically above the ensemble in what can only be described
as an anthem to the power of the torch singer to sustain romantic yearning while focusing male sexual emotion. As such, it sacralizes the American
musical theater star and sanctifies the very genre, an aim left in no doubt as
the postlude (for such it is) blazes forth with a blatant chord of the flat 7th
(the sequence is $^{\flat}$VII-iv-$^{\flat}$VII-IV-$^{\flat}$VI-V^7-I) before throbbing to a *pianissimo*
close. Kern never wrote another number quite like this, except perhaps in
Gentlemen Unafraid. He must have had an operatic ensemble in mind, but
the effect is more like something from a Bach Passion.

If the blues and *objets trouvés* represent one axis of signification in *Sweet
Adeline,* another crosses it; this can be only briefly described here but helps
bind the score into a satisfying whole. Reviewers of the Broadway production appreciated its period gaiety, "garnished . . . with captivating music and
decorated . . . with the fluent costumes and circular hats of the day," and
dwelled on its humor: the same review devoted two whole paragraphs to
Charles Butterworth as Rupert Day.[12] If Lulu and her songs are vintage stuff
on one level, Kern himself sets a firm, higher tone in certain other numbers.
"Play Us a Polka, Dot" is, for him, nothing special despite its eponymous
promise, but "First Mate Tom W. Martin (Poor Wet Fish)" is one of his
very best 6/8 marches, well complemented by "Out of the Blue," the catchy

modernity of its angular melody not quite belying a period ragtime flavor. However, in "Spring Is Here" the fun is forgettable, and two other character numbers, "Oriental Moon" and "Molly O'Donahue," were borrowed (from *The Cabaret Girl* and *Sitting Pretty*, respectively).

All the more, then, do Adeline's own songs stand apart from these tokens of frivolity in what for Kern is a new aura. Her very first refrain note sets the tone: the F sharp forming a chromatic $^{\sharp}\hat{2}$ appoggiatura over tonic harmony

Ex. 4.1. Some Girl Is on Your Mind.

in "Here Am I." Kern's late style, influenced by the demands of romantic intimacy in film music, first appears here; the gambit intrigued Alec Wilder and perhaps influenced Rodgers when he came to exploit romantic exoticism with his $\sharp\hat{2}$s and $\sharp\hat{4}$s in "Bali Ha'i." Notably absent in this new style is 1920s syncopation, lacking a single trace in the melody of "Here Am I." Morgan's tessitura is also a separating factor: not the chest belt of later torch singers, but a soprano soaring to g^2 or reaching soulfully down to b flat in the same breath of the key phrase "I'm a poor fool, but what can I do?" in "Why Was I Born?"[13] The fragile appeal of her registral span is clear enough in Morgan's recording of this song; in "Here Am I" the bottom B flat is stressed as early as the third note of the refrain, while the release reaches the top-G apex in one of Kern's most inspired sequences. It is inspired because of the cushioning 7–6 suspensions in its harmony, the perfect expression of Adeline's vulnerable innocence (they reappear in the same key in "Some Girl Is on Your Mind"), and because of the second four-bar statement, basically a 3rd lower but with subtly surprising changes, above all the sly move to C major, like an emblem of Adeline's depth and radiance (ex. 4.2). Wilder noticed that this song refrain posits a central dominant cadence, as for an ABAB form, but proceeds instead with a release applicable to the AABA type, making it an ABCA hybrid. Adeline's memorable release (and it is the release that returns in "Some Girl Is on Your Mind"), borrowed from an AABA form, expresses her first love, for the man who will break her heart,

Ex. 4.2. Here Am I (release).

while ABAB represents her sadder and wiser in "Why Was I Born?" — seemingly in accordance with Wood's theory of song forms. The distinction is also reinforced by musical meaning in that "Here Am I" is her inner voice articulating what is supposed to be a diegetic *poem*, as we are repeatedly reminded with its "Read this" cues. By the time she sings "Why Was I Born?" she is learning to put on a performance, for the whole song is diegetic, not just the words. Only her third number, "Don't Ever Leave Me," reverts to nondiegetic straightforwardness and an absolutely standard AABA form as in act 2 she anticipates settling down with Jim. It feels rather flat as a result, but these three stages of her life need the three songs. A fourth, objectifying her rather than her emotional property, is her diegetic show number "The Sun About to Rise," and another trinitarian symbol occurs when, at her lowest point after losing Jim, she starts the show again with a medley reprise of this song, "Why Was I Born?," and "Don't Ever Leave Me." A pleasing variation on Kern's finaletto technique in that all three reprises are sung by the same person and belong to the same character, the medley complements "Some Girl Is on Your Mind" with another symphonic touch, transplanted from the more common act 1 position and all the stronger for it.

Music in the Air

Kern and Hammerstein stayed with a Teutonic background for their next joint venture, but it was a brave decision to set it entirely in Germany, between the idyllic mountain village of Edendorf and the wicked city of Munich. Apart from *Blue Eyes* it is the only one of Kern's musicals to contain no American characters; there are not even any English-speaking ones. One might view it as Kern's answer to Friml and Romberg were *Blue Eyes* not the more obvious romantic candidate, for *Music in the Air*, while undoubtedly an operetta (the authors' subtitle was "a musical adventure"), is a modern pastoral, with no aristocrats, palaces or castles, no Cinderella-like transformations, no colonialism or exoticism, no overblown masculinity in uniform (unless one counts *Lederhosen*). The tensions in the double romance plot concern not class and race but province and metropolis, above all, amateur and professional. And grandeur of setting belongs to the provincial amateurs, the star couple being denizens of nothing more alluring than a music publisher's office. The plot is simple: the love of a young country couple, Karl and Sieglinde, blossoms on a hike to Munich, whither the girl's father, Dr. Walther Lessing, is venturing in order to sell a song to his old school friend the music publisher, on whose premises they meet the musical theater librettist Bruno and his prima donna partner, Frieda. Cross-couple temptation here and at the zoo leads in act 2 to an abortive debut for Sieglinde on the stage and for Walther in the pit and to a heavy sermon from the musical director about professional reality in the theater; Frieda returns to rescue Bruno's show, and in a final scene back in Edendorf Walther is seen to have learned from experience and Karl and Sieglinde are reconciled. Their rural community endorses them, much as in *Oklahoma!*—witness the very last spoken lines in the script, enunciated by the Burgomaster: "Wait a minute. We were in the middle of a council meeting. You can't break up a council meeting like this. We were going to decide about Karl and Sieglinde— Where are they? . . . Oh there they are!"

One might argue that politics should not have been whitewashed out of the plot but affairs of state acknowledged, as in Ivor Novello's *The Dancing Years* a few years later; it took Hammerstein until *The Sound of Music* to include the Nazis in an alpine fantasy. Were Kern and Hammerstein hoping for German production prospects? Adolf Hitler's accession to the chancellorship took place little more than two months after the show opened in New York on 8 November 1932, and its aftermath undoubtedly blighted a fine work. Nonetheless it did achieve a notable film in 1934 and a revival on the American West Coast in 1942, the German setting retained although a shift to Bohemia had earlier been agreed upon. For its Broadway revival in 1951, Bavaria finally gave way to Switzerland.

Music in the Air is Kern's second biggest published score, barely a dozen pages shorter than the Chappell *Show Boat*, and like *Sweet Adeline* it improves on *Show Boat* by not tailing off in the second act. It is also one of his best works, and in 1932 received a superb Broadway production—"I never have seen a musical play so well acted. Never in my life," wrote Alexander Woollcott.[14] The score salutes the musical classics of Europe at every turn, not so much with symphonic pretension as with the outpourings of a love letter to the bourgeois styles, types, and repertoire of the old world—arrangements of Beethoven, waltzes à la Richard Strauss, irresistible polkas, bustling light music, *gemütlich* romance melodies, a character called Sieglinde, a librettist called Mahler and much of the paraphernalia of his composing namesake such as bird calls and horn calls, *Ländler* and pedal-pointed chorales, and a symbolic wandering minstrel, Cornelius the bird breeder.

Pretension does arise with the labels that were attached to its eleven scenes in the opening night program, though not in the published score or libretto: "leit motif," "études," "pastoral," "impromptu," "sonata," "nocturne," "caprice," "rhapsody," "intermezzo," "humoresque," and "rondo." These deserve scrutiny and suggest that Kern might have wanted the whole score to be viewed as something analogous to a suite or a symphony. Whether this is really possible when he still writes concatenations and reprises of song forms rather than architectural spans hosting reconciled contrasts is a moot point. The shuffling and signification of the song modules are certainly complex and ingenious, though more on the basis of diegetics than musical form—which perhaps proves the point about what Hammerstein and Kern were aiming at all along, enhanced musico-dramatic *meaning*.

The first, "leit motif" scene shows Walther writing a polka based on two motifs, one borrowed from a linnet singing outside his window, the other, for its B section in the dominant, from the rhythm of his daughter's words as she bangs on his door with the breakfast tray. The polka becomes the song "I've Told Ev'ry Little Star" and is certainly the most important tune in the musical, whose plot begins with its onstage composition and ends with the arrival of its published sheet music several months later. "Études" is a set of diegetic numbers rendered by the Edendorf community during their demonstration in the schoolroom, in other words, a *divertissement* of their characteristic styles and genres. First comes a danced *Ländler*, followed by a note-for-note eight-part choral arrangement by Kern of the returning A and B sections of the slow movement of Beethoven's C major piano sonata, op. 2 no. 3, which segues into Walther's polka, arranged for the choir, now in as many as eleven parts, with Karl as soloist.[15] Then the mountain climbers sing a supplicatory hymn for their hike to Munich, followed by the Edendorf Walking Club Song, the 6/8 march "There's a Hill Beyond a Hill." The "pastoral" is the love scene between Karl and Sieglinde on the way. It begins as a tapestry of underscoring motifs, described by Hammerstein in his stage directions as "a lacy musical fabric of mountain echoes and woodland murmurings," and coalesces into Cornelius's song "And Love Was Born," very much the counterpart of Pompineau's "The Night Was Made for Love" in *The Cat and the Fiddle*. This entire scene is set to music — though not to singing. "Impromptu," the fourth and final scene of act 1, has the best music in the score, namely, the "improvised excerpts from Bruno's new piece 'Tingle-Tangle,'" as it describes them. Although these are not the only music in the scene and are not continuous, they do hold it together, first, after some lengthy dialogue, with a refrain of the glorious waltz "I Am So Eager," later with no fewer than 380 bars referring to the putative operetta in a single span, culminating with a reprise of "I Am So Eager." This is supposed to represent the first-act finale of Bruno's operetta. Kern, however, after further dialogue, adds a delicate finaletto on different, less locally dramatized musical material as a sequel with which to close his own act 1, pointedly nesting his musical structures in the process.

Kern's label "rondo" for the last scene of the musical is the most easily appreciated of the eleven, for the entire scene is accompanied by an incessant alternation of the eight-bar AB periods of a supposed popular song emanating infectiously from the pub piano. It underlines the entire notion of "music in the air," for it gets passed from one group of performers to another just as Walther and the Burgomaster think they have managed to stop it and reminds us that Edendorf is not so idyllic as to be unresponsive to the latest commercial hit. It is like a grotesque augmentation of a thirty-two-bar refrain, for there are thirty-two sections altogether, twenty-four of the A period in nine different keys interspersed with eight releases of the B section. This is the endlessly extendable form of the Busby Berkeley production routines to Harry Warren's music in the Warner Bros. films of the same era, though Kern got there first. But it is not a great tune, a fact which compromises the score as a structure. As for the remaining generic labels, they seem strained in act 2 and with the exception of this final scene apply more by analogy to the drama than to the music, for the musical divisions begin more and more to cut across the scenic ones in order to bind scenes together both with reprises and by covering a scene change. The latter occurs when "I Am So Eager" is used to fuse the orchestra pit debacle ("intermezzo") with the temporally and geographically contiguous activity of the prodigal star's return to her dressing room. The former develops a recapitulation structure that works on three levels and needs explaining.

First, there is the zoo scene, possibly the longest in the show with its thirty pages of virtually continuous scoring. This is musically focused on "One More Dance," though with much extra, previously heard material besides. This material might suggest a development section. More likely, the song's reprise for the "other" woman with different words ("That sounded funny—didn't it?—I mean the different words to the same air," Karl comments) or simply the parallelism of the couples and their developing situation gave rise to the label "sonata."[16] The second level of reprise is between scenes. The polka for the bear that ends the zoo scene returns two scenes later, its first theme introducing the scene instrumentally, its second forming the "Tra-la-la" trio to the main (new) number, "When the Spring Is in the Air." This is the scene called "caprice"—a plausible enough label for the song and its treatment as a ubiquitous popular number getting under all the characters' skins from restaurant and radio—and is itself a parallel to the intervening one ("nocturne"), for both take place in the women's hotel rooms later that night. However, this particular parallel is not musically underlined, probably to save such pointedness for the most important between-the-scenes musical reprise, that of the second act's hit song, "The Song Is You." This is featured in two further parallel scenes, the dressing room ones ("rhapsody" and "humoresque"), though in this case they are not consecutive; Bruno sings it to Sieglinde in the first and to and with Frieda in the second, itself a parallel to his vocal behavior in the zoo scene. And just as in a symphonic second subject the contrast between one statement and the other would be of tonality and maybe orchestration, here the scene titles do seem to indicate something comparable: the first time Bruno sings

"The Song Is You" it is fervently, to Sieglinde; on the second occasion, when Frieda and the audience know what he has been up to (warming up an old song used for his every conquest), each plays the other's game of flattering pretense, their real love a layer further beneath, and the song conveys both levels of understanding, its music and words as romantic as ever, its performance pure burlesque, with Anna the dresser trying to adjust Frieda's costume as the couple embrace. "How can you sacrifice this sensational melody which will not be heard by anybody with all this physical stuff going on?" Arthur Schwartz asked Kern in rehearsal. "The scene calls for it," Kern replied.[17]

The third and broadest level of recapitulation is between the acts. "In Egern on the Tegern See" grows from a sixteen-bar AC form (so to speak) as remembered by Marthe in act 1 to the real thing, a thirty-two-bar ABAC refrain with its delicious midway imperfect cadence to the lines "Look out across the water, / The calm contented water," when sung by Lilli to Walther's delight in the "caprice" scene of act 2. More importantly, the *Tingle-Tangle* excerpts return with diegetic semiplausibility (since it is at a rehearsal for this new operetta) as underscoring in the climactic orchestra pit scene, thereby leading into the "I Am So Eager" transition mentioned above. The *Tingle-Tangle* reprise is not wholesale, for the 6/8 and 3/4 sections (depicting the soldiers and the fair) are omitted, having been reprised already in the zoo scene, but it is thoroughgoing enough to be far more than opportunistic underscoring, emotionally and aesthetically speaking, and lends weight to the message that the show must go on, while the cut reminds us of what has supposedly been done to Walther's added music in the process. One number that is part of *Tingle-Tangle* and appears in both occurrences of the excerpts also spills over into the second dressing room scene in act 2: Frieda's Arietta ("I'm Alone"), reprised by her complete with the coda missing from the dress rehearsal we have just witnessed (compare pp. 98 and 192 of the score) because she can now hear it offstage ("Leave the door open! That's my music they're playing!"). Most suggestive of all, however, is the return of the act 1 Introduction's *scherzando* passage in E major with its consequent, the motif of the sun on the cuckoo clock, in the entr'acte, that is, at a parallel point after the intermission. This music, borrowed as we have seen from the Prelude to *Love o' Mike* by way of *Men of the Sky*, with its instrumental bustle really does feel like parts of a symphonic allegro exposition and recapitulation.

The score for *Music in the Air* is a connoisseur's delight. Such subtle touches as the similarity between the upward arpeggio in the final C section of "I'm Coming Home" and in "In Egern on the Tegern See"; the development of the "moonlight" musical analogue from that same arpeggio into the first phrase of "I'm Alone" (p. 96 in the score); the restrained but passionate love theme (the very first music in the score) arising innocently from the B section of Walther's polka (and its words), as though he as a widower is reliving his own love in his relationship with his daughter and prospective son-in-law (with echoes of Hans Sachs); and the quite gorgeous 3/8 instrumental verse to "One More Dance"—these are top-notch Kern. So is the deft modulatory pivot back to C major on the note B from the E major middle section of "The Song Is You." This has often been commented on, though its actual release into E major for the final Edendorf scene, the last time it is heard, has not. Other passages stand out. The diegetic composition of "I've Told Ev'ry Little Star" is perfect musical theater—it seems inconceivable that Hammerstein should have wanted to cut this scene. The close of act 1 surely takes inspiration from the close of *Der Rosenkavalier* or the end of act 2 of *Die Meistersinger* for a musical still life when three tunes (one by Bennett?—see chapter 1) sound quietly together as Walther, his old school friend Ernst, and the secretary Marthe sip wine, think of the past, and ponder the youngsters' crazy present. Then the octave transposition of the first two notes of "I've Told Ev'ry Little Star" deftly turns the tune into a valedictory horn call, a leading note quixotically jumps up an octave for its resolution, and a phrase from the trio to "There's a Hill Beyond a Hill" which was used in the "pastoral" scene as a second birdsong motif forms the cadence. Richard Strauss is also brought to mind in the daring appoggiatura B natural against B flat in the bass of the eighth bar of "I Am So Eager," the first of Kern's great waltzes, though the authors' way of making us accept in advance that the B natural is a "right" wrong note is a little obvious:

> BRUNO (*speaks after the 8th bar of 3/4 strain*): No—no—wrong note!
> (UPPMANN *stops playing when* BRUNO *checks him.*)
> FRIEDA: I should say it is.
> UPPMANN: What should it be?
> BRUNO: It should go:
> (HE *hums the entire phrase that Uppmann has just played, stressing the dotted half note of the eighth bar.*)
> FRIEDA (*after Bruno has finished his humming*): He means it's a "B" natural.[18]

Ex. 4.3. At Stony Brook.

Similarly egregious are countless passages of underscoring in which motifs are introduced or cross-referenced for psychological purposes. The sexual
awakening of Karl and Sieglinde at Stony Brook is one such, adding a new
technique in the form of Hammerstein's experimentation with rhymed, metric dialogue. This, like the show's title, was very much in the air at the time,[19]
Mamoulian employing it in the musical film *Love Me Tonight* of the same
year, 1932, and again as late as *Summer Holiday* (1948); it represents the author's determination to fuse music and word, music and thought as closely
as possible. The four bars in which Sieglinde expresses her admiration and
jealousy of Karl's worldly experience employ, as orchestral underscoring, a
rhythmic ghost of the song "We Belong Together," from which the last scene
of the musical will be constructed, and thus anticipate the young couple's
destiny.[20] They don't yet know this, and Sieglinde must be imagining the
music Karl would have heard in the theater. She goes on to imagine a *valse
lente* as she quizzes Karl further about the erotic appeal of the actresses; it is
similar to "Frieda's 'Mme Frou Frou' Reminiscence" accompanying her incipient flirtation with Karl in the next scene—but not the same, for "I didn't
see Madame Frou Frou!" Karl acknowledges, to Frieda's chagrin.[21] And Sieglinde's thoughts affect her speech: she rhymes and stresses to the rhythm of
the music; they both do (ex. 4.3). The technique is used again later and described by Hammerstein in the zoo scene as follows: "*The following speeches
are synchronized in counter metre to melodies played by the orchestra. It is
partly rhyme, partly blank verse, partly prose, read without too much cadence
and without any apparent consciousness on the part of the performers that it
is anything but prose.*"

Kern and Hammerstein, then, were taking their presentation of music
on the stage very seriously in 1932. The intricate web of motifs and cross-
references is in the same vein as Hammerstein's much earlier protestation, in

the program to *Rose Marie* (and closely echoed by Rodgers four years later in *Chee-Chee*), that "the musical numbers of this play are such an integral part of the action that we do not think we should list them as separate episodes." But the difference wrought by the intervening years, with the help of *The Cat and the Fiddle*, whose program had carried a similar disclaimer, is that by the time of *Music in the Air* the authors had become determined not just to weave a quasi-symphonic fabric but to "solve the problem of making musical utterance the natural medium of expression" once and for all. They did so, at least in theory, by having every single bit of singing in *Music in the Air* be diegetic, an extraordinary feat for such a large score.

Well, not quite every single bit. There are two delicious ironies in *Music in the Air*. The first is that, for a musical so much about music, the composer (of *Tingle-Tangle*) is written out of the picture: Kruger never appears, and Bruno has erroneously been taken to be a composer, rather than singing actor and librettist, by one reviewer at least and almost by Hammerstein himself to judge from several passages in the script. The second irony is that when the office scene hands us the excuse for some all-sung operetta (Bruno's demonstration of *Tingle-Tangle*), Kern makes him *sing* what as the character on the stage he is actually *speaking*, epitomized by such phrases as "And then the curtain / Comes down at the end of this scene," set catchily to the head motif of the splendid verse of "I'm Coming Home." In fact the example just given is not Bruno quoting the operetta dialogue (though he does this, singing, too) but describing the action. Altogether we have five layers of expression in the passage: Bruno speaking between musical phrases; Bruno speaking rhythmically to musical accompaniment (there are some crossed noteheads); Bruno singing a description; Bruno singing spoken dialogue; and Bruno singing an operetta song. He knows he is doing the first and fifth of these but not the second, third, and fourth, and it means that the refrain of the song is diegetic but the verse is not. This is melopoetic virtuosity indeed, to reverse the operatic "problem" and have what would be spoken in the operetta sung in the musical!

Three Sisters

A traveling photographer's three daughters marry a variety of types and classes: Tiny, the eldest, the village policeman; Dorrie, escaping the nomadic life, the lord of the manor; Mary, innocent and determined, a handsome but feckless concert-party entertainer. This may sound cosy and un-eventful, and the fact that *Three Sisters* struck some that way indicates that Hammerstein and Kern had not managed to make it *musically* consequen-tial enough. But others found it "strange, unusual," "a big, generous, original show," and surely what allows for its epic quality is that, like *Show Boat* but unlike *Sunny*, its central betrothals lead to an expanding time frame as the only way of showing their consequences, which include failure and a second chance.[22] This puts *Three Sisters* in the same genre as *Carousel* and *Allegro* but not *Oklahoma!* In *Three Sisters* all three couples suffer separation — by war. In its chronological sweep, from the carefree Derby crowds of 1914 through the First World War to 1924, and its openness of scale and carniva-lesque theme, including gambling, premarital sex, wedding day desertion, concert-party minstrelsy in and out of khaki, and the leisure pursuits of the English masses, *Three Sisters* could hardly contrast more with the contained, disciplined worlds and morals, whether theatrical or bucolic, of *Music in the Air*.

At the same time, it returns to some of the themes of *Sunny*—the circus girl, the swells and their lust for entertainment, the social mobility of a pretty daughter, the onstage marriage. But all in all one's impression is of ambi-tious realism on a broad canvas, indulged and developed here and through *High, Wide and Handsome* to *Gentlemen Unafraid*. If the men in *Three Sisters* are no more impressive than those in *Show Boat*—it is the women who are heroic—its time frame and spread of plot make it Hammerstein's only obvious theatrical follow-up with Kern of that show's epic scale; it is an important work partly because of this.

All the more pity, then, that it cannot be fully reconstructed from the sur-viving materials, for the music is scattered and incomplete. No piano/vocal score was published, and the orchestral material (scored by Bennett) and rehearsal copies have disappeared almost entirely, so the show could never be authoritatively revived or recorded. A stage direction such as the fol-lowing suggests the extent of lost underscoring: "*(Musical accompaniment has, of course, continued after the end of Eustace's refrain, creating a mood for the following scene. One or two lights go out in the background; slowly Tiny's head appears in the window, she looks out cautiously to make sure that Eustace is out of sight and earshot.)*" So does the comment of a reviewer who found that "Mr. Hammerstein likes Mr. Kern's music so much that he's always letting it run through his dialogue, so that words and music form a coherent pattern." Such loss is doubly frustrating because a recording was made in 1934 of an entire 7½-minute musical scene ("Derby Day: A Musical Impression") using the original singers and orchestra, and it is good stuff.[23]

Yet a provisional musical assessment can be made. The heavy, chromatic flavor of the romantic underscoring, pointing firmly toward Hollywood, can be gauged from such published passages as the introduction to "Lonely Feet" and the instrumental continuation of "What Good Are Words?" accompanying the intrusion of society folk prior to the resumption of Gypsy and Mary's tryst at the end of act 2 scene 4 (scene 1 in revision). Eight songs were published separately. Four others appeared in piano and orchestral selections and recorded dance band medleys and can be more fully reassembled from the lyrics in the scripts and from the Kern Collection additions. Most of the ensemble and extended numbers are, thankfully, also extant, though the final two, "The Gaiety Chorus Girls" with its pony ballet and "August Bank Holiday: A Medley," are completely lost. Most of this music is unique to *Three Sisters*, though "I Won't Dance" was reused in the film of *Roberta* and "Lonely Feet," along with its choreographic essence, in that of *Sweet Adeline*, both the following year, and several numbers had come originally from elsewhere. "What Good Are Words?" originated as "Cottage of Content" in *Men of the Sky*, and portions of the two fantasy sequences were drawn from *Sitting Pretty*—Mary's "My Lover, Come Out of the Shadows" from "On a Desert Island With You," "Dorrie Imagines" from "The Enchanted Train," its refrain turned into a waltz. The post-impressionist 9/8 coda of "What Good Are Words?" is something of a leit-motif for dreaming, not just in this work—it also closes act 1 at the end of the dream sequence, with a "silver rose" reminiscence tacked on—but across Kern's output: it had previously closed "Cottage of Content" and would be used twice again, as the coda of "Your Dream (Is the Same as My Dream)" in *Gentlemen Unafraid* (see the last bars of ex. 4.6) and *One Night in the Tropics*.[24]

In *Three Sisters* Kern was working with motifs more than ever before, and it is significant that the between-phrase fills of "Cottage of Content" were replaced in "What Good Are Words?" with a characterful pastoral motif in parallel 3rds owing little to popular song traditions (though it is additionally supposed to represent the distant ball music in the estate scene). It has modal (mixolydian) inflections, and other song forms get similarly intercut with culturally indicative motifs. In Gypsy's "Now That I Have Springtime," the Cockney George interpolates a cheeky dotted-note riposte ("Don't believe a word he is telling you") which adds two bars before the quadratic form can proceed and Gypsy can incorporate it into his own melody. It becomes George's motif, which in "Derby Day" he whistles to the crowd.[25] Gypsy's motif is the introductory vamp to this diegetic song, a bass ostinato with offbeat guitar chords: it represents him when he enters the dream sequence. Gypsy's other song, "Roll On, Rolling Road," has an impetuous unison polka motif between periods (see ex. 1.1) which equally expresses his wayfaring sex appeal and the eye contact of "Zenida the Algerian princess" in the adjacent booth. "Derby Day" includes another instrumental motif for Zenida, followed swiftly by passages for Dorrie and Eustace as they enter. Only the recovery of the rest of the incidental music would clarify whether these were developed as personal motifs. There is also evidence of a penchant for quodlibets in this score, for a manuscript of one of the Derby Day scene changes counterpoints "Hand in Hand," "Roll On, Rolling Road," and "You Are Doing Very Well," while in the act 3 opening similar treatment is rather clumsily accorded that last tune, the verse of "Dorrie Imagines," and "My Lover, Come Out of the Shadows," no doubt to keep all three sisters in our minds prior to their berceuse, which follows (ex. 4.4).[26]

Kern and Hammerstein had apparently wanted to write a musical about Englishness for Drury Lane once before, and in *Three Sisters* tokens of Englishness were exploited wherever possible. Witness the 9/8 eighth note motif for the bustle of Derby Day, the glutinous verse of the policeman's serenade, and the same song's introduction, a mouth organ signal for Eustace which is also the head motif of "What's in the Air Tonight?" Modality, already mentioned, is prominent among those tokens: "A Funny Old House" lands plump on the chord of the flat 7th at the end of its first phrase and utilizes an "English cadence" (another flat 7th) at the end of its second. The "Take me through the city" section of "Roll On, Rolling Road" is also modal (dorian), though it is not intended to sound English, with its unison gathering note from somewhere east of Vienna and its label "À la tzigane" when it first appears in the Prelude.[27] George's jaunty dotted rhythms would have accorded with Kern's feeling for Edwardian London, while those of the splendid melody sung by a chorus of strollers crossing the stage in Mary and Gypsy's "scene," "What's in the Air Tonight?," are more up-to-date, distinctly reminiscent of Eric Coates's *Knightsbridge* march, already a famous BBC signature tune in 1933. As for the perky "You Are Doing Very Well,"

Ex. 4.4. *Three Sisters*, quodlibet.

it has a "national song" feel about it because its first phrase holds traces of both "The British Grenadiers" and "The Bluebells of Scotland."

"Derby Day" is a combination of tone poem dispatched as a scene-changer (ending with a splendid horse race in sound) with a medley of songs squeezed onto a 78 r.p.m. record. Well worth the unusual effort it must have taken to get it preserved, cast and all, on record, this music shows Kern setting his personal stamp on the colorful and enticing theater setting, wise not to have done so in anything as hackneyed as an opening chorus or a "Derby Day" song. Effectively he offers a musical analogue for William Frith's famous painting of 1858, a populist Victorian classic. Gladys Calthrop's decor and Kern and Hammerstein's direction seem to have imitated elements of the painting, including the tents on the left of the stage, the grandstand in the background as seen from its Tattenham Corner viewpoint, and the proletarian figures perched aloft in order to see the race (figs. 4.2, 4.3).

Putting a painting on the stage, indeed putting Frith on the stage, was nothing new. Neither was staging the Derby, which had been done since 1822, though Hammerstein was bold in depicting Derby Day so soon after the light opera of that title by Alfred Reynolds and A. P. Herbert (Lyric Theatre, Hammersmith, 1932).[28] He knew the work and had perhaps read the *Observer*'s comment that *Derby Day* was "a Drury Lane piece offered in pocket-sized dimensions." He was also bold in his exploitation of Drury Lane's technological capabilities and traditions of spectacle. Did they go to his head? He had ample experience of it as a venue, for, as James Agate sourly observed when reviewing *Three Sisters*: "Mr. Hammerstein . . . reigns in our national theatre." Hammerstein shows (*Rose Marie*, *The Desert Song*, *Show Boat*, and *The New Moon*) had run there without a break from 1925 until nearly 1930, and another, *Ball at the Savoy*, immediately preceded *Three Sisters*. But this was the only time he had actually written a piece for the Theatre Royal, and it seems he drew rather self-consciously on some of its traditions. The family saga bore obvious similarities to Noël Coward's *Cavalcade*, which had played there two years earlier. The dense but reliable singing policeman Eustace Titherley (played by Stanley Holloway) became a pantomime figure when in the last act his progeny ran to unending sets of twins (six in the original script, later modified to three) and his burlesque song "Keep Smiling" was taught to the audience. The original script contained fourteen scenes, admittedly three fewer than *Show Boat* but encompassing a horse race, the Thames full of boats on August Bank Holiday in a set requiring amplification, a village common, a country estate, and a canteen in wartime France, not to mention interiors. A live horse and live geese appeared, a horse and cart bolted offstage, and Gypsy and George made off in a stolen car. Some of these effects, including Marsden's stolen car and the river, were abandoned or simplified (the river became a lock) before opening night. None of them was as audacious as Novello's television inventor and shipwreck in *Glamorous Night* the following year, but perhaps that was part of the problem, for anything at Drury Lane had to be spectacular. It is not clear whether Hammerstein used a stage revolve: MacQueen Pope claims that the only occasion on which one had been used at Drury Lane prior to 1945 was in an earlier musical, *Wild Violets* (1932–33).[29]

As well as Esmond Knight, who was to play Gypsy, *Wild Violets* had starred two of the eponymous sisters of 1934, the American Charlotte Green-

wood, best remembered as Aunt Eller in the film of *Oklahoma!*, and Adele
Dixon. Greenwood in her autobiography claimed that Kern was persuaded
to write *Three Sisters* for her after seeing the closing night of *Wild Violets* in
1933; this was a couple of months after the Derby. Together with Holloway,
Victoria Hopper as Mary, the youngest sister, and Eliot Makeham as their
father, this made for a strong cast. There was nothing but praise for the decor
and direction. Ralph Reader, England's answer to Busby Berkeley, choreographed the dream sequence and managed the crowd movement with some
of the verve he would later lavish on boy scouts in the annual Gang Shows.
The failure of *Three Sisters*, which ran for only two months, is not therefore automatically explained, given that critics were divided, unless Agate's
withering comments about "American inanity" were sufficient to damn it.
One could argue it was doomed from the start because of nationalist feeling,
not so much toward the authors as toward the cast: "There has been plenty

Fig. 4.2. William Frith, *Derby Day*.

of newspaper discussion about having a foreign cast," Leighton Brill wrote
to Hammerstein from London before the script was even complete. "They
absolutely disregard whom the play is by, but have said . . . that the national
theatre, Drury Lane, should have English actors treading the boards."[30]

Problematic *Three Sisters* was bound to be, but then so is *Show Boat*.
One difficulty was finding a focus for the stars—too many of them, with the
three sisters, in a plot in which only the deeply flawed male leads (Gypsy and
Eustace) were supposed to be singers. Each sister had her moments, Dorrie
in "Lonely Feet," which replaced her fantasy "Dorrie Imagines," and in "I
Won't Dance," Mary in her dream scena and her duet with Gypsy ("What
Good Are Words?"), Tiny in "You Are Doing Very Well" and "Somebody
Wants to Go to Sleep," Mary and Tiny together in "What's in the Air To-

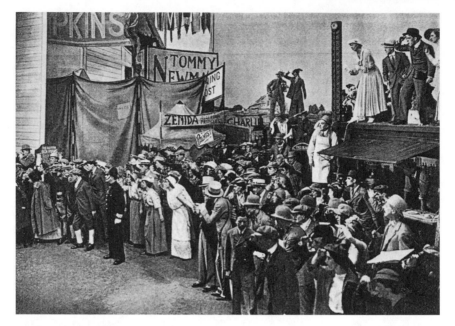

Fig. 4.3. *Three Sisters*, Derby scene.

night?" and "There's a Joy that Steals Upon You." But there was not much they could do together other than sing a lullaby reprise of "Somebody Wants to Go to Sleep" to Mary's baby at the beginning of act 3. And the third coupling, Dorrie's, was not properly expressed in song, bodged as it was between her seduction by Glainley and her later marriage to his friend Marsden after Glainley had passed her over (presumably so he could then be killed off as an airman, the only reference to wartime loss and suffering in the entire plot: *South Pacific* was still a long way off). Marsden and Glainley did join in "Here It Comes," another strangely mixolydian song, but that was about all, and that was cut before opening night. But it is difficult to believe that the carping about faulty Englishness was anything but spite projected onto other shortcomings, for the vernacular details ring true enough and were appreciated by some critics. Hammerstein had, after all, spent far more time in and around London than he ever did in Oklahoma, and his maternal grandparents were born in Britain. Kern knew the river and Londoners at play even better, and his wife's background was very close to that of the sisters. Such lines as the following, if hackneyed, are perfectly serviceable:

MRS. TITCHMARSH: Would you like to come inside, Mr. B, and 'ave me give
    you a little drop of somethin' to pick you up?
ALF: I don't mind if I do, Mrs. T.

—and the family characters and dynamics are genuinely touching at many
points, especially when Mary and her father have their sentimental tête-à-
tête at the end of act 3 scene 1. She abandoned with the baby, he lonely as
a widower, both understand that although he "was born in a shopkeeping
family, of course," the wayfaring urge has been transmitted from American
mother to English daughter, who will happily enter into the wandering life
with Gypsy and their own child if he will come back for her. He does come
back, and in his inarticulate anger is shamed into one good action when he
tends to the baby offstage. Reentering the room with its doll in his hand, he
ends the scene thus:

> GYPSY: First time I ever did anything for a kid . . . Please forgive me, Mary.
>   *(He clasps her about the knees. She puts her hand on his head and looks*
>   *out through the window.)*
> (CURTAIN)

This was apparently too sentimental for a Drury Lane audience and was
subsequently cut; but it confirms Gypsy as the prototype of Billy Bigelow in
Carousel, just as the whole setting of campground romance looks forward
also to *State Fair*. Once again we find ourselves bridging the pre-*Oklahoma!*
gulf and needing to view Hammerstein's work whole. But in 1934 British
first-nighters could ruin these closing lines that in the dress rehearsal had
reduced their creators to tears. "The audience just sat there and wrote a new
play, with the same words spoken in the same way"—it must have been this
passage Bennett meant when he recounted the episode. It was certainly the
one that devastated Knight, when, as he described it, "for the first time I got
the bird. It was a horrible experience." They had all reckoned without the
British gallery, which Wodehouse had faithfully described in the words of
one of his characters a decade and a half earlier: "There's a regular click,
you know, sir, over here in London, that goes to all the first nights in the
gallery. 'Ighly critical they are always. Specially if it's an American piece like
this one. If they don't like it, they precious soon let you know."[31]

Where does this leave Kern? One certainty is that only with *Carmen
Jones* did Hammerstein really learn to write lyrics that matched the dramatic realism for which he was striving, as the early thirties' preoccupation
with diegetic plausibility gave way to quasi-operatic soliloquy. *Three Sisters*

does not travel far along this road, and none of the emotional epiphanies would seem to have been enshrined in the lyrics or their music. "Derby Day," largely instrumental, is probably the best music in the score, though it is difficult to judge much of the rest. There is nothing quite as compelling in *Three Sisters* as Helen Morgan's music in *Sweet Adeline* or as fresh as the concerted numbers and *Tingle-Tangle* excerpts in *Music in the Air*. A cloying atmosphere too often overtakes the music, as in *Roberta*; critics noticed this, and it cannot be gainsaid, lovely though the score's most earnest moments are. But final judgment on the show should be suspended until the rest of the music turns up. One day it will, one hopes.

High, Wide and Handsome

The circus must have been deep in Hammerstein's blood. One notices all sorts of recurrent motifs, and the 1930 film of *Sunny* includes a scene of undressing in a caravan with the handing out of clothes, similar to Tiny's actions in act 1 of *Three Sisters*. A show caravan also triggers the plot of *High, Wide and Handsome*, rather more spectacularly when it explodes in flame in the opening scene, leaving the heroine homeless. Repeatedly in his work Hammerstein created or latched onto the medicine show life in one manifestation or another, from Ali Hakim in *Oklahoma!* to the holiday-making caravanners in *State Fair* and their bizarre equivalent, the girl living in a boiler, in *Pipe Dream*.

Kern went along with this amiably enough, never at a loss for jaunty razzmatazz, and must have understood instinctively two principles, perhaps fantasies, at work underneath these symbols. The first, fairly obvious, was the conflict between hobo and community, freedom and responsibility, entertainment or leisure and work. On this opposition would be built the folk musical, as Rick Altman has defined it with due cognizance of *High, Wide and Handsome* and its relation to *Oklahoma!* though understandably without reference to *Three Sisters*, the essential seriousness of whose "pastoral melodrama," the cutting of its "jocular vein" upset the London critics because they could not see that a new genre was in the making.[32] The other fantasy, more obscure, was the quest for masculinity and femininity in the one body. The grace and strength of gymnasts, the androgynous clothing and close, undifferentiated community of circus performers must for Hammerstein have represented some deep yearning and probably helps explain the strange generic mix of *High, Wide and Handsome*, the failure of *Very*

Warm for May, and then the staggering success of *Oklahoma!* Only girls danced in the dream sequence of *Three Sisters.* The one in *Gentlemen Unafraid* did include sufficient gender reversal that the authors felt obliged to comment on it in the script.[33] But it took *Oklahoma!* to make dancing cowboys acceptable to a bourgeois audience long suspicious of who went to see men in ballet and why.

If, then, the circus was one node of depiction for challenged masculinity and femininity in American culture, the western certainly became another. How extraordinarily they converged in *High, Wide and Handsome!* Working with the cult director Mamoulian, Hammerstein wrote the story and screenplay as an original. It was far from his first western, if one includes *The Desert Song* and *Rose Marie* as stories of adventurers in extreme terrain; nor was it Kern's, if one recalls *The Red Petticoat.* The story, in Tom Milne's succinct words, "concerns the true history of the discovery of the Pennsylvania oilfields in 1859, and the epic struggle waged by the poor farmer-prospectors against the railroad freight tycoons who resorted to every means in their power, financial and physical, to prevent the completion of the pipelines which would bring oil to every home in America."[34] This was musical comedy turning historical with a vengeance, tackling the birth of that particular capitalist interest that rings in our ears more insistently than ever today with each cry of "It's the oil, stupid!"—for the Titusville oil drillings were the first in modern times. Hammerstein's view of it was about as communist as he could get in 1937, when in lumpy but crucial dialogue he had his hero Cortlandt insist that the oil should belong to the whole world for its benefit and his antagonist Brennan observe that he could make it whatever price he chose for the benefit of shareholders through big business deals.

There is absolutely no sense of any of this in the music and lyrics (in which the word "oil" does not occur); Kern's contribution is therefore problematic. Several reviewers were measured in their assessment of his score, rating the songs between "disappointing" and "pleasant," "gay and tuneful" or "fetching" and avoiding superlatives.[35] The probable reason is that Kern was ill and lacked the control over it that he had evidently exercised in the studio from the film of *Sunny* onward. Almost certainly there would have been a battle of wills between him and Mamoulian, mavericks that they were, or coolness in order to avoid this. Mamoulian's suggestion of plagiarism from *Porgy and Bess* when he first heard one of Kern's tunes was hardly tactful, and who knows but that such a challenge, coming at the exact point of Kern's final commitment to Hollywood (he and Eva had just moved into their new house in Beverly Hills), contributed to his heart attack a month or so later?[36]

He must have been writing the songs in the latter part of 1936. One version of the title number, entitled "The Fields" and leading into a barn dance chorus of it complete with caller, is copyright 7 December 1936, and we should probably take this as postdating the song's primary treatment. Kern must have continued adding musical items right up until the date of his emergency, which was 21 March 1937: "Workmen's Chorus" (with lyrics by Bennett!) has a copyright date of 19 March. The film was released on 21 July, therefore probably filmed between March and May. Kern was prostrate for most or all of that period; Hammerstein was in Europe (hence the Bennett lyrics?) or back at Kern's bedside. It seems Mamoulian and the studio staff did what they liked with the music.

This involved casting aside quite a lot of it. An entire folder of manuscripts labeled "Unused Material" survives, most of it unique to *High, Wide and Handsome*.[37] Some of it apparently *was* used, but much of it was not, including an extensive underscore, "Awake and Bathe," for Sally's first morning on the farm; this seems to have been replaced with her unaccompanied rendition of "High, Wide and Handsome," which Grandma Cortlandt and her canary join in, allowing for Sally's flattery of her cracked voice to work on the old woman against her protestations. One can see why using music as a lever in the plot appealed to Mamoulian more than subliminal underscoring here, especially as it precedes Sally's aria to the chickens and pigs, which they too participate in, and thereby privileges diegetic singing for as long as possible—until she sings "Can I Forget You," in fact. But it is symptomatic of what happened to the film: Kern's *High, Wide and Handsome* is a modest suite of six published songs, not a rhapsody of narrative motivation. This might have been the upshot whatever his health, but it is worrying to hear such passages of melodramatic underscoring in the latter half of the film as the music for the shantyboat raid, with its repeated $3/4 \mid{}^\flat 3212\mid 1$ motif that sounds Russian, right for Mamoulian perhaps but not at all like Kern. It would appear by his own testimony that Bennett composed it.[38]

Even the songs suffer, for they are evenly rather than cumulatively spaced throughout the film and lack a real production number. The refrain of "High, Wide and Handsome," performed diegetically by Sally, accompanies the very opening shot of the film, but Randolph Scott was no singer, so we never hear its verse or witness a rendition by Cortlandt on his horse in cowboylike anticipation of a tryst with Sally as the lyrics, thoroughly

Oklahoma!-like in this respect, would seem to demand. One gets the impression that "Jerome Kern and Oscar Hammerstein's *High, Wide and Handsome*," as the opening credits promised, was a different film from the one Mamoulian shot. "The Folks Who Live on the Hill" is sung by Irene Dunne instead of by the man implied by the verse, again omitted, and pitched in a high key, D flat, which negates its lazy, hillbilly mood. Without the verse the cowboy vamp has no time to establish itself but feels more like a diegetic figure left over from the wedding dance preceding the scene, a clever but misplaced touch. Both these songs cry out for Alfred Drake and the dramaturgy of *Oklahoma!*, but Mamoulian had to return to the stage for that breakthrough in the folk musical.

One concludes, therefore, that whether with *High, Wide and Handsome* Mamoulian "wrecked a good historical Western by getting frivolous about it, or alternatively, wrecked a good musical by getting too serious about it" (both charges that might, *mutatis mutandis*, have been brought against Hammerstein in *Three Sisters*) was a matter of relatively little consequence where Kern's music was concerned; Milne argues positively, however, that the songs lubricate the clash of genres by providing moments of Brechtian alienation.[39] Whatever one's view, there is essentially only the little group of songs, some more effectively employed in the film than others, and an exceedingly mixed bag of underscoring. Toward the end of the film, as the astounding scenes of adventure and confrontation followed each other breathtakingly, music of any but the most generic kind became redundant. What really excited Mamoulian was *musique concrète*, the music of street sounds and, like a good Meyerholdian, the sound and sight of machinery. The soundtrack is at its best when we hear and see a forest of machinery being winched up the cliff, a train stopping on a bridge, or oil pipes being assembled and, in one spectacularly extended sequence, falling off a sled and sliding down a hillside with the most amazing noise.

The songs have their strengths. They form a nicely contrasted collection of supposed historical types, something musicals would increasingly be called upon to do with the growth of settings in the past. For once Kern can luxuriate with impunity in a polka ("Will You Marry Me Tomorrow, Maria?," complete with trio in the subdominant). Here Hammerstein matches Kern's sine-wave swings above and below the dominant in the title phrase—a 2nd, 4th, 5th, 3rd—with syllabic play of his own ("marry," "-morrow," "Maria"). Curiously, there is no waltz unless one counts "I'll Follow Your Smile" (as the "Wagon and Hilltop Scene" became in *Can't*

Help Singing). "Can I Forget You" is one of Kern's most cigar-shaped bal-lads, certainly retrospective in its rhythmic and modulatory primness (no hint of dance in the former, only dominant and subdominant for the latter) and thereby *volkstümlich* in a Victorian way. The *Jerome Kern Collection* calls it "rather like the songs of Stephen Foster," a similarity difficult to pin down unless "Jeanie With the Light-brown Hair" is brought to mind, with its F major 3-↓5-1 melodic shape for "light-brown hair" (compare Kern's 5|↑3--[2]|1 refrain opening) and similar release within an AABA form, Kern's falling (IV)6̂ (I)5̂ 3̂ 2̂ (II)î ↓(V)5̂ over eight bars, Foster's over the last two.

Moreover, several of the songs show Kern in possession of a careful and partly new agenda. The novelty is the paradox of suggesting mid-nineteenth-century pastiche with the most up-to-date twentieth-century traits he can muster. "High, Wide and Handsome" is a classic 2/4, its low, sleek lines thor-oughly contemporary though with the "oompah" model still plausible as an antebellum galop, especially in the verse. More striking is the extreme chro-maticism of Molly's "The Things I Want," with its anachronistic blues throb, emphasized on the soundtrack. At least one supposes it is anachronistic, al-though the connection of blues with lachrymose Victoriana should never be discounted. The singer has to negotiate a tritone, a diminished 4th and a diminished 6th within the first six notes of the refrain, their enharmonic co-nundrums nicely paralleled in the lyric reversal of not getting the things she wants and not wanting the things she gets. (The Kern/Hammerstein melo-poetics play similar tricks at the start of the refrain of "High, Wide and Hand-some": note the jumble of two *i*'s, three *d*'s and two *and*'s, further mixed up on immediate repetition as "I'm ridin' wide and high"—four *i*'s, two *d*'s, and one *and*; one *m* each. Kern's tune comparably interverts the first three scale degrees as 2/4 |1---|2--1|3-2-|--3-|2-1 before leaping to 4 and 5 for "wide and high.")

Most important, however, are what for want of a better term one might call community vamps—guitarlike figures suggestive of country or hillbilly music, blues or saloon: something lazy, rural, or sleazy, music from the dirty vernacular hinterland, be it white or black; a new sense of what is "out there" beyond the Appalachians. One country vamp, an "oompah" outgrowth, is in "Allegheny Al," this time pentatonic in the verse and suggestive of banjo picking. It is supplemented by melodic figures hinting at steamboat calls ("Steamboat 'round the bend" at the start of the verse, "He's a Beau Brum-mel" in the release; compare "Cotton Blossom" and "Captain Andy" in *Show Boat* and "Steamboat Comin'" in the *Portrait for Orchestra*). But the classic example is the introduction to the refrain of "The Folks Who Live on the Hill," another "oompah" variant. In 4/4 rather than 2/4 or 2/2, it suppresses the traditional "oompah"'s spring by grounding it with an initial chord and adding dotted-note repetition to the afterbeat. Curiously, nothing as indolent permeated the Rodgers and Hammerstein style; Kern's gambit, cowboy music by 1930s association and by no stretch of the imagination a real 1850s figure, suggests instead, as does the entire song with its loose-limbed, sprawling periods, Harold Arlen or Hoagy Carmichael. Hammer-stein might have taken the sentiment and scenario of the song from a Vic-torian ballad, but a musical prototype is less easy to pinpoint. Carmichael's "Two Sleepy People" dates from the following year. As Kern said to Ham-merstein of "The Folks Who Live on the Hill," "Unless you play the figure in the accompaniment it loses everything."[40] He was right, and his one little gesture set the syntactical seal on the folk musical with a single stroke as unforgettably as the word "folks" in the song's title.

Gentlemen Unafraid

Reenter Otto Harbach for Hammerstein's next major project after *High, Wide and Handsome:* another historical American drama, centred on up-state New York rather than Pennsylvania but taking place only one year later, its opening scene set at West Point in 1860. Other than *Roberta*, this was Kern's first college plot since *Leave It to Jane*, but an utterly different affair from both, involving conflicts of loyalty not to sporting teams but to fight-ing states: *Gentlemen Unafraid* concerns southern cadets who have a duty toward the north in the Civil War. But the parallels with *Roberta* are impor-tant, too, for the deep anguish suffered by young people in choosing their values as well as their partners for life was a favorite scenario of Harbach. A family man of sixty when he wrote *Roberta*, he handled patriotic choices and the complementary qualities of old and new worlds just as much as Hammerstein, be the contrast between southern tradition and northern con-science in *Gentlemen Unafraid* or European dignity and American efficacy in *Roberta* and *The Cat and the Fiddle*.

Several of *Gentlemen Unafraid*'s lead characters relate to those in *Ro-berta*. John Kent's mixture of moral solidity and gauchely awakening sexu-ality is divided between the hero, Bob Vance, symbol of the former, and his fellow cadet Bud Hutchins, strong, upright, and athletic but a disastrous dancer and terrified of women. Bud is the clown, a role that went to a young comedian, Red Skelton, at the start of a distinguished career just as that of Huckleberry Haines had gone to Bob Hope. (And Skelton would take over something of Haines's function in the 1952 film of *Roberta*, *Lovely to Look At*.) Linda is the siren, brittle and manipulative like Sophie but, unlike her, able to mature and earn her man by the end of the play.

Gentlemen Unafraid is thereby another *Bildungsroman*, a story about young persons' painful character development. But their pain and development are forced on them by civil war, and this makes it as ambitious a subject as Kern, Harbach, and Hammerstein ever tackled, even though it was by no means the first Civil War operetta. It includes the Gettysburg Address in act 2, followed by the death of Abraham Lincoln offstage after a cameo appearance by John Wilkes Booth, and a hint at the cycle of revenge that could perpetuate itself. (In a sense, Sondheim's *Assassins* begins where *Gentlemen Unafraid* leaves off.) Robert E. Lee appears in one scene, Edward VII as Prince of Wales is offstage at a West Point ball in another, and Bob has a private interview with Lincoln in a third. To write musical comedy dialogue for Lincoln was a risky business, but at least they did not ask him to burst into song: Hammerstein's fondness for accompanied rhythmic dialogue saves the day when Lincoln recites the title song, "Gentlemen Unafraid," to its tune in the orchestra, like "Here Am I" as a supposed poem. Whatever Harbach's role in all this, Hammerstein's stamp appears to be firmly on the show, for it explores the nature of conflict and the role of culture in fostering hatred, and although no one other than Lincoln actually dies, once again *South Pacific* feels both foreshadowed and necessary.

Gentlemen Unafraid is by definition Kern's least-known stage score in that only two of its songs were published, and then only later: "Abe Lincoln Has Just One Country" in 1941, when it became an anthem in aid of the U.S. Defense Bond and Stamp Drive, "Your Dream" in 1940, when reused in *One Night in the Tropics*. (A third, "De Land o' Good Times," was a reworking of "Mah-Jongg," of all things, from *The Beauty Prize*, published fifteen years earlier.) It is also one of his best, and its fortunes were constrained not by quality but by circumstance. Its operatic premiere engaged the wrong audience and critics: "There is not one page of impressive music-drama declamation in the entire score. . . . why the composer should have conceived the Civil War period in musical terms of the modern 'popular' idiom is puzzling," wrote the *Christian Science Monitor*. Furthermore, 1938 was a terrible time to present a musical about war and separation, Kern was still too ill to direct or publicize it (he did not attend the St. Louis premiere), and the first night of the open-air production was all but rained out. One hardly knows what to make of the presence among the dignitaries attending of Harry H. Woodring, secretary of war, or of the deep irony of Bud's speech to Betsy—this must surely be Hammerstein's—as they settle down to domestic bliss after the war: "Well, we won't fight among ourselves again. And there's nobody else to fight with," he asserts. "We don't ever get mixed up with Europe. We've got no colonies or anything. We've just got a nice, plain little country. Got our own cotton and coal and all the food we want— not a worry in the world. All we got to do is stay home and mind our own business." One imagines this made the audience uncomfortable in 1938. It would certainly make us uncomfortable today, almost a reason in itself for reviving the show.[41]

To turn the *Christian Science Monitor*'s censure on its head, as a musical *Gentlemen Unafraid* feels thoroughly modern, its tunes sleek and smooth, its book scenes confidently interspersed with those such as the first one at the West Point dance and its sequel in the garden in which underscoring is extensive or continuous, rising to song or chorus work where diegetically appropriate or subliminally acceptable. But there is a great deal of choral singing, possibly with one eye on the growing college market if Weill's *Johnny Johnson* and Aaron Copland's school opera *The Second Hurricane* of the previous two years were noted. *Johnny Johnson* had an antiwar theme and *The Second Hurricane* a multiracial one, both also represented in *Gentlemen Unafraid*, which was in any case rewritten for amateurs as *Hayfoot, Strawfoot* in 1942.[42] Even after that, when Kern and Hammerstein released their stakes in the material, Harbach carried on reworking it almost to the end of his life under various titles, with different music altogether (by Peter de Rose).

Gentlemen Unafraid, whose orchestrations are missing, was subject to thoroughgoing change, and *Hayfoot, Strawfoot* sported three entirely new, up-to-date songs, "The Kissing Rock," "Little Wily Miss," and "What's Become of the Night?," that one would pass over with reluctance. But the first-night score is the thing, except for some shifted numbers that represent an interim stage between it and *Hayfoot, Strawfoot* and almost certainly an improvement. One such shift entailed rescuing "Little Zouave" from near the end of the show, in act 3, to an initial position near the beginning as "Boy With a Drum." The Zouaves, originally a French Algerian regiment, sported a colorful Moorish uniform copied by the 5th New York Volunteer Infantry which became the epitome of masculine dash and bravery in the

American Civil War. A Zouave chorus drill would have been an obvious attraction as the third-act *divertissement* of an old-fashioned musical comedy, but its dramatic excuse in *Gentlemen Unafraid* is lame in the extreme: Pignatelli, Bud's bugbear as the Italian dancing master at West Point, has become a Zouave and continues to undermine Bud's desire for Betsy until Bud finally grabs her. As "Boy With a Drum," a most haunting tune and lyrics became a "thumping tattoo" casting over us the spell of war in all its heartache quite early in the show.[43] In *Hayfoot, Strawfoot* the number returns as part of "Interlude in the Dark" in act 2 to depict the fighting itself in place of "How Would I Know?" (ex. 4.5).

The sinuous triplets and smolderingly indolent melody of "Boy With a Drum," its minimum harmonic movement creating maximum effect in partnership with melodic dissonance, represent Kern's sophisticated late 1930s idiom, much in evidence in this score. (Conversely, he seems less concerned with nineteenth-century pastiche than in *High, Wide and Handsome* and in several places, as in the case of *Sweet Adeline*, imports period tunes instead.) "When a New Star" is as ingratiating as "Boy With a Drum," achieving its sumptuousness through an uncommonly broad harmonic rhythm, at root Viennese. The first eight bars of the refrain are all on the tonic, with very slow diatonic appoggiaturas in the melody. The next eight are on the dominant, with a 4–3 suspension every other bar and some nested diminished 7th appoggiatura chords. Repeated with a flat 7th added at bar 7 and a subdominant prefacing the dominant, this makes for a thirty-two-bar *abab* form. But it is broadened into a sixty-four-bar AABA because a sixteen-bar bridge follows. Altogether this gives a Hollywood gloss to the underscoring when the A sections of "When a New Star" (or "Our Last Dance," the same tune) accompany much of the romantic dialogue between Bob and Linda in the Garden Scene; surveying the Garden Scene as a whole one can see how its techniques, developed in or for film, now take precedence over the pseudosymphonic continuity of Kern's stage finalettos.

Two major differences from a finaletto are evident. While a patchwork of reprises plus the odd dance tune still forms the backbone of the musical continuity, it leads to a new song, in this case "Your Dream," and also includes the odd freestanding leitmotif. The Garden Scene begins by stringing together a sequence of offstage waltzes (apparently new), a bit of the opening polka, "Sweet Young Candidate," for Bud's embarrassed exit, the "dream" motif from *Three Sisters* for Linda's romantic entrance, "When a New Star" for her conversation with Bob, and a foretaste of her "Sweet as a Rose" as she expresses disdain for her dancing partners. Then there is genuine development as these last three items are interwoven with a thread of *melos* connecting them to accompany Linda's incipient self-realization when, during a very long speech, she says, "I've been hurt for the first time in my life."[44] Example 4.6 shows that melodic thread, which as it were discovers (through the developing variation of a motif shown by dotted brackets) that the different tunes are connected, just as Linda discovers that her actions and feelings have an effect on others and they in turn on her. The dream motif is, as in *Three Sisters*, rounded off with a "silver rose" figure as her torn scraps of dance card fall to the ground. She then sings "Sweet as a Rose in the Moonlight" as the verse for "Your Dream," whose refrain is Bob's reentry into the dialogue. This is followed by the dream motif as coda while they embrace, though this time the silver rose effect accompanies the eavesdropping cadets and girls as "they rustle back up the steps again, giggling." Linda and Bob go to a bench and hear glee club voices singing "Sweet as a Rose" offstage; they join in, and the head motif of "Your Dream" rings out on their last note to end the scene.

The second difference is that scene music such as this—"Make-believe" is its prototype—accompanies reflection and the characters' exploration of themselves and each other, rather than dramatic action arising from earlier self-presentation. As in the famous *Carousel* Bench Scene, what will happen to the characters later will happen less in music than it had in a musical comedy finale, but it will happen more because of the music that was in their heads when they first set themselves up for the outcome.

The actual songs of *Gentlemen Unafraid* were not necessarily all written for it. Even one that probably was, "Cantabile (A Song Without Words)," remained unused (and cannot be placed) and resurfaced the following year as "All the Things You Are" with a different introduction and transition from verse to refrain. The number for the Irish barmaid Betsy, "What Kind of Soldier Are You?," is catchy enough but would fit anywhere. "Your Dream" includes the down-home vamp from "The Folks Who Live on the Hill" and feels like material left over from *Riviera* or other films, as does "When You Hear That Humming," virtually a calypso. (Linda's "Mister Man," following the glee club verse "Many a Lofty Mountain," also has a touch of rumba about it.) "Abe Lincoln Has Just One Country" and the title song, on the other hand, would fit nowhere else. The former is not as stirring a patriotic number as one might have liked or expected, but with real singers makes its point and can expand into eloquence, which is how this show was designed.

Marziale

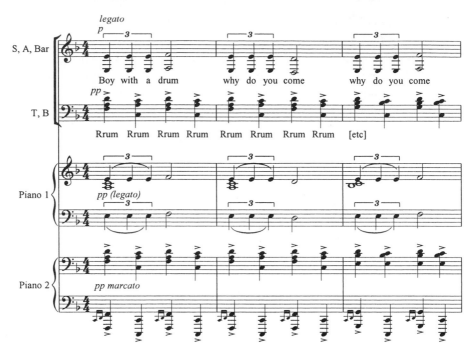

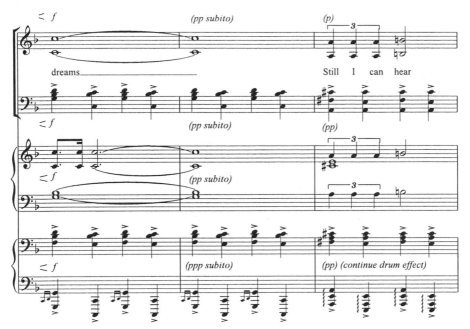

Ex. 4.5. Boy With a Drum.

The same capacity triumphs in "Gentlemen Unafraid" (a quotation from Kipling), succinct and understated but the show's hidden gem.[45] It had to be modest, for, as already mentioned, it is supposed to be a memorized poem, but its stalwart diatonicism could surely not have expressed the concepts of gentlemen and courage in any better way. The parallel triads and bass line in contrary motion (x in ex. 4.7) are perfectly simple and perfectly logical: the tiniest touch of C major neoclassicism within a vernacular framework. And the tune has fiber in its contours—again, a "classical" singer can bring this out, as Ben Bagley realized in *Jerome Kern Revisited*.[46]

Gentlemen Unafraid would nevertheless stand or fall by its ensemble numbers. Even "What Kind of Soldier Are You?" takes on a larger dimension when reused for the dream—or rather unconsciousness—ballet (when Betsy hits Bud over the head by mistake in a fight), a bitonal layer of parallel triads added between its ragged phrases as fills and a subsidiary section, "Shy Boy," following as Bud's nagging internal voice (silenced once and for all, the script tells us, when he finally embraces Betsy in the last scene of the musical). Like the dream sequence in *Three Sisters*, though this time ne-

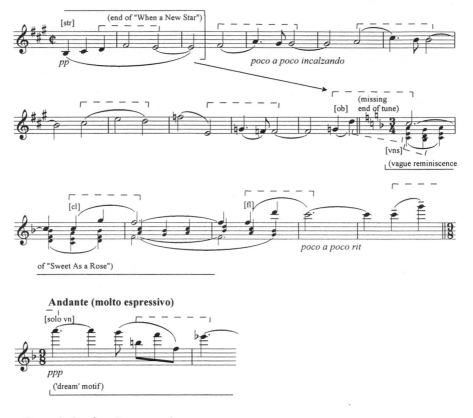

Ex. 4.6. Garden Scene, *melos.*

cessitating ballet dancers, the number ("Fantasie") is in two parts and acts somewhat like a finaletto in reprising earlier tunes. Bud and Betsy lead two of the other ensemble numbers, "When You Hear That Humming" and "Gaily I Whistle a Song (It's Gayer Whistling As You Go)," both attributed to Harbach as lyricist in one reliable source. The latter is a carefree tune in the "Pick Yourself Up" mold, its feel-good quotient inevitably recalling Walt Disney's *Snow White* of the previous year. But the big number is "How Would I Know? (I Wish Dat Dere Wasn' No War)." It comes as no surprise to learn that Hammerstein wrote the lyrics for this, and as does so much of his work, it raises the question of the representation of racial Others, in this case black slaves, by dominant whites. Liza, who leads the song, is less of a problem than her husband, Joe, stereotypically shiftless, sartorially ridiculous, and a virtuoso dancer (played by Avon Long), but still is uncomfort-

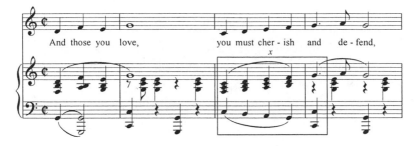

Ex. 4.7. Gentlemen Unafraid.

able in her function, she and her companions being the unwitting carriers rather than possessors of ironic perception. The song's standpoint is ignorance, which *we* are supposed to understand as deeper wisdom but *they* only suffer:

> YOUNG WOMAN: Whut she mean by dat?
> OLD WOMAN: She means 'bout Marse Bob fightin' against us.
> YOUNG WOMAN: But he done go wid de Yankees. Ain't dey fightin' *fo'* us?
> OLD WOMAN: 'Course dey ain't. De North is fightin' against de South. You is f'um de South, ain't you?
> YOUNG WOMAN: Dat's right. *(She looks puzzled, then turns to Liza)* Whut you make o' all dis, Liza?
> *(Pause. LIZA looks off, as if she hadn't heard)*
> LIZA: Doan ax me . . . Ignorant Darkies lak us doan understand sech things . . .
> *(There is a hush among the others as they listen to her—a silent pause, then she starts to sing)*

"How Would I Know?" is a terrific number nevertheless, at thirty-one pages of rehearsal score certainly one of Kern's biggest musical spans. Liza's stirring tune, in the rhythmic manner of "Battle Hymn of the Republic," builds irresistibly, and in 1938 full use seems to have been made of the forty-strong opera chorus, equally large dance ensemble, and two extra female choirs, one white and one black, drafted in for the occasion. The tableau climaxes twice, once for battle and the second time for defeat and Lincoln's voice-over speech. One can easily imagine Kern, jealous of *Porgy and Bess*'s corporate élan, wanting to match it here and in "De Land o' Good Times," which builds very much like "Can't Help Lovin' Dat Man." Perhaps he succeeded.[47]

Very Warm for May

Very Warm for May is about a stagestruck girl, May, who runs away from home to take part in a barn theater production in opposition to her Broadway *Wunderkind* brother. He despises summer stock but rescues the show when its comically experimental director walks out on it. He also falls productively in love with a representative of the amateur world, as does May.

In this show a new element, mockery, enters the equation. In 1939 it did Hammerstein and Kern no good, and it is difficult now to unpick both its motivation and the effect it must have had on the show's creative team and then on audiences. For *Very Warm for May* appears rather perversely to halt the development of the folk musical and reinstate the show musical with disastrous generic consequences. *Annie Get Your Gun* would eventually demonstrate how both genres could be fused by careful choice of historical setting, as, rather more ambiguously, would *Kiss Me, Kate* when it mixed up comic crooks with a production of a putative Shakespeare musical. There must have been a faint echo of *Very Warm for May* in *Kiss Me, Kate* when the latter's leading man was named Fred Graham, for Will Graham (the name changed from Jarman after the Boston tryout) is the former's *paterfamilias* with a gangsters' debt—or rather he was, until that strand of the plot was notoriously excised by the show's producer, Max Gordon.[48]

Were the narrative simplification and the loss of mortal danger underlying May's escape to the barn theater really responsible for the show's failure? Kern himself thought so. "In the original version," Bordman comments, "the first act ended with a stunned, compassionate Winnie consoling a terrified May with a touching reprise of 'In Other Words, Seventeen.' With the hoods and their imminent menace expunged the same finale sounded hollow and sugary." Without access to the first script, one can only guess that more important still were the low comic touches offsetting the pretentiousness of Ogdon Quiler's Progressive Playshop Theatre Guild, Inc., and its output: the emotional susceptibility of one of the gangsters, finally demonstrated when he sings half a refrain of "All the Things You Are," must have been unforgettable. One presumes that this was the character feebly modulated into the chaperone Kenny in the revision; sadly, although listed on the CD recording, Kenny's rendition of "All the Things You Are" has not been preserved.[49]

There is still plenty of comic obstruction in the revised *Very Warm for May*. But much of it borders on the self-referential, and this is where the

Fig. 4.4. *Very Warm for May*, L'Histoire de Madame de la Tour.

show would have split its audience, closing out those not in the know, a fatal divide in the half-incestuous, half- puritanical community that was the New York theater of 1939. Hammerstein could not handle innuendo, or was not expected or permitted to do so by his arbiters. With war already raging in Europe and soon to engulf the United States, it was no time to challenge a Broadway audience's masculinity.

Challenge it the show certainly did. When Hammerstein's stage directions describe the "18th century flavor contributed by the wigs and shoes" of the poolside rococo ballet rehearsal as "grotesquely diluted" by the participants' twentieth-century swimming trunks he was understating a spectacle that must have been outrageously camp (fig. 4.4). Ogdon Quiler, his name all too suggestive of the "odd" "queer" he most certainly is, throws one effete tantrum after another, the final one splendidly captured on the original cast recording when he laughs himself off the stage in act 2 like a latter-day Sextus Beckmesser: "What has become of my little play? . . . I thought I had something to say in the theatre, but I suddenly find my play invaded by strangers, who tell me I can't say it my way. Well, if I can't say what I have to say in my way, I don't want to say it at all! I don't want

to open the show! . . . I'm going to be a novelist. To hell with the theatre!"[50]

More insidious still is the suspicion that Quiler somehow represented
the temperamental, psychologically insecure Gordon and that Gordon's dis-
comfiture with Hammerstein and his team stemmed from this. As Cole
Porter had stated five years earlier,

> When Rockefeller still can hoard en-
> Nough money to let Max Gordon
> Produce his shows,
> Anything goes.

It took one to know one, perhaps.

Twenty years later, and in the right hands, *Very Warm for May* might
have become a cult experience like Sandy Wilson's *Valmouth* in Britain; ten
years earlier, the likes of Eddie Cantor might have gotten away with it. But
the very notion of commemorating Bessie Marbury, the lesbian producer of
the Princess Theatre shows, in a musical must have set Kern and Hammerstein off on the wrong foot; no doubt if Harbach had been involved he would
have been a restraining influence, for *Roberta* had unproblematically exploited a somewhat similar figure ("Aunt Minnie" rather than "Winnie") in
its title character. Winnie Spofford as played by Eve Arden is virtually a pantomime dame, but her interruption of Quiler's rehearsal with sandwiches all
round and her determination to glamorize May as a fallen young woman are
pure Marbury. Marbury's memoirs, published long before, had made much
of "my girls" with their "souls looking heavenward" and of her insistence on
"hot bouillion, coffee and sandwiches [being] provided for the members of
the staff, company and stage hands, when these long hours engendered all
this physical strain and fatigue." Whether, like Winnie, she was perennially
trying to palm vaudeville hopefuls off on her writers for theatrical relief is
less certain.[51]

There are also probable references to the authors themselves—perhaps
to Kern in the following exchange between Quiler and a local journalist:

> OGDON: Well, Mr. Hancock, you and all of Fairfield will soon be proud of
>   this child. The whole state of Connecticut will be proud of her. *(Pause)*
> HANCOCK: Why?
> *(The sound of his voice is such a distinct shock that all heads turn in his
> direction)*

This echoes Kern's advice to the young Paul Weston: "Young man, if you want to accomplish anything in this business you must remember that it is extremely important that you meet every suggestion with the word 'why?,' and say it loudly and in an annoying manner."[52] Hammerstein's pretensions toward epic chronology are brought to the fore in Quiler's comment "The entire story takes place in an old Connecticut garden; the action covering two hundred years . . . let that soak in!—Two hundred years!," and those toward epic scope of action when a little later he says, "[In] our civil war sequence . . . we accomplish in a few strokes what it takes four hours to do on the screen," an obvious dig at the imminent *Gone With the Wind* but also perhaps at *Gentlemen Unafraid*, whose shadow lurks in the dialogue being rehearsed on the following page of script.

Hammerstein probably recognized in Quiler the perilous line he himself trod between dramatic effectiveness and pretension when he described him at his first entrance as "up to a point, talented, beyond that point, phoney"; and he made sure that what since *Music in the Air* was becoming something of a personal trademark, the act 2 sermon, should clarify the point, as it does lyrically in famous later examples such as "Carefully Taught" from *South Pacific* and "The Farmer and the Cowman" from *Oklahoma!* In *Very Warm for May* there are two sermons, the first itself about clarifying points. When Quiler is taken to task for his dramatic surrealism, which necessitates a sofa and a chandelier mysteriously appearing in a forest, he protests, "I don't want it to be clear! I don't believe in coddling my audiences. They must learn to find out for themselves what a play is about," whereupon Johnny Graham, the Broadway realist, retorts with patronage aplenty, "Well, I know what you're driving at, but it ought to be written so that Kenny and Mr. Schlessinger can understand it." The second comes when Johnny, who has earlier acknowledged that he prefers excellence to originality ("I like things to be like other things—only much better"), counts sincerity among his ten commandments and lectures Liz on how to sing a song, the stage direction reading: "*He is worked up now. Here is something he feels deeply. Sincerity on the stage is his religion.*" But he makes Liz cry, and she accuses him of caring more for his profession than for people. Her brother is in love with his sister, who a few pages earlier has been accused by him of exactly the same failing. The story, then, is about the conflicting claims and values of professionalism and spontaneous human warmth, about whether "people like the Spoffords" can ever be "happy with people like the Grahams"; probably also about the Spoffords' old money and the newer social entrenchment of the Grahams (which makes it a pity they were not given Jewish names).[53]

This epiphany, which closes the last scene but two, was presumably in the mind of one reviewer who complained that the show "does not achieve a sense of direction until the last half hour of the vexing evening."[54] But is it the real theme of the musical?

By 1939, with Europe falling apart, the dramatic conflict in an American musical set in the present could only be about America itself, no longer about the relationship between the old world and the new. The simplest idea was to transfer such tensions to those between generations, and this is what Rodgers and Hart had done in *Babes in Arms* (1937). More than anything, *Very Warm for May* appears to be emulating their success with this show and their earlier *On Your Toes* (1936) with its modern ballet and genuine criminal thrill. May, "leftily dignified" and defying her theatrical elders in order to be part of a summer show in the New York hinterland, is not just very much in the mold of the *Babes in Arms* youngsters, but was played by Grace McDonald, still only eighteen, who had starred in *Babes in Arms* even younger. But Kern was ten years older than Hammerstein and less adaptable than he to a "young faces" approach necessitating at least some sympathy with idealistic politics; confusion in the show's viewpoint will easily have arisen.

The latent musical corollary to the generational theme in *Very Warm for May* is Tin Pan Alley facing swing. Yet what Quiler and his "progressive" art represent undercuts this, for it is never clear what his evening's entertainment actually consists of. (It is "a fantastic play that is never defined," that same reviewer protested—a series of "operettes," apparently.) Nor can we grasp his musical ideal. His obscurantism ought surely to demand difficult modern sounds, yet his composer, Raymond, is a popular songsmith. To compound this confusion, we are asked to believe that what Johnny stands for, the Broadway commercial show, represents artistic integrity while the psychologically probing aims of Quiler do not, beyond that certain point. Somewhere in the middle of all this, jazz seems to stand in for modernity— but is that modernity the slangy youth of May and her chums or the stuffy cerebration of Quiler? He is certainly not on the same wavelength as his players, as their giggles in his first rehearsal make clear, and if anything the music for his ballets suggests now a bygone romanticism, now a twee neo-classicism.

All show musicals run the risk of confusion when the diegetic point at issue is musical style, and here is a particularly potent example because the real stylistic pressures on Kern in this work were not those of the rival directors, Quiler and Graham, which he was somehow supposed to illustrate, but those of the contemporary Broadway he was trying to reconquer. His allegiance was to Tin Pan Alley but his obligation was toward the fashion of the decade, swing. Swing by now meant specialist scoring and arrangement, and this had already produced friction in *Swing Time*. Now Kern and Bennett drew on the vocal arrangements of the young Hugh Martin for the "hot" number "High Up in Harlem," and perhaps for the first time since the "Butterfly Ballet" in *Sally* a musical high point in a Kern stage show is scarcely his authorial property. There are four other factors in the score that make it what it is, and they all deserve consideration: a new orchestral sound, based on swing and including saxophones; a changing approach to song form; neoclassical modernism; and vocal performance practice.

Very Warm for May was Kern's first stage (as opposed to film) show with swing band scoring. Saxophones dominate the pit band's overture on the recording, and Bennett and Kern certainly knew how to update their textures and sometimes their forms accordingly, but at bottom it is voices that define the change of style. Grace McDonald's is the girlish belt of the screen teenager. A low chest-voice tessitura with discreet head-voice peaks can be savored in her performance of "That Lucky Lady," its insistent nadir pitch g sharp or a flat (though there is also a g natural), its apex a chested a^1 in the first B section, but rewritten sequentially, affording a head-voice b^1 and c^1, second time around in the $ABAB_1$ form. This is the vulnerable yet determined persona of a Judy Garland, its exploitation by Kern coinciding more or less with the release of *The Wizard of Oz* in August 1939. A new voice type for Kern, this particular song was probably not written for it, being first sung by Raymond a 4th higher in F major as "That Lucky Fellow." At the lower pitch McDonald must surely have been amplified to compete with the heavy orchestral scoring, and the recording suggests as much.[55] As Leighton Brill pointed out to Hammerstein during the casting process, "All our singers of today . . . have sung only before a mike." We find Kern vigorously resisting this type of singer at audition with accusations of "commonness," until, as Brill reports, "the news of . . . shows, such as . . . Larry and Dick Rodger's two, has at length stirred Mr. Jerome Kern to a point wherein he sees somebody good and he is willing to sign instead of stall."[56]

"That Lucky Lady" is slim and sleek in its lines, rising through a slow chromatic tritone across the insinuating, octave-doubled melody of its A section. "In Other Words, Seventeen" is less graceful. The pandiatonic emphasis on scale degree 2 is all very well (see the sonorous jazziness of the chording at the end of the B section of the refrain, giving a B$^\flat$-d-f-g-c^1 chord), but we are now a perfect 4th lower than the key and tessitura of an earlier Kern song whose melodic design this one strongly resembles, "Sitting Pretty," and "Sitting Pretty" was much more roundly contoured. Representing teenage gangliness is one thing, but the song's extra section inserted before the AC reprise is crass, and Hammerstein, with lyrics such as "I'm reading Karl Marx and Steinbeck too / Sprinkled with Hemingway," was foundering here.[57] May's other two first-act numbers show Kern departing from thirty-two-bar forms but failed to make their mark. "May Tells All," plunging straight in with a lilt as to a verse without a refrain, trips along for an irregularly grouped eighteen bars in its second half and sounds old-fashioned despite certain echoes of the song "On Your Toes." "Me and the Roll and You" is more interesting, with the rhythmic *chutzpah* of Schwartz and Dietz's later "That's Entertainment," but it was cut before the New York opening. Like "May Tells All" it consists of one melodic span that is neither verse nor refrain, and although the first twenty of its sixty bars sound prefatory, the next twenty-four feel more like a subdominant middle section than the main event until A major, not E, is confirmed as the song's tonic with the title phrase at the end of its final sixteen-bar period. This gives an ABC form subdividing aa$_1$bb$_1$bcb$_2$, the proportions eight, twelve, eight, eight, eight, eight, and eight bars. The tonal insecurity of the twelve-bar a$_1$ section leading from E to A is curious, for it sounds modal rather than modulatory, a modern touch perhaps attributable to emulation of Rodgers, perhaps not. (Ex. 4.8, which shows the last eight bars of this section, also demonstrates May's low tessitura, the big band sonorities of Kern's new Broadway idiom, and Hammerstein's attempt at teenage slang.)

Jack Whiting, who played Johnny, was basically a baritone crooner and on the recording sounds as though he too relied on amplification. "Heaven in My Arms" is a fine number, again formally novel and loose-limbed and fashionably casual in the way the melody sits on the harmony, for Johnny, coolly admitting "I like it here," enters on an upper leading note that descends by leap; his refrain ("On through the night") then begins an octave lower with |7-61|3---| as though a relative minor statement but harmonized |I--|ii^9-V^{13}-|, all of which suggests the microphone's smoothing assistance. "All in Fun," which he also sings, has an angular refrain head motif (|5$^\sharp$4↑$^\flat$3-|-) and a wide vocal range that again would have been difficult to

Ex. 4.8. Me and the Roll and You.

place securely without amplification and even with it precludes sustained phrases (Whiting's are very short).

There is no secondary comic couple in *Very Warm for May*. But there are quite substantial interpolations by Alvin's Orchestra (Matty Malneck, violin, Milton Delugg, accordion, and others in the original production). Dramatically irrelevant they may be, but they underline the theme of new versus old style in their hot renditions of classics like the *William Tell* overture, Negro spirituals, and Liszt's *Liebesträume*, all very well done. So does the vocal swing extravaganza "High Up in Harlem," essentially a jazzed-up schottische. This was cut, but an extraordinarily hot instrumental version of it replaced Delugg's first set piece in act 1 as "Harlem Boogie-woogie." These and Kenny's rendition of "All the Things You Are," a dance by Avon Long as the black servant Jackson (no associated music surviving), and Winnie's

Ex. 4.9. "Very warm for May" figure.

and Quiler's spoken monologues—Quiler sings, but Winnie does not—take the place of vaudeville song and dance in this show. Two substantial musical moves in the opposite direction, culturally upward toward ballet and opera, both concern ensembles, ultimately *Very Warm for May*'s most distinctive feature.

Quiler's work, as will already be apparent from earlier discussion, is most easily demonstrated as vocal ballet—singers' movement now "arty," purged of its vaudeville inheritance—and there are three examples of it: "Ogdon's Characterization" in act 1, and "L'Histoire de Madame de la Tour" and the "Brain Ballet (The Strange Case of Adam Standish)" in act 2. All three, plus Quiler's musical love scene centered on "All the Things You Are," begin with music of a *fête galante* cast; probably the best way of approaching them is as a vaguely Gallic neoclassicism on the one hand (as though Quiler were Jean Cocteau or Guillaume Apollinaire, his musical correlatives Erik Satie or Sergey Prokofiev), and on the other as Kern's last attempt to put his "Pierrot pantomime" idea of 1917 into action. "Ogdon's Characterization" begins with an innocuous "tempo di minuetto" tune, "L'Histoire de Madame de la Tour" with a sung gavotte, the "Brain Ballet" with a sighing *claire de lune* motif in parallel 3rds plus walking bass that becomes the verse of "In the Heart of the Dark." The gavotte is extended to form a self-contained ABABA number plus interlude before turning itself into a waltz.[58] More interesting than these is "All the Things You Are" in that in its introduction a *bergomasque* accompaniment figure supports a pseudo-baroque cantilena including the figure *x* (ex. 4.9), which represents the words "very warm for May," spoken against it during an antique lovers' conversational tryst a few bars later. Was this to have played a larger part in the musical? Possibly, but as the score stands it lacks motivic and formal development, and the most extended musical number is "Ogdon's Characterization." Here, after the minuet (in

E flat) and some dialogue interruption, a complete ABAC instrumental re-frain underscores the actors' first attempts to read their lines, starting with Miss Wasserman impersonating the musket (*sic*). Ogdon then demonstrates what he wants, in a second complete song, in the subdominant with sixteen-bar verse and AABC refrain of thirty-six bars. The C section is repeated by the chorus; Ogdon then has a new release, D, which returns to C, as though CCDC were itself a "lyric binary" unit, all about Mr. McGee as a weeping willow. Ogdon follows this up back in the tonic with a complete reprise of the first, "musket" refrain, explaining how to characterize the object (rather well, actually), and still in the tonic (F major) proceeds to describe Miss Hyde's babbling brook in yet another complete refrain, this time in $ABCA_1$ form. Finally, back in E flat, the three actors plus a fourth, Mr. Pratt as a picket fence, sing their characterizations in four-part counterpoint, Miss Wasserman to the complete tune of the opening minuet; this is topped-and-tailed with a vamp that makes the modernist pretension but burlesque actu-ality of Ogdon's creation abundantly clear.

This is not quite the "set of young lithe pantomimists" Kern had dreamed of, for they sing. Importing Hollace Shaw, coloratura soprano, was on the other hand perhaps the closest manifestation yet of the fantasy idea im-plicit in Kern's 1933 memo to Hammerstein, for as Carroll she and her male counterpart Charles (Ralph Stuart, tenor) represent the "heart voices" of the actors in Quiler's psychological dramas. This allows Shaw to vocalize as high as d^3 in "All the Things You Are," supported by Charles and a seven-part chorus, an extraordinary aural experience fully captured on the recording, though even she appears to be amplified. In a similar capacity she also sings "In the Heart of the Dark" as the focus of Quiler's "Brain Ballet." This has the sumptuousness of cabaret rather than, as with "All the Things You Are," that of operetta and has been rightly seen as a nod toward Porter. (Compare "In the Still of the Night.") McGlinn's recording reveals it as a great song, and it was apparently Eva Kern's favorite. For all the other ingratiating tunes in *Very Warm for May*—and they are more of a piece, as "charm songs," than in any other score by Kern—it is "All the Things You Are" that stands out. Every commentator on Kern has praised it, pointing out the boldness of its chromatic contours and modulatory sequences, the brilliant simplicity of its enharmonic return from bridge to A section, and the discernment of a public which could, despite these apparent obstacles, turn it into a hit. One thing they have not mentioned is the degree to which it is impover-ished without a twenty-four-bar section of its verse published at the time but omitted in the anthologies, whose truncated verse ends with an upward and downward 5th in the voice part (and has different words). In the original version (though "Cantabile" in *Gentlemen Unafraid* was different again) this is expanded to upward 6ths in the yearning, Borodin-like transition ("Ah, me! If my heart could only find a voice!"), repeated sequentially in the relative minor, and developed into an extended imperfect cadence which prepares the minor-key opening of the refrain and its initial melodic gesture much more romantically. Whether Kern and Hammerstein really underestimated the song's impact has to be doubted, however, when it closes the show, the inarticulate Kenny's reprise of it, ending act 2 scene 4, having previously set this up with his lines,

> De dearest tings I know
> Is what you are —
> Some day my happy arms will hold you
> And some day I'll know dat moment devine,
> When all de tings you are — are —

My God — dat's a beautiful song![59]

One can hardly say more.

CHAPTER 5

Kern and Hollywood

A New Era

IN 1928, *BLUE EYES* WAS RUNNING NICELY AT THE NEW PICCADILLY THE-
atre in London when it had to make way for a film, *The Jazz Singer.*
This, as is well known, was, if not the first talkie, the first film to combine visual with verbal and musical entertainment in a successfully alluring
way; the first film musical, in effect. Its ousting of a stage musical play from
a West End theater was highly symbolic.

Significant, too, was the simultaneity of *Show Boat* with the coming of
sound to film. Ferber's novel appeared in installments in *Woman's Home
Companion* between April and September 1926. It was widely noticed, became almost the first Book of the Month, and immediately attracted (silent)
film offers, for it was exactly the epic stuff of which mass-market films were
then made; they were attempting to attract a "better" audience by "imitating
the middle-class forms of the novel and legitimate theater."[1] Nothing, therefore, shows more clearly Kern's ambitious cast of mind in the mid-1920s than
his determination to appropriate *Show Boat* for his own purposes. The novel
appeared in book form in August 1926, and by November he and Hammerstein had purchased its "dramatico-musical" rights.

But something else had happened in August: on the sixth, Warner Bros.
had released their first Vitaphone evening in New York—a demonstration
of film with synchronized sound. Even if it was more a filmed variety concert than anything else, all the items being shorts, one would like to know
whether Kern was there and, if so, whether he sensed that the dictates of

musical theater were about to change forever. He may well have been present, for, concerned enough to attend a New York songwriters' meeting a few months later, which had been called "to discuss what might be an important development in the modern theater: sound pictures," he asked the assembly, "Have any of you heard this Vitaphone?" When one and all demurred, he said dismissively, "Well I have, and it will never amount to anything! Good day, gentlemen!"[2] This sounds like denial, occurring as it did only a week or so before he handed Bennett the "yards and yards of music" for *Show Boat*'s act 1 scene 1.

If Vitaphone *did* catch on—and Bennett judged it was sufficiently on Kern's mind that he could write a joke about it into his realization of *Show Boat* sketches: a passage marked for "English Horn and Vitaphone"—then it would have a variety of implications. The stage musical would have to alter its approach and subject matter in order to appeal to a much broader, less affluent, more transcontinental audience than the New Yorkers who had basked in musical comedy's reflexive portrayals; if it did not, packaged musical melodramas *with copyrighted songs*—this presumably is why the songwriters gathered to look into their future—would henceforward be the new, sole province of the screen. Conversely, film might achieve a technical sophistication (particularly in terms of dramatic continuity) and blend of music and narrative that left the musical stage outmoded and the ordinary person a much more discriminating critic of the genre. Or musical comedies might begin to expect a whole new afterlife in royalties from screened versions of their dramaturgy with the original music in the right places, and maybe with the original artists singing it, which was what was missing from the silent film versions of three of Kern's musicals that had already been made.[3]

Hollywood would all too soon demonstrate that it cared as little about the original music in the right places as it did about the original artists singing it, but, as if to prove that *Show Boat*, the stage show, had been conceived all along with the new medium of sound film in mind, it did choose that musical as a rare opportunity to come up with something approaching an authentic transformation of a Broadway production for the screen. This was in the 1936 Universal film, directed by James Whale, and it strongly suggests that with *Show Boat* Kern and Hammerstein had been aiming toward film all along. Shortened to less than two hours, the score, including three new songs (plus two more that were cut and are lost), and the new, tighter, closer-to-the-novel screenplay provided by Hammerstein together offer the most satisfying, balanced, and compelling version of *Show Boat* as drama achieved up to the present day. In almost every way it is superior to the stage version and its variants. Key performances, "very close to what they were on the stage," were captured, namely, those of Charles Winninger (Captain Andy), Helen Morgan (Julie), Irene Dunne (who played Magnolia on tour), and Sammy White (Frank); Robeson's as Joe was incorporated.[4] Baravalle again conducted, and Bennett's orchestrations were largely retained, to particular advantage in the second stanza of "Bill" with its halo of strings against a soft-focus Morgan, who gives the definitive performance of the song.

The songs are reduced in number, spread out fairly evenly as highlights, and very clearly offset against the spoken drama with its underscoring; in other words, there is no attempt to "integrate" them, the formal model being closer to musical comedy than in the stage version, though it is also boldly operatic in that Allan Jones's and Irene Dunne's trained concert voices transport us into an unashamedly unnaturalistic, romantic world with their first and third duets (though not with the second). Kern's three new songs are all important. "I Still Suits Me," for Joe and Queenie, promotes them musically to secondary couple, a bold, warm move which Robeson's and Hattie McDaniel's abilities more than justify. "I Have the Room Above Her," the extra love duet for Magnolia and Ravenal that shows the development of their wooing between "Make-believe" and "You Are Love," is among Kern's tenderest conceptions. In a scene to be cherished, Ravenal sings it quietly (so as not to be overheard by Parthy) to Magnolia's rinsed-out stocking hanging below his window, and even more quietly hums a coda of simple, intense beauty that later forms both their wedding march and underscoring for the newborn Kim in her cradle. Kim's birth scene is restored from the novel, along with excellent footage of the river in flood; the World's Fair scene is dropped from the stage show in favor of a montage of Chicago pleasure jaunts in which we realize for the first time, again in new accordance with the novel, how much Magnolia accepted and enjoyed the life—a crucial antecedent to her speech on receiving Ravenal's letter of desertion. Here Dunne's later film *Joy of Living* is foreshadowed. We also realize for the first time how central Captain Andy is to the entire enterprise, as a study of an old-time actor-manager, and why Winninger was Ziegfeld's highest-paid member of the troupe. Once in the middle of each act he rescues the diegetic show, first when the Backwoodsman wrecks it and Andy has to complete the plot on his own, second, and more important, when Magnolia is faltering in front of a hostile audience at her Trocadero debut. Winninger actually conducts the *ritardando* into the refrain of "After the Ball," and conducts it well, sweat glistening on his desperate forehead, as though his theatrical intervention saves the *music* for the diegetic audience, the singer, and us. He is the maestro, and the viewer, exactly in Magnolia's stage position as performer, is obliged to obey and succeed. This is real music theater. Even "Gallivantin' Aroun'," Magnolia's blackface number for the *Cotton Blossom* olio, should not be spurned (though it was nearly cut). In addition to the painful irony of its performance to a host of real blacks in the gallery it reminds us, since she does it so well, that her actual career, rapidly glossed over in the novel and all dramatic versions of it, would have been founded as much on blackface as anything else in that era of coon shouters. She was never the "Old Fashioned Wife" of the early Kern song she teaches to Kim in her elegant drawing room, not even on the stage, this last a subtle musical touch among others. "Gallivantin' Aroun'" returns to provide the musical finale, transformed into a spectacular revue number for Kim, drastically curtailed though this was.

Uncertain Genres

Until *Swing Time* appeared in August 1936, it was unclear what a Kern film musical should look and sound like. *Show Boat*, released in May 1936, was for all its glory an adaptation, as had been the sound film versions of *Sally*, *Sunny*, *The Cat and the Fiddle*, *Music in the Air*, *Sweet Adeline*, and *Roberta* before it. *Men of the Sky* seems never to have appeared with its entire score and went virtually unnoticed. *I Dream Too Much* (released November 1935) was an intriguing blend of melodrama and boudoir operetta—its plot has distinct similarities to that of *The Cat and the Fiddle*—that was not followed up. It was the sole fruit of any substance from Kern's second and third stays in Hollywood in 1934–35: writing "Lovely to Look At" for a much altered *Roberta* and title music for a pair of MGM straight dramas, *Reckless* and *The Flame Within*, hardly gave him a new profile to compensate for his Broadway silence. The musical was moribund during this period, languishing for lack of investment on Broadway and, with some notable exceptions, ousted from any developing role in Hollywood's tough-guy period. What one misses from Kern in both films is music that *heals* the characters—a musical's true vocation—for the title song of *Reckless* is indifferent and its only celebratory numbers are by others.

Both these films, as with Ramon Novarro in *The Cat and the Fiddle* and

Henry Fonda in *I Dream Too Much*, owe their sexual *frisson* to a weak, vulnerable, or irredeemable and very young playboy who is good to look at: Louis Hayward in *The Flame Within*, Franchot Tone in *Reckless*. If Hollywood was courting a gay or "fag-hag" audience, as had ballet for some time, it would later be followed up on the stage with *Pal Joey*; but Novarro's singing voice (the only one of the four to be heard) was weak, and for the young male to flourish in musical film, looks had to be sacrificed for performing ability, initially in the shape of Fred Astaire. All Kern's later film musicals, with the exception of *Centennial Summer* and the operatic *When You're in Love*, arguably, relied on at least one real musical comedy star or its equivalent to carry them—Fred Astaire, Ginger Rogers, Gene Kelly, Deanna Durbin, Allan Jones, Irene Dunne.

Might *Men of the Sky*, if released at any other moment, have been able to alter this fact? As noted, the film is lost. But its music and screenplay survive, and rather as with Gershwin in *Delicious* of the same year they offer a glimpse at counterfactual history in the shape of a stage musical rethought in cinematic terms with the composer's authorial voice fully in place, something that rarely if ever happened afterward on the screen.

In the first scene of *Men of the Sky*, the American tennis champion Jack Ames has just beaten his German friend Eric von Coburg and is talking to the Alsatian Madeleine, with whom both men are in love. As in the abandoned version of act 1 scene 3 of *Show Boat*, Kern attempts recitative over the movie's theme tune, "Ev'ry Little While," which represents the hotel orchestra's melody of the moment and Jack's response to it: "There's a message in that old melody they're playing—/ A message that I would like to be saying / If I but thought that you would hear me," he sings. This would hardly have worked among the first words uttered between the primary lovers in the film, and the script has them spoken instead, but it indicates the extent of musical authority in its creators' minds. (It also shows a rare indecision about the motivic shape of a melody: compare its |56123 opening with the |56713 published form of ex. 1.8.) More counterpoint emerges when Madeleine's father, a secret agent, explains to her that he has dedicated his life to France ever since he fought in vain to prevent Strasbourg from falling to the Germans in 1870 (it remained German until 1918); she is to be his spy when she stays with the von Coburgs for a month near Heidelberg (was this location Kern's doing?). She has just become engaged to Jack, but this destroys her hopes of following him to America, and she hums "Stolen Dreams" while her father, shuffling his papers, hums "La Marseillaise." The orchestra's staccato osti

Ex. 5.1. Stolen Dreams and La Marseillaise.

nato suggests he is already thinking of the Morse code messages he will be sending his countrymen (ex. 5.1). As often in Kern's music, the counterpoint makes for a somewhat impoverished tune, not to mention a typically feeble rhyme, "dreams" / "schemes," from Harbach.

But soon melodies are carrying rather more literal messages than Jack had envisaged, and this one ("Stolen Dreams"), intended as the title song of the film, bears the burden of the plot. Separated from Madeleine at the outbreak of the First World War and believing her sojourn with the von Co-burgs to represent her betrayal of their engagement, Jack signs up with the French as an aviator, and behind enemy lines in Prussian disguise he too carries spy messages. Madeleine turns out to be the sender, and they are re-united amidst great danger. They agree that when a shepherd's pipe is heard, she will play a gentle theme on the piano ("Stolen Dreams") if the coast is clear for him to retrieve the message she has deposited in the garden, but something more lively if it is not. After a while the German colonel begins to guess that her music is coded and, in von Coburg's anxious, conflicted presence, forces her to play "Stolen Dreams" against her will. However, she still has a card up her sleeve, the musical Morse code, and even though the colonel's sidekick recognizes what she is doing, Jack understands the code and has retrieved the message from the tree before they have time to find it:

> *(Just as she is lighting [a] cigarette for him [the Colonel], there is heard outside the playing of a shepherd's pipe. Her hand does not tremble—her eyes are steady—even though the Colonel's eyes are searching hers. She blows match out.)*
>
> MADELEINE: Listen—Isn't that a pretty motif. It is old Bartholomes—he plays like that every evening. *(She goes to piano)* I've often thought a lovely ballad could be built on that phrase.
>
> *(She plays the shepherd's theme over—then repeats it with accompaniment. Then develops it into a grayer mood.)*
>
> COLONEL *(shows he recognizes the lively tune)*: Very interesting—but I like something—more tender—that dream song—I heard you play—the last time I was here.
>
> *(She registers, again the shepherd's pipe is heard.)*
>
> COLONEL: Play! Fräulein!
>
> *(This time there is command in his voice. Eric is watching the situation anxiously. If she refuses to play, she admits guilt. If she plays,—what?)*
>
> *(Madeleine starts to play* Stolen Dreams *very tenderly. Eric looks relieved. Now she puts a little more emotion into her singing and as though to support the voice, she adds a few notes into the accompaniment. All watch with interest—especially Schmidt, who is sitting where he can see her hands.)*
>
> CUT TO PATHWAY OUTSIDE
>
> *(Jack, in Prussian uniform, is coming up the driveway seen in the light of the old lantern. Madeleine's singing comes to him. Now he stops and listens. He recognizes a change in the rhythm of the accompaniment. Now he beats with his right hand—showing he is getting the beats. He suddenly realizes that a message is being sent to him. He looks for Lantern.)*
>
> CUT TO ROOM INSIDE
>
> *(The picture just as it was before, only Schmidt has his notebook and pencil out and is jotting something down. He suddenly rushes to Colonel, who watches.)*
>
> SCHMIDT: She is sending a message.—"Danger—Don't come in"—"The lantern on the tree. Don't come in—The lantern on the tree."
>
> CUT TO LANTERN
>
> *(Jack is taking the envelope from behind the lantern.)*

Sadly, the music for this particular scene is absent from the Library of Congress score, but example 5.1 presumably gives some idea of it, as does the music cue for an earlier, unexpected entrance of the Colonel: here, from "Stolen Dreams," Madeleine swiftly segues into an energetic French waltz rather like those of Victor in *The Cat and the Fiddle*.

Immediately after the excerpt given above, Oscar, the witless male half of the secondary couple, recognizes Jack and gives him away. Both Jack and Madeleine are arrested and sentenced to death, though in a few last moments together, courtesy of von Coburg, they sing their reunion song, "Cottage of Content," in counterpoint with a four-part processional chorus from the chapel next to the prison, its bells pealing in the song's key of C major after the singing has stopped. The picture fades as the guards prepare to take Madeleine to the firing squad, and a drum roll and low percussive chords of B major, a final suggestion of code as well as of heartbeats, tattoo, or the actual firing, end the score, a closing modernist touch to integrate its operatic dimension. This was certainly intended as cathartic tragedy set to music, though there is still spoken dialogue in the final scene; it failed to impress one reviewer, however, who thought the captive Jack and Madeleine "are treated more as guests in church than enemies."[5]

Much of the *Men of the Sky* score would be reused, and, as noted, some of it originated elsewhere. But there is plenty of unique music too, and at 130 pages of piano/vocal score it should certainly be counted one of Kern's major works; he probably wrote more for it than for many, if not all, of the later films. "I'll Share Them All With You" and "Suzette" are the stuff of gay Parisian spectacle (see fig. 5.1 for Jack Whiting as Jack Ames, fourth from the left), and once again there is contrapuntal exploitation when the former tune is joined by a bugle call to barracks, as in *Carmen*. Other music includes the song "All's Well With the World," a foreshadowing of "Matchmaker, Matchmaker" from *Fiddler on the Roof*, and instrumentals for the two action interludes, cutting between identical cabaret and military formations, a neat filmic idea with its musical counterpart of a lively, "symphonic" collection of motifs (words are later added to these as "Flying Field").

All in all, *Men of the Sky* is a pivotal work in Kern's output in more senses than introducing him to his second career, the one in Hollywood. It was his first show with Harbach alone and links his 1920s idiom and its *belle époque* roots with his later style, for there are echoes of *Sunny* in the cabaret songs as well as foretastes of *The Cat and the Fiddle* in the use of two pianos

Fig. 5.1. *Men of the Sky,* Paris sequence.

(specified for part of the cabaret), a pianist as female lead, and the conflict of nationalities. It was the first of three "integrated" scores in which musical composition is their very subject. The battle ("Flying Field") music is similar to that of *Blue Eyes* ("His Majesty's Dragoons"), while the link with *Three Sisters* was more than expedient, for in both plots (as again in *Gentlemen Unafraid*) the leading couple is separated by war, and the passing of time creates an epic dimension (even felt with Shirley's unanswered letters in *The Cat and the Fiddle*). If in a traditional musical comedy everyone decides to go somewhere else at the end of act 1, in the musical play—and here, following *Show Boat*—parting follows betrothal: one person is separated, as in romance plots such as *The Winter's Tale*. Time has to pass, too, which lends "Ev'ry Little While," one of Kern's most haunting tunes, a sadness which was always part of his idiom but can now be crucial to the plot. (The screenplay is explicit about the dreadful depredations made by three years of war on the cafe musicians and others: they are starving.) One wonders even whether Kern was conscious of the parallel with *Tristan und Isolde* in prefacing a reunion in death with a lover's coded arrival on shepherd's pipe with its gay or sad melodic alternatives.

After the leaden locution of Harbach it is a relief to turn to the effortless, airy lyrics of Dorothy Fields in *I Dream Too Much*, presaging their vivacity in *Swing Time*. As stated above, the whole film needs (and lacks) a lift from musical comedy star turns, yet in many respects it is admirable, a faultless dramaturgical conception and severely underrated. Henry Fonda and Lili Pons play out what is narratively the best of Kern's musical problem pieces, following up the battle of styles of *The Cat and the Fiddle* and the battle of theatrical standards of *Music in the Air* with a battle of economic pride. Once again an ambitious, overserious operatic composer is made to realize that musical comedy is not demeaning, for his tunes are "just like Schubert," as a first-night admirer puts it, once updated in his wife's London production (an Ivor Novello kind of affair, all swirly waltzes, though Fonda's character, the composer Jonathan Street, is American). In fact the film's title number, which the admirer has just heard, is definitely not like Schubert, and must be Kern's most chromatic song, moving almost entirely by semitones for the first eight bars of the refrain and the first two of the verse.

In *I Dream Too Much*, because of the sustained focus on character psychology and motivation, showing from the start an ill-matched couple who thereby have all the more to teach each other through suffering and serial separations, one takes the plot seriously. But it is not satisfying as a musical. Most of the musical focus is on Pons as a young opera star, which at that time she really was—her sensational Met debut had occurred four years earlier. Pons's stratospheric coloratura (she used to sing the mad scene from *Lucia di Lammermoor* a tone higher than written) is witnessed plentifully, in "Caro nome" from *Rigoletto* at the start of the film, in the "Bell Song" from *Lakmé* in her triumphant operatic debut, a complete rendition in full production that slows the film's pace all too indicatively, and in some of Kern's music. "The Jockey on the Carrousel" ends on a top B, "I'm the Echo (You're the Song That I Sing)" on a top D in the scores (both with coloratura passages), "I Got Love" on top B in the film. Yet she proves, as few have proved since, that an opera singer can be a swing entertainer by singing the music straight. She does this in "I Got Love," during her nightclub phase (to her husband's displeasure), and a fine song it is, an outgrowth of "Can't Help Lovin' Dat Man" with jazz and swing underpinnings added and with much richer harmonies. Representative of Kern's attempt throughout this film to get away from verse/refrain structures, "I Got Love" still feels like an AABA module (the dominant return is focal). But its introduction serves as the B section, which returns as coda, its verse and refrain are blended through the long notes at the beginning of each phrase, with one of the verse phrases returning before the bridge, and it has two recapitulatory As. In other words, the form is much more complicated: $B^8x^4y^4x^4y_1{}^4A^8A^8y^2y_2{}^4B^8A^8A^8B_1{}^8$, the long notes giving it a circularity that belies even this scheme. At the same time, however, "I Got Love" signals the difficulty Kern will have modernizing his rhythm for swing, for it barely avoids stodginess, from which the band arrangement and Pons's compelling performance luckily redeem it. "The Jockey on the Carrousel" is, understandably enough, also circular in motivic construction, with a *moto perpetuo* ostinato and very French rhythms, though on the broadest front (a 120-bar song with 32-bar A sections) still an AABA conception. "I Dream Too Much" also departs from formal norms, for after a 24-bar verse comes a false 16-bar refrain before the real one.

Swing Time and the Return of Musical Comedy

Swing Time was the sixth of the Astaire/Rogers musical films for RKO. Porter (*The Gay Divorcee*) and Berlin (*Top Hat, Follow the Fleet*) had already contributed three of the scores, Kern a fourth with *Roberta*; Gershwin would compose one for *Shall We Dance* (and another, for *A Damsel in Distress*, starring Astaire without Rogers). All the films are classics, and if *Swing Time* divided its initial critics more than its predecessors—verdicts ranging from "the very best musical that these two have ever given their admiring public" to "a disappointment" blamed on Kern's having "shadow-boxed with swing . . . right now we could not even whistle a bar of 'A Fine Romance,' and that's about the catchiest and brightest melody in the show"—all cavils were relative to ongoing sublimity.[6]

From Kern's point of view *Swing Time* signaled the triumphant return of musical comedy to its central place in his output, if without the abundance of witty songs pertaining to a stage show (there are only five in *Swing Time*, plus one foreground and one background instrumental): "Like all descendants of Roman New Comedy (Shakespeare and stage musicals among them)," Gerald Mast comments, "the FredandGingers turn on structural symmetries . . . In *Swing Time* there are two weddings that don't take place (at the beginning and the end), and two times that the drawing of cuffs on a pair of pants delays those weddings, and two presumed fiancés, Margaret (Betty Furness) for Fred and Ricardo (Georges Metaxa) for Ginger, and two older but wiser sidekicks (Victor Moore for Fred and Helen Broderick for Ginger), and two nightclub owners competing for Ricardo's orchestra, and two cuttings of the cards for the services of that orchestra." *Swing Time* triumphs on this basis but also rehabilitates vaudeville. As Henry Jenkins has shown, Hollywood and its well-made plays, with their ever more bourgeois codes of genre and humor, progressively outlawed the anarchy of the silent screen, the slapstick of the circus, and the episodic pleasures of vaudeville, though these refused to bow out of its schemes and add a vital element of crazy delight to many an "integrated" film. *I Dream Too Much* is a perfect example of this survival, for it lacks a secondary, comic couple (and there is never a hint at alternative pairings), relying instead on Eric Blore and The Duchess, his trained seal that steals the show, trumping its subversion in death ("Ever had a seal die in your arms?" Blore asks Fonda dreamily when he is supposed to be serving drinks at a society party). Blore's "mad scene" duet on his flute with Pons in the flat above, and her stealing of the seal's fish hanging out of his window, are crazy precursors of the romantic setting of "I Have the Room Above Her" in the 1936 *Show Boat*.[7]

In a musical, music must steal the show, with or without trained seals, and *Swing Time* is the first of Kern's original film musicals (as opposed to the adaptations) in which it does this. At the outset, the film shows yet another uncertain mix of comedy and realism involving feckless, indigent males, much in need of female reconstruction, in a world of harsh urbanity. Astaire and Victor Moore ("Pop") make their penniless way in a goods truck to New York, where they immediately encounter cops, accusations of theft, a cigarette machine they storm, a dance school they crash, and a hotel room they can't pay for, indulging in deception on all these fronts. But it takes only Astaire's first, long-awaited break into song, indicatively as he sits on the floor following a self-induced pratfall (*willing* the musical comedy, as it were) and with a number entitled "Pick Yourself Up," to bathe the audience in glorious light music and sublime dancing rather than challenge them with an economically and psychologically driven plot. Both goofy and suave, its initial vamp (Astaire begins with no introduction) conveys the emotional reassurance of inner-part sustained half notes alongside quirky dislocations of rhythm (the not quite "oompah" figure, the end-stopped vocal phrases) and harmony (the false relation between A sharp and A natural). A Kern polka is perfect for this moment and is what "Pick Yourself Up" becomes:

the best of them all, however much indebted to that of Jaromír Weinberger's *Schwanda the Bagpiper* (which was noticed at the time and to whose inner-part chromaticism Bennett refers in his orchestration). Its impudent tonal overreaching is as inspired a burlesque touch as the traditional incorporation of bugle calls and the three one-bar insertions of pantomimic business in this otherwise thirty-two-bar AABA refrain. In fact all the impertinence has a structural side to it. The tonal overreaching, when the opening A section is repeated not in the tonic F major but a tone higher, in G, is pursued further in the B section, whose first four bars are higher again, in A flat major; but if one hears the preceding G continuing as a dissonant pedal underneath this (a common "landscape" background for dislocated bugle calls in symphonic music), it soon turns into a $^6_4$ C major triad as preface to the accented C^{b7} chord which is the dominant return to the A section in F major. The bugle call, accompanied by a lyric quotation from Rudyard Kipling ("[But] you'll be a man, my son!"), is only one item in the lexicon of finger-wagging advice Rogers gives Astaire, sung to a comparable lexicon of musical jingles, and in any case inverts the melodic shape and almost the rhythm of the passage at the words ". . . on the ground, / I pick." The dissonant mickey-mousing of "take a deep breath," as Astaire does just that, reminds us of the A flat tonic of the B section.

Swing Time as light comedy and as musical comedy has been well set up in the lengthy prelude to this first sung moment, particularly in a series of audiovisual gags. These include the severe ancestral portrait smiling in the fiancée's parental drawing room as all parties eventually laugh off Astaire's failure to arrive at his own wedding (another of Mast's symmetries, paired with the outbreak of laughing in the film's finale); not just the Jewish tailor's quaint "Rommy" vocabulary[8] and gesticulations when asked to add cuffs to Astaire's wedding trousers but his desperate reaching for reference manuals as if for Holy Writ when Pop asks him, "Why not?"; the bride's father's throwing away of the telephone receiver as though it were contaminated when Lucky's colleague blows him a kiss; the scratching and tossing of 78 r.p.m. records in Rogers's anger; and the New York policeman who somehow hears in the rhythm of a taxicab's horn Pop's bad-mouthing of him when his back is turned. As for the traditional musical comedy plot, from the start it concerns the three staples of money, marriage, and mistaken identity. The entire story is about Lucky's determination to marry his hometown girl and save enough money to do so when his friends have (rightly) done everything they could to prevent him. The thwarted wedding occurs spectacularly early, not halfway through but right at the beginning of the film; by its end—indeed, at its very end—another (that of Rogers to Metaxa) has also been thwarted, so that the rightful one can now take place. Money carries the action almost entirely. Astaire is nicknamed Lucky because of his gambling luck, symbolized by his lucky quarter, which he must not lose and which indicates his destiny when he gives it to Rogers on first sight, much to Pop's consternation (for Pop has determined to stick with him through good and ill, and so far it is all ill). Rogers is actually called Penny ("Though I'm left without a penny," Lucky sings in the opening line of "Never Gonna Dance"). Lucky's friends make him gamble to delay his wedding; when he wins, we witness his taste for it as he bids himself up with the bride's father so that he can have the challenge of making good financially and marry her with pride. But in the short term he has lost the bride, lost his bet, and lost his train fare to New York. An incidental ends with a bang just as Lucky thumps the cigarette machine and coins clink into the change tray, signaling the incipient rise in his fortunes. As Mast's critique makes clear, later moments of gambling keep the plot moving, not least in order that Pop and Lucky can both try to make what they see as an honest man of the other. But this is where the mistaken identity comes in. Not only does Penny mistake Lucky for a scrounger and petty thief, and then for a no-good gambler, but Lucky too thinks he needs to marry the bourgeois girl and acquire capital, whereas we and his friends know that he has mistaken his own identity. In virtually his first dialogue exchange, he wants to give up dancing for money making, whereas Pop, and gradually the audience, recognize him as an artistic risk-taker, the only credible corollary to the talents of a brilliant metropolitan dancer. He has to gamble everything not for Margaret and social acceptability but for Penny. His real security is not in stocks—or stakes, as his *faux pas* pronounces it in the interview with the bride's father—but in his feet and his dancing partner.

Musically, credit must go to Bennett for establishing the right continuity and tone, full of wit and easy energy, as accompaniment to much of this comic exposition. Three extended instrumentals, plus a concatenation of vamps for the beginning of the dancing lesson, precede "Pick Yourself Up." The first is the music of an unused song, "It's Not in the Cards," a reassuringly perky, Gershwin-like tune ([4/4] 34|565↑#2 #23|53-333|31-1|1161-6|555↑3-↓5|#4↑♭3↓4↑2|1) with which to commence proceedings and heard right from the start of the film's action as Lucky and his male vaudevillians dance off the small-town stage; it continues, intercut with tiny snatches of church music, during the delaying tactics while the wedding party waits. The second seems to have been largely Bennett's invention, a "Train Sequence" of 168 bars commencing as a lively 2/4 to accompany the locomotion and continuing as a 6/8 scherzo with the indigent couple's initial exploits in New York, stopping as they hit the jackpot with the cigarette machine (or rather with Penny as far as Lucky is concerned). Snatches of "Pick Yourself Up" are woven into it as Penny appears at the machine.[9] The third incidental, appropriately using the episode theme of "Never Gonna Dance," is diegetic novelty-piano underscoring to the dance school sequence, all very twiddly and fey. This is the perfect counterpart to Blore's fussy, officious school director and his ridiculous white picket fence around the dance floor, which Moore destroys in an attempt to woo Helen Broderick (Mabel) after eating her sandwich and losing her her job. "You're still fired," Blore snaps at Broderick, reminding us of ongoing financial imperatives, and with this classic musical comedy moment the first section of the film closes.

But this is to omit reference to that section's most important event, the dance chorus of "Pick Yourself Up," our first experience in the film of "sheer heaven," as Blore puts it, as Lucky saves Penny from dismissal by proving he can dance after all. Mast again reminds us that in this film at least Kern was working to a strict formula:

> In *Top Hat, Swing Time,* and *Shall We Dance?* there are three Fredand-Ginger duets. The first . . . is always Fred's invitation and Ginger's initiation, when she learns that dancing with Fred is like nothing else in the world. She tries to resist his invitation, then either joins because she must . . . or because it might be fun . . . Their dance begins tentatively, after either he or she sings the song's verse and chorus. She seems to try to copy his gestures and steps at first. Then, in the second chorus of the dance, the music and movement shift into double time and she can anticipate his steps even before he does them; she no longer needs to watch him to do exactly as he does . . . The second duet confirms this initial experience, reminding the couple (especially Ginger) of what is at stake in their union, often when the external obstacles that the narrative throws in their path threaten to block their union forever . . . these numbers feel the pressure of novelty, of coming up with some new variation on a pattern . . . "Waltz in Swingtime" is a paradox (a jazz waltz) . . . The third dance duet differs in the three films. Only in *Swing Time* is it a full and private duet, "Never Gonna Dance," an agonized mime of parting and separation.[10]

Swing Time—Analysis and Critique

"Pick Yourself Up" may conveniently be analyzed in detail as a representative Astaire/Rogers duet and for its rich amalgamation of codes and structures, in that to the interactive spectrum of decor, music, lyrics, spoken words, expressions, gestures, dance maneuvers, noises, and actions already present in live musical theater, musical film adds to it the camera's viewpoints and rhythm. As befits its tentative, early position in Fred and Ginger's romance, the number is not continuous: the music stops completely for dialogue at two points (fig. 5.2).[11] The first musical segment is their song, which with its two different verses makes for a one-and-a-half refrain module (xAABAyAA). Ginger is firmly in control of the situation and has only softened toward her accoster because he is on the floor, a hopeless nincompoop. Thus she sings the whole of the refrain and Fred sings only the verses, the first of them while still squatting. (He picks himself up at one of her commands to do so.) But as she loses musical control in bars 100 to 116 (the strain recedes into the background against spoken dialogue and then drops the melody too), Fred drags her down, literally. This hardens her to the point at which music must cease, and she reaches metaphorical rock bottom by losing her job after rejecting her pupil. Fred is forced to take decisive remedial action and drags her to the dance floor to show what he can really do. Thus begins the dance segment of the routine, to two complete musical choruses (the second a jazz paraphrase) separated by verse *y*, which on the larger level is like a B section because it culminates in a pointed dominant return. Here Fred and Ginger show their by now complete mastery of the pairing by twirling to a halt balletically before chorus three erupts in jazzy explosions. Ginger is then reinstated in her job, and Moore, trying to do the same for Broderick, similarly drags her to the floor for a burlesque version of what we have just seen, the camera and spoken dialogue shielding us from half of it and the music executing strictly no more than one thirty-two-bar refrain plus introduction and coda as chorus four.

The music, as can be seen, operates in broad arcs, in this case four choruses, but is also broken up into generally eight-bar sections. Dialogue breaks down into even shorter exchanges, sometimes with a camera shot each, and against this fragmentation runs the continuity and rhythmic development of the playing spaces. This takes the number from the cramped, hostile anteroom with its lack of privacy, its slippery floor, fragile gramophone records, and intrusive door jambs and furniture to the even less musi-

cal office, where Broderick's temper snaps. Fred has to negotiate a number
of doors and passageways in order to take command of the situation and
of the departing Rogers, but as if to match his unfaltering mastery of these
complex, claustrophobic spaces, the camera follows him into the frame and
out of them with Ginger in a single shot (shot 17). The dance floor with its
relaxing furniture and ubiquitous windows into other rooms announces our
first arrival at cinematic luxury in the film, but the triumphant follow-up
back in the office reminds us that money and career as well as romance still
have to be set up.

Shot 17 is followed up with the extended take of Fred and Ginger's
dance, all done in a single shot except for brief intercuttings of Ginger's and
then Blore's delighted and amazed faces. Astaire, the star who was paid a
good deal more than the director, made sure of this camera treatment, and
the preceding sung chorus is similarly respected in the lengthy shot 7, covering the whole of it until dialogue cuts in on the final half-refrain.[12] The
camera work thus underlines the music's breadth and flow, but as we can
see in figure 5.2 there is also a strong sense of contrapuntal overlap between
shots and musical sections at certain points, notably along the second row
of events where the music is broken off and then starts again. Significantly,
the burlesque afterpiece of Moore and Broderick is not given long shots; its
rhythm is more syncopated against the musical sections than one can tell
from figure 5.2, the cut into shots 32 and 33 actually taking place somewhat
after the musical breaks. Only once, to emphasize Fred's apparent submis-
sion and Rogers's assumed superiority, does the camera move vertically as it
pans up from him on the floor to her standing over him in shot 7; but there
are visual counterparts to the three falls framing the sung segment of "Pick
Yourself Up" (Fred falling before the song and dragging Ginger down with
him after it), and they involve the fence. Both Astaire and Moore lead into
their dance choruses through the absurd gate, which they swiftly open; after
aesthetic containment by the white fence (fig. 5.3), Fred and Ginger's dance
finally spills beyond it in breathtaking vaults that scarcely slow the steps—
out, in, and out again as they conclude. So excited is he that Blore too jumps
the fence as he runs after them. At the end of his dance, Moore manages to
get Broderick safely over it before trampling it with his own final leap.

The dance steps and movements and their relationship to the musical
sections remain beyond the scope of this study, though vital to the func-
tioning of the aesthetic whole, as Astaire and Hermes Pan understood well
enough when devising them. Of course as a tap dance the sequence is also

Top table

bars	0	4	8	12	16	20	24	28	32	36	40	44	48	52	56	60	64	68	72	76	80	84

routine segment	VAMP			SONG (**Chorus 1**)				
musical unit	(4 + ?6 bars) first waltz attempt--slip	(4 + ?5 bars) second waltz attempt--slip	(4 + ?8 bars) third waltz attempt; Fred falls	(18 bars) Fred's **verse x**	(8 bars) Ginger **A**	(8 bars) Ginger **A**	(8 bars) Ginger **B**	(12 bars) Ginger **A**
shot	1 MLS (Fred and Ginger)	2 MCS	3 MLS ↓ / 4 CU G / 5 F / 6 G	7 MCS (Fred on floor) ...pans up to Ginger		zooms out, reframed for couple		
playing space	anteroom							

Bottom table

bars	84	88	92	96	100	104	108	112	116	116	120	124	128	132	136

routine segment	SONG (cont.)				TAP DANCE (**Chorus 2**)	
		Ginger insults Fred; Blore fires her.	Cut to Broderick insulting Moore; Blore fires her; Fred intervenes.	Fred forces Ginger onto dance floor to show what he's learnt.		
musical unit	(16 bars) Fred's **verse y**	(8 bars) dialogue A instrl	(8 bars) **A** Ginger falls		(6 bars) **intro**	(8 bars) **A** they dance	(8 bars) **A** vigorous taps added
shot	7 (cont.) zooms in for CU of couple	8 G ↓↑	9 Bl	10 back to Ginger and Fred on floor	11 + Bl / 12 F G / 13 / 14	15 MCS MBBl	16 MCS	17 +F+G pan	18 to floor → camera watches dance from side of ballroom, behind fence	20 continuation of 18 after brief shots of Ginger's face	22 = 18
playing space	anteroom (cont.)			office	...to floor	dance floor

140 144 148 152 168 172 176 180 184 188 192 196 200 204 208 212 216 220 224 228 232 236

TAP DANCE (cont.)

Blore rushes
to congratulate
them.

Chorus 3 (jazz paraphrase)

(8 bars) **B** dance continues	(8 bars) **A** dance continues	(16 bars) **verse y** balletic *rit.* on last 4 bars	(8 bars) **A**	(8 bars) **A**	(8 bars) **B**	(16 bars) **A**	(16 bars) **coda**

24 (cont.) camera continues to follow Fred and Ginger around the ballroom floor from the periphery   ... they vault the fence, three times   ↑   ↑   ↑

	25 BI	26 BI ↑	27 all 5	28 all 3

dance floor (cont.)   office

---

240 244 248 252 256 260 264 268 272 276 280 284 288 292

BALLROOM DANCE (Chorus 4)

Moore decides
to have a go
with Broderick.
           "You're still
fired!"

(8 bars) **intro** M/B take floor	(8 bars) **A** under dialogue	(8 bars) **A** M/B viewed	(8 bars) **B** ditto with dialogue	(8 bars) **A** dialogue continues	(14 bars) **coda** M/B leave floor; he tramples fence; dialogue
29 MCS Moore and Broderick: → camera follows them onto the floor	30 → 31 MCS Fred, Ginger and Blore	32 MLS Moore and Brod	33 CU Blore	34 MCS F+G 35 BI 36 MCS F+G	37 M/B 38 ↑ ↑! 39 MCS triumph 40 CU BI 41 MCS M/B

office (cont.)   ... alternating with dance floor

Fig. 5.2. "Pick Yourself Up"—the routine.

Fig. 5.3. Fred Astaire, Ginger Rogers, and the fence in "Pick Yourself Up."

part of the musical arrangement, for in this case dance is sound as well as sight, with its rhythmic underlines, missed beats, agogic accents, cross-rhythms, and decorative triplet figures. It complements the orchestration and sometimes stands in for it during "stop time" silences (this happens toward the end). No wonder such an interdisciplinary feast as the musical film has been called the most complex of all art forms.[13]

Furthermore, although *Swing Time* is no longer strictly farce (even if both of Penny's prospective husbands lose their trousers), mechanical ingenuity is still at a premium. The financial engine of the plot is impeccably complicated and full of crazy logic: the hero thinks he has to cease gambling not because he is losing too much but because he is gaining too much.[14]

Orchestras, conductors, and not one but two nightclubs change hands at the turn of a roulette wheel and produce reverses with perplexing swiftness, as also does the shortest of dialogue exchanges in the snow scene (in which each couple thinks the other wants to be left alone) when suddenly Ginger, not Fred, is the emotionally cold party. Mechanical ingenuity, rephrased as virtuosity of conception, operates on many another front. The glorious deco sets revel in their victory over three-dimensional abstract space, that of Raymond's casino nicely contemplated in the overlapping curves of the Venetian blind through which we witness Fred and Ginger's exit at the end of "Waltz in Swing Time."[15] And while the affinity between swing music and deco architecture is more one of association than aesthetic logic, the "Waltz in Swing Time" does conquer metric space comparably with its incessant hemiolas and more complex cross-rhythms (notably 3 + 3 + 2 + 2 + 2 eighth notes across two bars). "Bojangles of Harlem," Astaire's novelty production number (there was one in every film), is remarkable less for occasioning his sole appearance in blackface than for the routine of dancing with his own triple shadow. The mechanical ingenuity here is very literal, for at first one wonders whether it is a triple light projection of his actual dancing and accordingly scrutinizes the technical perfection. A gag gives the game away—it is not—which leaves one studying the three shadows to see if they are still mechanically multiplied. Another gag confirms that they are not either.

The musical corollary is thematic cross-reference and counterpoint. Perhaps no other musical film of its time matches their exploitation here. At the thematic zenith is the simultaneous combination of "The Way You Look Tonight" and "A Fine Romance," heard twice (first in the opening titles) but probably noticed only once, in the closing shot of the film as Fred and Ginger finally embrace, he singing the latter and she the former song, the only time they ever sang in counterpoint. Musically speaking this was the simple but important destiny of *The Cat and the Fiddle*'s musical plotting—and of course an idea that Kern could not repeat without compromising dramatic freshness. He chose this moment, and for once came up with two tunes that fit in perfect counterpoint without either of them having to sacrifice character (ex. 5.2). Indeed, "The Way You Look Tonight," the one that until its B section foregoes syncopation for this purpose, won Kern his first Oscar. (One must assume the counterpoint was Kern's and not Bennett's or that of the musical director, Nat Shilkret; the fit is too good to have been coincidental.) Further cross-reference occurs as snatches of "Pick Yourself Up" are heard against "A Fine Romance" when Fred sings it; this could well have

Ex. 5.2. *Swing Time,* counterpoint.

been Bennett's work or that of the arranger, who according to Arlene Croce
was Edward Powell, rather than Kern's. The tune of "A Fine Romance" also
invades "Waltz in Swing Time," as do the lyrics "Pick yourself up, / Dust
yourself off." (Fields seems to have been fond of lyrical cross-reference and
elaborated on the phrase "a fine romance" as "La Belle romance" and "perfectly swell romance" in "Never Gonna Dance." Croce discovered in her
interviews that it was Kern and Fields who later had these phrases inserted
into the dialogue of the snow scene.)[16] The first ending bars of "A Fine
Romance" (and, more important, the accompaniment figure of its unused
verse) replicate the introduction and coda figure of "The Way You Look
Tonight," which represent Fred's diegetic preluding when he first plays it on
the piano.

All five songs—"Pick Yourself Up," "The Way You Look Tonight," "A
Fine Romance," "Bojangles of Harlem," and "Never Gonna Dance"—are
exploited as underscoring or diegetic dance band material at some point
or other. The tutti refrains for opening and end titles and lead-ins to the
many nightclub scenes give an almost liturgical, hymnlike solidity to the
overall musical experience, especially as Bennett could draw on a larger-
than-Broadway orchestra for them: eight reeds, giving banks of up to four or
five saxophones or four clarinets when needed, three trumpets, three trom-
bones, percussion, harp, guitar, two pianos, and up to nineteen strings.[17] The
web of cross-reference and the overall spread and balance of musical num-

bers also give a symphonic dimension to the score, if the analogy with a Lisztian four-in-one symphonic poem be permitted and the many incidentals treated as developmental or, in the case of the "Train Sequence," episodic. "It's Not in the Cards" and "Pick Yourself Up" belong to the expository section: what second subject was ever more delightful than "Pick Yourself Up"? The two counterpointed tunes, "The Way You Look Tonight" and "A Fine Romance," occur in two love scenes which can be thought of as intermezzi separated by a dance movement, "Waltz in Swing Time." As Lucky redoubles his efforts to win the girl he really loves, the two most impressive musical movements occur, a scherzo-finale pair comprising "Bojangles of Harlem" and "Never Gonna Dance." The former comes immediately after his first kiss with Penny, the latter is a threnody of farewell and failed persuasion and accordingly characterized as a blues, therefore chorale-like at bottom. The most persuasive and musically discursive unit in all this is the snow scene, almost continuously underscored in a manner producing a central slow movement encasing "A Fine Romance." It is all the more delicious for coming immediately after the central book scene in the film, by contrast a minute, economical gem of mechanical accomplishment pivoting every strand of the plot.

The snow scene begins with the two couples' arrival at the New Amsterdam Inn only to find it derelict. Probably it was Bennett who devised the impressionist, whole-tone incidental figuration on flutes, clarinets, harp, celesta, piano, xylophone ("lightest possible hammers"), marimba, and occasional cascades of staccato, muted violins *divisi a 4*, which are the very image of snow falling off branches and human shivering. From this a musical-box tune emerges every once in a while that could possibly have been triggered by the jauntiness of "Pick Yourself Up," but a sustained melody follows; it is first announced piecemeal and hesitantly on strings as Lucky wonders what to do about Penny nestling against his shoulder to keep warm (and Pop wonders whether they ought to go home to prevent this), then played straight through. This is the verse to "A Fine Romance," never sung in the film, though it was intended to be, with a full set of lyrics by Fields for Penny, exasperated at Lucky's inexplicable coolness in what is now an acknowledged romance. Penny wanders a little way off while this is playing, to the rustic gazebo whither she entices Lucky as the whole-tone figuration returns, more insistently *ostinato* as the romantic impasse deepens. Again she tries to break it by snuggling up to Lucky, and he cannot help responding as he embraces her from behind, showing her how to flap her arms against her body to keep warm. To signal this rise in the emotional temperature, an extremely tender harmonic arrangement of the B section of "The Way You Look Tonight" begins on strings and continues through the returning A section as far as the downward octave, whereupon the low tonic (î) turns into 3̂ (that is, modulates down a major 3rd) for the refrain melody of "A Fine Romance"; this is perfectly synchronized with Penny's comment, "It's more than an experience. It's sort of like a—a romance, isn't it?" to which Lucky replies, "As we say in French, 'La Belle romance,'" to which Penny adds "La swell romance." This is extremely tight motivic working, for the notes for the words "perfectly swell romance" in "Never Gonna Dance" are grafted onto the melodic line at this point.

The spun line breaks here, for Pop, obeying earlier instructions, interrupts them, reminding Lucky to draw away. This is too much for Penny, who stands up and suggests they go home; leaning on a tree and straight off with no preliminaries save introductory four-chord gestures on strings, she launches into two refrains of "A Fine Romance." The second half of her first refrain is filmed from above, and the snow plentifully falling is mirrored in the return of impressionistic pointing in the accompaniment. The first half of her second refrain in this "sarcastic love song" is more ironically orchestrated, the pointillism now on trumpets with Robinson mutes. The lines from the song "You're calmer than the seals in the Arctic Ocean, / At least they flap their fins to express emotion" gain a priceless dimension as Lucky flaps his arms in a deadpan manner as he had previously taught Penny to do.

Penny sits again, on another rustic bench, and accuses Lucky of being cold. This now is too much for him, and to a violin cantilena that blossoms into further four-chord gestures, all very much in *Siegfried Idyll* style, he grabs her as though to kiss her, the harmonies now warm and dominant-based rather than cool and whole-tone. But a crescendo on a dominant 9th climaxes on another icy whole-tone chord as Pop, ever-watchful, hits him with a snowball, further musical symbolism at the minute, pantomimic level. Only single notes are left hanging as Lucky wonders how to cancel Pop's sentry duty and decides to retaliate. A variant dominant 9th preparation (literal, where the snowball is concerned) and whole-tone impact accompany the return volley, which hits Mabel. Lucky is obliged to rush off and apologize to her, whereupon Pop, with firmer intervention, spills the beans about the fiancée to Penny. Seconds later Lucky, passing him on his way back, releases him too late from his obligation and understandably has "Pick Yourself Up" running through his mind at the sudden rebuttal he now receives from Penny. But his song is a third refrain of "A Fine Romance," snatches of "Pick Yourself Up" jogging along as countermelody on the muted trumpets as though laughing at him. The scene closes on the final chord of "A Fine Romance" with the opposite sound to nature's musical delicacy: the noise of the starter and windshield wiper motor of the car, throwing the elements in his face as blown snow. The scene has lasted nine minutes, most of them set to music, whether Kern's, Powell's, or Bennett's.

The biggest and most important numbers in *Swing Time*, however, are the three dance routines subsequent to "Pick Yourself Up": "Waltz in Swing Time," "Bojangles of Harlem," and "Never Gonna Dance," paralleling (though not taking place in all three of) the New York nightclub settings. Given these settings, Kern was having to write the most up-to-date, jazzy music possible. Did he succeed? or does the criticism of shadowboxing with swing hold? I noted the misgivings about both the quality and authorship of "Waltz in Swing Time" in chapter 1. Kern got unusually touchy when he realized that Astaire was finding Hal Borne's musical constructions more apposite to his choreographic needs than Kern's while devising the production numbers. Bordman makes heavy weather of refuting Borne's criticisms of Kern and authorial claims to parts of "Bojangles of Harlem." To quote in full from his interviewer, Croce: "When the song arrived on Hal Borne's piano rack, it was in 2/4 time. 'I played it for Fred, and he had kind of a strange look on his face,' Borne recalls. 'That was the trouble with Kern. His melodies were the greatest but his syncopation was corny. It was corny *then*. Fred said, "I like the melody and the lyric is just fine, but why don't we swing it? Then we can come back to 2/4." But it still wasn't right. And it wasn't long enough. I added a section, which I played on an upright piano. It was based on a vamp idea that kept going up different keys. That was not a harpsichord, it was a doctored piano, and that was not Kern, it was me. We always had to do these things in production numbers.'"[18] The added section is no big deal, just a boogie-woogie vamp with *minore* Jewish tag à la "Forty-Second Street," and Borne's last sentence would apply to virtually any film and many a Broadway routine, as would "Why don't we swing it?," the customary broader-tempo version of the refrain. As shown in chapter 1, even a Kern holograph sketch would not prove who authorized what. What Kern definitely did write, and publish, is a perfectly memorable and serviceable song, the low opening tessitura of its refrain—a Broadway tenor line now the melody—exactly right for the soulful world of Harlem that Bojangles represents, the key changes for each limb equally apposite to the kaleidoscopic perspectives of a deco production number (and with E major binding verse and refrain).

"Never Gonna Dance" does show the strain that would in all likelihood have overwhelmed Kern, and possibly Fields as well, had another of their songs for the film, "Swing Low, Swing High," been used. "Swing Low, Swing High," a chaotic attempt at the rhapsodic freedom of jazz in both melody and words, was wisely discarded.[19] But the strain is put to advantage in "Never Gonna Dance," failure built into its very title. Here is an intriguing context. From the first bars of its introduction we sense the "serious," that is, non–musical comedy, music of Gershwin, and the *Swing Time* music would have been among the first Kern wrote after the opening of *Porgy and Bess* in October 1935. It is his equivalent of "Oh, Bess, Oh Where's My Bess?" Yet if Kern had anticipated that his rambling seventy-six-bar song, in ABACxA rondo form, would form the basis of an extended dance structure, in the film it is cleverly used merely to prove that words will never reconcile Penny to Lucky. The tune is too gangling, the lyrics too much of a mouthful, each section a new, futile, inorganic attempt by Lucky to convince Penny that his heart will remain with her. He tries too hard, and their real threnody begins only when she once more takes control and begins to walk down the staircase—to the tune not of "Never Gonna Dance" but "The Way You Look Tonight." For a while they walk around the dance floor side by side to this melody, recapitulating their first assignment in the dance school. In the syncopated B section they begin to dance, and when, after an instrumental extract of "Never Gonna Dance," the tune switches to "Waltz in Swing Time," one realizes that the musical culmination of the film is not one song but a typical Kern finaletto, as Croce points out (though she is wrong in pinning that label on the later reprise of "A Fine Romance"). Uniquely, we have an unsung but danced version of the formula; "steps from the Waltz are quoted," Croce observes, before "Never Gonna Dance" returns once more as the fourth and last finaletto section.[20] It ends in unmitigated sorrow, Astaire's pose after Rogers rushes out virtually that of a classical dancer lamenting at the tomb of a nymph. This is the eleventh hour, not the end of act 1, and with the exception of *Men of the Sky* Kern's closest approach to tragedy.

South of the Border

I Dream Too Much was Kern's last dramatic work set in Europe. By 1936, a war was being fought in Spain and the rest of Europe was rearming, three of its major countries prey to right-wing dictators. The United States, past or present, would be the setting for the majority of Kern's remaining musicals, but after *Swing Time* a run of four out of five films (the fifth being *High, Wide and Handsome*) continued to fight introspection by celebrating Latin America and the exotic south. Two films, *One Night in the Tropics* and *You Were Never Lovelier*, did obeisance to the good neighbor policy by being set largely or wholly in Hispanic territory, the former in the mythical capital San Marcos of some unspecified country, the latter in Argentina.[21] *When You're in Love* begins in Mexico with an expatriate artist, Cary Grant as Jimmy Hudson, and an Australian prima donna, the opera singer Grace Moore as Louise Fuller. Fuller lacks a visa for U.S. entrance; a marriage of convenience ensues, recapitulating the immigration theme of *Sunny*. *Joy of Living* stars a wealthy shipowner, Douglas Fairbanks Jr. as Dan Brewster, with his own South Pacific island who woos a musical comedy singer, Irene Dunne as Margaret Garret. At the end of the film they elope to the paradise island, though the scenes are concerned only with New York.

Two of the four films, *When You're in Love* and *You Were Never Lovelier*, suffer authorially because they showcase Latin band music at the expense of Kern's songs. However attractive and colorful the mariachi numbers in *When You're in Love*, thirty minutes or more elapse before we hear a note of Kern (though the same would be true of *Swing Time* without "It's Not in the Cards," as Croce points out).[22] And then it is for only two songs, since operatic repertoire also obtrudes, as does "Minnie the Moocher," in ways that closely parallel *I Dream Too Much*. Moore belts "Minnie the Moocher" as Pons did "I Got Love," again rather successfully, but in this case the song is not by Kern. In *You Were Never Lovelier*, while Buenos Aires is clearly a substitute for Europe and the heroine's French ancestry is carefully stressed (and heard), Xavier Cugat's band and songs are prominently featured, and Kern's score is not as comprehensive as one would wish in this otherwise excellent musical. *Joy of Living* has four Kern songs, but three of them are over before the film is midway, and musical silence accompanies much of its second half. The fourth film, *One Night in the Tropics*, critically condemned by all, nevertheless contains a better spread and abundance of material. It gets off to a good musical start with an attractive light-music incidental

(|122771|6775563|5--.3|2) — is this "Simple Philosophy," listed in the opening credits? — and ends with another comprehensive, unpublished quadruple-time number, "Farandola," with its lively 6/8 chase section. But in the four intervening songs there is no first-class material, "Back in My Shell" being particularly feeble.

When You're in Love and Joy of Living both recapitulate the battle between work and love, musical career and partnership, fought out in I Dream Too Much. But unlike I Dream Too Much, these films concern a woman who has to be taught and strongly resists being taught more folksy values by a "real" man (Grant or Fairbanks): the retreat from feminized culture as the Depression recedes and war approaches is easily sensed. Both Grant and Fairbanks worship their stars, then brutally teach them to give up the stage for marriage or at least place their career second to their husband's more intuitive, therefore more healthy, appreciation of culture and nature. Both marriages, like that of I Dream Too Much, are hasty and prove right only after considerable strife, but whereas in I Dream Too Much it was the woman who had to take control, in the later films the man never makes a faltering move and simply has to wait for his wife to submit to his superior judgment, already demonstrated, and fly to his arms. The balance and charm of musical comedy evaporate as this hardening of cultural values takes its effect; it seems somehow right that the songs bow out as Joy of Living proceeds, in a film that paradoxically introduces insufferable longueurs in the scenes in which Brewster is supposed to be teaching Garret how to have fun.

Joy of Living introduces a heavily reflexive note when the last few bars of the second refrain of "You Couldn't Be Cuter," near the beginning of the film, are sung by Brewster and cronies in a dockside bar while staring appreciatively at a sheet music cover of the actual published song, Kern's and Fields's names clearly visible. The film, then, is supposed to be about Joy of Living as a stage show. Under this pretense Kern and his world do not come off very well, for the opening sequence is a chorus of "What's Good About Good-night?" as first-night finale to the stage show, like the finale of I Dream Too Much full of operetta claptrap as though it were White Horse Inn. At the end of the film Garret summarily leaves the show (and her dreadful theatrical family) with no hint of musical regret. When You're in Love undermines musical theater still further. If Street's tunes in I Dream Too Much were "just like Schubert," Grace Fuller's song festival, over which not even her lover takes precedence, is experienced as a ghastly, open-air stadium distension of real Schubert but certainly not real culture when "Ständchen" is sung with a huge *mise-en-scène* of deco classicism and droopy chorus maidens. "Our Song," previously sung in the woods to an appreciative audience of owls, deer, rabbits, and a raccoon, is then presented to the bovine human masses, the stage decked out with rank upon rank of chorus minstrels in mock-medieval costume, clearly a *fête galante* extravaganza but one to put *The Passionate Pilgrim* to flight.

In *Joy of Living* the songs, all four of them performed by Dunne, are never sung straight or developed into a musical comedy routine and seem to be the comic interludes of a straight actress (which she was increasingly becoming). Barring opening production numbers, in all three of *I Dream Too Much*, *Joy of Living*, and *When You're in Love* the first Kern song is sung to children, another indication of family values rising uppermost. The idea and its execution in "The Jockey on the Carrousel" are cute enough, but "The Whistling Boy," one of Kern's Alpine waltzes (the whistling toy was a piece of Swiss machinery?), is sung by Fuller to literally hundreds of children as though in some nightmare version of *The Sound of Music*, which is a pity, for the song itself is attractive. "You Couldn't Be Cuter" is sung by Garret, accompanying herself on a toy piano, to her sister's nauseating twins, who refuse to fall asleep and take over the second refrain when she does. The next song in *Joy of Living*, "Just Let Me Look at You," is first heard as Garret rehearses its scene in her limousine, the instrumental accompaniment played on a portable gramophone as her admirer hangs onto the back of the car and they stare each other out through the rear window. He forces her to repeat it after outrageously hauling her up in court for annoyances; at first she is so angry she sings it really badly but, realizing she can charm the judge, starts again, seductively enough for a subliminal orchestra to be heard by her audience. "What's Good About Good-night?" is given its solo version in the radio studio, where she is broadcasting it (live, of course) with full orchestra and po-faced conductor in tails. As she receives news of Brewster's imminent departure she accelerates the second refrain far beyond the hapless conductor's ability to catch up; by the last chord she has long finished and is out of the studio. Dunne is a brilliant comic actress in these scenes, but the music deserves better treatment. Nor does it get it in the fourth and final song, "A Heavenly Party," which she sings to diegetic piano accompaniment in a recording booth at a fair. When she finishes, a punter does a jazzy retake of it in the style he says Maggie Garret would have used—shades of *Show Boat*'s transformations of "Can't Help Lovin' Dat Man." Yet these are good songs in their way, which is generally Kern's smooth, economical Hollywood way with melody and voice-leading. The B section of the AABA "You Couldn't Be Cuter" begins to sound like a Rodgers and Hammerstein jogtrot and integrates a momentarily flattened $\hat{3}$ with flat $\hat{7}$ and $\hat{6}$ leading back down to the dominant over $^\flat VI^7$, nicely counteracting its otherwise excessive perkiness. All of the *Joy of Living* songs except "What's Good About Good-night?" feature the now idiomatic quarter-note triplets beloved of crooners and violin breaks, though in "A Heavenly Party" they are contrasted with nervous dotted notes in the verse (apposite to Dunne as Garret but never heard in the film) and surprisingly exhilarating eighth-note triplets in the published refrain fills. "Just Let Me Look at You" feels at the start of its refrain too similar to "A Heavenly Party," both playing on harmonic parenthesis with ii-V progressions, but in the B section of its ABA_1C form reverts to the melody of the verse, to great effect when departing from it for the midway fox-trot cadence. "What's Good About Good-night?" follows up Kern's modulatory proclivities in some of the *Swing Time* songs when a passing but important flat $\hat{3}$ in the opening phrase of the ABA_1B_1 unit (there is no verse) is recapitulated for A_1 with that note as tonic, in G flat major.

In *One Night in the Tropics* musical comedy conventions return with a vengeance, yet to curiously unintegrated effect. Money drives every inch of the plot, which sees Steve's best friend, Jim (Allan Jones), doing everything he can to make Steve's fraught engagement to Cynthia result in marriage, opposition from both family and old flame notwithstanding. This is because he has a bet on it he cannot afford to lose, in the form of a "love insurance" policy he has taken out for Steve on his father's ailing company and an underwriter's reluctance. The underwriter, Roscoe, sets his minders onto the leads to make sure they go through with it, which they do in South America with a narrative twist—the policy turns out to be valid because both parties will have married by the requisite date, though not to each other. Wodehouse's crooks are back in evidence with Abbott and Costello as the minders, and the shotgun wedding takes place amid mayhem.Yet Jones's romantic voice and songs (including "You and Your Kiss") are quite wrong for his bachelor exploits with Steve and the comic speed with which the film began. Mickey, an Irish singer, sings "Remind Me," a Latin number, with fake Spanish accent in a New York bar long before they have embarked for South America, which confuses the codes further. "Your Dream (Is the Same as My Dream)" was imported from *Gentlemen Unafraid* as a song long and broad enough (a forty-eight-bar ABA with modulations aplenty) to demand proper emotional treatment at a crux in the plot, all sentiments being meant for a character other than the one being sung to. But no such treatment eventuates in the film, for Nancy Kelly's voice as Cynthia is weak, and Steve, the most overwrought of the four leads at this point, does not sing at all.

You Were Never Lovelier and the New Hollywood

You Were Never Lovelier is the opposite of *One Night in the Tropics* in its bid, above all, for a harmonious blend of ingredients. Its narrative premises are still those of musical comedy insofar as marriage, money, and mistaken identity remain crucial. Astaire as the New York dancer Robert Davis, whom we last saw in a Kern film as a too successful gambler, opens this one as a spectacular loser at the Palermo race track in Buenos Aires; and here we shall see his line from *Swing Time* "You never give the orchids I send a glance!" in action. His moral identity takes most of the film to establish, at least with the rich, peppery hotelier Eduardo Acuña (Adolphe Menjou), who persists in regarding him as beneath contempt. He is mistaken for the suitor who daily sends orchids and love letters to Rita Hayworth as Maria, Acuña's second daughter, in reality a ruse by her father to get her to fall in love, until they really begin to fall for each other. Money is at the root of Davis's complicity in the father's deception, for he needs a dance contract at his hotel, and naturally his lack of it accounts for much of Acuña's hostility toward him. But the real motivation of the curious plot is Acuña's own marriage, celebrating its twenty-fifth anniversary, for, like his favorite daughter, he is passionate and sentimental (of French parentage, in fact) underneath his brittle exterior and projects his own romantic frustrations onto her—he invents the story about her waiting for her Lochinvar—because he knows he himself was second-best choice of his wife, Delfina:

> EDUARDO: Maria is going to wait until the right man comes along.
> DELFINA: Why should she? I didn't.[23]

He also knows he never managed to conquer his prior flame, Maria's godmother, Señora Castro, after whom Maria is named. Thoroughly chivalric, he has remained faithful to Delfina all these years but revels in writing the letters. "Wedding in the Spring," plausibly Breton in style, confirms his love of old-world music and values when played at the anniversary party and makes him the poetic image of the troubadour Astaire has to become before Maria will accept his love. This is probably why, unconsciously, he responds to Astaire's singing when he first hears it early in the plot at his eldest daughter's marriage, for Astaire's wedding song "Dearly Beloved" becomes the opening greeting of all his subsequent love letters. (It is also constantly on his daughter's mind from the moment she first hears it, as the underscoring and her eventual reprise of it confirm.)

This is a far cry from the farcical treatment of elders in *Oh, Boy!*, and the only sustained farce in *You Were Never Lovelier* concerns Fernando, Acuña's long-suffering and very camp secretary. The older generation is being taken seriously or at least treated affectionately. Something very similar happens in *Centennial Summer* three years later, in which again old parental jealousies bestir the plot in newer times, and in *Cover Girl*, whose Gallic father figure (Otto Kruger as John Coudair, owner of a fashion magazine) once more pulls the strings of youth in acknowledgment of generational folly. Is it a recognition that the audience for musicals was aging? That couples who had experienced only peace must stay together through the tribulations of war? That with the youngsters away at the front, the parents needed the consolation of self-depiction? Probably all these factors played into the equation.

Other features also assign *You Were Never Lovelier* more to the developing genre of romantic rather than classic musical comedy. The songs are now far more subliminal than in a traditional backstager, and of the three ballads, only "Dearly Beloved" is diegetic. This is largely a matter of ever more dictatorial studio notions of blend and mix, affecting vocal performance practice, orchestration, the provision of underscoring, and camera work. The incidental music is still crisp and attractive in the opening scene and for the anniversary party, and Astaire the dancer can still command his own style of presentation, which he does in the magnificent "Audition Dance" and in "The Shorty George," whose routine we witness in rehearsal with Cugat's band. But Astaire the singer is now subject to the overall gloss and sheen of a Hollywood package. In *You Were Never Lovelier*, still in black and white, this works well on the whole, for which one should be thankful, but the close-ups in the romantic songs, particularly when Hayworth is being filmed, make for meticulous lip-synching and therefore a conversational, musically disembodied croon as the norm. However well Hayworth does the lip-synching, her vocals dubbed by Nan Wynn, Astaire has to sing "I'm Old Fashioned" and "You Were Never Lovelier" more slowly and less performatively than he ought; in each case his commercial recordings of the songs are preferable to the soundtrack on account of their clean, forward instrumental accompaniment and a recognizable sense of pace, all but extinct in the new Hollywood song style.[24]

Rarely do Kern's songs in his last four films respond optimally to the studio's treatment, except when Deanna Durbin sings them. Conversely, the best production numbers in *You Were Never Lovelier* are compositionally weak, "The Shorty George" amenable enough to its jazz routining but devoid of melodic or harmonic interest, "Audition Dance" (not Kern's work?) musically desultory. The best position between studio schmaltz and generic dance music is filled by Cugat and his band, excellent performers and honestly filmed. When Astaire asks for "The Shorty George" to go a little faster, it actually does, and to view a real conductor performing "Wedding in the Spring" with (one judges) the actual players and singers on the screen is a rare pleasure, characteristic Kern authentically presented. Kern's contribution overall certainly amounts to the "exceptionally fine" score that Astaire found it, but one rather puts up with the presentation of the ballads for the sake of their musical qualities.[25] Significantly, Bennett, whose last Hollywood assignment for Kern was *Joy of Living*, did not orchestrate this film. Conrad Salinger, wizard of the MGM approach (though this is from Columbia), did, along with Leigh Harline and Lyle Murphy.

All three ballads are fine songs, among Kern's best for the screen. ("These Orchids," unpublished, is hardly a fourth, though it informs a good deal of underscoring.) "Dearly Beloved" keeps its harmonies on the wing—there are repeated references to angels in the lyrics—until the very last chord, the only plain root-position tonic triad we hear. "I'm Old Fashioned," a Kern classic, makes great virtue of its titular credo, applicable enough to Kern himself at this stage of his career, and underlines Maria's Frenchness, the ostinato patter and pert dominants of the introduction complementing the same rhythms and insistent tonics of "Wedding in the Spring," her parents' and grandparents' song. "I'm Old Fashioned" is surely Kern's final tribute to the bittersweetness of the *fête galante*, for within the contained solidity of its harmonies and developmental phrasing there is heartache in the 4–3 appoggiatura on the second "love," in its 7–6 counterpart in the tenor one bar later, and in the relative minor imperfect cadence to which these lead. This last is again followed, as in "Dearly Beloved," by an oscillating pair of ii-V progressions, this time as tonal parenthesis (in the dominant), because it switches back to the tonic for the structural ii-V marking the halfway point of the refrain (ex. 5.3 [a]).[26] The form of the song is difficult to label, and to describe it as $A^8(=a^4a_x^4)B^8A_1^8(=a_1^4c^4)A_2^{12}(=a^4b_y^4a_2^4)$ hardly solves the problem. The cellular phrase structure continues in the c section with Kern's most teasing sequence, for bars two to four of example 5.3 (b) all contain tonal surprises. There are various ways of hearing these four bars, but all of them are harmonically kaleidoscopic. And Johnny Mercer's lyrics avoid redundant duplication of the melodic phrasing. The phrase "old fashioned," which cannot be rhymed, accompanies a rhythmic motif which saturates the refrain, but Mercer staves off the obvious corollary (that "you're old fashioned" too) until its very last statement, in between refusing to rhyme the motif at all even when he might have done so to other words. Mercer also understands what to do with the sequence of example 5.3 (b). He avoids more than one repetition of the alliterative gerund ("sighing sighs / holding hands"), itself not quite a congruent duplication, following it up instead with a single two-bar phrase moving progressively away from the initial formulation: "heart," following "hands," loses its gerund, "hands" is not even rhymed as a separate word but as part of "understands." Altogether this is a fine example of maximum melopoetic interplay before a moment of return.

"I'm Old Fashioned" is routined in the new Hollywood style. It begins as distant underscoring to the lovers' garden tryst, emanating ostensibly from the two younger sisters as they try to get Davis back into romantic mood after he is nearly shot by Señora Acuña. This is largely on strings, with solo violin, very beautiful in its way, and one refrain passes, varying Kern's harmonies in the sequence and shading off into amorphous introduction for the last few bars. When Maria enters to sing her verse, all sense of tempo and span is suspended, the orchestral commentary after the word "saint" being more picturesque than decorous, though it does not actually violate the periodicity. Davis adds words (and dotted rhythms) to the accompaniment figure under the word "quaint," and Maria then sings the refrain. Lavish string countermelody is present from the start, and a welter of eighth notes on xylophone illustrates "the sound of rain upon a window pain" of the B section. Paradoxically, amid all this rococo detail, the harmonies of Kern's sequential passage are simplified. An added eighth-note upbeat to the A section stupidly negates the Gallic downbeat phrasing carefully engineered by Kern. A good deal of portamento, in voice and on strings, surrounds the culminating $^6_4$ on the word "stay." But a basic slow fox-trot tempo has been established, and it is retained for the ravishing ballroom dance refrain in the subdominant (A flat major) which follows. The innocent Frenchness of the song is lost, however, all traces of old-fashionedness gone by the second dance refrain, jazzed up in a faster tempo with a meaningless Hispanic break of a few bars

a)

b)

Ex. 5.3. I'm Old Fashioned.

and some terminal extensions (and an unrelated key, G major). One appreciates the quality materials of the orchestration, but tactful this studio idiom was not.[27]

This is all the more the pity because Kern wrote the film's magnificent title song (see ex. 1.8) in such a way that it cries out for the sumptuous ballroom dance treatment dubiously afforded "I'm Old Fashioned." This could have become a rhapsody to match "Never Gonna Dance." Robert's vocal performance of it follows a symphonic underscore that blends into an instrumental refrain of the song, of gossamer texture as in "I'm Old Fashioned," while he and Maria talk. He sings the verse plus one refrain, at which point one longs for the *sul G* violin cantilena that will surely follow (and which does on Astaire's "cover" recording). Nothing but a brief fade-out to dialogue ensues, however: the dance was cut by the studio. When a routine is finally accorded the song in the final moments of the film, Kern's melody is alienated by a specious tie-in of Hispanic features and reprise fragments of most of the film's numbers. *You Were Never Lovelier* delights, but with a little more discretion it could have stunned.

America Past and Present

The United States was at war by the time *You Were Never Lovelier* was created, and it appears to be set in the present; in strong contrast to its sister film *You'll Never Get Rich*, however, no wartime references disturb the romantic comedy, though one or two were intended. "On the Beam," a suave quickstep not unlike "That's Entertainment," is a sixty-four-bar AA_1BA_2 song full of references to flying, which make its additional similarity to the sleek lines of "High, Wide and Handsome," a horse-riding song, understandable. Lines such as "Time's flying by / And I'm flying high" in the first A section are followed up in the release with "I'm like the B-NINETEEN loaded with benzedrine[;] / When I come on the scene / I bust a hole in the sky." The form of this C major song is subtle, but "On the Beam" was cut. "Windmill Under the Stars," published in 1942 with lyrics by Mercer, could have been intended for the film, for it includes a Breton reference (Acuña's family is supposed to be from Brittany). But it was more probably written as a freestanding song of tribute to a beleaguered Europe, like "The Last Time I Saw Paris" and "Forever and a Day." Its dream of "the sweet air of liberty" returning to Spain, Holland, and France would have caused *You Were Never Lovelier* to jump uncomfortably out of its frame, reminding the audience that, far from living happily ever after, Robert and Maria would be separated soon after their marriage as he was called up.

Cover Girl, by contrast, managed to "make way for to-morrow" by including wartime service in the plot and having as its leading male character one who had already been called up but has been invalided out. Danny McGuire (Gene Kelly), owner of a modest Brooklyn nightclub, has seen action in Libya, but the nature of his disability is never specified, despite his doorman asking him about it. Given the extremities of endurance associated with North Africa in the Second World War we are probably meant to suppose psychological abandonment by his mates, or abandonment of them, since Kelly had previously been typecast as a weak young man who has to make good (or fails to do so, in *Pal Joey*). His first film, *For Me and My Gal* (1942), subjected him to the potent scenario of self-injury to avoid the draft. In *Cover Girl*, in which he bitterly says, "I love parties" when sent to one by an apparent rival, he has above all to learn to trust people again rather than expect a slight from good teamwork. This he can still enjoy with his girlfriend Rusty Parker (Rita Hayworth) after she becomes momentarily famous as the girl on the cover of *Vanity*'s fiftieth anniversary issue if only he has faith in her and in himself to keep her. The fact that she has been "called up" to Manhattan does not automatically mean that her head will be turned, though she too has to discover the strength of her loyalty and can do so only through being tested. (She is tested right to the altar, where she abandons her producer fiancé.) There are no guarantees in battle, but there is hope, which McGuire spurns, demeaning himself and her in the process. Phil Silvers as his vaudevillian sidekick Genius maintains hope where he fails, by reminding him to continue casting the spell over their weekly "ersters" until they find a "poil," which happens just in time for it to be sent to Rusty as a wedding gift (pearls at a wedding signaling bad luck, though they seem not to grasp this).

The pearl ritual stresses endurance against the odds, and *Cover Girl* is plain propaganda at many points. There are sailors in the nightclub audience in the opening scene, and backstage immediately after it Danny says to Genius, "The bigger the gripe, the better the army" as the girls grumble about his demands on them. A telegram on the doormat means bad news in wartime, and—who knows, to avoid assumption of bereavement?—Genius says, "Maybe it's a draft notice" as Hayworth picks up one addressed to her. It is in fact her theatrical summons, but the exchange at any rate stresses the inevitability of parting, which Kelly has to accept just as Marjorie had to in

Toot-Toot! The First World War, *Toot-Toot!*'s setting, is never directly invoked as a lesson of history in *Cover Girl*, but the idea of history repeating itself and coming out right on both occasions drives the subplot of Coudair's infatuation with Maribelle, Rusty's grandmother, forty years earlier. But again, this is with no guarantees, and until the climax of the film we are left to form our own assumptions about the outcome of the rich boy's 1904 courtship of the music hall girl, while the riddle of what the innocent girl feels and really wants is the precise point of Coudair's search for the right bridal face on the cover of his magazine.

There are naturally corollaries in song and dance to the propaganda and parables. Kelly's famous "Alter Ego Dance" (based on the song "Long Ago") is a sure sign that we are to take him as mentally, not physically, unfit for service. It ends violently when he throws a trashcan through a plate glass window in hatred of his own image: anger had to be released somewhere in a film about wartime, and this was a most creative way of doing so within the musical comedy form. Genius's diegetic vaudeville number, "Who's Complaining?," is all about bearing up under wartime shortages (and, conversely, superabundance of women), celebrated in a riot of lyrical cleverness from Ira Gershwin ("Because of Axis trickery / My coffee now is chicory / And I can rarely purloin / A sirloin"). The film's title song begins with the words "Soldiers and civilians." This is not in the published sheet music, but in "Make Way for To-morrow" the situation is reversed: "Listen all, this is Vict'ry calling 'Make way! / Make way now for that better day ahead'" proclaim the first lines of the verse in the sheet music, whereas in the film the words are "Listen all, this is Genius calling 'Hear ye!'" The point could not have been labored endlessly, however, and the production number "Put Me to the Test" is, despite its title, about a modern version of medieval chivalry, not warfare. (It was composed by Kern to the lyrics of an old Gershwin song left over from *A Damsel in Distress*.) Another take on the film's message of gallantry and endurance, it is heard twice, first in the big dance number for Kelly and Hayworth, done as a nightclub item, second in a comic rendition by Kelly and Silvers as vaudevillians broadcasting from the back of a moving army truck.

Morale in wartime also relies on a firm vision of better times, and the lyrics of "Make Way for To-morrow" urged their hearers to "Let ev'ry heart be a drum beating for great days to come." But a film about things "long ago (and far away)," to quote the title of *Cover Girl*'s chief ballad, was just as important a part of Kern's war effort as one about the present and the future.

Can't Help Singing, a musical western, concerns the headstrong daughter of a senator during the gold rush days of 1849 who runs away from home and follows her lieutenant fiancé all the way to California, only to fall for the freer and easier man who helps her evade parental capture and get there. By the time she arrives in Sonora she has four men apparently pursuing her: her father, her alibi (a rich prospector called Jake Carstair), Lieutenant Robert Latham, and the new flame, Johnnie (Robert Paige), to whom she commits. This makes for a colorful, crowded finale in the town square with a bit of a fight before destinies are agreed upon. The dazzling costumes and Hispanic architecture with its shady balconies and fountain spouting wine must have lifted wartime spirits wonderfully to a mythical place where "In this new Eldorado, there's free avocado for ev'ryone, / And there's none that weighs under a ton / In this fabulous clime," to quote the words of Kern's new, whimsical lyricist, Yip Harburg, from the song "Californ-i-ay."

It makes sense to think of *Cover Girl* and *Can't Help Singing* as a pair occupying Kern for most of 1943 and part of 1944. Generically, they show a cinematic approach that has in many ways returned to stage wisdom and procedures by hardening once again into the contrasting types of musical comedy and operetta. *You Were Never Lovelier* was still trying to circumvent such traditional loyalties, whereas *Cover Girl* is very much the vaudeville backstager and *Can't Help Singing* the closest Kern ever got to a film operetta. Music is crucial to the plot of the one (there would be no story without Rusty singing and dancing in Danny's nightclub in *Cover Girl*) and entirely incidental to the other (based as it was on a novel about the trek westward) except insofar as Johnnie first falls for Caroline (Deanna Durbin) singing in her open-air bath in Independence, Missouri, before he has set eyes on her. Yet it is *Can't Help Singing* that is all about singing, for Durbin's magnificent voice, the one and only gateway to her personality, is the box office attraction, and she is trilling away in her pony and trap within minutes of the film's opening. It is a story entirely about American rural endeavor, about working the land for national enrichment and security rather than for personal quirkiness and greed; unlike *The Red Petticoat*, it opens not in the far west with its rough miners but with the first shipment of gold being delivered to the government in Washington. All Durbin's singing occurs and is filmed out-of-doors, stressing her music and her personality as an extension of nature, if a little obviously like Curly's in "Oh, What a Beautiful Mornin'." The words "Humming bird, mocking bird, listen to me" are the film's lyric portal, opening the verse of its title song, and on her first appearance even the horses are trotting in time to the music. In "Any Moment Now" a deer listens to her, as with "Our Song" in *When You're in Love*. This was the musical contract longed for in the barnyard scene of *High, Wide and Handsome* but never sustained in that film.

Given Durbin's unique qualities, Kern, for the first time in his career, and the studio team could indulge in music as opera. This has its burlesque side, as when the townsfolk exaggeratedly join in with Durbin's warbling of the joys of spring in the bathhouse scene, including the man with the whiskers in outrageous falsetto, and even a postmodern touch when the reprise of "Californ-i-ay" includes the lyric line "Each scene is recorded" as if in *buffa* commentary on the preceding action. But Durbin vocalizes a tumescent coda to the first sequence of "Can't Help Singing" in proper earnest, as though it were the last movement of the Schumann piano concerto, and Paige eggs her on in vocal duet when this recurs in the bath scene. In "More and More" one phrase is marked "melody silent in accomp." in *colla voce* obeisance (very rare in Kern's output). At the end of the film, after its finaletto has run through parts of "Californ-i-ay" and "Elbow Room," the assembled wedding guests listen while Durbin reprises "More and More," descending the balcony staircase to her waiting husband. With another coda (which Paige actually instigates) supplanting its last four bars, her arioso extension, as they clasp hands and, after a fermata, she sings in close-up "because I love you and because I live for you," is a moment of pure operatic persuasion before she literally leads the guests with a final refrain of "Can't Help Singing." Coming less than a year before Kern's death, it affords the viewer a pang of regret after all that he never pursued a more operatic path.

Can't Help Singing also presented Kern with his first opportunity in years to write waltz songs, breaking the duple-time tyranny of the films in particular from the later 1930s and early 1940s. Without any doubt, it was Rodgers in "Oh, What a Beautiful Mornin'" from *Oklahoma!* who not only liberated him to do this but provided the blueprint for a new type of waltz melody with more persuasive, inflected harmonies to complement the simpler vocal rhythms and contours that now relied not on chromaticism, dotted-note cross-rhythm, and runs of eighth notes but on matter-of-fact trails of quarter notes interspersed with half notes and heavily end-stopped dotted half notes, a more folksy, *al fresco* interpretation of the genre. The result was that Kern's best waltzes—"Can't Help Singing," "Californ-i-ay," "Up With the Lark"— come from his last two films. The second phrase of "Can't Help Singing" is strikingly similar to the first of "Oh, What a Beautiful Mornin'." Both make special use of flat $\hat{7}$, and Kern follows it up a few bars later with a flat $\hat{6}$, a good example of the musical "added value" these late waltz songs pursue.

"Elbow Room," the blacksmith's song, is another number in *Can't Help Singing* that seems to stress that the mid–nineteenth century was an age in which people sang, together, singly, and with technical awareness. Whether the music is or is not intended as diegetic hardly seems to matter. In the 1940s Brooklyn of *Cover Girl* different contexts are needed to persuade us that it is the most natural thing in the world for characters to dance, together, singly, and with technical delight, along a street of tenement houses. If Astaire's dancing had always been either a diegetic display or a follow-on from a conversational song, Kelly's is always a matter of immediate self-presentation, of showing off in his natural medium of expression, and he needs no song to get him from dialogue to display. When performing thus in combination with other characters, he makes such expression into the prototype of a modern, that is, classic, production number.

"Make Way for To-morrow" is Kern's first and only number of this type, and again it stems from stage traditions, those of song-and-dance men and the strutting of blackface minstrelsy but also of the vaudeville "concept" act such as those chronicled in *Gypsy*. Novelty numbers like "Bongo on the Congo" and "Cleopatterer" had implied these traditions but tacked the comic movement onto the end of the song; in "Make Way for To-morrow" the dancing *is* the song, and it begins when Danny, Rusty, and Genius, still seated at the bar of Jo's oyster house, swivel round on their stools. The number is still diegetic, signaled in two ways. First, it is carefully set up by having the diner's pianist playing "Make Way for To-morrow" from the start of the scene and having the trio enter in theatrical high spirits: rhyming "Jo" with "show" in the first exchange as though this is their natural mode of interaction when in public, they perform their oyster ritual as soon as they sit down. Second, it is important that such a display be witnessed by characters in the narrative as well as by the film audience. Their audience is first the other diners, to whom they address their opening exhortations in song and dance and who stand up and peer out of the windows when they move to the yard, then the cop on the beat, followed by the kissing couple, the milkman, and the drunk. At the same time it is fantasy, in that the milkman is capable of joining in choreographically. The fantasy level is mirrored in their lightning succession of make-believe props as they move toward the street: first the garbage can lids, a diner's breadstick, and a pail as cymbals, fife, and drum of a marching band (fig. 5.4); then the tea chests as hustings; then

Fig. 5.4. "Make Way for To-morrow."

two oars as string basses in a jazz band; then the oars plus the pail again for
bailing out an imaginary boat; the mailbox as a tribal drum; the milkman's
imaginary horse; and a plucked flower plus a thrown flowerpot as adjuncts
to courtship. All these need rhythmic pantomimicry in sound, precise to
the microsecond. Their quick-march footsteps are maintained throughout,
and even the throwing of the breadstick into the pail is timed for an audible
musical offbeat. Sometimes musical sound is suspended for a short cadenza,
comparable to a tap break, as with the "Yackety-yak" mocking of the lovers
and the sounding of the milkman's horn, but never is the song's periodicity
lost, except insofar as its thirty-four-bar refrain is elided for the last two bars
with an eight-bar interlude for the imaginary band after the first chorus.

    At virtually all times, then, the carnival of orchestration and instrumen-
tal paraphrase, changing radically every few bars as the vaudevillian enact-
ment moves on, is superimposed on the regular course of verse or refrain.
The overall form is four and a half choruses of the refrain; a sixteen-bar verse
sung after the first; two pantomimic eight-bar interludes (after choruses one

and two); and a twelve-bar coda. The rhythm of the vaudeville enactments partly duplicates these periods, partly overlaps with them, partly produces small-scale syncopations, as when the slapped-oar jazz mimicry begins a bar or so before the musical refrain; this is closely comparable with the typical rhythms of camera shots discussed with reference to figure 5.2, and in this instance the overall pattern of concepts and number of bars for the outdoor portion of the routine is as follows: band (8), hustings (16), jazz (4), boat (8), alleyway and policeman (30), street (8), lovers (8), Indians (8), milkman (16), flowers (24), drunk (16), steps (12). Only the first two refrains and the verse are sung, as though the encounter with the policeman after the second refrain has silenced but not immobilized the performers for the rest of the routine.

All of this is a matter of exceptional vaudeville talent (Kelly, Hayworth, and Silvers) allied to studio wizardry from the director, designers, cameramen, and musical staff. Kern and Ira Gershwin will have had little or nothing to do with it once they had written their song as published, so where musical films are concerned, above all films such as this, one is left with assessment of the songs and of the routines as separate aesthetic entities, no obvious overlap or mutual responsibility between them affecting the argument.

At the same time, there has to be a continuum of idea and symbolism between the smallest musical phrase and the biggest production element in order for a song to feel right in its routined context, and "Make Way for Tomorrow" illustrates this well. The majority of the vaudeville concepts—the military band, the election speech, the boat being rowed toward distant land with its lookout patrol, even the disrupted lovers—relate to America's war in 1944–45. The lyrics plant victory references additional to the one cited earlier: "Strike up the band," "Over here, over there" (referring to the First World War song), and "Let there be music for all," this last set to a modern fanfare figure which is later strenuously extended with augmented and half-diminished chords in the struggle, not without pain, toward diatonic victory on the word "world" (ex. 5.4).

Kern's final film, *Centennial Summer*, as a vernacular costume drama shares obvious features with *Can't Help Singing* and begins almost identically, with a U.S. president (Ulysses S. Grant rather than Zachary Taylor) making a boring outdoor speech to a crowd on the steps of an imposing porticoed building on the east coast. But thereafter the similarities rapidly fade, and, far from being a western, *Centennial Summer* offers instead a suitable opportunity for judging how urban romantic comedy in musicals settled

Ex. 5.4. Make Way for To-morrow.

down after *You Were Never Lovelier.* One can accordingly argue that each of Kern's last three films represents one genre in its newly negotiated cinematic settlement: backstage musical comedy, operetta, and romantic comedy, in every case with an added "folk" element in response to wartime social (though not racial) leveling. All three films, as noted, were responding very obviously to folk-saturated progenitors: *Oklahoma!* in the case of *Can't Help Singing, Holiday Inn,* vehicle for "White Christmas," in the case of *Cover Girl,* and *Meet Me in St. Louis* in the case of *Centennial Summer.*[28]

    Centennial Summer shares the same problem as *Meet Me in St. Louis,* that of an undernourished score, here not Kern's fault but that of 20th Century–Fox in its seeming determination to let major songs slip by as casually and unnoticed as possible; the studio prided itself in press releases that "not one of the eight Jerome Kern songs is presented in the conventional setting of the theatre or any other phase of entertainment."[29] All three of the film's ballads suffer from this, two of them crooned privately by Julia (Jeanne Crain), the third presented by a generic singer in a restaurant and repeated chorally by the assembled diners. The three other principals, Philippe (Cornel Wilde), Ben (William Eythe), and Julia's older sister Edith (Linda Darnell), are simply not singers. At least *Meet Me in St. Louis* had a musical star, Judy Garland, and one magnificent production number for her, "The Trolley Song." *Centennial Summer* has no production number at all barring its belated acknowledgment, toward the end, of Philadelphia's sizable black community in "Cinderella Sue," sung and danced in a saloon by Avon Long and a group of children as passing buskers.

It does, however, have a great deal of music, and some fine Kern tunes. Thus if one can stomach the lack of musical foreground it is worth appreciating how it disposes its background score, which is in the "classic," Technicolor-era manner of a subliminal symphony intercut with very residual obligations to the Broadway musical. The fifty-four music cues evident from listening to the film are listed in figure 5.5. The numbering is not precisely that of the studio, for in figure 5.5 occasional discontinuities are amalgamated (as in cue 9), continuities are sometimes separated out because different themes need identifying within them (see cues 1–3, 22–24, 34–36, 38–41, and 42–43), and diegetic music that would probably not have been prerecorded (cues 6 and 32) is included. The studio's collection of music cues numbers thirty-four.[30]

Centennial Summer concerns the two headstrong daughters of an eccentric but upstanding Philadelphia couple at the time of the 1876 exposition. When their mother's cosmopolitan sister Zenia comes to visit, they outmaneuver each other in their unedifying attempts to court her French nephew; no more easily can their father handle Zenia's charms, though she manages to do him a much-needed professional turn. There are only five major songs, listed in bold, and they are spread out fairly evenly across the film, two of them reprised toward the end. Four of these songs were published (four seems to be the norm in Kern's last years), the fifth ("The Right Romance") was not. A further song, "Two Hearts Are Better than One," sung by Philippe, was published but cut from the film. In an effort to make Kern's contribution look substantial, the studio pressbook also listed parts of the title music ("Centennial" and "Long Live Our Free America") and "Railroad Song" among the numbers. These are indeed integral Kern songs, with lyrics, but there are other tunes by him too, all instrumental. One of them is "Two Dachshunds" (see fig. 1.5), in the event never used for the dogs, though they appear in the film, but for their owner, Aunt Zenia, or rather her letter. The music for the fancy-dress ball, one component of which, the "Polka," has already appeared elsewhere (see cues 13 and 20), includes the gorgeous "Waltz," barely heard under the dialogue but worthy of Lehár, with

1. "Centennial" title ([3/4] 5|1-1|-56|135|61)
2. "March" title
3. "Long Live Our Free America" title ([2/2]|4---|3-$^\sharp$2-|3-55|-77)
4. "Hail to the Chief"
5. *"Up With the Lark" scherzando underscore*
6. "All Through the Day" Ben and ukelele
7. "Railroad Song" ([6/8] 5653-5|↑3-33-2|1-53-5|4--2)
8. *"All Through the Day" romantic underscore*
9. *"Two Dachshunds" scherzando letter underscore*
10. *"The Right Romance" romantic underscore*
11. **"The Right Romance"** ([3/4] |333|3-↓5|5-6|6)
12. *"Two Dachshunds" scherzando letter re-reading underscore*
13. *"Polka" underscore*
14. *[Unidentifiable underscore]*
15. "Centennial" underscore
16. *"Railroad Song" scherzando underscore*
17. **"Up With the Lark"** ([3/4] |1-1|713|6-3|231|)
18. *"Up With the Lark" romantic underscore*
19. "Centennial" choral underscore
20. "Polka" scherzando underscore
21. "Clocks" scherzando underscore
22. "All Through the Day" romantic underscore
23. "In Love in Vain" romantic underscore
24. *Waltz ("The Right Romance"?) romantic underscore*
25. **"In Love in Vain"** ([2/2] 616|11-2|1765|6713|2)
26. "The Right Romance" waltz
27. "In Love in Vain" waltz
28. "All Through the Day" waltz
29. **"All Through the Day"** ([2/2] |3-21|5--6|565↑3|2)
30. "All Through the Day" waltz
31. "The Right Romance" waltz
32. "Railroad Song" Jesse whistle
33. *"Railroad Song" burlesque march underscore*
34. *"The Right Romance" romantic underscore*   }
35. *"All Through the Day" romantic understore*   }
36. *"In Love in Vain" romantic underscore*   }
37. French party entrance march and fanfare
38. "Polka" quadrille ([2/4] |77122|143)
39. "Two Dachshunds" quadrille ([2/4] |363363|222—see fig. 1.5)
40. Third quadrille (6/8)
41. "Polka" and "Two Dachshunds" repeated
42. Minuet
43. Waltz ([3/4] |3--|4-2|5--|↓1--|↑6--|7-6|1--|5)
44. Galop
45. "Up With the Lark" waltz
46. "In Love in Vain" waltz
47. *"The Right Romance" romantic underscore and* **vocal reprise**
48. **"Cinderella Sue"** ([2/2] 1.♯1.6̣|5---|--1.♯1.6̣|5)
49. *"Cinderella Sue" scherzando underscore*
50. "Up With the Lark" **vocal reprise** *and scherzando underscore*
51. *"All Through the Day" romantic underscore*
52. *"Railroad Song" and "Up With the Lark" romantic underscore*
53. *"Up With the Lark" scherzando underscore*
54. *"Up With the Lark" end title*

Fig. 5.5. *Centennial Summer,* music cues.

an entirely authentic nineteenth-century galop to follow. This was also an authentic succession of dances for a ball, and the preceding quadrille (cues 38–41) is a correct sequence.

There are three layers of musical presentation in the film (see fig. 5.5): that of the main songs (in bold) and those of supplementary diegetic material (in roman) and subliminal underscoring (in italics). The subliminal underscoring cannot be simply equated with background music, for the latter can include the diegetic material, as in the ball scene (cues 37–46), while there seems to be a deliberate differentiation of volume levels in the studio mix for each of these three layers. Other than at the ball, diegetic music mostly appears near the beginning of the film, to establish its credentials as a plausible subject for a musical (see cues 1–4 and 6–7).[31] This is in the mold of *Meet Me in St. Louis*, except for the fact that apart from "Hail to the Chief," the American presidential song, it would appear that only Kern's own music is used for the purpose. Kern distinguishes himself in *Centennial Summer* by resisting for once his serial temptation to mix in the real songs of his youth, presumably because this film is dated slightly further back.

Subliminal underscoring carries an enormous weight, as can be seen from the total of twenty-six cues devoted to it, almost half the total. It can be perceptually divided into two types, romantic and burlesque, the latter labeled *scherzando* in figure 5.5 so as to emphasize its quasi-symphonic function. As in a five-movement symphony, there may be a scherzo and a romance function among the "inner" movements of film music (enclosed not so much by other music, except for the opening and end titles, as by expository and concluding dialogue scenes), and a dance element that could be interpreted as either. In film music these types of cue are generally not presented continuously as musical movements but fragmented and separated into smaller sections. There may, however, be a balance between the types: *Centennial Summer* has ten *scherzando* or burlesque cues, twelve romantic ones, and fourteen diegetic dances. The large number of dances, while perfectly in accordance with the scenario, may reflect Kern's early suggestion that "the entire score be composed in waltz time to enhance the period flavor," anticipating a comparable Sondheim ploy by nearly forty years, as Bordman pointed out. Separated the cue types may be, but they coalesce into almost the equivalent of musical movements spread over the entire film: a bunch of preludial diegetic numbers, as stated above (cues 1–7), expository commentary on the characters and the plot, mostly in subliminal underscoring (cues 8–25), a first suite of dances in the restaurant scene (cues 26–31), the plot's thickening (cues 32–36), a second suite of dances at the ball (cues 37–46), and the narrative crux, episodic relief ("Cinderella Sue"), and denouement (cues 47–54). This makes for six such groupings overall, largely of one type of music each, subliminal underscoring dominating every other "movement" (nos. 2, 4, and 6). The quasi-symphonic intentions of the groupings are most apparent in cues 34–36, bracketed together in figure 5.5 as a continuous rhapsody of instrumental anguish revisiting the three main ballads one by one as the three main characters (Julia, Edith, and Philippe — Ben is little more than a stooge) approach their nadir of romantic entanglement. Their elders (Harriet, Zenia, and Jesse) mirror this love triangle, but in them we take it less seriously — hence the whistling and the burlesque march (cues 32–33) and the elegance of dancing (cues 37–46) as their strand of the plot comes to a head.

A musical item is missing from figure 5.5. It is a little waltz coda, [3/4] 234$^{\#}$46|5--|↓56$^{\flat}$7$^{\#}$73|1, very similar to the verse of "Dearly Beloved." Initially belonging to "The Right Romance," it is tagged onto the other two ballads at one point or another and used to link dances at the restaurant. It adds a dimension of cross-reference by symbolizing the round dance of love in which the leading characters get swept up, whirled from one to another without quite mastering the ironies of their own game. It is wistful and at the same time somehow cheeky, reminding us of both the pain and the fun involved in Quaker Philadelphia's learning at last how to enjoy itself *à la française*.

Kern's Last Songs

Like Gershwin, Kern found a new simplicity of style in some of his last songs, written for Hollywood. It is felt mostly in the abandonment of syncopation (though some songs still use it, especially in *Cover Girl*), in the primacy of plain rhythms, and in textures less reliant on "oompah" vestiges for their sense of motion. Verses also cease to be pert generators of energy and character and in some of the wartime sheet music, published in small format, have been relegated to the back cover, presumably to save paper. Sure, there are duds ("In Love in Vain" one of the more obvious), but in most cases these late songs are among Kern's most rewarding, with never a hint of melodic exhaustion or self-repetition. Hymnlike, sacralized sentiment for a patriotic decade might explain this attainment of "cigar-shaped" melody, as also might the predominance of narratives set in the nineteenth century, before the victory of black-influenced popular culture, but neither would account for the candor of "Long Ago," in Bordman's view "Kern's last great masterpiece."[32] Its casualness comes from the dissonant lie of the melody athwart diatonic harmonies at the beginning of the refrain: the first line ends on an added 7th, the second on an added 6th, and only one third of the notes in the first eight bars are consonant with the simple harmonies. Its passion resides in the way this melodic approach creates long phrases, which despite the implied suspensions manage to rise over the course of the refrain nearly an octave above the melodic headnote, an 11th above the nadir pitch, in a long-term *minor* arpeggiation (F, A flat, C, E flat) in this major-key song.[33]

The A flat is the headnote of the second limb of the refrain, simply the initial A section transposed up a minor 3rd, though after three bars Kern deftly returns to the tonic, or rather to V^7 of V in the tonic. Writing voice parts that despite the obvious difficulties (in this case a melodic tritone) somehow guide and sing themselves smoothly through the most unexpected modulations without losing tunefulness is perhaps the major manifestation of Kern's genius in this late period. Almost every song contains at least one such harmonic sideslip. "All Through the Day" transposes the first four bars of the final A section in an otherwise conventional AABA refrain up a minor 3rd (again from F major into A flat major) and arranges melodic pivot notes at each end to keep the singer secure. "Sure Thing," in E flat with a twenty-eight-bar refrain, arrives at the mediant (G major) after sixteen bars, but on its dominant rather than its tonic, and this turns into an interrupted cadence, the chord of E minor nevertheless leading smoothly to one of F minor as ii of V. "Any Moment Now" includes in the bridge a neat variant on the expected descending sequence, when its first two bars are simply reinflected with flats on the same pitches—only the third and fourth bars move down, and even here there are the usual "tonal" modifications. The bridge of another AABA song, "Cover Girl," begins with its tonic, B flat, enharmonically pivoting into B major as A sharp, and four bars later the ensuing phrase is repeated down a semitone. "Up With the Lark," an irresistible waltz song every bit the equal of "I'm in Love With a Wonderful Guy," is delightfully adventurous. In twenty-four bars it visits four unrelated major keys, G flat, D, D flat, and C before returning to its tonic of B flat. But the most seductive gesture comes in "Cinderella Sue," a song utterly beguiling in its catchy simplicity because once, just once, it winks a knowing eye, when an added flat 7th opens the door to a parenthetic Neapolitan (ex. 5.5). Harburg's lyrics, typical of his capacity for whimsical enchantment, reflexively perfect the

Ex. 5.5. Cinderella Sue.

moment as it "Passes by," reduced to exclamation ("And, oh my!") as the "miracles" of digression and safe return "occur."

Several times the studio balked at Kern's tonal experimentation. "Once in a Million Moons," probably its most extreme example, was cut from *Can't Help Singing* (see ex. 5.6 for its ending). So was "There'll Come a Day," which includes outlandish enharmonics in the A section of the refrain, as Bordman observes, and, as with "Any Moment Now," an inflected alternative to sequence in the bridge. "Two Hearts Are Better than One" was a considerable loss, for its soft-shoe lilt affords a new side to Kern's contemporaneity, though fitting the airport lounge ambience of the fashion magazine's lobby in *Cover Girl* far better than Philippe's assault on Victorian Philadelphia in *Centennial Summer*. Its changing tonal vistas and brazen glide back to the tonic from a key that has casually strayed a semitone away feel like the musical equivalent of a fashion model's latest sartorial challenge as she turns on the catwalk (see ex. 5.7). If there was a thread of connoisseurship running through Kern's appreciation of feminine display from *Roberta* to *Cover Girl*, offering him more than one plot in which beauty is serially paraded, it seems

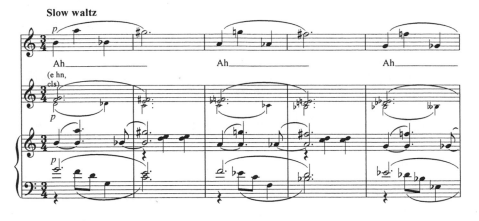

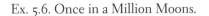

Ex. 5.6. Once in a Million Moons.

fitting that the very last known photograph of him, taken three days before he collapsed, has him studying costume designs for the 1946 *Show Boat* revival.[34] Here was a man who appreciated the good things in life. Bespoke voice-leading to clothe a shapely melody was definitely one of them.

The gilt folder in the Library of Congress, clearly pertaining to *Centennial Summer* but consisting mostly of material never placed in the film or not written for it, reminds us both that there was a great deal of wastage on any major project and that virtually any judgment about style and period has to remain provisional where Kern is concerned, for older songs continued to jostle new ones in his portfolio at all stages of his career. "All Through the

Ex. 5.7. Two Hearts Are Better Than One.

Day" was not necessarily a 1940s song, if, as Bordman states, it was "salvaged from an earlier collaboration with Hammerstein," and indeed it sounds similar to "Can I Forget You" from *High, Wide and Handsome. Cover Girl* may well contain more songs than "Sure Thing" first worked on with Ira Gershwin in 1938, while the residue from that occasion continued to be published long after Kern's own death (though some of it remains in manuscript).[35]

Indeed, Kern's last films afforded him the opportunity to look back on a forty-year career. *Centennial Summer* contains its antiquarian moments. The parallels between *Can't Help Singing* and Kern's debut musical, *The*

Fig. 5.6. John Coudair and Tony Pastor admiring Maribelle at the theater in 1905.

Red Petticoat, would reward sustained consideration. Both were westerns about gold mining, both focused on the heroine, both explored operetta, *The Red Petticoat* uncertainly, *Can't Help Singing* with a sure hand as though to set an old record straight, and both reserved a prominent place for "Dutch" humor. In *Cover Girl* John Coudair enacts the forty-year retrospect more patently on Kern's behalf, and although it is not specified, the implication is that something of Kern himself was written into the vignette of the young masher hosted in his stage box by the famous impresario (Tony Pastor— standing in for Charles Frohman?). Maribelle, supposedly in 1905, sings not just Kern's "Sure Thing" and "Let's Have a Little Kiss," new songs written for the film, but also, in a later scene though in flashback to the same period, an English song, "Poor John," in a Cockney routine with Coudair again look- ing on. As Andrew Lamb points out, this song would have held particular memories for Kern of his first visit to London.[36] But, more important, we are reminded of Kern's evening at the Palace Theatre on 12 February 1906 (figs.5.6, 5.7).

Fig. 5.7. Millie Legarde flirting with Bertie Hollender, Kern, Raymond Howard, and Powers Gouraud from the stage of the Palace Theatre, London, while singing "How'd You Like to Spoon With Me?," 12 February 1906. Courtesy of Andrew Lamb.

Arthur Freed clearly understood Kern's affection for the songs of his youth, both his and others', and for all Kern's anxiety about how MGM would treat his musical biography when they broached the topic with him in 1945, he will have had little hesitation in opening up his trunk to the producer. We hear close to forty-five of Kern's tunes, dating from 1905 to 1945, during the course of *Till the Clouds Roll By*, though it was perhaps a blessing that Kern did not live to witness how some of them and his life story were presented.

Works by Jerome Kern

Unless otherwise noted, all works are Broadway musicals.

1911   *La belle Paree* [7 songs]
1912   *The Red Petticoat*
1913   *Oh, I Say!*
1914   *The Girl from Utah* [7 songs]
1915   *90 in the Shade*
        Nobody Home
        Very Good Eddie
1916   *Theodore and Co.* [London, 4 songs]
1917   *Have a Heart*
        Love o' Mike
        Oh, Boy!
        Leave It to Jane
        Miss 1917 [7 songs]
1918   *Oh, Lady! Lady!!*
        Toot-Toot!
        Rock-a-Bye Baby
        Head Over Heels
1919   *She's a Good Fellow*
        Zip, Goes a Million [Worcester, Mass.]
1920   *The Night Boat*
        Hitchy Koo: 1920
        Sally
1921   *Good Morning, Dearie*
1922   *The Cabaret Girl* [London]
        The Bunch and Judy

1923   *The Beauty Prize* [London]
       Stepping Stones
1924   *Sitting Pretty*
       Dear Sir
1925   *Sunny*
       The City Chap
1926   *Criss-Cross*
1927   *Lucky* [with Harry Ruby]
       Show Boat
1928   *Blue Eyes* [London]
1929   *Sweet Adeline*
1931   *Men of the Sky* [film]
       The Cat and the Fiddle
1932   *Music in the Air*
1933   *Roberta*
1934   *Three Sisters* [London]
1935   *Reckless* [film]
       I Dream Too Much [film]
1936   *Swing Time* [film]
1937   *When You're in Love* [film]
       High, Wide and Handsome [film]
1938   *Joy of Living* [film]
       Gentlemen Unafraid [St. Louis]
1939   *Very Warm for May*
1940   *One Night in the Tropics* [film]
1941   *Scenario for Orchestra* [concert work]
1942   *Portrait for Orchestra: Mark Twain* [concert work]
       You Were Never Lovelier [film]
1944   *Cover Girl* [film]
       Can't Help Singing [film]
1946   *Centennial Summer* [film]
       [*Till the Clouds Roll By*, "biopic"]

Notes

CHAPTER 1. Introducing Kern

1. Gene Buck, master of ceremonies, evening concert at the California Coliseum, San Francisco, 24 September 1940, on *Carousel of American Music* (Music and Arts CD-971, 1997), CD 3, track 11; unknown host, first broadcast performance of *Portrait for Orchestra*, 7 June 1942, Library of Congress Recorded Sound Collections, tape RXA 9746 A; Abram Chasins, interviewer, WQXR radio broadcast, New York, November 1961; introductory voiceover, Paramount radio promotional trailer for *High, Wide and Handsome*, Library of Congress Recorded Sound Collections, tape n.c.p. 3784; Arthur Hamilton, Academy of Motion Picture Arts and Sciences centennial tribute to Jerome Kern, 1985; telegram from President Harry S. Truman, CBC memorial radio broadcast, 9 December 1945, quoted in Ewen, *World of Jerome Kern*, 145; Hon. Philip J. Philbin, eulogy on Kern, House of Representatives, 26 March 1946, quoted ibid.; Ewen, *Story of Jerome Kern*, 3.

2. Bosley Crowther, *New York Times*, 6 December 1946, 27.

3. Personal communication from William Harbach.

4. There are two current anthologies of Kern songs, the *Jerome Kern Collection* and *Jerome Kern Rediscovered*, whose musical content is identical. The reprint edition is *Jerome Kern: Collected Songs*; see the bibliography for details of these items and the published scripts and piano/vocal scores. Suskin lists eighteen published piano/vocal scores in his *Catalogue* (xxi), but for three (*The Beauty of Bath, The Kiss Waltz*, and *Theodore and Co.*) Kern was not the principal composer, while *Oh, Boy!*, which seems only to have been published in Sydney, Australia, was merely a bound collection of nine of the separately published songs. *Show Boat* has been engraved in three different versions: see Block, *Enchanted Evenings*, 319–21, for the differences between the Harms and Chappell scores. Full scores surviving in the Library of Congress Kern Collection comprise *The Cat and the Fiddle, Criss-Cross, Dear Sir, Leave It to Jane, Lucky, Music in the Air, Roberta*, parts of *Rock-a-Bye Baby, Sally, She's a Good Fellow, Show Boat, Sitting Pretty, Sunny, Very Good Eddie, Very Warm for May*, and *Zip, Goes a Million*.

Love o' Mike is in the Shubert Archive; *Sweet Adeline* is with the Rodgers and Hammerstein Organization; *Oh, Boy!, Oh, Lady! Lady!!*, and *Have a Heart* have been revived from sources elsewhere. *Six Plays by Rodgers and Hammerstein* (New York, 1959) is the published edition of their scripts.

5. See the bibliography for details of the recordings discussed in this paragraph and the previous one. Pearl's *Showboat . . .* presents the seven vocal tracks issued in 1928. "All the Things You Are" is on *Broadway Showstoppers* (EMI CDC 7 545862, 1992).

6. See the bibliography for full details of the books on Kern. Factual details in the present book are taken from Bordman and Lamb unless otherwise indicated.

7. Freedland, *Jerome Kern*, 1.

8. Note that there were two different editions of this book, for the London and New York markets. Citations in the present work are from the London edition.

9. Randall's work (see the bibliography) is supplemented by D. Chatfield, "Jerome Kern and the Princess Musicals" (M.A. diss., University of California at Davis, 1981); R. Friedman, "The Contributions of Harry Bache Smith (1860–1936) to the American Musical Theatre" (Ph.D. diss., New York University, 1976); Philip John Martin, "Development and Interpretation of the Elements of Integration in the Princess Theatre Musicals" (Ph.D. diss., University of Utah, 1993); Reuel Keith Olin, "A History and Interpretation of the Princess Theatre Musical Plays: 1915–1919" (Ph.D. diss., New York University, 1979); Jeffrey Hilton Smart, "The Internal Development of the Princess Theatre Musical Shows" (Ph.D. diss., University of Missouri, Columbia, 1991); Rebecca Strum, "Elisabeth Marbury, 1856–1933: Her Life and Work" (Ph.D. diss., New York University, 1989).

10. Bordman, *Kern*, 24.

11. NBC *Biography in Sound* radio documentary on Kern (29 November 1955), Library of Congress tape RWB 7571 A1-4.

12. In 1919, Saddler wrote to Kern about "Victor the fatuous," but Kern admired or at least envied Herbert for having done his own orchestrations. See the Library of Congress Kern Collection additions, box 3, Saddler correspondence, item 5; Ferencz, ed., *The Broadway Sound*, 65.

13. Fordin, *Getting to Know Him*, 60; Bordman, *Kern*, 24–25.

14. Quoted in Bordman, *Kern*, 39.

15. "The inexhaustible Mr. Kern," *New York Times*.

16. Leonard Spigelgass observed, "Jerome Kern disliked all of them . . . Irving Berlin was beneath their contempt." This is quoted from Samuel Marx and Jan Clayton, *Rodgers and Hart: Bewitched, Bothered and Bedevilled* (London, 1977), 237, by John M. Clum in *Something for the Boys: Musical Theater and Gay Culture* (New York, 1999), 54. Clum assumes that "them" and "their" refer, respectively, to lower- and upper-class Jewish songwriters.

17. Lamb, *Jerome Kern in Edwardian London*, 23; Don Walker to Gayle T. Harris, 12 February 1982, Library of Congress Don Walker Collection, box 2.

18. Francis may have been British but was certainly working in New York on *Fluffy Ruffles*. On *The "Mind the Paint" Girl*, see Peter Bailey, "'Naughty But Nice': Musical Comedy and the Rhetoric of the Girl," in *The Edwardian Theatre: Essays on Performance and the Stage*, ed. Michael R. Booth and Joel H. Kaplan (Cambridge,

1996), 36–60; Joel H. Kaplan, "Edwardian Pinero," *Nineteenth Century Theatre* 17 (1989), 20–49.

19. On *The Merry Widow*, see Orly Krasner, "Birth Pangs, Growing Pains and Sibling Rivalry: Musical Theatre in New York, 1900–1920" in *The Cambridge Companion to the Musical*, ed. William A. Everett and Paul R. Laird (Cambridge, 2002), 29–46. A *Waltz Dream* opened in New York on 27 January 1908, in London on 7 March. Kern's three interpolations were probably for the London production, though they may have joined the New York one later.

20. "Kern as Interpolator," Randall, *Becoming Jerome Kern*, 20–77.

21. Lamb, *Jerome Kern in Edwardian London*, 27–33; newspaper clipping, *New York Herald*, ? June 1910, Kern Collection adds, box 3, Correspondence, item 9.

22. Gershwin, however, was able to take up the river setting again in *Primrose*, his 1924 show for London.

23. Ewen, *World of Jerome Kern*, 47–49; Eva died before this was published, however, so Ewen may be revealing more than she would have wanted left on the record; Kern Collection adds, box 2, folder 7; Ferencz, ed., *The Broadway Sound*, 142.

24. Bordman (*Kern*, 47–48) specifies only five songs for *The Rich Mr. Hoggenheimer*, but see Suskin, *Catalogue* (125) for the eight.

25. All theaters and dates henceforward refer to New York unless otherwise specified.

26. See Randall, "*The Red Petticoat* (1912): Jerome Kern's First Full Score and Emerging Aesthetic for Integrated Musicals," *Becoming Jerome Kern*, 185–219.

27. Bordman, *Kern*, 90; Grossmith, "GG," 116; Bordman, "Jerome David Kern," 469.

28. Quoted in Bordman, *Kern*, 81–85.

29. Ibid., 87–88. For Smith, see John Franceschina, *Harry B. Smith: Dean of American Librettists* (New York, 2003).

30. Ferencz, ed., *The Broadway Sound*, 67.

31. Wodehouse and Bolton, *Bring on the Girls*, 16–19.

32. Davis, *Bolton and Wodehouse and Kern*, 171.

33. 31 March 1942, Library of Congress Hammerstein Collection adds.

34. Bordman, *Kern*, 139.

35. Henry Jenkins, *What Made Pistachio Nuts? Early Sound Comedy and the Vaudeville Aesthetic* (New York, 1992), 116.

36. Gilbert Seldes referred to them as "the Globe productions," comparing them with the Princess shows. See Seldes, "Plan for a Lyric Theatre in America," *The 7 Lively Arts* (New York, 1924; rev. ed., 1957), 153–63 (159).

37. See Andrew Lamb, *Leslie Stuart: Composer of Florodora* (New York, 2002), 240–44.

38. Bordman, *Kern*, 158; George Gershwin to Max Abramson, 12 September 1918, Library of Congress Gershwin Collection, box 64, folder 2; Seldes, "Plan for a Lyric Theatre in America," 3.

39. Richard Rodgers, *Musical Stages: An Autobiography* (New York, 1975; 2d ed., 1995), 20.

40. *Till the Clouds Roll By*: three scripts, Arthur Freed Collection, USC.

41. The statement about speed, as recalled by Bennett (though it must have come

from Saddler or Kern himself), is an extract from a Chappell booklet on Kern with an article by Rodgers that was in preparation in July 1952 (see Chappell and Co. to Oscar Hammerstein, 30 July 1952, Hammerstein Collection adds). On the pianism, Guy Bolton and Edna Ferber were interviewed for *Biography in Sound*, and Kern's playing can be heard on *Carousel of American Music*, CD 3, track 12 ("Smoke Gets in Your Eyes") and the Paramount *High, Wide and Handsome* trailer ("The Folks Who Live on the Hill"). Kern himself said of using the piano for composition, "Years ago, I found that wandering aimlessly about on the keyboard is largely ineffective and a decided deterrent to so-called originality. Subconsciously, the fingers seem to fall into well-worn and familiar channels. Countless melodies of mine have been notated on menus, envelopes and endless bits and scraps of stray paper. Mind you . . . the keyboard as a mechanical aid is important . . . musical history has been made by such slaves to the piano as Richard Wagner and Igor Stravinsky" (Kern to Vaughn DeLeath, 3 May 1938, Library of Congress Gershwin Fund Collection). Hammerstein's statement is from his "Jerome Kern," 166.

42. Graham Wood, "The Development of Song Forms in the Broadway and Hollywood Musicals of Richard Rodgers, 1919–1943" (Ph.D. diss., University of Minnesota, 2000), 12; "Sitting Pretty" sketch and professional copy: Kern Collection, box 71, folder 13.

43. Ferencz, ed., *The Broadway Sound*, 90, 97, 103. The material in the Kern Collection, box 58, folder 19, is indeed Kern's holograph sketch, in pencil at first, then ink as it proceeds. Its progression looks identical to the published score, i.e., Kern had everything worked out, in this case with fairly precise accompaniment details. Bennett did not have to make much up. Bennett's full score is in box 57, folder 8. The parts (box 67, folder 1) are also extant, with scoring for flute, oboe, two clarinets, bassoon, two horns, two trumpets, trombone, tuba, drums, violin 1 (three stands), violin 2, viola, cello, double bass (one stand for all these)—there is no harp in this number. They are mostly on Harms no. 2 paper, showing many signs of heavy use, and mostly in the same hand, though three hands or more can be identified altogether, mostly on the wind parts, as though extras came in toward the end to help on these (if the string ones were done first). The item is no. 20. There is, further, a copyist's piano/vocal score of five pages (box 59, folder 4), presumably made from Bennett's fair copy for the Tuesday morning rehearsal once Hammerstein had written the lyrics.

44. Kern Collection adds, box 3, item 7a; box 33, folder 6. On Miller in California, see the liner notes, *Jerome Kern Melodies*, volume 2, 8.

45. Ferencz, ed., *The Broadway Sound*, 98–99, 159, 254–55; Bordman, *Kern*, 358. Bennett's tributes are Variations on a Theme by Jerome Kern (1934) and Symphonic Study (1946)—see David Ewen, *The Lighter Classics in Music* (New York, 1961), 168.

46. Kern Collection, box 12, folder 9.

47. *Biography in Sound*; *Can't Help Singin*,' 53–54; Randall, *Becoming Jerome Kern*, 94–96; Wood, "The Development of Song Forms," 20.

48. They are incorrectly attributed to Berton Braley in *Collected Songs*, vol. 14.

49. *Lyrics by Oscar Hammerstein II*, 4–5.

50. Ferencz, ed., *The Broadway Sound*, 65–66, 287; Kern Collection, box 34, folder 13. The fills may have been Kern's because Saddler has used this pencil copy to

annotate the additional filigree work he intends to put into the orchestration (and there are comments on routing, too).

51. Ferencz, ed., *The Broadway Sound*, 74.

52. See Randall, "Drama in Miniature: Composing Dramatically Effective Songs," *Becoming Jerome Kern*, 78–133.

53. Ibid., 80–81.

54. Hammerstein, "Jerome Kern," 154–55; Oscar Hammerstein to ?William Hammerstein, 1929 (Hammerstein Collection adds).

55. Banfield, "Scholarship and the Musical," 191–92.

56. Grossmith, "GG," 185, 189.

57. At this stage the show was entitled *Vanity Fair*. Script in the possession of Gerald Bordman.

58. Most medley overtures and some reprise finalettos nevertheless repeat one of the tunes at the end.

59. Crittenden, *Johann Strauss and Vienna*, 200.

60. Kern Collection adds, box 3, Frank Saddler full scores.

61. George J. Ferencz: "Saddler, Frank," in *The New Grove Dictionary of Music and Musicians, 2d ed.*, ed. Stanley Sadie and John Tyrrell (London, 2001), vol. 22, 81; Saddler to Kern, 1 March 1912, Kern Collection adds, box 3, Saddler correspondence, item 2; Kern Collection, box 95, folder 30.

62. Saddler to Kern, May 1919, ibid., item 5, and 27 July 1919, item 7.

63. The McGlinn Collection score of "Whip-poor-Will" (a song from this show which never reached Broadway), presumably based on the Library of Congress parts (Kern Collection, box 94, folder 6), confirms this. The violins and cellos comprise two desks each.

64. Ferencz, ed., *The Broadway Sound*, 113; Dorothy Parker, "A Succession of Musical Comedies: The Innocent Diversions of a Tired Business Woman," *Vanity Fair*, April 1918, 69.

65. Hammerstein, *Biography in Sound*.

66. Bordman, *Kern*, 304.

67. Ewen, *World of Jerome Kern*, 96; *Philadelphia Public Ledger*, 11 December 1927, 11.

68. Peter Noble, *Ivor Novello: Man of the Theatre* (London, 1951), 60; HMV 04181 and D425.

69. Henson never made it into *The Cabaret Girl*, however, for he was ill before the first night and had to be replaced by Norman Griffin.

70. Banfield, "Scholarship and the Musical," 186–87; Hammerstein, "Jerome Kern," 157.

71. *The Play Pictorial* 53, no. 316 (1928), iii; James Ross Moore, "Girl Crazy: Musicals and Revue Between the Wars," in *British Theatre Between the Wars: 1918–1939*, ed. Clive Barker and Maggie Gale (Cambridge, 2000), 99.

72. Harbach said it was a houseboat *in* Florida. See Otto Harbach, oral history memoir, New York Public Library, transcript T-MSS 1993-038, box 21, folder 7.

73. Simon, "Jerome Kern," 25.

74. See Richard Barrios, *A Song in the Dark: The Birth of the Musical Film* (New York, 1995), 230–35, and Edwin H. Bradley, *The First Hollywood Musicals: A Critical*

Filmography of 171 Features 1927 through 1932 (Jefferson, N.C., 1996), 87–90, for important accounts of this film. Bradley in particular is indispensable for the 1929 *Show Boat* (166–69), the 1930 *Sunny* (119–21), and *Men of the Sky* (285–86).

75. This makes Harbach's statement "HAVE LYRICS ALL FINISHED" in a telegram to Jack Warner of 25 February from Florida seem odd. It could be, however, that the dates on the scores are those of the studio arranger. Kern and Harbach may have written the songs earlier, prior (for example) to the 18 June Hollywood screenplay.

76. *Men of the Sky* folder, Warner Bros. Collection, USC.

77. It has also been stated that Kern appeared as an extra.

78. *Variety*, 21 July 1931, 34.

79. See Banfield, "Scholarship and the Musical," 197–200.

80. Harbach, interview.

81. Fordin, *Getting to Know Him*, 125–26.

82. See Gordon and Funke, *Max Gordon Presents*, 140–56; Ralph Reader, *It's Been Terrific* (London, 1953), 121, and *Ralph Reader Remembers* (Folkestone, 1974), 172–73.

83. Kern to Mrs. Joseph Cooper, 5 May 1934, New York Public Library, PerfArts-Music JPB 91-46 no. 1; Fordin, *Getting to Know Him*, 128.

84. Ewen, *World of Jerome Kern*, 119–22; *Till the Clouds Roll By* scripts, USC; Fields, *Biography in Sound*.

85. Ferencz, ed., *The Broadway Sound*, 76, 101, 103, 256; Hammerstein, "Jerome Kern," 154; Dietz, *Dancing in the Dark*, 64; List, "Jerome Kern and American Operetta," 435.

86. Hammerstein, "Jerome Kern," 155, 170; Gordon, *Max Gordon Presents*, 159–60; *Can't Help Singin'*, 51; Harbach, oral history memoir, box 21, folder 7.

87. Ferber, *A Peculiar Treasure* (New York, 1939), 305, and *Biography in Sound*; Gordon, *Max Gordon Presents*, 145–46; Harbach, oral history memoir; *Portrait for Orchestra* broadcast.

88. Hammerstein, "Jerome Kern," 170; Arthur Hammerstein to Oscar Hammerstein, n.d. (1934?), Hammerstein Collection adds; Isaac Goldberg, *Tin Pan Alley: A Chronicle of the American Popular Music Racket* (New York, 1930); Dietz, *Dancing in the Dark*, 65; Kern Collection adds, box 3, item 15.

89. List, "Jerome Kern and American Operetta."

90. Carl Engel, "Jazz: A Musical Discussion," *Atlantic Monthly* (August 1922), 185.

91. 23 January 1939, Hammerstein Collection adds.

92. Gordon, *Max Gordon Presents*, 213–15.

93. Ewen, *World of Jerome Kern*, 100. Kern's nationalism was made evident in a letter to Bart Pfingst: "Looking backward [at my older shows]," he wrote, "I am astonished to find that the locale of nearly all of them was not America . . . I mention all this because much of the gratification I get out of the success of 'Show Boat Scenario' is because of the place in the sun that has been accorded American popular music, and I think any future symphonic treatment should be confined to American subjects as well as idioms" (15 March 1942, New York Public Library, Walter Slezak papers, box 1, folder 9).

94. Personal communication from Michael Feinstein.

CHAPTER 2. Kern and Musical Comedy

1. For a full account of the two Fred Stone shows, see Mordden, *Make Believe*, 55–59.

2. *Sunny*, Chappell script, 31, 33; *Head Over Heels*, script, Tams-Witmark Collection, University of Wisconsin, Madison, Box 650A, 2-32.

3. Unpublished script, Tams-Witmark Music Library, 2-40 to 2-41.

4. Liner notes, *Gershwin: Kern: Porter*, 6.

5. Stanley Cavell, *Pursuits of Happiness: The Hollywood Comedy of Remarriage* (Cambridge, Mass., 1981), passim.

6. Ferber, *Show Boat*, 173.

7. *Head Over Heels*, 2-10.

8. Unpublished script, Tams-Witmark Music Library, 1-2-53; Hugh Wheeler, *Sweeney Todd: The Demon Barber of Fleet Street*, script (New York, 1991), 73.

9. Unpublished script, Tams-Witmark Music Library, [1-]6; Wodehouse, *The Small Bachelor*, 78–79.

10. "I wrote 50,000 words of *The Small Bachelor* before I came to the start of *Oh, Lady*" (Wodehouse, *The Small Bachelor*, 6).

11. The rare books mentioned in Mr. Cooley Paradene's letter to Sinclair Hammond (Wodehouse, *Bill the Conqueror*, 129–30) match *The Library of Jerome Kern*, vol. 1, 27–31, 62–63, very closely.

12. Wodehouse, *Bill the Conqueror*, 32; id., *The Adventures of Sally* (London, 1922, Penguin 1986), n.p.; id., *A Damsel in Distress* (1919; repr. Penguin 1961), 28, 52, 160–61, 204, 224.

13. Quinton, "P. G. Wodehouse and the Comic Tradition," xiv–xv.

14. Ibid., xiii.

15. *Oh, Boy!*, 1-1-5; *Oh, Lady! Lady!!*, [1-]3; *Oh, Boy!*, 1-1-47.

16. Biographical prefatory material to Wodehouse's novels in Penguin editions; David Jasen, "Introduction," *P. G. Wodehouse: Four Plays* (London, 1983), xiii; unpublished script, Lord Chamberlain's Play Collection, British Library, 59.

17. For the criteria and terminology of dramatic segmentation on this level, see Manfred Pfister, *The Theory and Analysis of Drama* (Cambridge, 1988), 234–39.

18. The Tams-Witmark script is from 1923, the Tams-Witmark Music Library score a collation from unpublished and published sources and undatable.

19. For the *Oh, Boy!* original cast recordings, see *Music from the New York Stage*, vol. 4, CD 1, tracks 2–4.

20. *Oh, Boy!*, 1-1-23.

21. *Oh, Boy!*, 2-42.

22. Basil Boothroyd, "The Laughs," in *Homage to P. G. Wodehouse*, ed. Thelma Cazalet-Keir (London, 1973), 68; Hall, "Incongruity and Stylistic Rhythm in P. G. Wodehouse."

23. *Oh, Boy!*, 2-26 to 27.

24. Wodehouse's typed lyrics, though not the printed vocal score, have a full stop after "I've something to tell you," with a capital "B" for "Between," which starts a new line (Kern Collection, box 34, folder 25); the score has "that you all know about," surely incorrect.

25. However, Wodehouse's typed lyrics have "I am in love" and, second time around, "all about, / So people say," with the contraction and the deletion of "so" as pencil emendations. Therefore it looks as though Kern or Wodehouse decided the contraction was preferable, and the music was altered accordingly.

26. "That!" is actually underlined in the typed lyrics.

27. Oral history memoir, box 21, folder 7.

28. Wodehouse, *Bill the Conqueror*, 100–101.

29. Day's lyrics (*Complete Lyrics*, 78) are not quite right. These are from the Lord Chamberlain's Play Collection script, 86.

30. See Banfield, "Scholarship and the Musical," 195, for a musical example from this song.

31. Kern Collection, box 33, folder 4.

32. See Andrew Lamb, "From *Pinafore* to Porter: United States–United Kingdom Interactions in Musical Theater, 1879–1929," *American Music* 4 (1986), 45.

33. See Lewis A. Erenberg, *Steppin' Out: New York Nightlife and the Transformation of American Culture, 1890–1930* (Chicago, 1984), 158–71.

34. *Jerome Kern in London, 1914–23*, side 1, track 6.

35. J. B. Priestley, *English Humour* (London, 1929), 44.

36. *American Popular Song*, 37; *Music from the New York Stage*, vol. 3, CD 3, track 13.

37. Shubert Archive, *Love o' Mike* clippings file, 12 November 1917.

38. The overture's manuscript (Kern Collection, box 18, folder 26) looks like Saddler's hand but is credited to Stephen O. Jones in the finding aid; at least it is contemporary. As usual, the copyright lines look like Kern's italic hand. Interestingly, the paper is English.

39. Bordman, *Kern*, 178; *New York Times*, 23 May 1918, 11; unpublished script, Tams-Witmark Music Library, 1-2 and 2-58.

40. Seldes, *The 7 Lively Arts*, 153.

41. Rebecca A. Bryant: "Shaking Things Up: Popularizing the Shimmy in America," *American Music* 20 (2002), 169.

42. *Music from the New York Stage* vol. 4, CD 2, track 23; see also Stephen Banfield, "Stage and Screen Entertainers in the Twentieth Century," in *The Cambridge Companion to Singing*, ed. John Potter (Cambridge, 2000), 67.

43. Edward A. Berlin, *Ragtime: A Musical and Cultural History* (Berkeley, Calif., 1980), 107.

44. Mordden, *Make Believe*, 27; unpublished script, Tams-Witmark Music Library, 1-34 and 1-51. See also Charles Hiroshi Garrett, "Chinatown, Whose Chinatown? Defining America's Borders with Musical Orientalism," *Journal of the American Musicological Society* 57 (2004), 119–73.

45. *Good Morning, Dearie*, 1-42.

46. Grossmith, "GG," 211.

47. The counterpoint is not present in the finale in the published score, but its lyrics are specified in a stage direction in the published libretto.

48. See Kern Collection, box 1, folder 1, for "The Arrow"; Marshall, *Top Hat and Tails*, 56, for the comedy routine.

CHAPTER 3. Kern the Romantic: Three Shows

1. Grossmith, "GG," 177–79. The recordings of Temple and Dickson can be heard on *Jerome Kern in London, 1914–23*; of Miller (for the film soundtrack only, nine years later) on *The Song Is . . . Jerome Kern*, track 14, and various other historical compilations.

2. *New York Times*, 24 September 1924, 21.

3. Bordman, *Kern*, 258.

4. Mordden, *Make Believe*, 37.

5. Max Dreyfus to Hammerstein, 8 April 1937, Hammerstein Collection adds.

6. Kern to Hammerstein, 30 June 1942, 2 October 1942, and 3 May 1943; ?Leighton Brill to Oscar Hammerstein, 3 December 1935; all Hammerstein Collection adds.

7. Wodehouse and Bolton, *Bring on the Girls*, 152–72; Bordman, *Kern*, 246; website http://www.ibdb.com/person.asp, accessed 7 September 2004.

8. Kern letter of 30 August 1933, quoted in Day, *Complete Lyrics*, 366; Wodehouse and Bolton, *Bring on the Girls*, 170.

9. Bordman, *Kern*, 246. "Dwight Frye [is] known to cinema buffs because he played Renfield in Universal's Dracula film seven years later. You remember—the guy who goes nuts and eats spiders?" (Mordden, *Make Believe*, 105).

10. P. G. Wodehouse, *Wodehouse on Wodehouse* (London, 1980), 249; Day, *Complete Lyrics*, 333–67, for the *Pat* and *Sitting Pretty* lyrics; unpublished script, Tams-Witmark Music Library, 2–5; liner notes, *Sitting Pretty*, 13–14.

11. At some point, however, Steiner went through Bennett's orchestrations adding trombone and converting the third violin part to first viola.

12. Liner notes, 16; Kern Collection, box 71, folder 6. The sketches, rehearsal scores, and orchestral material for *Sitting Pretty* are in the Kern Collection, boxes 68–71.

13. Wodehouse, *Bill the Conqueror*, 50.

14. In the Tams-Witmark rental score serviceable lyrics have been added. Are these Wodehouse's, rediscovered? Day's edition omits them. They lack humor and finesse but accomplish the action neatly. The available (Tams-Witmark) script appears to be a 1970s or 1980s copy done on electric typewriter and does not correspond to the one referred to by McGlinn (liner notes, 17), for the lyrics of the opening number are not present. Nevertheless, it seems unlikely that much if anything has been altered to make the show a rental production.

15. *Sitting Pretty*, 1–9.

16. A second orchestration of this song and several others, for three saxophones, two trumpets, trombone, drums, violin, banjo, double bass, and piano, survives (Kern Collection, box 70, folder 7) from the Dolly Sisters' road tour of *Sitting Pretty*. It reminds us that the hinterland might hear a very different sound from Broadway.

17. Wodehouse, *Bill the Conqueror*, 41–48; *Sitting Pretty*, 1–13.

18. *Sitting Pretty*, 1–18.

19. Ira Gershwin, *Lyrics on Several Occasions* (London, 1977), 120.

20. *Sitting Pretty*, 1–33, 1–42; Wodehouse, *Bill the Conqueror*, 255–56.

21. Liner notes, 17.

22. *Sitting Pretty*, 1-45.

23. There was, however, an attempt to turn this scene into a ballet using some of the same music scored by Steiner—or would it have appeared later, given that it also includes "Shadow of the Moon," "On a Desert Island With You," and "Worries"?

24. The piano/vocal rental score has the chorus singing the refrain's accompaniment figure as countermelody in "Days Gone By."

25. *Sitting Pretty*, 2-27; 2-33 to 34; 2-36.

26. Anderson reorchestrated the second half of the song's verse, however, and it is this version that is heard on the recording.

27. *Sitting Pretty*, 2-39.

28. Ibid., 2-43.

29. Ewen, *Story of Jerome Kern*, 75.

30. Mordden (*Make Believe*, 206) cites some precedents.

31. Alisa Roost, "Before *Oklahoma!*: A Reappraisal of Musical Theatre During the 1930s," *Journal of American Drama and Theatre* 16, no. 1 (Winter 2004), 5; Kern to Vaughn DeLeath, 3 May 1938, Gershwin Fund Collection.

32. Lehman Engel, *The American Musical Theatre* (New York, 1967), 39.

33. Kreuger's *Show Boat* and the liner notes to the 1988 recording are indispensable, as are Block and Mordden below. For book chapters, see Lawrence Berlant, "Pax Americana: The Case of *Show Boat*," in *Cultural Institutions of the Novel*, ed. Deirdre Lynch and William B. Warner (Durham, N.C., 1996), 399–422; Block, "*Show Boat*: In the Beginning" (*Enchanted Evenings*, 19–40); Citron, "Hammerstein, 1927–1928"; John Graziano, "Images of African Americans: African-American Musical Theatre, *Show Boat* and *Porgy and Bess*," in *The Cambridge Companion to the Musical*, 63–76; Mordden, "Go, Little Boat: The All American Musical Comedy" (*Make Believe*, 205–32); Swain, "First Maturity"; and Linda Williams, "Posing as Black, Passing as White: The Melos of Black and White Melodrama in the Jazz Age," in *Playing the Race Card: Melodramas of Black and White from Uncle Tom to O. J. Simpson* (Princeton, 2001), 136–86. In addition, all four of the Kern biographies have at least one chapter on *Show Boat*. Articles include Breon, "*Show Boat*," and McMillin, "Paul Robeson, Will Vodery's 'Jubilee Singers,' and *Show Boat*."

34. Kreuger, "Some Words About 'Show Boat,'" 18.

35. Ziegfeld to Kern, quoted in Bordman, *Kern*, 283.

36. While beyond the scope of this book, a comparison with shows of the 1920s on black subjects such as *Deep River* and even *Golden Dawn* ought to be made. See Mordden, *Make Believe*, 140–42; McMillin, "Paul Robeson," 63–64.

37. The *Show Boat* material is in the Kern Collection, boxes 55–67.

38. Ferber, *Show Boat*, 102.

39. Mast, *Can't Help Singin'*, 62.

40. Several authors attribute all this to the filling in of a perfect 4th with one extra note, and Block (*Enchanted Evenings*, 30) compares the various ramifications with the second subject of the first movement of Dvořák's *New World Symphony*.

41. All subsequent references are to the engraved Chappell piano/vocal score of 1928.

42. I owe this insight to a student, Rachel Sanders-Hewett.

43. *The Ultimate* Show Boat, CD 1, track 3.

44. It is not by Kern. Kreuger (*Show Boat*, 57) says it is an old Bohemian melody.

45. Chappell script, 13.

46. See Banfield, "Scholarship and the Musical," 186–88.

47. Early unpublished script, Library of Congress ML50.K43S3 1927, 1-15.

48. Chappell script, 16.

49. In an early version Parthy actually appeared here. See Block, *Enchanted Evenings*, 38–39.

50. Chappell script, 17; Ferber, *Show Boat*, 143.

51. *Kern "Showboat," "Sunny,"* track 2.

52. Citron, "Hammerstein, 1927–1928," 69–70; Ferber, *Show Boat*, 48, 82–83, 91–92; Harry T. Burleigh, *The Celebrated Negro Spirituals: Arranged for Solo Voice* (London, 1917).

53. The recording, not issued in 1928 for contractual reasons, was included on a 1977 World Record Club LP album (SH240) of *Show Boat* and *Sunny* with their original London casts.

54. *The Ultimate* Show Boat, CD 1, tracks 9 and 13; Kreuger, *Show Boat*, 74, 103; Ferencz, ed., *The Broadway Sound*, 98–99; WQXR radio broadcast, 11'45".

55. Bennett's fill and harmonies are heard in what must be "Ol' Man River"'s earliest recording, with the Whiteman band and Bing Crosby, made in January 1928, and also in Al Jolson's of March 1928 (*The Ultimate* Show Boat, CD 1, tracks 1 and 5). Presumably the song had been published by then.

56. *Lyrics*, 21–22.

57. The arrangements, for his Jubilee Singers as the black chorus, were done by Will Vodery (see McMillin, "Paul Robeson," 63–64).

58. It was a reuse of "If We Were on Our Honeymoon" from *The Doll Girl*. All uncanonic *Show Boat* material is on the 1988 recording, complete with lyrics and liner notes.

59. Mordden, *Make Believe*, 208; *Kern "Showboat," "Sunny,"* track 5; *The Ultimate* Show Boat, CD 1, tracks 7, 8, and 15.

60. Liner notes, *Show Boat*, 31.

61. Ibid., 28.

62. The "Ol' Man River" refrain was evidently the only creative way in which the presence of Joe and Queenie throughout the miscegenation scene, carefully engineered by Hammerstein, could be acknowledged. He wanted them to witness Vallon's and his community's hatred of their race and the audience in turn to witness their silent witnessing of it and described their continuing presence on stage after Captain Andy has cleared out all the gawping onlookers: "Only PARTHY, MAGNOLIA and ANDY are left on the stage, and JOE and QUEENIE stand in the pit—holding each other's hands, transfixed, dumb, vaguely hurt" (early script, 1-46). Or is this an example of not letting African Americans speak for themselves, not giving them a discursive awareness of their own oppression? (See chapter 4 for a recurrence of this problem in *Gentlemen Unafraid*.)

63. Ferber was well aware of the parallels between the melodramas onstage and

those backstage in her novel—see *Show Boat*, 107–09. The plays were probably William Henry Smith, *The Drunkard* (1852); Ellen Wood, *East Lynne* (1861); and Mary Jane Holmes, *Tempest and Sunshine* (1854) (these last two novels that, like *Show Boat* itself, would have been dramatized). But who wrote *The Parson's Bride?* It appears in Ferber (124–27). Did she invent it?

64. The rehearsal tunes are "My Old Kentucky Home," "I Dreamt [that] I Dwelt in Marble Halls," and "In the Gloaming" (early script, 1-36 to 39, 1-69; Chappell script, 47). "Love's Old Sweet Song" is "Just a Song at Twilight." "I Dreamt that I Dwelt in Marble Halls," from Michael Balfe's opera *The Bohemian Girl*, Gustav Lange's "Blumenlied," and a *melo* for the villain appear in the published scores (Chappell, pp. 130–31).

65. Early script, 1-77.

66. McGlinn, liner notes, 33.

67. Mordden (*Make Believe*, 229) points out how this ruins that song's diegetic role, McMillin ("Paul Robeson," 54) that in the earliest script it was to be sung by Magnolia defiantly to her mother with the words "Can't stop me now, / There's no use to try" (which reappeared in the 1946 revival).

68. "Show Boat," *The Play Pictorial* 53, no. 316 (2 July 1928), 2.

69. It was indeed composed (by Sol Bloom, later a congressman) for the Columbian Exposition and danced there (by "Little Egypt"). See James J. Fuld, *The Book of World-Famous Music*, 5th ed. (Mineola, N.Y., 2000), 276–77.

70. Citron ("Hammerstein, 1927–1928," 64) points out that *Oklahoma!* also has only one new song in act 2. This is not strictly true.

71. McGlinn (liner notes, 50, 52–53) explains that scenes 3 and 4 were reversed in the 1927 production because the designer, Joseph Urban, could not find a way of accomplishing the set changes; thus the Trocadero rehearsal scene was supposed to have come after the convent scene, not before it. To have these two scenes (3 and 4) represent simultaneity was a blatant fudge on Hammerstein's part. As McGlinn points out (liner notes, 30), even a convent school would hardly keep its pupils locked away on 30 December. And why was Ravenal still hanging around in Chicago two weeks after fleeing his wife and his responsibilities? The early script (2-22) makes it clear that it was the letter and convent scenes (2 and 3) that were supposed to be simultaneous, thereby achieving a nice parallel to the simultaneity of scenes 2 and 3 in act 1.

72. Early script, 2-25 to 28. In the 1929 film Julie is Hetty Chilson, a neat elision. Mordden (*Make Believe*, 210) points out, however, that Ferber leaves it ambiguous whether Julie is one of the working girls or more of a clerk.

73. *The Ultimate* Show Boat includes her three recordings, dating from 1928, 1932, and 1938 (CD 1, tracks 6, 14, and 22). All retain the published key of B flat major. The 1928 recording, made while she was creating the role of Julie, was conducted by Baravalle and uses the stage orchestration. So does Marie Burke's of the Drury Lane production, also recorded in 1928. Finck gets a splendidly ethereal aura of string sound out of Bennett's scoring for the refrain in stanza two.

74. Early script, 2-33.

75. "Apache Dance" is by Jacques Offenbach and comes from *Le Roi Carotte* (1872), where it forms the act 3 entr'acte.

76. Kreuger, liner notes, 17; early script, 2-47; Chappell script, 87.

77. Liner notes, 29–30. But Mordden (*Make Believe*, 221) says flatly, "I don't believe this story . . . nobody talked the touchy Kern into anything."

78. McGlinn, liner notes, 28–29, 32.

79. Oral history memoir, 553.

80. Gordon, *Max Gordon Presents*, 147.

81. Mordden, *Sing for Your Supper*, 221–25; A. E. Wilson, "About Love and Music," *The Star*, 5 March 1932, 3; E. A. Baughan, "This 'Hi-diddle-diddle' Stuff," *The Era*, 9 March 1932, 9; James Agate, "Key to Musical Comedy," *First Nights* (London, 1934), 84; Oral history memoir, 556.

82. Oral history memoir, 551–53, 555; unpublished script, Lord Chamberlain's Play Collection, British Library, 2-4-1.

83. See the Kern Collection, boxes 1–7, for the musical materials.

84. "The Inexhaustible Mr. Kern."

85. British Library script, 1-2-3 and 2-1-6.

86. *Americans in London*, track 9.

87. Strictly speaking, the first *j* should be reversed.

88. Agate, *First Nights*, 84.

89. Rodgers, *Musical Stages*, 145; British Library, Lord Chamberlain's Play Correspondence Index.

90. There were changes of name for the British script, and it includes a good deal of piecemeal shortening, but the omissions are minor crossings out within the same flow of dialogue. The outcomes are unaffected.

91. Script, 2-3-6.

92. *Americans in London*, track 12.

93. In the MGM film of *The Cat and the Fiddle* (1934) this song is one of Shirley's compositions, and Victor tries to rewrite it for her using the main melody rather than the four-bar refrain.

CHAPTER 4. Mostly Hammerstein

1. P. Filmer, V. Rimmer, and D. Walsh, "*Oklahoma!*: Ideology and Politics in the Vernacular Tradition of the American Musical," *Popular Music* 18, no. 3 (1999), 381–95 (382); *Variety*, 5 January 1944, 234; Fordin, *Getting to Know Him*, 209.

2. Fordin (*Getting to Know Him*, 161) simply says Hammerstein was weak on structure. Hammerstein testified: "I am still a strong believer in the unscientific method of picking up a 'bicycle built for two' and riding it to a destination—without a map" (Hammerstein to Kern, 18 January 1939, Hammerstein Collection adds).

3. Surely "consummation"? Perhaps his handwriting was unclear to the typist.

4. Kern Collection adds, box 2, item 17.

5. Kurt Weill to Lotte Lenya, 12 August 1944, quoted in J. Galand, "Introduction," *The Firebrand of Florence*, critical edition of the score by Kurt Weill (New York and Miami, 2002), 20.

6. W. A. Darlington, "Mary Ellis as Singer," *The Daily Telegraph*, 20 May 1933, 6.

7. Gordon, *Max Gordon Presents*, 145; Rodgers, *Musical Stages*, 207; Bordman, *Kern*, 305; Victor 22199, recorded 16 October and 12 November 1929.

8. See J. Peter Burkholder, "Patchwork in Tin Pan Alley Songs," *All Made of*

Tunes: Charles Ives and the Uses of Musical Borrowing (New Haven, 1995), 322–27, for a discussion of the practice with particular reference to George M. Cohan; Randall, *Becoming Jerome Kern*, 116–18, for quotation in Kern.

9. The overture tunes, in order, are "They All Follow Me," unidentified, "Daisy Bell," "The Band Played On," "I'd Leave Ma Happy Home for You," "Break the News to Mother," unidentified, "Hello! Ma Baby," "Tell Me, Pretty Maiden," and "I Want to Be a Military Man." The use of "You're the Flower of My Heart, Sweet Adeline" is anachronistic, since the show's date is 1898 and the song was not published until 1903. "A Hot Time in the Old Town Tonight" was published in 1896, and Kern returned to it repeatedly, for it features also in *Show Boat* and *The Red Petticoat* (see Randall, *Becoming Jerome Kern*, 192, 218).

10. On style modulation, see Peter Dickinson, "Style-modulation: An Approach to Stylistic Pluralism," *Musical Times* 130 (1989), 208–11. The political background is strengthened in the 1935 film, which adds a spy strand to the plot.

11. "Don't Ever Leave Me" was published in 2/2, but in the Tams-Witmark copyist's score it is presented in 4/4. T. B. Harms also published two versions of the refrain's accompaniment, one more pulsating than the other.

12. J. Brooks Atkinson, "The Play: The Gay Nineties," *New York Times*, 4 September 1929, 38.

13. It appears, however, to be pitched a semitone lower, insofar as one can tell from transcriptions of old recordings.

14. Beatrice Kaufman and Joseph Hennessey, eds., *The Letters of Alexander Woollcott* (London, 1946), 97.

15. This arrangement, by Bennett, can be heard as it sounded under Hyam Greenbaum in the original London production on *You Must Remember This: The Great Theatre Songs* (Conifer CD 75605 52284 2, 1996), although the soloist is Mary Ellis, who as Frieda did not perform the song in the show.

16. Chappell script, 68.

17. Bordman, *Kern*, 332–33.

18. Script, 31–32.

19. See Galand, *The Firebrand of Florence*, 19, and Mordden, *The Hollywood Musical* (New York, 1981), 68–69.

20. In fact it is not a variant of "We Belong Together" but part of an unpublished song called "Thank You for Loving Me" that Kern seems to have envisaged using in *The Forbidden Melody*, his "unknown" show with Harbach.

21. The connection between Sieglinde's imagined waltz and *Mme Frou Frou* is made manifest when the two women sit down in mutually suspicious sociability at the zoo cafe, for here the themes are juxtaposed.

22. M. Willson Disher, "Musical Play Experiment," *Daily Mail*, 10 April 1934, 15; B.B., "English Life Depicted by Americans," *Daily Mirror*, 10 April 1934, 7.

23. *Three Sisters*, revised script, Rodgers and Hammerstein Theatre Library, 1-33; "Musical Cavalcading," *The Bystander* 122, no. 1583 (17 April 1934), 112–13; *Americans in London*. Bordman (*Kern*, 348–49) states that Kern conducted the recording, but according to Bucky Willard's liner notes for the CD transfer, "personally supervised by Jerome Kern" was the phrase on the 78 r.p.m. label, and the conductor was the Drury Lane musical director Charles Prentice.

24. "Pony ballet" was a type of kick-line routine invented by John Tiller. This one was in drag, or would have been had not merely a rehearsal been shown. The dream sequence was labeled a "scena" and included singing, with flowing movement (choreographed by Reader) rather than ballet dancing for the chorus girls and balletic costume but not movement for Gypsy.

25. In Bennett's piano score of "Derby Day," another hand has scribbled "Yiddish" above the dotted-note motif and "Anglo Saxon" above Gypsy's resumption of "Now That I Have Springtime." George, as an East Ender, would quite likely be Jewish. See Andrea Most, *Making Americans: Jews and the Broadway Musical* (Cambridge, Mass., 2004), 108, for consideration of a similar Hammerstein character, Ali Hakim, as the comic Jewish pedlar, a traditional stage type; also Tim Carter, *Oklahoma! (1943): The Making of an "American" Musical* (forthcoming).

26. The various motifs can be heard on *Americans in London*, track 17, 1′42″, track 18, 0′00″, 1′06″, 1′12″, and 1′23″; see Kern Collection adds, box 2, items 8g and 8m for the quodlibets.

27. Leighton Brill to Oscar Hammerstein, 21 December 1933, Hammerstein Collection adds; track 17, 0′10″, 0′49″, and 1′58″ for the "Derby Day" sections.

28. Any number of "Derby Day" songs had been published, and the British Library holds three from the previous decade. A later light music classic, *Derby Day*, came from the pen of Robert Farnon in 1955 and an overture from that of William Alwyn in 1960. On staging the Derby, see Andrew Horrall, *Popular Culture in London c.1890–1918: The Transformation of Entertainment* (Manchester, 2001), 49–51. The London Coliseum had staged a play called *The Derby* in 1904 which went much further than *Three Sisters* and showed the actual race with real galloping horses.

29. Kurt Gänzl, *The British Musical Theatre* (Basingstoke, 1986), vol. 2, 365; "The American Alliance," *Sunday Times*, 15 April 1934, 6; *Three Sisters*, original script, Lord Chamberlain's Play Collection; W. MacQueen Pope, *Theatre Royal, Drury Lane* (London, 1945), 317. On Drury Lane spectaculars, see Horrall, *Popular Culture in London*, 93.

30. Greenwood, *Never Too Tall*, 180 (Greenwood says this was in September 1933, but her dates are unreliable and according to MacQueen Pope [ibid.] the show closed on 8 July 1933); "The American Alliance"; Leighton Brill to Oscar Hammerstein, 22 December 1933, Hammerstein Collection adds.

31. Revised script, 2-3-3; original script, 144, 180; Ferencz, ed., *The Broadway Sound*, 142; Esmond Knight, *Seeking the Bubble* (London, 1942), 79; Wodehouse, *A Damsel in Distress*, 22. Several commentators have said the gallery was out to get *Three Sisters* because Adele Dixon had too little to do. Freedland remarks of *Show Boat* that at Drury Lane "a letter was received by the President of the Gallery First Nighters . . . [protesting] at the employment of colored American artists in London while an embargo had been placed on the employment of English actors and actresses in New York" (93), which accords with Brill's comments quoted above and suggests they would have regarded Greenwood as gratuitous.

32. Altman, *The American Film Musical*, 298–316; "The Drury Lane Show," *Sunday Referee*, 15 April 1934, 8.

33. "There should be a suggestion of a satirical reverse on the old-fashioned 'Royce' number wherein a chorus of boys worked with a girl principal, dancing with

her by turns, lifting her high above their heads. In this case it is the girls lifting the boy" (unpublished revised script, Rodgers and Hammerstein Theatre Library, 1-6-65).

34. Tom Milne, *Rouben Mamoulian* (London, 1969), 106.

35. Green, *Rodgers and Hammerstein Fact Book*, 465–66.

36. Bennett's description of Mamoulian's behavior during production bears this out. See Ferencz, ed., *The Broadway Sound*, 156–57.

37. Kern Collection adds, box 1, item 39.

38. See Ferencz, ed., *The Broadway Sound*, 156. Yet some passages (for example, the |737-| motif) do sound like Kern. And the studio's trailer is puzzling, for it includes a good two minutes' worth of incidental music, mostly without voiceover, claiming that "Jerome Kern has written this dramatic musical interlude, as colorful as the desperate conflict that inspired it" (Library of Congress tape, 2′56″). Given that Kern himself is playing the piano on that same trailer, whom are we to believe? The interlude is in any case quite different from anything that appears in the film.

39. Milne, *Mamoulian*, 110.

40. Fordin, *Getting to Know Him*, 148.

41. Undated cutting in Hammerstein Collection adds; revised script, 2-6-50.

42. This title is taken from lines in the lyrics to "Hoe-down" in the first scene, chanted by cadets as they try to sort out their feet in the dance. Its significance lies in the fact that certain recruits in the American Civil War were supposedly so rustic they did not know their left foot from their right for drill purposes, and a piece of hay was tied to the left boot, a piece of straw to the right, to help them.

43. Bordman, *Kern*, 376.

44. Revised script, 1-3-35A.

45. The phrase appears in the dedication poem to *Barrack-Room Ballads*. See *Rudyard Kipling's Verse: Definitive Edition* (London, 1940), 83–84.

46. Vol. 3, track 13.

47. Revised script, 2-3-29 to 34, 2-6-51; Green, *Rodgers and Hammerstein Fact Book*, 468–69.

48. Gordon, *Max Gordon Presents*, 213–17; for details of the plot and its changes, see Bordman's liner notes to the original Broadway cast recording.

49. Kern to Hammerstein, 10 April 1942, Hammerstein Collection adds; liner notes. The original cast recording comes from a studio broadcast undertaken as a plug for the show and aired on NBC's WJZ station.

50. Recording, track 12; revised script, Rodgers and Hammerstein Theatre Library, 2-3-6 to 7.

51. Recording, track 4 (revised script, 1-2-30 to 33); Elisabeth Marbury, *My Crystal Ball: Reminiscences* (New York, 1923), 234–37.

52. Ewen, *World of Jerome Kern*, 10.

53. Revised script, passim.

54. Brooks Atkinson, *New York Times*, 18 November 1939, 23.

55. Liner notes; recording, tracks 1 and 7 (2′41″).

56. Brill to Hammerstein, 17 and 22 July 1939, Hammerstein Collection adds.

57. Kern nevertheless found as he worked on the show that "the tune has become inescapable with me. It haunts me more than any of the other new lot" (Kern to Hammerstein, 4 May 1939, Hammerstein Collection adds).

58. The recording (track 6) picks it up halfway through the interlude.

59. Revised script, 2-4-3.

CHAPTER 5. Kern and Hollywood

1. Neal Gabler, *An Empire of Their Own: How the Jews Invented Hollywood* (New York, 1988), 24.

2. Ferencz, ed., *The Broadway Sound*, 97–98.

3. *Oh, Boy!*: Pathé Exchange, 1919; *Oh, Lady! Lady!!*: Realart Picture Corporation, 1920, starring Bebe Daniels; *Sally*: First National, 1925.

4. Ferencz, ed., *The Broadway Sound*, 151.

5. *Variety*, 21 July 1931, 34.

6. Louella O. Parsons, "Swing Time," *Los Angeles Examiner*, 23 September 1936; Frank S. Nugent, "Swing Time," *New York Times*, 28 August 1936, 21.

7. Mast, "When E'er a Cloud Appears," 147; Jenkins, *What Made Pistachio Nuts?*

8. Sigmund Romberg was celebrated for his English malapropisms.

9. Of "It's Not in the Cards," Arlene Croce, working from interviews with the creative team of *Swing Time*, states that "the music we hear is not the song that Kern and Fields wrote." So is it not by Kern at all? See Croce, *Fred Astaire and Ginger Rogers Book* 109. Titles such as "Train Sequence" are taken from the manuscript full scores in the RKO Collection at UCLA, *Swing Time* Music Files M-58, M-59, and M-60.

10. Mast, *Can't Help Singin'*, 149–51.

11. Abbreviations: MLS = medium long shot; MCS = medium close shot; CU = closeup; F = Fred; G = Ginger; Bl = Blore; B = Broderick; M = Moore; ↓ = fall; ↑ = jump over fence (⤉ = unsuccessful).

12. Astaire was paid $85,000. The director, George Stevens, earned $56,403.33, slightly less than Rogers ($59,880.78). Moore was paid $40,666.67, Broderick $9,550. By contrast, the entire orchestral costs amounted to $42,982.50, only half Astaire's fee, and this included the "arranging" fee (presumably Bennett's but including Powell and others?), which was $5,000. The "music rights" cost $62,000, which may have represented Kern's flat fee of $50,000 (he gained royalties over and above this) plus extras. See RKO Collection, file P-67, folders 1 and 3; Bordman, *Kern*, 357.

13. Altman, *The American Film Musical*, ix.

14. Credit for the plot mechanics must be given to Allan Scott, reviser of Howard Lindsay's screenplay. See Croce, *Fred Astaire and Ginger Rogers Book*, 108.

15. Howard Mandelbaum and Eric Myers, in "New York Nights: Night Clubs," *Screen Deco* (Bromley, 1985), 101–05, explain the historical nightclub referents and give full descriptions of *Swing Time*'s three cabaret settings. The refurbished Silver Sandal set is the climax but at $8,000 cost less than that of Raymond's nightclub ($10,000). The New Amsterdam Inn set at $7,000 was nearly as expensive as these (P-67, folder 4).

16. Croce, *Fred Astaire and Ginger Rogers Book*, 108, 107, 109. Hal Borne, Astaire's rehearsal pianist, inserted the "Fine Romance" section of "Waltz in Swing Time."

17. This would have made a total of thirty-eight players, specified by Bennett for the "End Title" cue. The number of musicians used to record different sequences varied, as the production files indicate, but perhaps Bennett didn't get them all, for

thirty-six were used for "MAIN and END TITLES," according to the production files (P-67, folder 3). Bennett's scores also specify the names and therefore the doublings of the wind players: Reed, DeBoucher, Moll, Moore, Cheever, Green, Stall, Bayer (M-59, folder 4). These names occur elsewhere in the archives.

18. Croce, *Fred Astaire and Ginger Rogers Book*, 112.

19. RKO Collection, M-60, folder 6.

20. Croce, *Fred Astaire and Ginger Rogers Book*, 108.

21. Bordman (*Kern*, 386) locates San Marcos in the West Indies.

22. Croce, *Fred Astaire and Ginger Rogers Book*, 109.

23. *You Were Never Lovelier*, Columbia DVD, 46′00″.

24. Astaire recorded six songs from *You Were Never Lovelier*: "Dearly Beloved," "You Were Never Lovelier," "I'm Old Fashioned," "On the Beam," "The Shorty George," and "Wedding in the Spring." They can all be heard on *Fred Astaire: Golden Greats*.

25. Fred Astaire, *Steps in Time* (New York, 1959), 253.

26. Another French touch, the momentary whole-tone sonority at the start of bar twelve, is absent from later printings, where the G sharp is omitted.

27. Later there are a couple more refrains of "I'm Old Fashioned" as diegetic underscoring to the fancy dress ball.

28. Intriguingly, Idell's *Centennial Summer*, like *Meet Me in St. Louis*, is divided into four parts, one for each season of the year. Which came first?

29. *Jerome Kern's* Centennial Summer: *In Technicolor*, studio pressbook, 12.

30. Kern Collection adds, box 3, items 16 and 17.

31. The diegetic ceremonial music acts as a kind of metonym for the actual music commissioned by the 1876 exhibition, mentioned in the novel as "copies of the *Centennial March* written by the great Wagner, the *Centennial Hymn* composed by Whittier, the *Centennial Cantata* by Sidney Lanier" (Idell, *Centennial Summer*, 186). In the novel, not only the president but Theodore Thomas's orchestra is inaudible at the opening ceremony (194).

32. Bordman, *Kern*, 399.

33. See Forte, *The American Popular Ballad*, 25–26 for a guide to the terminology.

34. It is reproduced in Kreuger, *Show Boat*, 156.

35. Bordman, *Kern*, 403. "Sure Thing" began as "Hard to Replace"; see Robert Kimball, *The Complete Lyrics of Ira Gershwin* (London, 1994), 282, 308–14.

36. Lamb, *Jerome Kern in Edwardian London*, 42.

Bibliography

PRIMARY SOURCE COLLECTIONS

Brandeis University Library
British Film Institute, London
    Unpublished screenplay of *High, Wide and Handsome*
British Library, London
    Lord Chamberlain's Play Collection: unpublished scripts, censorship
        correspondence
Cinema-Television Library, Doheny Memorial Library, University of Southern
        California, Los Angeles
    Roger Edens Collection
    Arthur Freed Collection
    Greenwood, Charlotte. *Never Too Tall*, unpublished autobiography. 1941.
    MGM Collection
    Alfred Newman Collection
    20th Century–Fox Collection
    Warner Bros. Collection
The Harburg Foundation, New York
    Unpublished scores
Interviews and private collections
    Gerald Bordman
    Michael Feinstein
    James J. Fuld
    William Harbach
Ira and Leonore Gershwin Trusts, San Francisco
    Unpublished scores
Library of Congress, Washington, D.C.
    Copyright deposits, music
    Copyright deposits, scripts

Gershwin Collection
Gershwin Fund Collection
Hammerstein Collection
Hammerstein Collection uncatalogued additions
Jerome Kern Collection (see Library of Congress website for downloadable
    catalogue)
Jerome Kern Collection uncatalogued additions
McGlinn Collection
Recorded Sound Collections
Warner Chappell Collection
New York Public Library, Performing Arts Library, Lincoln Center
Billy Rose Theatre Collection
Music Collection
Otto Harbach Papers
Paramount Theatre Library, Oakland
Rodgers and Hammerstein Theatre Library, New York
Unpublished scripts
Unpublished piano/vocal scores
Shubert Archive, New York
Clippings files
Correspondence files
Illustrations files
Files on *The Golden Widow, King of Cadonia, The Kiss Waltz, Love o' Mike,*
    Oh, I Say! and *The Red Petticoat*
Tams-Witmark Music Library, New York
Unpublished scripts
Unpublished piano/vocal scores
University of Birmingham Library, Special Collections
Theatre Collection
University of Bristol
Theatre Collection
University of Wisconsin, Madison
Tams-Witmark Collection
Young Research Library, University of California at Los Angeles: Special Collections,
    Arts
RKO Collection

Books, Articles, and Dissertations

Altman, Rick. *The American Film Musical.* Bloomington and Indianapolis, Ind., 1987.
Babbitt, Milton. "All the Things They Are." *I.S.A.M. Newsletter* 14, no. 2 (May 1985),
    8–9.
Banfield, Stephen. "Scholarship and the Musical: Reclaiming Jerome Kern." *Proceed-
    ings of the British Academy* 125 (2004), 183–210.
Block, Geoffrey. *Enchanted Evenings: The Broadway Musical from* Show Boat *to Sond-
    heim.* New York, 1997.

Bordman, Gerald. *Jerome Kern*. New York, 1980.

———. "Jerome David Kern, Innovator/Traditionalist." *The Musical Quarterly* 71 (1985), 468–73.

Breon, Robin. "Show Boat: The Revival, the Racism." *The Drama Review* 39, no. 2 (1995), 86–105.

Citron, Stephen. "Hammerstein, 1927–1928." In *The Wordsmiths: Oscar Hammerstein 2nd and Alan Jay Lerner*, 62–85. London, 1996.

Croce, Arlene. *The Fred Astaire and Ginger Rogers Book*. London, 1972.

Davis, Lee. *Bolton and Wodehouse and Kern: The Men Who Made Musical Comedy*. New York, 1993.

Day, Barry. *The Complete Lyrics of P. G. Wodehouse*. Lanham, Md., 2004.

Dietz, Howard. *Dancing in the Dark: An Autobiography*. New York, 1974.

Ewen, David. *The Story of Jerome Kern*. New York, 1953.

———. *The World of Jerome Kern: A Biography*. New York, 1960.

Ferber, Edna. *Show Boat*. 1926; reprint, New York: Penguin, 1994.

Ferencz, George J., ed. *"The Broadway Sound": The Autobiography and Selected Essays of Robert Russell Bennett*. Rochester, N.Y., 1999.

Fordin, Hugh. *Getting to Know Him: A Biography of Oscar Hammerstein II*. New York, 1977.

Forte, Allen. "Ballads of Jerome Kern." In *The American Popular Ballad of the Golden Era: 1924–1950*, 52–85. Princeton, 1995.

Freedland, Michael. *Jerome Kern*. London, 1978.

Gordon, Max, with Lewis Funke. *Max Gordon Presents*. New York, 1963.

Green, Stanley. "Jerome Kern." In *The World of Musical Comedy*, 4th ed., 50–65. San Diego, 1980.

———. *Rodgers and Hammerstein Fact Book*. New York, 1980.

Grossmith, George. "GG." London, 1933.

Hall, Robert A., Jr. "Incongruity and Stylistic Rhythm in P. G. Wodehouse." *Annali* (Istituto Orientale di Napoli, Sezione Germanica) 11 (1968), 135–44.

Hammerstein II, Oscar. "Jerome Kern, Songwriter, Perfectionist." *Vogue*, February 1945, 154–57, 166, 168, 170.

Idell, Albert E. *Centennial Summer*. New York, 1943.

"The Inexhaustible Mr. Kern." *New York Times*, 21 January 1917, section 2, 5.

Jasen, David A. *The Theatre of P. G. Wodehouse*. London, 1979.

Josephs, Norman. Essay review of Bordman, *Jerome Kern*. *Popular Music* 1 (1981), 169–75.

Kislan, Richard. "Jerome Kern." In *The Musical: A Look at the American Musical Theatre*, 2d ed., 112–27. New York, 1995.

Kreuger, Miles. *Show Boat: The Story of a Classic American Musical*. New York, 1977, reprinted with new introduction 1990.

———. "Some Words about 'Show Boat.'" In McGlinn, *Show Boat*, EMI recording, liner notes, 1988, 13–24.

Lamb, Andrew. *Jerome Kern in Edwardian London*. 1981; revised and enlarged as I.S.A.M. Monographs no. 22, Brooklyn, N.Y., 1985.

The Later Library of Jerome Kern. New York, 1962.

The Library of Jerome Kern: New York City. 2 volumes. New York, 1929.

List, Kurt. "Jerome Kern and American Operetta." *Commentary* 3 (1947), 433–41.

Lyrics by Oscar Hammerstein II. 2d ed. New York, 1985.

McGlinn, John. Liner notes. See below, "Commercially Released Recordings."

McMillin, Scott. "Paul Robeson, Will Vodery's 'Jubilee Singers,' and the Earliest Script of the Kern-Hammerstein *Show Boat.*" *Theatre Survey* 41 (2000), 51–70.

Mast, Gerald. "When E'er a Cloud Appears in the Blue: Jerome Kern." In *Can't Help Singin': The American Musical on Stage and Screen,* 49–65. Woodstock, N.Y., 1987.

Mordden, Ethan. *Make Believe: The Broadway Musical in the 1920s.* New York, 1997.

———. *Sing for Your Supper: The Broadway Musical in the 1930s.* New York, 2005.

The Play Pictorial 1–63. London, 1902–33.

Quinton, Anthony. "P. G. Wodehouse and the Comic Tradition." In *P. G. Wodehouse: A Comprehensive Bibliography and Checklist,* edited by Eileen McIlvaine, Louise S. Sherby, and James H. Heineman, ix–xx. New York, 1990.

Randall, James. "Becoming Jerome Kern: The Early Songs and Shows, 1903–1915." Ph.D. dissertation, University of Illinois, 2004.

Simon, Robert. "Jerome Kern." *Modern Music* 6, no. 2 (January-February 1929), 20–25.

Sondheim, Stephen. Liner notes, *The CBS Album of Jerome Kern: Paul Weston and His Orchestra.* 2 LPs, Columbia C2L-2, 1957.

Suskin, Steven. *Berlin, Kern, Rodgers, Hart and Hammerstein: A Complete Song Catalogue.* Jefferson, N.C., 1990.

Swain, Joseph P. "First Maturity." In *The Broadway Musical: A Critical and Musical Survey,* 15–49. New York, 1990.

Wilder, Alec. "Jerome Kern (1885–1945)." In *American Popular Song: The Great Innovators, 1900–1950,* 29–90. New York, 1972.

Wilk, Max. "'All the Things You Are:' Jerome Kern." In *They're Playing Our Song: Conversations with America's Classic Songwriters,* 30–40. 1973; rev. ed. New York, 1991.

Wodehouse, P. G. *Bill the Conqueror.* 1924; reprint, London, 1996.

———. *The Small Bachelor.* 1927; reprint, London, 1987.

———, and Guy Bolton. *Bring on the Girls.* London, 1954.

PUBLISHED SHEET MUSIC

The Beauty Prize, piano/vocal score. London and New York: Chappell and T. B. Harms, 1923.

Blue Eyes, piano/vocal score. London and New York: Chappell and T. B. Harms, 1930.

The Cabaret Girl, piano/vocal score. London and New York: Chappell and T. B. Harms, 1922.

The Cat and the Fiddle, piano/vocal score. London and New York: Chappell and T. B. Harms, 1932.

Good Morning Dearie, piano/vocal score. New York: T. B. Harms, 1922.

Have a Heart, piano/vocal score. New York: T. B. Harms and Francis, Day and Hunter, 1917.

Jerome Kern Collection. Santa Monica, Calif.: Welk Music Group, 1988.

Jerome Kern Rediscovered. Miami, Fla.: Warner Bros. Publications, 2000.

Jerome Kern: Collected Songs. Boca Raton, Fla.: Masters Music Publications Inc., n.d.,
   16 volumes of facsimile reprints, 1906–19.
Music in the Air, piano/vocal score. London and New York: Chappell and T. B. Harms,
   1933.
Oh, Lady! Lady!!, piano/vocal score. New York: T. B. Harms, 1918.
Roberta, piano/vocal score. New York and London: T. B. Harms and Chappell, 1933.
Sally, piano/vocal score. London and New York: Chappell and T. B. Harms, 1921.
Show Boat, piano/vocal score. New York: T. B. Harms, 1928; London: Chappell, 1928;
   New York: Welk Music Group, 1946.
Stepping Stones, piano/vocal score. New York: T. B. Harms, 1924.
Sunny, piano/vocal score. London and New York: Chappell and T. B. Harms, 1934.
Very Good Eddie, piano/vocal score. New York: T. B.Harms, 1915.

Published Libretti

Sunny. London: Chappell, 1934.
Show Boat. London: Chappell, 1934; New York: Rodgers and Hammerstein Theatre
   Library, 1962.
Blue Eyes. London: B. J. Simmons, n.d.
Music in the Air. London: Chappell, 1936.

Commercially Available Films on DVD

Can't Help Singing
Cover Girl
Show Boat. MGM, 1951.

Swing Time
Till the Clouds Roll By
You Were Never Lovelier

Commercially Released Recordings (Selective List)

Americans in London in the 1930's. Encore ENBO-CD #3/92, 1992.
Ben Bagley's Jerome Kern Revisited. 3 CDs, Painted Smiles Records PSCD-111, -113,
   -134, ?–1992.
Early Kern: Broadway and London / 1907–1925. Rialto Records CD, 1991.
Fred Astaire: Golden Greats. 3 CDs, Disky MP 790902, 2001.
The First Rose of Summer: Rare Early Theatre Songs by Jerome Kern. 42nd Street Moon
   CD, MBR 04003, 2004.
Gershwin: Kern: Porter: Overtures—Film Music, conducted by John McGlinn. 2 CDs,
   EMI 5 68589 2, 1995.
[Gloria's Romance] Our Musical Past, Volume 2: *Two Silent Film Scores.* Library of
   Congress CD OMP-103, n.d.
Jerome Kern Gems. Victor Light Opera Company vocal medleys. Box Office LP C-31,
   recordings from 1938.
Jerome Kern in London. World Record Club LP, SH 171, 1973.
Jerome Kern in London, 1914–23. World Record Club LP, SHB 34, 1976.
Jerome Kern in London and Hollywood. Rialto Records CD, 1992.

Jerome Kern Melodies: Played by the Gordon String Quartet. 3 78 r.p.m. discs, Decca
    A-293, 1942.
A Jerome Kern Showcase. Pearl, PAST CD 9767, 1991.
Jerome Kern Treasury, conducted by John McGlinn. EMI Angel 7 54883 2, 1993.
Kern Goes to Hollywood. First Night Records, OCR CD6014, 1985.
Kern "Showboat" [sic], *"Sunny"—Rodgers "Lido Lady."* Pearl, GEMM CD 9105, 1994.
The Land Where the Good Songs Go: The Lyrics of P. G. Wodehouse. Harbinger CD,
    HCD 1901, 2001.
Leave It to Jane. AEI-CD 038, 1997.
Music from the New York Stage: 1890–1920. 12 CDs, Pearl GEMM CDS 9050–9061,
    1993.
Musical Ladies and the Music of Jerome Kern. Encore ENBO-CD #4/92, 1992.
*[Portrait for Orchestra] Andre Kostelanetz and His Orchestra: The Music of Fritz Kreisler,
    Richard Rodgers and Jerome Kern.* Vocalion CD, CDUS 3015, 2000.
Show Boat, conducted by John McGlinn. 3 CDs, EMI 7 49108 2, 1988.
Sitting Pretty, conducted by John McGlinn. 2 CDs, New World Records 80387–2,
    1990.
The Song Is . . . Jerome Kern. ASV CD AJA 5036, 1990.
The Songs of Jerome Kern. ASV CD AJA 5377, 2001.
The Theatre Lyrics of P. G. Wodehouse. Folkways Records RFS 601, 1981.
The Ultimate Show Boat. 2 CDs, Pearl GEMS 0060, 1999.
Very Good Eddie. DRG Records, CDRG 6100, 1977.
Very Warm for May, original Broadway cast recording. AEI-CD 008, 1985.

Permissions

Librettos

Stage directions from the unpublished script for *The Cabaret Girl*
By Pelham Wodehouse and George Grossmith
Reprinted with permission of A. P. Watt on behalf of The Trustees of the Wodehouse Estate.
All Rights Reserved. International Copyright Secured.

Excerpts from the unpublished script for *The Cat and the Fiddle*
By Otto Harbach
Used by permission of the Betty Kern Miller Trust
All Rights Reserved. International Copyright Secured.

Excerpts from the unpublished script for *Gentlemen Unafraid*
By Oscar Hammerstein II and Otto Harbach
Used by permission of the Betty Kern Miller Trust
All Rights Reserved. International Copyright Secured.

Excerpts from *Leave It to Jane*
By Guy Bolton and Pelham Wodehouse
Reprinted with permission by the Tams–Witmark Library, Inc.
All Rights Reserved. International Copyright Secured.

Excerpts from the unpublished screenplay for *Men of the Sky*
By Otto Harbach
Used by permission of the Betty Kern Miller Trust
All Rights Reserved. International Copyright Secured.

Lyrics

"Californ-i-ay"
Words by E.Y. Harburg
Music by Jerome Kern

"Can't Help Singing"
Words by E.Y. Harburg
Music by Jerome Kern

The Cat And The Fiddle
Words by Otto Harbach
Music by Jerome Kern

"The Chaplin Walk"
Words & Music by Jerome Kern, Schuyler Greene & Otto Motzan
Music by Jerome Kern

Cover Girl
Words by E.Y. Harburg
Music by Jerome Kern

"Why Was I Born?"
Words & Music by Oscar Hammerstein & Jerome Kern

"Sympathetic Someone"
Words by Anne Caldwell
Music by Jerome Kern

"That Peculiar Tune"
Words & Music by Schuyler Greene & Herbert Reynolds
Music by Jerome Kern

"Way Down Town"
Words & Music by Anne Caldwell
Music by Jerome Kern

"Who's Complaining?"
Words by Ira Gershwin
Music by Jerome Kern

"Whose Baby Are You?"
Words by Anne Caldwell
Music by Jerome Kern
© Copyright 1920 T. B. Harms & Company Incorporated.
Universal Music Publishing Limited (50%)/Chappell Music Limited (50%).
Used by permission of Music Sales Limited.
All Rights Reserved. International Copyright Secured.

"Windmill Under The Stars"
Words & Music by Anne Caldwell
Music by Jerome Kern
© Copyright 1942 Universal Music Publishing Limited (50%)/Copyright
Control (50%).
Used by permission of Music Sales Limited.
All Rights Reserved. International Copyright Secured.

"A Year From Today"
Words by Pelham Wodehouse
Music by Jerome Kern
© Copyright 1924 T. B. Harms & Company Incorporated.
Universal Music Publishing Limited (50%)/Chappell Music Limited (50%).
Used by permission of Music Sales Limited.
All Rights Reserved. International Copyright Secured.

"You Said Something"
Words by Pelham Wodehouse
Music by Jerome Kern
© Copyright 1917 T. B. Harms & Company Incorporated.
Universal Music Publishing Limited (50%)/Chappell Music Limited (50%).
Used by permission of Music Sales Limited
All Rights Reserved. International Copyright Secured.

"You're The Only Girl He Loves"
Words & Music by Jerome Kern and George Hobart
© Copyright 1912 Universal Music Publishing Limited (50%)/Copyright
Control (50%).
Used by permission of Music Sales Limited.
All Rights Reserved. International Copyright Secured.

Music

"Every Girl In All America"
Words & Music by Berton Braley
Music by Jerome Kern
© Copyright 1940 Universal Music Publishing Limited (50%)/Copyright
Control (50%).
Used by permission of Music Sales Limited.
All Rights Reserved. International Copyright Secured.

Garden Scene
Music by Jerome Kern
Used by permission of the Betty Kern Miller Trust
All Rights Reserved. International Copyright Secured.

"The Gay Lothario"
Words & Music by C. H. Bovill
Music by Jerome Kern
© Copyright 1908 Universal Music Publishing Limited (50%)/Copyright
Control (50%).
Used by permission of Music Sales Limited.
All Rights Reserved. International Copyright Secured.

"Good Morning, Dearie"
Words & Music by Anne Caldwell
Music by Jerome Kern
© Copyright 1921 Universal Music Publishing Limited (50%)/Copyright
Control (50%).
Used by permission of Music Sales Limited.
All Rights Reserved. International Copyright Secured.

Head Over Heels
Music by Jerome Kern
Used by permission of the Betty Kern Miller Trust
All Rights Reserved. International Copyright Secured.

"I've Told Ev'ry Little Star"
Words by Oscar Hamerstein II
Music by Jerome Kern
© Copyright 1932 T. B. Harms & Company Incorporated, USA.
Universal Music Publishing Limited.
Used by permission of Music Sales Limited.
All Rights Reserved. International Copyright Secured.

"Ol' Man River" (sketch)
Music by Jerome Kern
Used by permission of the Betty Kern Miller Trust
All Rights Reserved. International Copyright Secured.

"Once In A Million Moons"
Words by E.Y Harburg
Music by Jerome Kern
© Copyright Harms T B Company.
Chappell Music Limited (50%)/ Universal Music Publishing Limited (50%).
Used by permission of Music Sales Limited.
All Rights Reserved. International Copyright Secured.

Overture to *Sitting Pretty*
Music by Jerome Kern
Used by permission of the Betty Kern Miller Trust
All Rights Reserved. International Copyright Secured.

"Play Us a Polka, Dot"
Music by Jerome Kern
Used by permission of the Betty Kern Miller Trust
All Rights Reserved. International Copyright Secured.

Polka from *Oh, I Say!*
Music by Jerome Kern
Used by permission of the Betty Kern Miller Trust
All Rights Reserved. International Copyright Secured.

Portrait For Orchestra
Music by Jerome Kern
© Copyright 1942 Universal Music Publishing Limited.
Used by permission of Music Sales Limited.
All Rights Reserved. International Copyright Secured.

"Roll On, Rolling Road"
Words by Oscar Hamerstein II
Music by Jerome Kern
© Copyright 1934 Universal Music Publishing Limited.
Used by permission of Music Sales Limited.
All Rights Reserved. International Copyright Secured.

"Sitting Pretty"
Music by Jerome Kern

"Sitting Pretty"
Music by Jerome Kern, orchestrated by Robert Russell Bennett

End credit to *Swing Time*
Music by Jerome Kern

Three Sisters
Music by Jerome Kern

"Two Dachshunds"
Music by Jerome Kern

Very Warm for May
Music by Jerome Kern

"What's the Use?"
Music by Jerome Kern

"Why Don't They Dance The Polka?"
Words & Music by Harry Smith
Music by Jerome Kern

"You And Your Kiss"
Words by Dorothy Fields

Music by Jerome Kern
© Copyright 1940 Universal Music Publishing Limited (50%)/Copyright
Control (50%).
Used by permission of Music Sales Limited.

Music and Lyrics

"Ain't It A Grand And Glorious Feeling"
Words by Pelham Wodehouse
Music by Jerome Kern
© Copyright 1917 T. B. Harms & Company Incorporated.
Universal Music Publishing Limited (50%)/Chappell Music Limited (50%).
Used by permission of Music Sales Limited.
All Rights Reserved. International Copyright Secured.

"Boy With a Drum"
Lyrics by Otto Harbach
Music by Jerome Kern
Used by permission of the Betty Kern Miller Trust
All Rights Reserved. International Copyright Secured.

The Cat And The Fiddle
Words by Otto Harbach
Music by Jerome Kern
© Copyright 1931 Universal Music Publishing Limited.
Used by permission of Music Sales Limited.
All Rights Reserved. International Copyright Secured.

"Cinderella Sue"
Words by E. Y. Harburg
Music by Jerome Kern
© Copyright 1944 T. B. Harms & Company Incorporated, USA.
Universal Music Publishing Limited (50%)/Chappell Music Limited (50%).
Used by permission of Music Sales Limited.
All Rights Reserved. International Copyright Secured.

"Drift With Me"
Words by Harry B Smith
Music by Jerome Kern
© Copyright 1916 T. B. Harms & Company Incorporated, USA.
Universal Music Publishing Limited.

"Ev'ry Little While"
Words by Otto Harbach
Music by Jerome Kern
© Copyright 1931 Universal Music Publishing Limited.

"Gentlemen Unafraid"
Lyrics by Oscar Hammerstein and Otto Harbach
Music by Jerome Kern
Used by permission of the Betty Kern Miller Trust

"Here Am I"
Words by Oscar Hammerstein
Music by Jerome Kern
© Copyright 1929 Universal Music Publishing Limited.

"Honeymoon Lane"
Words by Herbert Reynolds
Music by Jerome Kern
© Copyright 1913 Universal Music Publishing Limited (50%)/Copyright
Control (50%).

"I'm Old Fashioned"
Words by Johnny Mercer
Music by Jerome Kern
© Copyright 1942 T. B. Harms & Company Incorporated.
Universal Music Publishing Limited (50%)/Chappell Music Limited (50%).

"Journey's End"
Words by Pelham Wodehouse
Music by Jerome Kern
© Copyright 1922 T. B. Harms & Company Incorporated.

Prose

Excerpts from Otto Harbach: Oral History Memoir, New York Public Library
By William Harbach

Excerpts from "Jerome Kern and American Operetta" by Kurt List reprinted from
Commentary, May 1947, by permission; all rights reserved.

Unpublished message from Kern to Frank Saddler on score

Unpublished memo from Kern to Oscar Hammerstein II
19 May 1933

Excerpts from unpublished letter from Kern to Vaughn DeLeath
3 May 1938

Excerpt from unpublished letter from Kern to Oscar Hammerstein II
23 January 1939

Excerpt from unpublished letter from Kern to Oscar Hammerstein II
4 May 1939

Excerpt from unpublished letter from Kern to Bart Pfingst
15 March 1942

Excerpt from unpublished letter from Kern to Oscar Hammerstein II
31 March 1942

Images

Claude Bragdon, Act 2 design for *Oh, Lady! Lady!!* Used by permission of Peter Bragdon

Photograph of Dury Lane production of *Show Boat*
Reproduced by permission of The Institute of the American Musical, Inc.

Photograph of Jerome Kern
Reproduced by permission of Getty Images.

William Frith's *Derby Day*
Reproduced by permission of Tate, London 2005

Photograph of *Very Warm for May*, Act II
Reproduced by permission of AEI Records

General Index

Abbott and Costello, 64, 282
accompaniments and vamps, 31, 33, 39, 42, 60, 61, 62, 104, 107, 113, 115–16, 117, 144–45, 150, 170, 192, 195, 221, 232–33, 237, 264, 274, 277, 281, 292, 300
African-American influences, 61–62, 103, 117–20, 145–46, 158, 162–63, 167, 206–7, 256, 301
"After the Ball," 173, 176, 256
Agate, James, 180, 184, 223, 224
"Alexander's Ragtime Band." See Irving Berlin
alienation techniques, 116, 231
Allegro. See Rodgers and Hammerstein
American history, 175–76, 206, 229, 233–35, 279, 284, 288–300
American musical comedy and musical theater, identity of, 17–18, 22–23, 47, 49, 50, 74, 76, 77–78, 94, 146, 155–56, 163–64, 199, 245–46
amplification, 55, 117, 133, 223, 247–48, 251
Anderson, Hilding, 138, 149, 318 n26
Annie Get Your Gun. See Irving Berlin
"Apache Dance." See Jacques Offenbach
The Arcadians. See Lionel Monckton
Arden, Eve, 244
Arlen, Harold, 62, 233
arrangements, 24, 26, 66, 246–47, 274, 276; dance-band, 44, 61–62, 122–24, 146, 263, 274; string quartet 64

art deco, 120, 184, 273, 278, 281, 325 n15
[Ascherberg,] Hopwood and Crew, 10, 13
Assassins. See Stephen Sondheim
Astaire, Adele, 45
Astaire, Fred, 3, 45, 49, 55, 62, 65, 152, 257, 263–78, 283–88, 293, 325 n12, 325 n16, 326 n24, fig. 5.3; films with Ginger Rogers, ix, 54, 55, 129, 184, 263–78, fig. 5.2, fig. 5.3

The Babes and the Baron. See Herbert Haines
Babes in Arms. See Rodgers and Hart
Bach, Johann Sebastian, 107, 207; "Sheep May Safely Graze," 158
"backstage" musicals, 175, 180, 203, 242, 284, 291, 296
Ball at the Savoy, 223
ballet, 76, 89, 103, 126, 229, 246, 249–51, 257; dream ballets, 201–3, 221, 225, 229, 239–40, 251, 323 n24
"The Band Played On," 322 n9
Baravalle, Victor, 167, 255, 320 n73
Barratt, Augustus: Kitty Grey, 12
Bartholomae, Philip, 18
"Battle Hymn of the Republic," 241
Baughan, E. A., 180, 203
The Beauty of Bath, 309 n4
Beethoven, Ludwig van, 212, 213
Belasco, David, 16, 199
Bendix, Max, 132

Index of Kern's Works